ECOHUMANISM AND THE
ECOLOGICAL CULTURE

ECOHUMANISM

AND THE ECOLOGICAL CULTURE

The Educational Legacy of
Lewis Mumford and Ian McHarg

WILLIAM J. COHEN

With a Foreword by FREDERICK R. STEINER

TEMPLE UNIVERSITY PRESS
Philadelphia • Rome • Tokyo

TEMPLE UNIVERSITY PRESS
Philadelphia, Pennsylvania 19122
tupress.temple.edu

Copyright © 2019 by Temple University—Of The Commonwealth System
   of Higher Education
All rights reserved
Published 2019

Text design by Kate Nichols

Library of Congress Cataloging-in-Publication Data

Names: Cohen, William J., author.
Title: Ecohumanism and the ecological culture : the educational legacy of
   Lewis Mumford and Ian McHarg / William J. Cohen ; with a foreword by
   Frederick R. Steiner.
Description: Philadelphia : Temple University Press, [2019] | Includes
   bibliographical references and index. |
Identifiers: LCCN 2018043417 (print) | LCCN 2018060125 (ebook) |
   ISBN 9781439918296 (E-book) | ISBN 9781439918272 (cloth : alk. paper) |
   ISBN 9781439918289 (pbk. : alk. paper)
Subjects: LCSH: Human ecology—Study and teaching. | Environmentalism—Study
   and teaching. | Environmental education. | Education—Philosophy. |
   Mumford, Lewis, 1895–1990. | McHarg, Ian L., 1920–2001.
Classification: LCC GF26 (ebook) | LCC GF26 .C64 2019 (print) | DDC
   304.2—dc23
LC record available at https://lccn.loc.gov/2018043417

♾ The paper used in this publication meets the requirements of the American National
Standard for Information Sciences—Permanence of Paper for Printed Library Materials,
ANSI Z39.48-1992

Printed in the United States of America

9 8 7 6 5 4 3 2 1

To my teachers at Penn
Who opened up new horizons
That made the difference

JOHN C. KEENE
ANTHONY R. TOMAZINIS
and
IAN L. McHARG

Contents

Part II. Planning and Design: The Fusion of Theory and Practice

Part III. Ecology and Human Ecology in Planning and Design Education: A History of an Interdisciplinary Curriculum, 1936–2000

Part IV. Future Prospects for Education
in the Ecological Culture

Foreword

Redesigning the Nature of the Academy

O VER TACOS AND COFFEE around an Austin, Texas, conference table, a group of earnest architects and I engaged in a spirited conversation. My companions were advocating ecological literacy for their profession, a worthy goal in my view. I asked them what they had in mind, as architecture curricula are notoriously dense and long. Whereas conventional bachelor's degrees typically take four years and one hundred twenty credit hours, professional architecture undergraduate degrees require about five years and one hundred sixty credit hours. Meanwhile, in most disciplines, master's degrees take one to two years and require thirty credit hours, but graduate architecture degrees often cover at least three years and sixty to seventy credit hours—the equivalent of a doctoral degree in most fields. Academic architects are terrific at adding requirements but not at reducing them. Allied fields of architecture, including landscape architecture and planning, typically hold longer than normal degree expectations. In any case, my architect friends believed that another course or a module would suffice to achieve ecological literacy.

The only design or planning curricula ever to achieve ecological literacy were Ian McHarg's landscape architecture and regional planning programs at the University of Pennsylvania (Penn), where students were required to take courses in ecology, geomorphology, soils science, hydrology, and human ecology after taking prerequisite courses in introductory biology and geology. These subjects in addition to climatology, remote sensing, writing, and various mapping and landscape representation experimentations were also integrated into studios taught by designers, planners, environmental scientists, and ethnographers, and the studios involved considerable firsthand site investigation. Landscape architecture students were also expected to take a summer field ecology course; regional planners took environmental law and an advanced biology course, such as limnology or plant physiography.

That's literacy.

Having been a student in McHarg's program and having now spent a lifetime in the academy, I remain amazed that McHarg was able to pull it off. McHarg and his team not only advanced ecological thinking in design and planning but also created a truly interdisciplinary department. The coming together of arts and sciences to inform the design and planning professions is much discussed but rarely achieved.

Neither McHarg nor Lewis Mumford, his mentor, had a conventional education, and neither was bound by traditional disciplinary territories. McHarg pretty much skipped high school and college, entering graduate school at Harvard University via an apprenticeship in landscape architecture, military service, and a correspondence course in town planning. His views about education and ecology were also informed by his boyhood walks in his native Scottish countryside. Mumford took courses at City College and the New School and without earning a degree became an eminent author and college teacher at Stanford University, Penn, and Harvard. A keen observer of the city, he called the streets of Manhattan his university. McHarg and Mumford craved knowledge about the cultural and the natural processes that shape human settlements.

McHarg and Mumford inspired this book's focus on the more exploratory wing of the Penn Department of Landscape Architecture and Regional Planning: the master of regional planning (MRP) degree. Although regional planning remains part of the department's name, the degree established by McHarg, which can be viewed to some extent as an homage to Mumford, has ceased to exist. Having first grown from the fertile seed bank of 1960s idealism and then rocketed through the environmental decade of the 1970s, the degree fits, as William Cohen illustrates, within Mumford's ecohumanism.

On New Year's Day 1970, President Richard Nixon signed the National Environmental Policy Act into law. Almost five months later, the first Earth Day (then an Earth Week), led in Philadelphia by McHarg and his students, took place. The year before, McHarg had published *Design with Nature*, with an introduction by Mumford. Thousands of young people, including me, read the book and were drawn to landscape architecture and its more radical sibling, regional planning. McHarg's reinvention of planning first through ecology and then through human ecology elevated an understanding of how we relate with each other, other species, and our surroundings to the center of the process of planning.

In several ways, McHarg's ideas about ecological determinism and fitting our designs and plans to nature's constraints and opportunities echo the theories of his mentor's mentor. Also a son of Scotland, Patrick Geddes believed that organisms, including humans, can participate in their own evolution. This idea was the basis for Geddes's approach to town planning and, subsequently, for McHarg's regional planning. According to this view, we are determined by ecology, but we are also active agents of change through our interactions with people, other organisms, and our environments.

In this book, Cohen tells an engrossing story about McHarg's ecologically grounded MRP program at Penn—from its inspiration by Mumford, through its various heydays, to its disappearance. In the process, academic planning lost its more risk-taking, experimental position and grew more conservative in substance, if not in political leaning. Although the degree is gone, the Geddes-Mumford-McHarg interdisciplinary approach to planning and design remains influential and relevant.

I allow myself to imagine a world built by ecologically literate architects, a world where the wounds from past buildings are healed and people thrive in healthy, safe, and productive built environments with other species. Similarly, I indulge an image of an academy where the arts and sciences coexist and advance together in a diverse ecosystem of trust, learning, and wisdom. I can only hope for an ecological culture in which people embrace knowledge as a means to pass on the planet in sound condition to future generations. Cohen tells the story of such hope and imagination as they were pursued for a time in a quest for life. As he notes, a Second Enlightenment holds the promise of renewing this pursuit for an ecological culture.

—FREDERICK R. STEINER
    Dean and Paley Professor
    School of Design
    University of Pennsylvania

Acknowledgments

THESE ACKNOWLEDGMENTS are more than just a thank-you. They are my personal recognition of many individuals who gave me inspiration, encouragement, and technical support. Each one, in his or her own way, helped to steer this book to completion and finally to publication.

This book is dedicated to the three most important people during my life as a graduate student at the University of Pennsylvania. John Keene would become not just one of my professors but also my adviser, dissertation supervisor, confidant, and friend. I relied on John's careful guidance to keep me moving in the right direction; he was truly indispensable to my success at Penn. Tony Tomazinis was chairman of the Department of City and Regional Planning when I made application to the graduate program. He declared me a "special student," since I was entering academia after many years as a practicing planner. This new life phase would open up many doors, and Tony smoothed every step of the way. Studying with Ian McHarg became my singular motivation to return to graduate school at Penn. I had originally encountered his presence—that indefatigable charisma and uncompromising devotion to an ecological ethic—at the first Earth Day lecture at the University of Delaware, in April 1970. Not until several decades later would I be in his company as one of his students, when he would solidify my understanding of "man and environment." Ian's life work has become my own mission—to perpetuate his insistence on the necessity of ecological planning and design.

More than just a dear friend and professional colleague for the past forty years, Gerald F. Vaughn has really become my intellectual companion. He has pushed, critiqued, and become so fully committed to the finalization of this book that I might think of him as a co-author. No one gave me more hope than Jerry; through countless discussions, he pointed me in the right direction, challenged my thinking, and offered innumerable suggestions that shaped this publication. Jerry and his late wife, Patti, provided unselfish support, for which I will always be grateful.

Fritz Steiner and I first met many years ago through a telephone conversation. It would be the beginning of an important, growing collaboration and friendship. Through the many times and circumstances that challenged my ability to keep the fire burning, Fritz stayed with me, offering advice and encouragement. As a student of Ian McHarg's, Fritz has been an indefatigable proponent of McHarg's theory and method. His stature in the field of ecological planning and design is universally recognized, and I am especially honored that he agreed to write the Foreword to this book.

Several of my closest friends and family members have given their time, energy, and advice to make this work possible. Chris Zelov, with whom I have helped produce several documentary films to promote Ian McHarg's prescription of ecological planning and design, has been a kindred spirit, ally, and adviser. Don Callender read and commented on chapter drafts, giving me hope that the project really could be completed. Jim Harker, Esq., gave advice on copyright issues. John Schoonover, photographer extraordinaire, took my photo for the book cover. And finally, I am grateful to my daughter, Rebecca, who patiently sat by my side as we checked bibliographic entries.

The University of Pennsylvania Architectural Archives in the School of Design, which houses Ian McHarg's papers, has been a critically important source of information. For several years, I have relied on the invaluable help of Bill Whitaker, curator, to point me in the right direction in accessing papers and documents. Nancy Thorne, former archivist, and Heather Isbell Schumacher, current archivist, made sure that I had every archived document that I needed. Thanks also go to Allison Olsen, digital archivist, for her careful attention to detail.

At Monmouth University, which holds Lewis Mumford's personal library, George Germek, special collections librarian, was particularly helpful and courteous in guiding me through the collection—even allowing me to put my fingers on Lewis Mumford's typewriter. Scott Knauer, director of Galleries and Collections opened up Lewis Mumford's wonderful array of original sketches and drawings.

I am grateful to the Kislak Center for Special Collections, Rare Books, and Manuscripts at the University of Pennsylvania, which holds Lewis

Mumford's and Sophia Mumford's papers. I appreciate the cooperation and help of John Pollack, library specialist. Dean Robert Wojtowicz, the literary executor of the Mumford collections, was wholly supportive in allowing me to publish photographs from these sources, and Gina Maccoby, literary agent, made it happen.

University of Delaware Archives and Records Management provided the photograph of McHarg's 1970 Earth Day lecture, and Lisa Gensel was instrumental in securing permission to include it.

At the Division of Rare and Manuscript Collections at Cornell University Library, thanks are due to Peter Corina for his research and assistance.

Several people were especially generous with their time and resources. Yipeng Peng, a graduate student in the Penn Department of City and Regional Planning, who served as my research assistant during the summer of 2017, meticulously corroborated the manuscript's citations to the McHarg Papers at Penn's Architectural Archives. Harvey Shapiro, a McHarg student in the 1970s, sent me previously unpublished photographs, especially from McHarg's visits to Japan. Charlie Fifer drew my conception of the "Layer Cake in the Contemporary Idiom," which appears in Chapter 12. Carolee Kokola provided a photograph that she took during the dedication of the plaque honoring McHarg at the Penn School of Design ceremony in April 2000.

Two members of the Temple University staff provided technical assistance to an author who, at times, has been confounded by the growing complexity of computer technology. Shawn Ta in Instructional Technology and Steve Campbell in the Tyler School of Art and Architecture bailed me out of many difficulties. CC Thomas, a member of the American Society for Indexing, carefully prepared the Index of Names and the General Subject Index.

I extend my appreciation to the Graham Foundation for Advanced Studies in the Fine Arts, which provided a grant to support manuscript research and publication.

Temple University Press has been incredible to work with. From the beginning, when I first approached Editor in Chief Aaron Javsicas to see whether there might be interest in publishing this book, his support and guidance have been unwavering. Aaron introduced me to a staff with outstanding ability and professional dedication. My sincere thanks go to Nikki Miller, former editorial assistant, for her initial involvement in preparing this book for publication review. Gary Kramer, publicity manager, and Ann-Marie Anderson, marketing director, have been a delight to work with. Kate Nichols, art manager, designed the interior. Kate Levy designed the expressive and dynamic cover. Irene Imperio Kull, advertising and promotions manager, deserves thanks for her promotional skill. Joan Vidal, senior production editor, provided astute attention to detail to make sure that everything went just right. I relied immensely on her sound judgment. Finally, Heather Wilcox, copyeditor, must receive my highest praise for her comprehensive review; though her queries were at times quite a challenge to respond to, her efforts were essential to the readability of this book.

Introduction

IN APRIL 1965, the Conservation Foundation convened a conference in Warrenton, Virginia, to discuss "future environments of North America." At that conference, Lewis Mumford, one of the most respected public intellectuals of the twentieth century, was called on to make "closing remarks." After several days of presentations, Mumford said, "The 'probable' future is not necessarily the actual future at all. It is always a summary of the past, and all its predictions are predictions about the past, not about the future. The other future is that based on possibility."[1] For Mumford, that "possibility" was the idea that to secure human survival, we must transition from a technological culture to an ecological culture. An extension of this transition is the current hybridization of technology with ecology—known as *ecotech*—that has effectuated a direction for the twenty-first century.

Mumford's various writings in books, journals, and magazines as well as his many association memberships offer clear evidence that unless we are able to control technological advancement, our basic humanity will be severely and negatively affected. Moreover, Mumford was clearly a multidisciplinary thinker in the intellectual tradition of the Scottish Patrick Geddes, whom he referred to as "master." Geddes had pursued a variety of disciplines, including biology, botany, sociology, economics, and town planning. According to his biographer, the sociologist Marshall Stalley, Geddes "could never limit himself to one discipline and was forever relating his life and his knowledge to the

---

1. Lewis Mumford, "Closing Statement," *Future Environments of North America*, ed. F. Fraser Darling and John P. Milton (Garden City, N.Y.: Natural History Press, 1966), 718.

ecology of nature and of mankind."[2] Such a perspective leads to the conclusion that Geddes was an *ecohumanist*, and his entire career would serve as an example to those who followed him—especially Lewis Mumford and Ian McHarg.

SUCH INTERDISCIPLINARY THINKING combined with empirical observation first attracted Mumford to Geddes, as he explained: Geddes "taught me how to take in the life of cities . . . not as a mere spectator or as a collector of statistics or a maker of abstract models, but, to begin with, as a citizen and a worker, participating in the total life of a community, past, present, and prospective."[3] However, another attraction piqued Mumford's interest: education. Geddes promoted the development of the whole person, not so much through classroom experiences but through life experiences gained by observation and analysis.

Those who are intellectually endowed to seek, to invent, to create, and to learn seem to have a natural affinity to pass that endowment on to others. In a unique way, the best educators have developed the capacity to constantly broaden the net for knowledge, continually challenging current thinking and theories with viable alternatives. So it was with Mumford and McHarg.

This book does not focus on Mumford as a classroom teacher or educator in the traditional sense, although he did serve as a visiting professor at several institutions during his career; rather, it assesses his conception of an educational philosophy, grounded in human ecology—or, as it would evolve into, *ecohumanism*. This philosophy would be the cornerstone of embracing the necessity of moving toward an ecological culture. Mumford's ecohumanism, as an educational philosophy, would have its greatest influence on and fullest expression in a graduate curriculum pioneered by McHarg, the renowned landscape architect and regional planner at the University of Pennsylvania (Penn). Mumford's relationship with and mentoring of McHarg would become the key elements toward the advancement of a new way to achieve an ecological culture—through an educational curriculum based on fusing ecohumanism to the planning and design disciplines.

To Mumford, the intellectual, and McHarg, the educator, nothing less than an ecological imperative began with an understanding of natural systems and extended to embrace human systems. This imperative would be the guiding mantra to ensure success in planning, designing, and developing regions and cities. It would be the crucial variable for cultural survival. And

---

2. Marshall Stalley, *Patrick Geddes: Spokesman for Man and the Environment* (New Brunswick, N.J.: Rutgers University Press, 1972), xiii.

3. Lewis Mumford, *Sketches from Life: The Autobiography of Lewis Mumford* (New York: Dial Press, 1982), 155.

survive we shall if the Mumford-McHarg prescriptions can be passed to future generations. Thus the pivotal role of education moves into the forefront beginning in the elementary levels. However, we must earnestly develop university and college curricula that recognize that converting the technological culture to the ecological culture is the only path to follow if we wish to preserve our unique humanity and continue to have a suitable habitat.

The Holistic Nature of Ecohumanism

Lewis Mumford was a thinker, historian, social critic, and philosopher; Ian McHarg was a landscape architect, regional planner, doer, and educator. Both shared a rejection of *reductionism*—a philosophy that concentrates on looking at parts to describe and understand the world rather than viewing the world holistically. Conversely, they promoted an acceptance of *holism*— a philosophy that emphasizes the interaction between many parts of the whole, thus focusing on systems and the interrelationships of their parts. The common denominator at the base of their respective life's work was simply *ecology*—or, perhaps more specifically, *human ecology.* Mumford and McHarg dedicated themselves to making us aware that in a universe of complexity, an inextricable bond develops between people and their environments, and the human pursuit of building towns, cities, and even regions rests on essential principles of how people can best relate and adapt to a natural environment. Mumford promoted this philosophy through a voluminous output of writing, encompassing books and journal and magazine articles. McHarg advocated this idea through the development of a graduate curriculum in landscape architecture and regional planning, first based on natural systems ecology and later expanded to incorporate the human dimension.

When Mumford wrote *The Culture of Cities* (1938), he expressed the notion that humans—the organisms—are not strictly implicated in an "environment in space," which "has its own line of growth, . . . its own curve of development, its own span of variations, its own pattern of existence," but are "also implicated in time, through the biological phenomena of inheritance and memory; and in human societies it is even more consciously implicated through the necessity of assimilating a complicated social heritage which forms, as it were, a second environment."[4] This is the starting point to configure an acknowledgment of the interconnection of the two "environments"— the natural and the human. Pushed a bit further, this acknowledgment becomes the key element in fashioning an understanding of the *boundaries* of ecohumanism that combine the scientific knowledge of ecology with human

---

4. Lewis Mumford, *The Culture of Cities* (New York: Harcourt, Brace, 1938), 300.

social values. This in turn gives rise to the *concept* of ecohumanism, which can be succinctly defined, as suggested by professor of ecology, evolution, and behavior Philip Regal, as implying "insight into patterns of connectedness among individuals and between individuals and institutions and with the non-human environment."[5] Additionally, "the humanist commitment to the ethical and material quality of the human condition means that the earth must be regarded as home and habitat."[6] The human in nature therefore becomes the guiding light in understanding what we are and what we may become. We are, in the context of nature, "parts of this earth, having developed or evolved as aspects of nature; engaging in the natural processes shared by all life."[7]

FROM THEIR INITIAL MEETINGS during McHarg's student days at Harvard University in the late 1940s, when he heard Mumford lecture, an intellectual power drew the two men together. In 1954, McHarg began a career in higher education with his appointment as an assistant professor of landscape architecture and city planning in the Graduate School of Fine Arts (today known as the School of Design) at the University of Pennsylvania. Mumford was a visiting professor on the same faculty. The men formed a strong collegial bond, and Mumford's growing influence on McHarg's intellectual development became profound—so profound that McHarg's curriculum would rise to international prominence as an interdisciplinary model for the graduate education of planners and designers as well as environmental studies scholars.

This book explores Mumford's vision of embracing ecohumanism as the principal facilitator to move a technological culture toward an ecological culture and McHarg's formulation and implementation of that vision through an interdisciplinary graduate curriculum. Mumford set the stage, as it were; McHarg choreographed the actual performance. The emphasis on Mumford's and McHarg's educational legacy shows the importance of using ecohumanism as an educational pedagogy to train the next generation of planners and designers, who will shape the ecological culture.

Structure and Organization of the Book

The essential thrust of this book is that Mumford's insistence on changing a technological culture into an ecological culture had its most important

---

5. Philip J. Regal, "Ecohumanism: Refining the Concept," in *Ecohumanism*, ed. Robert B. Tapp (Amherst, N.Y.: Prometheus Books, 2002), 62.

6. Ibid.

7. Harvey B. Sarles, "The Human in the Context of Nature," in *Ecohumanism*, ed. Robert B. Tapp (Amherst, N.Y.: Prometheus Books, 2002), 215.

formulation from an educational perspective in McHarg's graduate curriculum at the University of Pennsylvania. The intertwining of a number of circumstances and experiences that both men shared illuminates the movement from ecohumanism as a Mumford-based philosophy to McHarg's human ecology–based graduate educational curriculum. Thus, in the sense of Mumford's mission, this foundation would be the key to educating future planners and designers, as well as others, to facilitate the direction of an ecological culture in how we plan, design, and build our communities and human settlements.

Educational curricula emerge from a guiding objective (or vision); they then evolve, incorporating feedback from faculty and students. Such is true in the history of how McHarg fashioned and carried out the graduate educational curriculum at Penn that serves as this book's case study.

THE BOOK IS DIVIDED into four parts and thirteen chapters. Part I reviews foundation themes—or pathways—that provide a contextual framework that highlights the eventual interface between Mumford and McHarg as a composite of a rich intellectual history. Chapter 1 provides a justification for ushering in what is described as a *Second Enlightenment* based on the philosophical and operational concept of ecohumanism. Chapter 2 gives an overview of a number of historically important planning and design perspectives. Chapter 3 probes the essence of the thinking that shaped Mumford's ecohumanism, especially in regional planning and education, which in turn becomes key to ascertaining Mumford's influence on McHarg's development and establishes the Mumford-McHarg relationship that carries ecohumanism to ecological planning. Two roles are identified: (1) the contribution of architect and planner Artur Glikson, which transitions Mumford's perspective from ecological vision to practice, and (2) the role of Ian McHarg, which provides the ecological link between practice and education.

Part II, in Chapters 4 and 5, examines the difference between a practitioner and an educator; McHarg's theory and method of ecological planning; his distinction between ecological planning and ecological design; and, finally, the fusion of ecological planning with regional planning, which becomes important to deciphering the bridge between education and practice. *Design with Nature*, the brief but powerful title of the 1969 book that became McHarg's landmark contribution to the planning, design, and environmental literature, is also discussed. It is an indispensable representation of a theory and a method that has direct applicability to planning and designing human settlements. The Mumford influence became paramount, and designing with nature became McHarg's mantra—one that he pursued and extolled with a religious fervor.

Part III, in Chapters 6–10, presents the historical development of the curriculum at the University of Pennsylvania that would incorporate ecology and then human ecology into the education of regional planners and landscape architects. The history of this pedagogical development—told here for the first time—stands as a story of its own. And it is an important case study because McHarg sought compatibility between theory and practice in regional planning and landscape architecture. The curriculum would go through a number of iterations, which are presented in detail to assess the strengths and weaknesses that emerged over time and the evolution of the acceptance of using ecology in this educational milieu. The curriculum would become a tangible product of advancing Mumford's dream through McHarg's action to ensure the transition from a technological culture to an ecological culture. Chapter 11 closes Part III with a retrospective assessment of McHarg and the events that influenced the curriculum.

Part IV, Chapter 12, begins by focusing on an overview of McHarg's legacy in practice and education, since a number of existing academic curricula in not only environmental planning but also environmental studies, landscape architecture, geography, architecture, and environmental engineering can be traced to his human ecological curriculum at Penn. Many faculties at colleges and universities earned their academic credentials in McHarg's Department of Landscape Architecture and Regional Planning and were instrumental in establishing or contributing to the development of interdisciplinary programs encompassing environmental planning and education at other institutions. The Penn curriculum may not have been replicated exactly, but outside programs have been modeled on its approach and method. For the future, the prospect is high that not only planning but also environmental design, community development, and the broader-based environmental studies programs will continue to be modeled on the Penn curriculum. Certainly, modifications and the infusion of new technological tools will be incorporated to improve data collection and analysis, but the pedagogical underpinnings are likely to remain definably "McHargian," pervaded with Mumford's ecohumanism.

Chapter 13 concludes the book by exploring a number of engagements for ecohumanism and its role in moving toward an ecological culture. These include a justification for moving into a Second Enlightenment in the areas of technology, planning, design, development, and education. Also considered is a future ecohumanism graduate curriculum as the basis for training the next generation of planners and designers to lead us into an ecological culture, thus securing the educational legacy of Lewis Mumford and Ian McHarg.

PART I

PATHWAYS TO THE ECOLOGICAL CULTURE

1

Emergence of a Second Enlightenment
for the Ecological Culture

A SCIENTIFIC REVOLUTION BEGAN in the late sixteenth and early seventeenth centuries that was highlighted by the application of new methods of observation and experimentation to understand the evolving role of humans and the laws of nature. The works of Francis Bacon, Galileo Galilei, and René Descartes, among others, revolutionized Western thinking in advancing human knowledge about our place in the world. The Enlightenment would emerge in the seventeenth century as the Age of Reason, promoting a rational and real-world inquiry to apply knowledge for human benefit. Underscoring this movement—which generally would cover the period from the Glorious Revolution in England in 1688 to the defeat of postrevolutionary France in 1815—was the concept that a focus on science, conceived as the pursuit of rationality, could reveal nature as it is and show how it could be conquered or manipulated. Moreover, the Enlightenment was a challenge to existing authority, seeking to liberate "the human mind, an inspiration to leaders and followers worldwide, a method for effective change, and a framework of values by which that change can be measured."[1]

Of importance, social and political Enlightenment philosophers, such as David Hume, John Locke, Adam Smith, Voltaire, and Jean-Jacques Rous-

---

1. James MacGregor Burns, *Fire and Light: How the Enlightenment Transformed Our World* (New York: St. Martin's Press, 2013), 7.

seau, vehemently rejected the religious and spiritual dogmas that had been so prominent during the Renaissance and the Reformation. They held to the dictum, as the English poet Alexander Pope stated, that "the proper study of mankind is man." Consequently, this perspective became "characteristic of the whole philosophy of the Enlightenment, not only in the practical sense . . . but also in the theoretical view . . . [that] as a whole, aims to base all knowledge upon the actual processes of [human] physical life."[2]

The founders of the new American Republic were fully immersed in the Enlightenment. All of them, but particularly Benjamin Franklin and Thomas Jefferson, were acutely aware that by studying the past, they would better understand the present—and this understanding would serve as the basis to optimally plan for the future. The founders were also aware of a unique and poignant fact of history—that no culture or society is immune from decline and extinction. They had read Edward Gibbon's monumental historical work produced during the Enlightenment, *The History of the Decline and Fall of the Roman Empire* (1776–1788); that work told them that the Romans gave up political liberty to become masters of the world, but as they became overextended through an insatiable quest to conquer new lands, their empire declined. Moreover, the course of history before the Roman Empire had already witnessed the decline of a number of once-powerful civilizations from ancient Egypt to the Babylonian Empire, from ancient Israel to the Persian Empire, and from Greece's Golden Age to the Macedonian Empire of Alexander the Great.

Knowing that so many great civilizations and empires of the past had eventually reached their limits and declined, the American founders took special effort to shape a social and political system that they believed would last through the centuries. They devised a new system of democracy that would become the crucial foundation for the new American civilization: *Novus Ordo Seclorum*, a new order of the ages.

ALTHOUGH THE CHIEF INTELLECTUAL THRUST of the Enlightenment can be said to have reached its apex early in the nineteenth century, its primary focus on continually improving the human condition through a rational and scientific perspective persists to this day. Enlightenment scholars planted the seeds; their successors have been tasked with harvesting new fruit for the betterment of mankind.

In a practical sense, we measure improvement in the human condition as progress over previous ages and previous ways of living. As a direct

---

2. Wilhelm Windelband, *A History of Philosophy: Renaissance, Enlightenment, and Modern*, vol. 2 (New York: Harper Torchbooks, 1958), 447.

result of Enlightenment thinking, the rational-destiny notion of human progress has guided how we plan and design the most notable of human settlements—our cities; it has also influenced how educational systems are constructed. This guise of progress has also smoothed the way for technology to accelerate its forward motion to improve our places to live. The machine, in the broadest context, has become the indispensable means to help and advance the human condition, proffering new artifacts to improve life and, of course, achieve even higher levels of progress. This situation, as we will see, would become the catalyst that propelled Lewis Mumford's advocacy of ecohumanism.

Progress, as a pragmatic ramification to living a better life, continued its march forward into the twentieth century. Human achievements in science, technology, and knowledge reached new heights. The voyage into cyberspace opened even newer and more exciting avenues of progress. Yet as each new threshold was reached, the challenge to push even further was always there. There was no ultimate threshold of achievement and success, only new plateaus to reach.

As ever more doors to discovery and progress opened, a definable sense of loss began to unfold. Were we simply proceeding too fast? Was the machine, the invention of human genius, actually pushing us into a new reality by making us subservient to its functional role? Were we allowing—consciously or unwittingly—the overwhelming success of our progress to begin to negatively affect essential components of our humanity? Were we losing the composite of a spiritual and functional relationship between man and nature?

IN 1970, ALVIN TOFFLER, a former editor of *Fortune* and a visiting scholar at the Russell Sage Foundation, published what would become a landmark book. As early as 1965, Toffler had coined the term *future shock* to "describe the shattering stress and disorientation that we induce in individuals by subjecting them to too much change in too short a time."[3] In *Future Shock*, he specifically addresses modern technologies, including the digital and communication revolutions that were beginning to have a worldwide effect on culture. He argues that a balance needs to exist "not merely between rates of change in different sectors, but between the pace of environmental change and the limited pace of human response."[4] Toffler's challenge to education is succinctly stated: "Its prime objective must be to increase the individual's 'cope-ability'—the speed and economy with which he can adapt to continual change."[5]

---

3. Alvin Toffler, *Future Shock* (New York: Random House, 1970), 2.
4. Ibid., 3–4.
5. Ibid., 403.

Another shock wave came in 1987, this time specifically leveled at the university educational establishment. Allan Bloom, a professor of political philosophy at the University of Chicago, assailed the form and substance of higher education as the "closing of the American mind" in a book that was critically reviewed by supporters and dissenters alike. In *The Closing of the American Mind*, he argues that a crisis in liberal education is "a reflection of a crisis at the peaks of learning, an incoherence and incompatibility among the first principles with which we interpret the world, an intellectual crisis of the greatest magnitude, which constitutes the crisis of our civilization."[6] Bloom is concerned about misguided curricula that do not encourage students to think, especially about the lessons of the past or about how to understand ideas in a historical context.

In a historical perspective, "how to think" became a major theme promoted by the American philosopher and educational reformer John Dewey (1859–1952). His writings are especially relevant in the education of planners, architects, and landscape architects today because they challenge the rational-idealist tradition by promoting empirical knowledge—that experience is realistic knowledge, not abstract knowledge. This approach creates a true symbiosis between thought and action and establishes "a new accent on the learning process as it actually unfolds within the intellectual life of the student."[7] The relationship of "how we think" in the context of education has been described as training in intelligence or having the ability to assess a situation to be able to change it for the better. Professor of philosophy John Passmore describes it this way: "This necessitates an education which is at once practical, since we must know how to change the world, and liberal, since we must know in what 'the better' consists. But this, too, can only be discovered experimentally, not by pure contemplation."[8] Dewey's position that nature and culture are mutually intertwined gives him credence as an ecohumanist in the Mumford tradition. Additionally, he did not simply develop philosophical positions that would be relegated to speculation but "always connected his observations and reflections with experiences in the dynamic and diversified contexts of life. It is this attitude, among other things, that we should take up today and make productive for our time."[9]

---

6. Allan Bloom, *The Closing of the American Mind* (New York: Simon and Schuster, 1987), 346.

7. Paul Fairfield, *Education after Dewey* (London: Continuum International Publishing Group, 2009), 39.

8. John Passmore, *A Hundred Years of Philosophy* (London: Gerald Duckworth, 1957), 118n.

9. Jim Garrison, Stefan Neubert, and Kersten Reich, *John Dewey's Philosophy of Education: An Introduction and Recontextualization for Our Times* (New York: Palgrave Macmillan, 2012), 109.

Toffler and Bloom give us cause for concern and offer some measure of hope for societal systems and educational institutions to critically examine how they are functioning. Dewey gives us the guideposts for "how to think" that are fundamental in any educational milieu. Collectively, these men offer us the reality and the challenge for twenty-first-century approaches to education and pave the way for our embrace of ecohumanism in education.

A Second Enlightenment: Prerequisite for the Ecological Culture

In the summer of 2006, I traveled to England and Scotland with Christopher Zelov, the founder and director of the Knossus Project, and Phil Cousineau, a San Francisco–based writer, to conduct a series of interviews in preparing a documentary film that would be followed by a publication. On one occasion at the University of St Andrews in Scotland, we were surrounded by a number of fertile and fresh minds who had been exploring new challenges to inculcate an ecohumanism approach to a rapidly changing world. Graham Leicester, the director of the International Futures Forum, opened our eyes—and our thinking—in a way that would establish a poignant justification and foundation for a transition from a technological culture to an ecological culture.

Leicester told us, "Mere survival actually doesn't inspire any of us. It would be a start, but it's not enough. Our sense of future consciousness is that the thing that we want to and need to maintain and sustain is human aspiration."[10] To make this new direction perfectly clear and understood, Leicester drew on "the metaphor of the enlightenment" to make sense of our current complex reality. He explained that we are subject to "rapid technological change, new interconnectedness, speed of advance; we are in a world we don't understand anymore. The old rules no longer seem to apply. The new rules haven't been discovered. What we need is a Second Enlightenment."[11]

After releasing the documentary film *City21: Multiple Perspectives on Urban Futures* (2008), Zelov, Cousineau, and I prepared a publication that would bring together in a written format the countless ideas and concepts that we had garnered from Scotland and elsewhere. We could not forget Leicester's "golden nugget" invoking the notion of a Second Enlightenment. As a result, we titled the publication *City21: The Search for the Second Enlightenment*, and I

---

10. Graham Leicester, "The St. Andrews Conversation," in *City21: The Search for the Second Enlightenment*, ed. Phil Cousineau and Christopher Zelov (Hellertown, Pa.: Knossus Project, 2010), 169.

11. Ibid., 171.

wrote, "What is now needed is a Second Enlightenment to begin to wean us from the rational-technical notion as the key framework for human progress that so gloriously characterized the first Enlightenment. . . . The singular focus of this new re-conceptualization must emphasize advancing ecology in planning, designing, and building cities of the future. . . . [I]t holds as the highest value the interconnectedness between man and nature."[12]

In the challenge to move toward an ecological culture, the acceptance of the premise and the necessity of a Second Enlightenment is the first step. It will not be easy, but it is a growing necessity—and reality. We could think of such a metamorphosis as an "ecological enlightenment," as described by professor of environmental studies and politics David Orr, which has its foundation in the 3.8 billion years of evolution. According to Orr, "When we get it right, the larger, ecologically informed enlightenment will upset comfortable philosophies that underlie the modern world in the same way that the Enlightenment of the eighteenth century upset medieval hierarchies of church and monarchy."[13]

THE PRESCRIPTION for a Second Enlightenment as the foundation to an ecological culture will, by necessity, induce a paradigm shift. When Thomas Kuhn first wrote his poignant masterpiece *The Structure of Scientific Revolutions* (1962), he found after a close examination of the history of science that the generally accepted models, rules, or patterns by which we do things (normal science) are constantly subject to competition and change. A process of competing ideas and methods inevitably will alter our accepted models, rules, and patterns, resulting in the emergence of a new paradigm (the new normal science).

Paradigms are also representative of traditions, which are difficult to alter, especially when they provide a level of comfort and satisfaction to the current generation of adherents or practitioners. Yet when an accepted way of solving problems does not fully solve the problems it attempts to address, the ensuing "failure" opens the door to finding a new way to solve the old problems. For Kuhn, this process engenders a "crisis" that paves the way for a paradigm shift: "The significance of crises is the indication they provide that an occasion for retooling has arrived."[14]

---

12. William J. Cohen, "Envisioning a Second Enlightenment: Advancing Ecology in Planning, Designing, and Building City21," in *City21: The Search for the Second Enlightenment*, ed. Phil Cousineau and Christopher Zelov (Hellertown, Pa.: Knossus Project, 2010), 26.

13. David W. Orr, *The Nature of Design: Ecology, Culture, and Human Intention* (New York: Oxford University Press, 2002), 4.

14. Thomas S. Kuhn, *The Structure of Scientific Revolutions*, 4th ed. (Chicago: University of Chicago Press, 2012), 76.

We can find a parallel perspective to the Kuhnian notion of paradigm shift in historian Arnold Toynbee's assessment of the nature and pattern of civilization growth. Toynbee writes, "In a growing civilization a challenge meets with a successful response which proceeds to generate another and a different challenge which meets with another successful response."[15] This process will continue, according to Toynbee, "until a challenge arises which the civilization in question fails to meet—a tragic event which means a cessation of growth and what we have called a breakdown. Here the correlative rhythm begins."[16]

We could, to a great degree, ascribe an organic view of change that emerges out of the work of Kuhn and Toynbee. In each case, systems or civilizations move along a continuum. They are circular, not linear. In effect, there is no stopping point: paradigms grow, develop, and are modified to achieve a new formulation; civilizations confront new challenges and either become reoriented or fail, only to be revived to start the process again.

However, one additional aspect of civilizational change needs to be accounted for. The historical reality is that many societies and civilizations have directly caused their own declines, collapses, or abandonments. It has been suggested that ecological problems—or unintended ecological suicide—have been at the forefront in affecting a society's sustainability. In a monumental work, professor of geography Jared Diamond argues that eight categories of behavior have been responsible for past societies' undermining their environments: (1) deforestation and habitat destruction, (2) soil problems (erosion, salinization, and soil fertility loss), (3) water management problems, (4) overhunting, (5) overfishing, (6) effects of introduced species on native species, (7) human population growth, and (8) increased per-capita impact on people.[17] According to Diamond, many of the problems that facilitated societies' declines or abandonments developed from their failures to anticipate. Political bodies and citizens are guided by group decision making, and Diamond identifies four areas at the center of bad decision making: "First of all, a group may fail to anticipate a problem before the problem actually arrives. Second, when the problem does arrive, the group may fail to perceive it. Then, after they perceive it, they may fail even to try to solve it. Finally, they may try to solve it but may not succeed."[18]

---

15. Arnold J. Toynbee, *A Study of History: Abridgement of Volumes I–VI by D. C. Somervell* (New York: Oxford University Press, 1946), 548.

16. Ibid.

17. Jared Diamond, *Collapse: How Societies Choose to Fail or Succeed* (New York: Viking Penguin Group, 2005), 6.

18. Ibid., 421.

IF WE THINK ABOUT our present civilization, juxtaposing the Diamond analysis, we can positively identify a "crisis" (in Kuhn's term) or a "breakdown" (in Toynbee's term). Today, we are facing challenges that have been stewing for several decades. They are manifest in our cities through the replacement and destruction of our historic and cultural fabric; they are manifest in our suburbs and rural hinterlands, as evidenced by sprawl, traffic congestion, and diminishing natural areas; they are manifest in the attitudes and actions of economic development and expansion that threaten the intrinsic need to maintain that symbiosis between people and nature. As a result, we are now facing the reality that we may have created more problems than we can reasonably solve. Are we at the brink of eco-suicide, or are we living with a schism between aspirations and reality?

Even in our educational system, we can discern a breakdown between aspirations and reality. University curricula rise and fall, experience high points and low points, and have their successes and failures, as recounted in the history of the ecological and human ecological curriculum at the University of Pennsylvania in Part III.

IN ANOTHER TIME, Lewis Mumford wrote a poignant statement and posed a question when the challenges of contemporary living were being tested not just in America but throughout the world: "For people do not believe in what they see unless the things they see correspond to what they believe."[19] He promotes his idea of a "faith for living" to become a "rational statement; so that which is mutely felt may be shared and understood. . . . But now comes the next question: how is this faith to be embodied? What old interests must be restored; what new fields of activity staked out?"[20]

For Mumford, the direction must be based on *biotechnics*, which refers to "an emergent economy, already separating out more clearly from the neotechnic (purely mechanical) complex, and pointing to a civilization in which the biological sciences will be freely applied to technology, and in which technology itself will be oriented toward the culture of life."[21] We can discern that Mumford is arguing for a paradigm shift, since "in the biotechnic order the biological and social arts become dominant: agriculture, medicine, and education take precedence over engineering," and instead of "depending solely upon mechanical manipulations of matter and en-

19. Lewis Mumford, *Faith for Living* (New York: Harcourt, Brace, 1940), 8.
20. Ibid., 231–232.
21. Lewis Mumford, *The Culture of Cities* (New York: Harcourt, Brace, 1938), 495. Mumford acknowledges that Patrick Geddes first coined the terms *biotechnic* and *neotechnic*.

ergy [biotechnics] will rest upon a more organic utilization of the entire environment."[22]

Mumford's biotechnicism found a secure niche in what Ian McHarg would foster as ecological planning. In his 1969 introduction to McHarg's *Design with Nature*, Mumford states that "it is only during the last half century that any systematic effort has been made to determine what constitutes a balanced and self-renewing environment, containing all the ingredients necessary for man's biological prosperity, social cooperation and spiritual stimulation."[23] The linkage was set, as Mumford continues that the name of this effort is "ecology" and that "Ian McHarg, while trained professionally as a town planner and a landscape architect, might better be described as an inspired ecologist."[24]

Closing One Door and Opening Another

About the time Mumford was writing *The Culture of Cities* (1938), something was taking place in the theory and the practice of architecture that would have a monumental impact in the twentieth and twenty-first centuries. A distinguishable movement in the shifting sands of paradigm change would affect not only architecture but also how our cities and regions would be planned and built. It began as a countermovement that rejected the historically based design concepts of the classic Beaux-Arts tradition in architecture and the City Beautiful movement in city planning, and it would ignite and fuel what would inevitably be called *suburban sprawl.*

The thrust—or paradigm—to plan, design, and build in a new, modern way would unshackle the designer and planner from the nostalgic dictums of the past; it would establish a new pattern and a completely different way to fashion our built environment. This new path forward was spearheaded by the most important progenitor of the Modernist movement or International School, Swiss-born architect Charles-Édouard Jeanneret-Gris (1887–1965). His book *Toward an Architecture* first appeared in 1923, by which time he had assumed the fictionalized moniker by which he would be best known, Le Corbusier. He was distinctive and bold in the ways he broke away from what had been and staked out a whole new way to design, plan, and even build. He was a true iconoclast, and he launched a paradigm change in architecture, design, planning, and development, as he proclaimed:

---

22. Ibid., 496.
23. Lewis Mumford, introduction to *Design with Nature*, by Ian L. McHarg (Garden City, N.Y.: Natural History Press, 1969), vi–vii.
24. Ibid., vii.

A great epoch has begun.
There exists a new spirit.
Industry, overwhelming us like a flood which rolls on towards its
destined ends, has
Furnished us with new tools adapted to this new epoch, animated
by the new spirit.
Economic law inevitably governs our acts and our thoughts.
We must create the mass-production spirit.[25]

The Modernist movement was directly responsible for producing an entirely new landscape as well as rearranging community aesthetics. Our communities would be functionally designed and mass produced similar to a machine. The change on the American landscape was relentless: the rise and pervasiveness of suburbia, the commercial strip centers, the regional shopping malls, the massive industrial parks, and the ubiquitous spread of highway systems would now create their own statement of technological supremacy. This style became dominant, unquestioned, and worshiped. It is still with us today.

Mumford bemoaned this new reality in a 1962 article in *Architectural Record*, wherein he claims that Le Corbusier did "put forward what seemed a fresh and original conception of the City of Tomorrow" and united the design and planning principles that "dominated the modern movement in architecture and city planning: the machine-made environment, standardized, bureaucratized, 'processed,' technically perfected to the last degree."[26] Mumford's critical analysis was that "by mating the utilitarian and financial image of the skyscraper city to the romantic image of the organic environment, Le Corbusier had in fact produced a sterile hybrid."[27]

McHarg would pick up and add fuel to Mumford's critique of Le Corbusier and the modernist architects and planners as he saw the exclusion of any incorporation or, at the very least, an understanding of ecology when he wrote, "The fallacies of modern architecture and its planning ideas are now clear. All reveal the same fatuous, faceless prisms, equally inappropriate for all people, all places, and all times."[28]

---

25. Le Corbusier, *Towards a New Architecture*, 13th ed. (London: John Rodker Publisher, 1931), 6. The original publication went through a number of editions, with the first English translation appearing in 1927 under this title.

26. Lewis Mumford, *Architecture as a Home for Man: Essays for Architectural Record*, ed. Jeanne M. Davern (New York: Architectural Record Books, 1975), 115, 117.

27. Ibid., 117.

28. Ian L. McHarg, *A Quest for Life: An Autobiography* (New York: John Wiley and Sons, 1996), 84.

MUMFORD WAS NOT an architect; neither was McHarg. So how do trained architects feel about the design supremacy championed by Le Corbusier and his cohorts that mirrors the values of a technological culture? James Wines, a cutting-edge architect and educator, has become a leader and unabashed spokesman for a "new iconography." It is not a radical perspective, but it comes to grips with a new understanding and a new direction that will, by necessity, be a cornerstone of the ecological culture. It will open a door to redesigning our human habitat.

Wines's work is internationally known for its commitment to the integration of the arts and the fusion of buildings, landscapes, and public spaces with their surroundings and environmental contexts. According to Wines, "Whereas Le Corbusier referred to the house as 'a machine for living in'— acknowledging his debt to industrial sources—there is a new generation of architects who regard the earth itself as the ultimate 'machine' and the human habitat as an extension of Gaia, or the earth as a living organism."[29] The replacement of an ego-centric design approach with an eco-centric approach is the first step toward achieving sustainable design, or, as Wines calls it, "environmental architecture." Such a shift has three purposes for Wines: "First, to advance the purely selfish motive of survival by a cooperation with nature; second, to build shelter in concert with ecological principles as part of this objective; and third, to address the deeper philosophical conflicts surrounding the issue of whether we really deserve the luxury of this existence, given our appalling record of environmental abuse."[30]

For Wines and others like him, a new "unified eco-philosophy" is a necessary countermovement to "those traditions of technocentrism and anthropocentrism that have dominated this century more than any other."[31]

THE DOOR IS CLOSING on the American suburban sprawl milieu. It will not cease to be relentlessly built and expanded, but it will be challenged to swerve in a new direction. The reality, as architectural historian Dolores Hayden writes, is "that since the early nineteenth century, suburbs have been important to the process of urbanization and economic growth, perhaps as important as the crowded centers of cities."[32] The technological culture shaped us in a way and gave us assurance that the promise of suburbia

---

29. James Wines, *Green Architecture* (Köln, Germany: Taschen, 2000), 9.
30. Ibid., 20.
31. Ibid., 61.
32. Dolores Hayden, *Building Suburbia: Green Fields and Urban Growth, 1820–2000* (New York: Pantheon Books, 2003), 17.

would indicate achievement of the American dream. This promise has been true for many, and for that reason alone an upheaval of the established development pattern and lifestyle amenities will, in all likelihood, never happen. However, cracks in the mirror have been growing for some time. The prospect of an ecological culture gives hope for a new direction—or, at the very least, an alternative direction.

THE PERVASIVENESS of the American suburban land use pattern—arguably the Modernist movement's most significant gift to contemporary American culture—has opened up many opportunities for economic growth and development. Yet at the same time, it has brought with it increasing problems, such as unyielding traffic congestion, declining open space, damaging impacts on natural resources, and a definable loss of a sense of place, among many others.

How many books and journal and magazine articles have been written in the last four decades that thoroughly dissect the shortcomings of American suburban sprawl? One of the more blatantly critical writings about the hysteria of suburbia comes from journalist James Howard Kunstler. He describes, in part, the end result of the impact of modernism on our suburban landscape: "Eighty percent of everything ever built in America has been built in the last fifty years, and most of it is depressing, brutal, ugly, unhealthy, and spiritually degrading."[33] Despite the rage, suburban sprawl remains. Kuhn was right; once patterns are set, they are difficult to change.

Mumford and McHarg offer their own critiques of suburbia. Mumford's is more measured and less emotional, since he sees the loss of community life as the significant characteristic. He explains, "Plainly, in the great metropolises for the past century, family and neighborhood association have largely become residual facts. Excess of numbers, a constant influx of strangers, frequent shifting of domiciles, lack of identifiable boundaries or common centers for meeting, all lessened the stabilizing processes of neighborhood life."[34] On the other hand, McHarg condemns "the neon shill, the ticky-tacky houses, the sterile core, [and] the mined and ravaged countryside. This is the image of anthropocentric man."[35]

Stemming from the critiques and negative assessments of modernism

---

33. James Howard Kunstler, *The Geography of Nowhere: The Rise and Decline of America's Man-Made Landscape* (New York: Simon and Schuster, 1993), 10.

34. Lewis Mumford, *The City in History: Its Origins, Its Transformations, and Its Prospects* (New York: Harcourt, Brace and World, 1961), 499.

35. This quotation was included in McHarg's narration of the film *Multiply and Subdue the Earth*, produced in 1969; it also appears as the frontispiece in his autobiography, *A Quest for Life*.

and its legacy, suburban sprawl, a countermovement arose in the 1980s. Architects, landscape architects, planners, urban designers, and developers in the New Urbanism movement began to challenge the status quo, advancing new ways to address such issues and seeking new directions to guide growth. New urbanism became an organized countermovement to the customary way we plan, design, build, and even redevelop communities. Urban designer Jonathan Barnett frames the concern of the New Urbanists this way: "The old methods for managing urban growth and change don't work as well as they used to; often they don't work at all."[36] As would be expected, New Urbanism has had its detractors and doubters, but it does offer a new direction, clearly challenging taken-for-granted and established trends. As Barnett has stated, "it calls for new design concepts to meet new situations."[37]

Constructing Ecohumanism

The planning and design professions—including city and regional planning, architecture, landscape architecture, and urban design—have, over many years, explored the environment-human relationship. After all, planning for better cities and designing more human-based environments have been the chief justifications we have for undertaking planning and design in the first place.

Understanding the environment and the human dimension is to place in perspective the relationship between the two. I must dismiss at the very beginning the notion that natural systems and human systems are antithetical. Intellectually, they may be construed to be, but in terms of evolutionary biology, they really form a whole—a system that strives for balance but often never fully achieves it. This pursuit of balance, as one might say, in the *world of nature* propels us to find that optimal expression of our *human nature*. So the ultimate synthesis, at least from an intellectual point of view, is to acknowledge the concept of *ecology*.

The concept is simple; the application is a bit more complex. *Ecology* in its basic construct is the relationship of an organism to its environment. If we can compound this definition and add the human dimension, it follows that *human ecology* adds the culture component in understanding the relationship of people to their place and to their environment.

One additional refinement is needed before we begin to explore the en-

---

36. Jonathan Barnett, "What's New about the New Urbanism?" in *Charter of the New Urbanism*, ed. Michael Leccese and Kathleen McCormick (New York: McGraw-Hill, 1999), 5.

37. Ibid., 7.

vironment and human dimensions, which enters the realm of what may be described as schools of thought: *humanism* and *environmentalism*. A humanistic perspective is principally interested in comprehending the full array of the human dimension—values, cultural norms, lifestyles, and even the rationale behind our planning, designing, and building of human settlements. Environmentalism stresses the elements inherent in the natural world and how they become associated with the survival of species and even the destiny of the planet itself. By combining the two, we can find that they are inextricably linked under the rubric of *ecohumanism*—a perspective that has its foundation in accepting that the ecology of the environment is an essential human value and that human progress and environmental stability will become two indispensable aspects of our survival.

To gain an overview of the various viewpoints of the environment and human dimensions as they specifically relate to planning, designing, and building human settlements—villages, towns, cities, and even regions—this book presents the threads of thought and action that highlight this relationship. So let us begin.

2

Planning and Design Perspectives
for the Ecological Culture

AMERICAN INTELLECTUAL HISTORY has provided a rich journey in exploring the relationship between humans and their interactions with the natural environment. Philosophers and artists, biologists and anthropologists, geographers and economists, writers and sociologists, foresters and lawyers have all made their mark in this intellectual journey. They have, within the confines of their specific disciplines or endeavors, attempted to first understand the natural environment and then contemplate how that same environment is changed by humans or, conversely, how the environment modifies human behavior. Finally, there arises an intellectual synthesis: the pursuit of comprehending the full measure of the environment-human relationship.

Interpretations of Nature

Beginning in eighteenth-century Britain and extending into nineteenth-century America, an interpretation and representation of nature emerged that was known as the *picturesque*. This term was "formulated into an aesthetic category . . . with particular application to landscape scenery, landscape painting and garden and park design."[1] It is the "persistent archetype

1. John Dixon Hunt, "Picturesque," in *The Dictionary of Art*, ed. Jane Turner (New York: Grove, 1996), 740.

of the garden," as landscape architect James Corner points out, that "portends an ecological consciousness that is simultaneously useful and symbolic, one that is rooted not in an external world of nature but with a particular culture's mode of *relating* to nature."[2] The evolution of the picturesque would capture the interest of poets, writers, and, perhaps most dramatically, landscape painters. In establishing the philosophical underpinnings of the picturesque, the writings of William Gilpin, Richard Payne Knight, Uvedale Price, and Humphry Repton had special influence. Associations of the written word with landscape painting can be found in the works of William Kent, Capability Brown, J. M. W. Turner, and John Ruskin. It allowed the picturesque to be brought into visual representation.

What led to this fascination with the picturesque? To begin with, the variety of shapes and forms found in nature captivated humans who could envision, design, or project how those shapes and forms could best be arrayed to achieve an optimal level of satisfaction or appreciation. The picturesque was an intellectual as well as an intuitive process. It was a representative form for expressing nature, establishing a distinction between the *beautiful*, thought of as harmony and regularity, and the *sublime*, thought of as including elements of danger and irregularity. Both aspects of the picturesque could be thought of as combining all the dimensions of nature that could be envisioned in the human consciousness. In the final analysis, the picturesque depended on the mind, the imagination, and an individual's sensitivity to interpret nature, encompassing the totality of its awesomeness, beauty, wonder, and excitement. In a very real way, the picturesque appealed to the senses by conceptualizing views of nature that humans could then adapt to enhance their living environment. The history of the picturesque as representational art emphasizes something akin to a social categorization of beauty. It was conceived not only to replicate nature but also to improve it—in the mind of the viewer—thereby evoking a full spectrum of potential or idealized human responses to a landscape aesthetic and how that aesthetic would optimize the use and enjoyment of a built environment.

NOT SURPRISINGLY, as the dawn of the American Industrial Revolution approached in the early nineteenth century, people's views of nature were influenced by new perspectives and values. New cities were being built, and older ones were expanding. The dominant attitude regarding nature was that vast undeveloped terrain, from sea to shining sea—the great American

---

2. James Corner, "Ecology and Landscape as Agents of Creativity," in *Ecological Design and Planning*, ed. George F. Thompson and Frederick R. Steiner (New York: John Wiley and Sons, 1997), 87; emphasis original.

wilderness—offered what seemed to be unlimited opportunities for growth and progress. This era witnessed "a new, national understanding of beauty in space," as historian John Stilgoe has said. This "new standard of spatial beauty—or visual quality—ruled the national imagination. Land in agricultural equilibrium—land cleared of wilderness and defended against the evils of weeds and blights and the return of wilderness—was land likely to remain fertile."[3]

Nineteenth-century America also witnessed a rising cry of concern about the increasing congestion, overcrowding, and industrial ugliness of the burgeoning cities. It was a literary age, and romantic writers extolled, in verse and prose, the wonders of nature. Escape to the country, they urged. There, you will find peace, solitude, and a world far away from the industrial horrors of the city. Many of these writers invoked poetic metaphors that depicted the American landscape as primal nature, as American studies professor Leo Marx so adroitly discusses. In this regard, the American sensitivity was to look at the landscape as "remote and unspoiled, and a possible setting for a pastoral retreat." This notion of the pastoral then became "invested with a new relevance and new symbols."[4] I suggest that in light of Marx's thesis, the classic ideals of the picturesque went through a metamorphosis. This time, there was a new, pragmatic concept of nature as a landscape aesthetic—the pastoral.

The rise of transcendentalism was, in many ways, a literary companion to the picturesque. Ralph Waldo Emerson and Henry David Thoreau led the way in exalting the wilderness and the amenities of nature. They firmly believed that without reference to nature, eternal truth could not be known. Succinctly stated, transcendentalists held, "If men and women would transcend the petty, dehumanizing, commercial burdens of their lives, they must maintain creative contact with the diffused presence of God in nature."[5] Thoreau's transcendentalism included a kind of holism that coalesced a strong sense of spirituality with a keen ability to observe how organisms related to each other and their environment. "In this holism," says intellectual historian Roderick Nash, "Thoreau professed what might be termed 'theological ecology'—God held things together."[6]

---

3. John R. Stilgoe, *Common Landscape of America, 1580–1845* (New Haven, Conn.: Yale University Press, 1982), 206.

4. Leo Marx, *The Machine in the Garden: Technology and the Pastoral Ideal in America* (London: Oxford University Press, 1964), 35, 46.

5. Joseph M. Petulla, *American Environmental History*, 2nd ed. (Columbus, Ohio: Merrill, 1988), 238.

6. Roderick Frazier Nash, *The Rights of Nature: A History of Environmental Ethics* (Madison: University of Wisconsin Press, 1989), 37.

THE HUDSON RIVER school of painting, especially the nature landscapes of Thomas Cole and his student Frederic Edwin Church, brought about a popular visual awareness of the beautiful, the sublime, and the picturesque in nature. The nation was entering an age in which the fine arts helped create a new hope that would become embodied in planning for utopian communities and the early suburbs. One could argue a direct relationship evolved between the romantic yearnings of the poets, writers, and painters and the growing demands for new development, especially as was opening up beyond the traditional cities and towns. These new developments offered new challenges—and, indeed, new choices. A synthesis was created by merging the romantic ideal and the depiction of a landscape aesthetic into the realm of plan making. The greatest advocate of this fusion was Andrew Jackson Downing, a horticulturalist and garden designer who incorporated the concept of landscape as an embodiment of nature, representing the beautiful aspects of nature in a planned—or controlled—manner.

The idea—or, if you will, the ideal—of the representation of nature gained prominence as an important design component of planning, as illustrated in an early-twentieth-century text that was used in the landscape architecture curriculum at Harvard University by Professor Henry Hubbard. In his text, we can decipher an intentional inclusion of the aesthetic elements of nature as an essential component of landscape design. Hubbard stresses that "designs must be, as far as humanly possible, both interpretations of natural character and effective pictorial compositions."[7] Although he discusses elements of the beautiful as contrasted with the picturesque, he continues, "In our present speech much of [the] acquired meaning of [the picturesque] has been again lost, and the word is used more in its simpler sense [as an effect that might be produced by a picture], although some of the associational flavor remains, as in the antithesis of 'picturesque' to 'pastoral' scenery in some discussions of park design."[8]

As the development of cities, towns, and the early suburban communities accelerated after the turn of the twentieth century, an environmental context for the representation of nature became, for the most part, one aspect of planning. With these changing times, new variations were shaped. The old garden aesthetic—so fundamental to the origin and perpetuation of the picturesque—merged with a new conception of functionality. As John Nolen, America's quintessential town planner in the early twentieth

---

7. Henry Vincent Hubbard and Theodora Kimball, *An Introduction to the Study of Landscape Design* (New York: Macmillan, 1927), 71.

8. Ibid., 78.

century, stated, "Any city that is worthy of the name is concerned primarily with use and secondarily with beauty. But if there is a reasonably high standard in providing the useful improvements of a town or city, it will invariably be found that utility and beauty go hand in hand and are virtually inseparable."[9]

The Scientific Field of Ecology

The development of a broad multidisciplinary movement under the rubric of ecology offered the promise of understanding the natural environment, natural forces, and the impact of modern technology on the environment. Ecology, as a scientific field, can be traced to ancient times and involves an analysis of perceptions to understand how humans and their environment interact. Moreover, it has, over time, engaged a community of scholars from a wide range of disciplines who have sought to decipher social and institutional changes that have influenced or altered people's relationship to the environment. In the broadest sense, technological change, resource use, and human adaptation have become the basic concerns of this understanding.[10]

Ecological concepts were being developed in eighteenth-century England around the idea of the "plentitude of nature," incorporating notions of food chains and equilibrium. Environmental historian Donald Worster describes this early conceptualization of ecology as including two traditions. The first was the arcadian perspective toward nature that "advocated a simple, humble life for man with the aim of restoring him to a peaceful coexistence with other organisms."[11] Worster terms the second early conception of ecology an "imperial tradition," represented by the work of Francis Bacon, the Enlightenment philosopher of the scientific method, and Carl Linnaeus, the founder of the science of botany. The principal tenet of the "imperial tradition" was that humans' domination over nature could be secured through the exercise of reason and hard work.[12]

The word *ecology* derives from the Greek *oikos* and means a house or place to live in. Ernst Haeckel, a nineteenth-century German biologist, is generally credited as being the first to use the term *ecology* in his study of

---

9. John Nolen, *New Town for Old: Achievements in Civic Improvement in Some American Small Towns and Neighborhoods* (Boston: Marshall Jones, 1927; Amherst: University of Massachusetts Press, 2005), 11 (page citation is to the reprint edition).

10. See Lester J. Bilsky, ed., *Historical Ecology: Essays on Environment and Social Change* (Port Washington, N.Y.: Kennikat Press, 1980).

11. Donald Worster, *Nature's Economy: The Roots of Ecology* (San Francisco: Sierra Club Books, 1977), 2.

12. Ibid. See pp. 3–55 for a thorough treatment of these two traditions.

plants, *The History of Creation* (1868). However, ecology as a scientific mode of inquiry did not become fully established until the beginning of the twentieth century as an important branch of the botanical sciences. The first major works include Eugenius Warming's *Oecology of Plants* (1909) and two textbooks by F. E. Clements, *Research Methods in Ecology* (1905) and *Plant Physiology and Ecology* (1907).

The writings of Charles Darwin and Alfred Russel Wallace (a contemporary advocate of the idea of evolution) establish the theoretical parameters for modern ecology, first in the scientific fields and later in the social sciences. This frame of reference—promoted by Darwin in *On the Origin of Species* (1859)—advances three essential conceptions. First, there is a web of life in which organisms adjust or seek adjustment to one another. Second, this adjustment process is a struggle for existence. And finally, the environment consists of a complex set of conditions that influence the adjustment process.

Ecology, embracing the biological perspective, is commonly broken down into three disciplinary branches: *plant ecology*, begun with the works of Haeckel in the nineteenth century and Warming in the early twentieth century; *animal ecology*, which had its beginning in the early twentieth century, principally through works by C. C. Adams (*Guide to the Study of Animal Ecology* [1913]) and V. E. Shelford (*Animal Communities in Temperate America* [1913]); and *human ecology*, which incorporates a natural science preoccupation with relationships to social science concerns and issues.

Today, ecology is considered to be the study of the relationship of organisms to the environment. In most cases, an ecological context is often associated with the natural sciences, particularly biology. The term *ecosystem* also developed out of the biological sciences and was first used in 1935 by Sir Arthur Tansley, a British botanist.[13] The ecosystem concept therefore expanded the essential term *ecology* to embrace a more focused, organizing principle in evaluating or studying the biological and nonbiological aspects of a total environment.

The Human Field of Ecology

During the late nineteenth and early twentieth centuries, sociologists, anthropologists, and geographers picked up on the ecology theme and began to develop the epistemological basis for the study of what would become

---

13. See Frank B. Golly, "Historical Origins of the Ecosystem Concept in Biology," *The Ecosystem Concept in Anthropology*, AAAS Selected Symposium, 92 ed. Emilio F. Moran (Boulder, Colo.: Westview Press, 1984), 33–49.

known as *human ecology*. This social science twist on a discipline primarily derived from plant and animal ecology was used as a more comprehensive approach to understanding human relations. Sociologist Amos Hawley defined the development of human ecology from the biological sciences as "the study of the form and the development of the community in human population" that became "a logical extension of the system of thought and the techniques of investigation developed in the study of the collective life of lower organisms."[14] Moreover, evidence suggests that as social science used the concept of ecology to study human affairs, natural science was not oblivious to the human or cultural dimension. In 1935, noted botanist J. W. Bews first published *Human Ecology*, wherein he summarizes the environment-culture connection by concluding that ecology involves three variables. First, he argues, ecology is a science: "It analyzes and investigates the phenomena of nature." Second, ecology has a comprehensive viewpoint of its own, "a special way of regarding the ultimate reality of life and nature." In this sense, ecology may be regarded as a philosophy. Finally, according to Bews's description, ecology may be viewed as an art, since it "provides a plan, a pattern into which can be fitted everything that we know of man, his responses, his activities, and his works."[15]

"Human behavior never occurs except in a cultural milieu," stated sociologist William Ogburn, and the social heritage could not grow except by the group activities of biological humans. Ogburn believed in a distinction between the cultural and the biological: "It is sometimes desirable to know how much behavior of biological man in a cultural environment is determined by activities of the biological equipment and how much is shaped by culture."[16]

Human ecologists see a link between humans as biological forms and humans as cultural expressions. But what is of concern here is that from the viewpoint of human ecologists, humans as cultural expressions are paramount. Here enters the interplay between human ideas, values, beliefs, and even dreams—dreams of the perfect and the ideal—with the wide variety of manifestations that influence the creation of the human habitat and adaptation to the environment.

It is fair to say that the initial explication of the concept of human (and later social or cultural) ecology, especially as it examines people's activities

14. Amos H. Hawley, *Human Ecology: A Theory of Community Structure* (New York: Ronald Press, 1950), 68.

15. J. W. Bews, *Human Ecology*, rev. ed. (New York: Russell and Russell, 1973), 300.

16. William Fielding Ogburn, *Social Change with Respect to Culture and Original Nature* (Gloucester, Mass.: Peter Smith, 1964), 13, 39.

and relations in a community context, rests in two disciplines: sociology and anthropology. Cultural (or human) geography and land (or resource) economics have also engaged in similar conceptual relationships. The writings that the Chicago school of urban sociology produced between 1915 and 1940 explore questions of human interactions in the urban setting. In 1925, Robert Park, Ernest Burgess, and Roderick McKenzie first published their collective work, *The City*, which contains "both theoretical expositions and interpretative essays about the cultural patterns of urban life."[17] The bridge between human ecology and plant and animal ecology can be highlighted by McKenzie's summary view that the spatial relationships among humans "are the products of competition and selection and are continuously in [the] process of change as new factors enter to disturb the competitive relations or to facilitate mobility." As a result, "Human institutions and human nature itself become accommodated to certain spatial relationships of human beings."[18] Hawley would later define the institutional organization of community—as an ecological factor—as "the structure of relationships through which the localized population provides its daily requirements. In some instances the bounds of ecological organization and of community are coterminous, in others ecological organization extends well beyond the limits of a single community embracing two, three, or any number of communities."[19] In the final analysis, human ecology, especially as it has become embraced by a number of social science disciplines, is really a synthesis. Conservationist Paul Sears succinctly stated this view when he argued that human ecology "is not so much a specialty as a scientific activity which must draw upon a wide range of specialties."[20]

---

17. Morris Janowitz, introduction to *The City*, ed. Robert E. Park, Ernest W. Burgess, and Roderick D. McKenzie (Chicago: University of Chicago Press, 1967), viii.

18. Roderick D. McKenzie, "The Ecological Approach to the Study of the Human Community," in *The City*, ed. Robert E. Park, Ernest W. Burgess, and Roderick D. McKenzie (Chicago: University of Chicago Press, 1967), 64. An interesting divergence from this classic sociological view was written many years later by Canadian ecologist Pierre Dansereau: "Food, space, housing, services, recreational facilities, etc., can all be distributed according to a plan which is more ecological than sociological, if one considers the origin of the resource needed for each one of these needs." Pierre Dansereau, "An Ecological Framework for the Amenities of the City," *Diogenes* 98 (Summer 1977): 12.

19. Hawley, *Human Ecology*, 180. Cf., James A. Quinn, *Human Ecology* (New York: Prentice Hall, 1950), and Walter Firey's representation of human ecology as it relies on human behavior to be a wholly rational act in *Land Use in Central Boston* (Cambridge, Mass.: Harvard University Press, 1947).

20. Paul B. Sears, "Human Ecology: A Problem in Synthesis," *Science* 120, no. 3128 (1954): 961.

Nature and Human Systems

Anthropologist Marston Bates writes that ecology can be considered "as a pervasive point of view rather than as a special subject matter . . . whereby the organism is regarded as a whole unit functioning in its environmental context." As a consequence, there is a "carry over from the biological sciences [that] might thus be especially helpful in relating the concepts of the one field to those of the other."[21]

According to anthropologist June Helm, "The ecological approach in anthropology proceeds from the first aspect or level of the adaptive system—man in adjustive and exploitative interaction, through the agency of technology, with his inorganic and biota milieu. But this level had immediate implications for the second aspect of the adaptive system, that of the relations between men."[22]

In anthropology, according to John Bennett, "cultural-environmental research was not considered ecological until Julian Steward first used the term 'cultural ecology' in the late 1940s." However, Bennett continues, "there are many ecologies in anthropology, if we use the word as a general referent for studies of organism-environmental interrelations."[23] In his pioneering work, Julian Steward cites Hawley's "most recent and comprehensive statement of social ecology" that relies on identifying that "man reacts to the web of life as a cultural animal rather than as a biological species," which conforms to "the widely accepted anthropological position that historical factors are more important than environmental factors."[24] The essence of Steward's contribution rests on his identification of the "culture core—the constellation of features which are most closely related to subsistence activities and economic arrangements. The core includes such social, political, and religious patterns as are empirically determined to be closely connected with these arrangements."[25] Consequently, "cultural ecology pays primary attention to those features which empirical analysis shows to be most closely involved in the utilization of [the] environment in culturally

---

21. Marston Bates, "Human Ecology," in *Anthropology Today: An Encyclopedic Inventory,* ed. A. L. Krober (Chicago: University of Chicago Press, 1953), 701.

22. June Helm, "The Ecological Approach in Anthropology," *American Journal of Sociology* 67, no. 6 (1962): 637.

23. John W. Bennett, *The Ecological Transition: Cultural Anthropology and Human Adaptation* (New York: Pergamon Press, 1976), 2.

24. Julian Steward, *Theory of Culture Change: The Methodology of Multilinear Evolution* (Urbana: University of Illinois Press, 1955), 34.

25. Ibid., 37.

prescribed ways. . . . It considers that the entire pattern of technology, land use, land tenure, and social features derive entirely from culture."[26]

In anthropologist Clifford Geertz's "empirical analysis," he concludes, "The necessity of seeing man against the well-outlined background of his habitat is an old, ineradicable theme in anthropology, a fundamental premise. But until recently this premise worked out in practice in one or two unsatisfying forms, 'anthropology' or 'possibilism,' and the turn to ecology represents a search for a more penetrating frame of analysis within which to study the interaction of man with the rest of nature than either of these provides."[27]

Geertz applies ecosystem theory to agricultural ecology. To him, "the guiding question shifts from 'Do habitat conditions (partly or completely) cause culture or do they merely limit it?' to such more incisive queries as: 'Given an ecosystem defined through the parallel discrimination of culture core and relevant environment, how is it organized?' 'What are the mechanisms which regulate its functioning?'"[28] From the perspective of cultural (or human) ecology, Geertz relies on evaluating the nuances of a systems approach and cause-and-effect factors that acknowledge the interdependence of cultural phenomena with the environment.

One of the essential points that reinforces Stewart's culture core concept and a systems approach for its use is found in the work of anthropologist Robert Redfield, who contrasts parts and wholes. Although Redfield is not a cultural ecologist, his studies of the "the little community" provide a way for the anthropologist and sociologist to intuit the "whole" and then decipher the "parts." In this way, interrelations can be understood—a system is constructed.[29] Redfield also discusses human-environment relationships as not simply factual but mental: "In towns and cities men build their environments into their very houses and streets so that the land and the weather are pushed outside of the system. And in every community, primitive or civilized, what most importantly surrounds and influences the people are the traditions, sentiments, norms, and aspirations that make up the common mental life. . . . The world of men is made up in the first place of ideas and ideals."[30]

Bennett's *The Ecological Transition* must be considered the crucial contribution from cultural anthropology that solidifies the link between ecology

26. Ibid.

27. Clifford Geertz, *Agricultural Involution: The Process of Ecological Change in Indonesia* (Berkeley: University of California Press, 1963), 1.

28. Ibid., 10.

29. Robert Redfield, *The Little Community* (Chicago: University of Chicago Press, 1955), 27.

30. Ibid., 29–30.

and human ecology in the context of a systems approach. To Bennett, the ecological transition is "the progressive incorporation of Nature into human frames of purpose and action."[31] Moreover, he defines cultural ecology as the "study of how and why humans use Nature, how they incorporate Nature into Society, and what they do to themselves, Nature and Society in the process."[32]

AS THE DISCIPLINE OF GEOGRAPHY became an academic focus in the early twentieth century—the first North American department of geography was established at the University of Chicago in 1903—its components were diversified into specialized branches, such as geomorphology, climatology, and biogeography. In his presidential address to the Association of American Geographers in 1922, Harlan Barrows proclaimed, "Geography should concentrate on those themes which lead towards synthesis, with an economic regional geography occupying a central place."[33] Geography as human ecology would become an increasingly important perspective, especially with the development of the field of landscape geography, which seeks to understand the physical and human elements of a region within a spatial context. Specifically, "landscape geography focuses on the human experience of being in landscape. . . . Further, there is explicit acknowledgement that landscapes, like regions, reflect and affect cultural, social, political, and economic processes."[34] Nuances to this approach capture geographer Yi-Fu Tuan's idea that space becomes place when it develops meaning.[35] Additionally, "the manner in which various societies or historical periods 'perceive the environment,'" in the view of John Brinckerhoff Jackson, a pioneer in the field of landscape studies, becomes "another way of saying how [one defines] the man–nature relationship."[36]

An integrative element exists between geography and resource (or land) economics, which also attempts to explain human relations with the environment, primarily as they imply human thought and meaning relative to environmental resources. As characterized by resource economist Gerald

---

31. Bennett, *The Ecological Transition*, 3.

32. Ibid.

33. Arild Holt-Jensen, *Geography: Its History and Concepts* (Totowa, N.J.: Barnes and Noble Books, 1982), 117.

34. William Norton, *Human Geography*, 3rd ed. (Toronto: Oxford University Press, 1998), 26.

35. Yi-Fu Tuan, *Space and Place: The Perspective of Experience* (Minneapolis: University of Minnesota, 1977), 136.

36. John Brinckerhoff Jackson, *A Sense of Place, a Sense of Time* (New Haven, Conn.: Yale University Press, 1994), 89.

Vaughn, "Human adaptation to the environment implies purposive action, and individual behavior collectively becomes social action usually resulting in public policy and programs. The dynamics of human adaptation constitute the largely unexplored frontier of behavioral geography and behavioral economics."[37]

Similar to sociologists, resource economists have clearly made a connection between human ecology and land use. However, they emphasize the idea of the scarcity of land resources and how that variable affects the competition for their allocation. Land economist Roland Renne explains the relationship this way: "An impersonal competition for existence occurs among human beings just as it does among plants and animals. Competition also occurs between man and other forms of life in his environment, but it is most ruthless between man and man."[38]

The Environmentalists

A number of movements rose and fell as a response to the environmental damage created by the Industrial Revolution during the nineteenth and well into the twentieth centuries. These movements shared philosophical and ethical attributes that challenged the dominant scientific world view, which generally viewed humans as supreme over nature.

The period between 1860 and 1915 saw the emergence of a body of thought that Worster calls *environmentalism*, which had as its central premise the view that "man's welfare depends crucially on his physical environment."[39] Proponents of this new recognition of the environment included Vermont lawyer George Perkins Marsh, landscape architect Frederick Law Olmsted, geologist Nathaniel Shaler, horticulturalist Liberty Hyde Bailey, and Harvard president Charles Eliot, among many others. They all believed in raising environmental awareness and emphasized that planning must be undertaken to reverse the negative externalities of unchecked development in a burgeoning industrial society.

After 1930, a new wave of naturalists and scientists emerged to provide further evidence and analysis of the importance of protecting and preserving our natural resources. Prominent among them were Paul Sears, *Deserts on the March* (1935); Henry Fairfield Osborn, *Our Plundered Planet* (1948); Rachel

---

37. Gerald F. Vaughn, "The Geography of Resource Economics," *Land Economics* 70, no. 4 (1994): 518.

38. Roland R. Renne, *Land Economics: Principles, Problems, and Policies in Utilizing Land Resources*, rev. ed. (New York: Harper and Brothers, 1958), 316.

39. Donald Worster, ed., *American Environmentalism: The Formative Period, 1860–1915* (New York: John Wiley and Sons, 1973), 2.

Carson, *Silent Spring* (1962); Murray Bookchin, *Our Synthetic Environment* (1962); Barry Commoner, *The Closing Circle: Nature, Man, and Technology* (1971); and Aldo Leopold, *A Sand County Almanac and Sketches Here and There* (1949).

Bookchin's *Our Synthetic Environment* was published in 1962, the same year as Carson's *Silent Spring*, which many believe signifies the beginning of the environmental movement. Both works focus on the troubling condition of the natural environment: Carson warns of the dangers of overuse of pesticides, while Bookchin describes "not only the harmful effects of pesticides, but the serious environmental deterioration under industrial capitalism—chemical food additives, changing patterns of disease, the pollution of the atmosphere, rivers and lakes, the harmful effects of radioactive wastes, soil erosion, low-quality food and the degradation of the urban environment."[40] This dire assessment spurred a new awareness of what was happening to our environment, but Bookchin also provided a new and radical wrinkle to the growing sense of environmentalism. As professor of anthropology Brian Morris writes, "Bookchin sought to develop a coherent, synthetic philosophy and social theory that was holistic, radical and libertarian and to which he gave the name 'social ecology.'"[41]

Leopold pushed the twentieth-century context of environmentalism to a new, radical plateau when he passionately proclaimed the need for a land ethic and the view that people must become members of the land-community, not its conquerors. Leopold's contribution was especially important in opening a new understanding of the human-nature relationship, as described by historian Nash: "What he proposed would have necessitated a complete restructuring of basic American priorities and behavior. His philosophy also involved a radical redefinition of progress. The conquest and exploitation of the environment that had powered America's westward march for three centuries was to be replaced as an ideal by cooperation and coexistence."[42]

Organic and Empirical Traditions

Many planners and designers are representative of organic and empirical traditions that embrace an ecological awareness, but the following brief perspective outlines an intellectual line of descent encompassing the infu-

---

40. Brian Morris, *Pioneers of Ecological Humanism: Mumford, Dubos and Bookchin* (Montreal: Black Rose Books, 2017), 170.

41. Ibid., 198.

42. Nash, *The Rights of Nature*, 73.

sion of ecology and human ecology into the practice of planning human settlements. It sets the stage to more fully explore the Lewis Mumford–Ian McHarg relationship in fostering an ecohumanism approach to planning that specifically focused on regional planning.

Frederick Law Olmsted (1822–1903)

Usually regarded as the father of American landscape architecture, Olmsted's reputation would be secured by only one project—the creation of a new ecological environment out of unused swampland in New York City that would be named Central Park (1858). His legacy for designers and planners is not that he (along with colleague Calvert Vaux) simply produced landscape plans but that he did so with artistic imagination and naturalistic design.

Olmsted's work spans a variety of landscape and planning challenges. Examples of his voluminous output include urban parks (in addition to Central Park): Prospect Park, Brooklyn (1865–1888); regional design: the Boston Park System (1875–1895); community design: Riverside, Illinois (1868–1869); campus design: Stanford University (1886–1889); and urban design: World's Columbian Exposition, Chicago (1890–1893).

A complete assessment of Olmsted's many diverse landscape planning projects identifies certain "traits" that would make him a landmark for future generations: "First, Olmsted had a sense of the necessity for a balanced relationship between man and the natural world. . . . Second, Olmsted's work showed an almost unbelievable amount of foresight."[43] He advocated the healing power of nature in much the same way as the transcendentalists. In fact, Olmsted "felt that natural beauty, when it was possible to find it, was even more restful than man-made imitations of nature."[44]

Ebenezer Howard (1850–1928)

Howard, the progenitor of the Garden City movement after the turn of the twentieth century, emphasized reconciling humans to their social and natural environments. His vision of the Garden City aimed to bring the advantages of the town and the country together to create the city as a humane place. Thus, a composite of the cultural amenities of the city with

---

43. Julius Gy. Fábos, Gordon T. Milde, and V. Michael Weinmayr, *Frederick Law Olmsted, Sr.: Founder of Landscape Architecture in America* (Amherst: University of Massachusetts Press, 1968), 13.

44. Ibid., 43.

the environmental amenities of the country would offer the best of both worlds. Howard's "invention" of the Garden City as a planning direction for new communities was a rejection of the deterioration of city life that was taking place in the industrialized urban centers in Europe. He argued that places could be made whole, humane, and environmentally pleasing. Of significance, according to Howard's associate Frederic Osborn, was the "central idea" "that the size of towns is a proper subject of conscious control."[45]

The first Garden City plan was finished in 1904 for Letchworth, England, by architects Raymond Unwin and Barry Parker. Since that time, Howard's influence has proven to endure in many places and cultures. The American response to the Garden City movement in England was to produce a number of plans and built communities that replicated the Garden City ideal. Notably among them were Forest Hills Gardens, New York, built in 1912 and planned by Frederick Law Olmsted Jr. with architectural designs by Grosvenor Atterbury. Radburn, New Jersey, became the prominent Garden City example by the end of the 1920s, planned and designed by architects Clarence Stein and Henry Wright. From an institutional perspective, the American Garden City had its greatest support with the establishment of the Regional Planning Association of America (RPAA), which functioned between 1923 and 1933. What distinguished the RPAA from the English Garden City movement was "its insistence on regarding housing and planning goals in terms of (to use Lewis Mumford's phrase) an 'organic ideology' of the human environment."[46] Mumford was one of the key organizers, along with Stein, Catherine Bauer Wurster, Wright, and Benton MacKaye.

Patrick Geddes (1854–1932)

An important early thrust in formulating an empirical approach to planning, predicated on ecology, began with the work of Scottish biologist turned town planner Geddes. In 1884, Geddes sounded an ecological warning: "When any given environment or function, however apparently productive, is really fraught with disastrous influence to the organism, its modification must be attempted, or, failing that, abandonment faced."[47]

---

45. F. J. Osborn, ed., preface to *Garden Cities of To-Morrow*, by Ebenezer Howard (Cambridge, Mass.: MIT Press, 1965), 10.

46. Stanley Buder, *Visionaries and Planners: The Garden City Movement and the Modern Community* (New York: Oxford University Press, 1990), 166.

47. Philip Boardman, *The Worlds of Patrick Geddes: Biologist, Town Planner, Re-educator, Peace-Warrior* (London: Routledge and Kegan Paul, 1978), 4.

Between 1904 and 1914, through his philosophy and fieldwork, Geddes developed the idea of integrating what he described as "place, work and folk" as a means to understand the interactions between humans and their environment. By refusing "to see a clear separation between theory and practice, planning and participation, thought and action," Geddes "viewed place in terms of people and their life, [relating] physical planning to the natural environment."[48] He was a unique thinker who would significantly influence the eventual development of an ecological approach to planning. Philip Boardman, Geddes's biographer, describes his comprehensiveness this way: "Geddes's life shows a constant interpenetration of the general and the particular, the philosophical outlook and the scientific outlook, the universal and the regional."[49] In effect, Geddes laid down the basic structure that would later become the basis for an ethnographic perspective for planning. Through the emergence of human ecological planning in the 1970s, the Geddes concept of "place, work and folk" became a fully operationalized method incorporated into contemporary planning.

Lewis Mumford (1895–1990)

One of the best-known intellectuals of the twentieth century, Mumford wrote on a wide range of topics and issues. His particular contribution for the purposes of this book revolves around regional planning, architecture, American cultural history, technology, and his advancement of ecohumanism in city and regional planning and education. In *The Culture of Cities* (1938), he expresses the notion that humans—the organism—are not strictly implicated in an "environment in space," which "has its own line of growth, . . . its own curve of development, its own span of variations, its own pattern of existence"; we are "also implicated in time, through the biological phenomena of inheritance and memory; and in human societies it is even more consciously implicated through the necessity of assimilating a com-

---

48. Marshall Stalley, *Patrick Geddes: Spokesman for Man and Environment* (New Brunswick, N.J.: Rutgers University Press, 1972), xiii.

49. Philip Boardman, *Patrick Geddes: Maker of the Future* (Chapel Hill: University of North Carolina Press, 1944), xi. One of the early proponents of Geddes's work was sociologist, economist, ecologist, and philosopher Radhakamal Mukerjee, who studied with Geddes in India between 1914 and 1915. Mukerjee argued for the "give-and-take between Man and Environment or between culture and region," predicated on his view that "in human evolution we have reached a stage where genotypes of individuals not only fit themselves to or select their suitable environments but also can control and change the environments for themselves and for the species in terms of their own values." Radhakamal Mukerjee, *The Philosophy of Social Science* (London: Macmillan, 1960), 25.

plicated social heritage which forms, as it were, a second environment."[50] In essence, societal development and growth must be predicated on a clear acknowledgment of the interconnection of the two "environments." Mumford held that all aspects of the environment, consisting of communities, cities, and regions, are governed by organic rules of growth related to their function. If those limits are exceeded, then we invite catastrophe. Modern technology must be subordinated to human needs rather than be thought of in purely economic terms.

Benton MacKaye (1879–1975)

Trained as a forester, MacKaye became an important intellectual ally of Mumford's in promoting the concept of the connection between ecology and regional planning. People must control the metropolitan invasion, MacKaye writes in *The New Exploration* (1928), and think of regional planning as applied ecology. He believed that the "environment . . . provides a sort of *common mind*—the total life which every life must share: it is the least common denominator of our inner selves."[51] Clearly, in the tradition of Geddes, MacKaye saw the benefits of pursuing a more realistic understanding of the human-environment relationship that would shape the settlement pattern of the region. This theme would later be incorporated in the work of Artur Glikson and Ian McHarg.

Artur Glikson (1911–1966)

Israeli architect and planner Glikson conceptualized regional planning as incorporating ecology from Geddes, Mumford, and MacKaye. In the introduction to a work of collected essays, *The Ecological Basis of Planning* (1971), Mumford writes that the German-born Glikson "was primarily concerned not to display technical virtuosity or superficial esthetic originality, but to provide a setting that would do justice to the complexities of nature and the varied needs of human life."[52] Glikson himself stressed that "land planning should become an attempt at balancing a measure of environmental belongingness with a measure of free mobility, at shaping a rhythm in the transition from movement to rest and vice versa, and at establishing by

---

50. Lewis Mumford, *The Culture of Cities* (New York: Harcourt, Brace, 1938), 300.

51. Benton MacKaye, *The New Exploration: A Philosophy of Regional Planning* (New York: Harcourt, Brace, 1928; Urbana-Champaign: University of Illinois Press, 1962), 134 (page citations are to the reprint edition); emphasis original.

52. Lewis Mumford, ed., introduction to *The Ecological Basis of Planning*, by Artur Glikson (The Hague: Martinus Nijhoff, 1971), xxi.

the introduction of environmental changes a meaningful and valuable relationship between men and their landscape."[53] This focus, he continued, "requires the development of Regional Planning into Regional Design."[54]

In the essay "Planning with the Land," Glikson presents the notion that an ecological approach and a human ecological approach need to be manifest in planning. He writes, "It is the function of Regional Land Planning first to open our eyes to environmental values, next to prepare for the immense work of re-creating the human environment, which, if we regard the future with hope, will be one of the central tasks of the coming era."[55]

Ian L. McHarg (1920–2001)

A landscape architect and regional planner, McHarg emerged in the latter half of the twentieth century as the principal advocate to "design with nature."

Mumford's unique influence led to the crucial intellectual partnership that would advance McHarg's work as he developed a graduate curriculum in landscape architecture and regional planning that was first based on ecology and later incorporated human ecology at the University of Pennsylvania (Penn) from 1969 to 1973 and 1973 to 1979. McHarg's academic work stretched over to the practical as he infused ecology in the first planning projects undertaken by his consulting firm, Wallace, McHarg, Roberts and Todd.

McHarg's first iteration of a curriculum in regional planning incorporated a natural systems knowledge to planning and design—ecological planning—which he promoted with a religious fervor. His second iteration incorporated the human dimension—human ecological planning—that would effectuate the bridge to an ecology-humanism approach to planning and design, the direct result of Mumford's influence.

The Mumford-McHarg connection was critical in the movement to first establish and then effectuate ecohumanism and the ecological culture, especially with regard to education. This book examines the impact of that connection.

---

53. Ibid., 43.
54. Ibid.
55. Artur Glikson, "Planning with the Land," in *The Ecological Basis of Planning*, ed. Lewis Mumford (The Hague: Martinus Nijhoff, 1971), 44.

3

The Shaping of
Lewis Mumford's Ecohumanism

L EWIS MUMFORD has been referred to as a visual as well as a verbal thinker. Accordingly, "he believed in the superiority of empirical knowledge, acquired through direct contact with the material world."[1] Mumford had a vast knowledge and broad array of interests that encompassed many subjects, from architecture to city planning, from art to technology, from social thought to morality.

He was indeed a "public intellectual," a thinker and writer who addressed a "literate and general audience about questions and issues and concerns undefined or categorized by conventional academic and professional disciplines."[2] An overall assessment holds that Mumford "tried to formulate a comprehensive social theory for the twentieth century, weaving organismic philosophy, human ecology, and intellectual history into a unique and highly personal vision."[3] According to professor of art history Robert Wojtowicz, "As a philosopher, historian, and critic, Mumford channeled his intellectual

---

1. Arthur P. Molella, "Mumford in Historiographical Context," in *Lewis Mumford: Public Intellectual*, ed. Thomas P. Hughes and Agatha C. Hughes (New York: Oxford University Press, 1990), 41.

2. This description is given by Russell Jacoby in *The Last Intellectuals: American Culture in the Age of Academe* (New York: Basic Books, 1987), 5.

3. Andrew Jamison and Ron Eyerman, *Seeds of the Sixties* (Berkeley: University of California Press, 1994), 87.

energies into the pursuit of a single life goal: eutopia, the good place, to be located in the here and now."[4] And toward the end of his career, according to Wojtowicz, Mumford "regarded utopia—the 'perfect place'—as nearly the polar opposite of eutopia."[5]

If we are going to cast Mumford as an *ecohumanist*, then it becomes indispensable to gauge his intellectual contribution as a composite of three areas of concern—the natural physical environment, the organic world, and human society—that pervaded his life's work and that continually found their thematic appearance in his writings, be they about technology, architecture, art, cultural history, regional planning, morality, or education. It has been said that "the hallmark of Mumford's life and work [wa]s balance and wholeness. In asserting the need for balance in the region, the community, and the individual, he emphasized the close interaction of these levels of human organization."[6]

Technics and the Renewal of Life

Rosalind Williams, a professor of the history of science and technology, has written that "for Mumford it is a fundamental and unwavering principle that life, not external mechanism of any kind, determines historical destiny." However, as history has proven, "the great leap of modern machinery and industry is therefore the external, material, secondary expression of underlying desires and interests that are the primary determinants of history."[7] A companion identification could think of Mumford as an ecological historian, although he was not an environmentalist in the common use of the descriptor. Rather, throughout much of his earlier writings, he engages a fundamental "ecological understanding of the ebb and flow of human history."[8] As a result, his environmental—or ecological—philosophy is "deeply historicist[, as] he believed that the forces of history were

---

4. Robert Wojtowicz, *Lewis Mumford and American Modernism: Eutopian Theories for Architecture and Urban Planning* (New York: Cambridge University Press, 1996), 162. Wojtowicz is Lewis Mumford's literary executor.

5. Ibid.

6. Park Dixon Goist, "Seeing Things Whole: A Consideration of Lewis Mumford," in *The American Planner: Biographies and Recollections*, ed. Donald A. Krueckeberg (New York: Methuen, 1983), 250–251.

7. Rosalind Williams, "Lewis Mumford as a Historian of Technology in *Technics and Civilization*," in *Lewis Mumford: Public Intellectual*, ed. Thomas P. Hughes and Agatha C. Hughes (New York: Oxford University Press, 1990), 47.

8. Ramachandra Guha, "Lewis Mumford, the Forgotten American Environmentalist: An Essay in Rehabilitation," in *Minding Nature: The Philosophers of Ecology*, ed. David Macauley (New York: Guilford Press, 1996), 210.

moving in the direction of a cleaner environment, a more benign technology, and a more democratic social order."[9]

AMONG HIS INCREDIBLE WRITING OUTPUT, two volumes stand out to recount and describe the personal and introspective Mumford. In 1979, he published what he characterized as "a personal chronicle" under the title *My Works and Days*. In this work, he writes that his "own beliefs challenge those who think there is no turning back on the road that mankind is now travelling, no possibility of changing our minds or altering our course, no way of arresting or redirecting the forces that, if they are not subdued, will bring about the annihilation of man."[10] This statement is Mumford's way of explaining his position, which projects his acute knowledge of history and offers hope for the future of humankind. In his words, it is not as "a prophet of doom but as an exponent of the Renewal of Life that [he has] faced the future."[11]

The second volume that provides insight into Mumford's intellectual development is *Sketches from Life*, his autobiography published in 1982. In one passage, he relates how his experience teaching a university course served as the impetus for his most creative and productive literary series.

Between 1932 and 1935, Mumford was invited by Professor Robert MacIver to teach a course at Columbia University in the evening division titled "The Machine Age in America." Mumford recounts that "no academic courses similar to mine as yet existed in the United States, though I had written more than one brief essay on the influence of modern science and technology on the arts, beginning with a piece in *The New Republic* called 'Machinery and the Modern Style' [1921]."[12] He writes that this course at Columbia would "urge [him] to widen [his] entire technological and social perspective."[13] Even the choice of the term *technics* would open the door to the eventual production of a series of books, exploring in depth technology as well as natural and human ecology—the singular thrust of Mumford's ecohumanism.

In his "personal chronicle," Mumford says, "My point of departure in analyzing technology, social change and human development, concerns the nature of man. . . . Technocratic man is no longer at home with life, or with

---

9. Ibid., 216.

10. Lewis Mumford, *My Works and Days: A Personal Chronicle* (New York: Harcourt Brace Jovanovich, 1979), 16.

11. Ibid.

12. Lewis Mumford, *Sketches from Life: The Autobiography of Lewis Mumford* (New York: Dial Press, 1982), 448.

13. Ibid., 449.

the environment of life, which means that he is no longer at home with himself."[14] Professor of cultural history Leo Marx describes Mumford's use of the term *technics* rather than *technology* as "the umbrella category of tools and utensils that figure in all of recorded human history."[15] Mumford borrowed the term from Patrick Geddes, according to Marx, enabling him "to stress the relatively brief history, hence the distinctiveness, of machine technologies. This is particularly important today, when in popular discourse the word 'technology' is assumed to refer almost exclusively to technologies developed in the modern era, since the widespread diffusion of implements driven by various forms of mechanized motive power."[16]

IN HIS MATURATION into a new and more encompassing direction in his thinking and writing, Mumford "felt the need for a period of detachment and solitude, as well as for fresh scenes and other people . . . [for the basic reason that] 'Withdrawal and Return' was the essential key to the most creative periods of every historic culture."[17] Inevitably, he would produce a new set of books on related themes that he called The Renewal of Life series.

The four volumes that compose the series span almost two decades of Mumford's fertile career—from 1934 to 1951—and consist of the following: *Technics and Civilization* (1934), *The Culture of Cities* (1938), *The Condition of Man* (1944), and *The Conduct of Life* (1951). Mumford's biographer and professor of history Donald Miller calls the series "one of the great intellectual undertakings of our time."[18]

In the first volume of The Renewal of Life series, *Technics and Civilization*, Mumford establishes the springboard that would propel his investigations and analysis for all four volumes: "During the last thousand years the material basis and the cultural forms of Western Civilization have been profoundly modified by the development of the machine."[19] He expands this thesis by claiming that Western culture has exhibited "the compulsive nature of the urge toward mechanical development without regard for the actual

---

14. Mumford, *My Works and Days*, 469, 472.

15. Leo Marx, "Lewis Mumford: Prophet of Organicism," in *Lewis Mumford: Public Intellectual*, ed. Thomas P. Hughes and Agatha C. Hughes (New York: Oxford University Press, 1990), 175.

16. Ibid.

17. Mumford, *Sketches from Life*, 450.

18. Donald L. Miller, *Lewis Mumford: A Life* (New York: Weidenfeld and Nicolson, 1989), 299.

19. Lewis Mumford, *Technics and Civilization* (New York: Harcourt, Brace, 1934), 3.

outcome of the development in human relations themselves."[20] His view is that the resulting impact of such a compulsion is "plainly disastrous."[21]

Mumford's description of the "Technological Complex," as he calls it, has endured and can be divided "into three successive but over-lapping and interpenetrating phases: eotechnic, paleotechnic, and neotechnic."[22] These three time periods can be described as eotechnic (the use of wind, water, and wood) from 1000 to 1750, paleotechnic (the development of the use of coal, iron, and steam) from 1700 to 1900, and neotechnic (advances in the use of electricity, hard alloys, and lighter metals) from 1820 through the present. The crux of Mumford's typology is that "up to the neotechnic period technological progress consisted in renouncing the organic and substituting the mechanical: this reached its height around 1870."[23]

Twenty-five years after writing *Technics and Civilization*, Mumford would write his own critique. Although he confesses that "the whole outlook and tone of the book, as well as the underlying philosophy, seem even more definitely dated," he clarifies that "its very being was probably more important than any special contribution: for what text and illustrations joined in saying was that technics was not merely the product of engineers, inventors, workmen, capitalists, scientists, but the expression of a whole society."[24] Notwithstanding its "original defects . . . [and] whatever further shortcomings time has disclosed," Mumford writes, "it still unfortunately possesses its original distinction."[25]

An Emerging Ecohumanism

Mumford had, one might say, an intellectual love affair with the machine. His extensive reading and travels brought about a new and revealing awareness as he progressed through his writing career. He held that tools and utensils that have been part of humanity's trek through history "were, in the main, extensions of his own organism: they did not have . . . an inde-

---

20. Ibid., 365.

21. Ibid.

22. Ibid., 109. Mumford here acknowledges that Patrick Geddes first described the two phases, paleotechnic and neotechnic; however, Mumford felt that a "period of preparation," which he called eotechnic, needed to take place before the neotechnic phase.

23. This statement is contained in a letter that Mumford wrote to James Henderson on August 8, 1933, and is cited in Molella, "Mumford in Historiographical Context," 59.

24. Lewis Mumford, "An Appraisal of Lewis Mumford's 'Technics and Civilization' (1934)," *Daedalus* 88, no. 3 (1959): 534, 535.

25. Ibid., 535–536.

pendent existence." Following from this thinking, he believed that "the tool [or, more properly, the machine] brought man into closer harmony with his environment, not merely because it enabled him to re-shape it, but because it made him recognize the limits of his capacities."[26]

In his "Summary and Prospect" in *Technics and Civilization*, Mumford urges not for the abandonment of the machine, as it might improve or advance human activity, but for "the rebuilding of the individual personality and the collective group, and the re-orientation of all forms of thought and social activity toward life." This approach, he believes, "promises to transform the nature and function of our mechanical environment and lay a wider and firmer and safer foundation for human society at large." The next step in this reorientation consists of bringing technics "more completely into harmony with the new cultural and regional and societal and personal patterns we have co-ordinately begun to develop." After all, he concludes, "Nothing is impossible."[27]

IS THERE AN URGENCY to embrace ecohumanism? In his classic work *The Closing Circle*, noted biologist and research scientist Barry Commoner proffers, "To survive on earth, human beings require the stable, continuing existence of a suitable environment. Yet the evidence is overwhelming that the way in which we now live on earth is driving its thin, life-supporting skin, and ourselves with it, to destruction."[28] And this statement was made in 1971. What about today? We have become aware of the call from many quarters to create sustainable and resilient communities. We are continually bombarded with mass media accounts of continued threats to our places of habitat and our environment, coupled with either a conscious or unwitting violation of the ability of a given area to accommodate human activity or development. The changing climate is real, and many places throughout the world are experiencing its effects, including increased flooding in communities that historically have not flooded, quirky weather patterns that are exacerbated by "pop-up storms" that seem to come out of nowhere, and a rising sea level that is reconfiguring many coastal areas.

If these circumstances illustrate where we are today, what will we become? What are the challenges that must be faced? Psychologist David Schafer has argued, "The imperative to 'improve the human environmental

---

26. Mumford, *Technics and Civilization*, 321.
27. Ibid., 433–435.
28. Barry Commoner, *The Closing Circle: Nature, Man, and Technology* (New York: Alfred A. Knopf, 1971), 14.

circumstances' means that ecohumanism *must* enlist the most able among us to engage others, no matter how reluctant they may be at first, to join in a public dialogue about the issues of the human environment that affect us all and our prosperity."[29]

If the environment is the natural world of our human habitat, what about the world we shape and mold that also is a component of our human habitat? We are living in a technological culture—a culture that has become permeated by our attachment to the machine. The locomotive and the automobile are machines that greatly served our increasing needs for mobility and easier lives. Machines are for living, Mumford believed. However, is there a threshold beyond which the machine becomes paramount? In describing "The Metropolitan Milieu" in 1934, Mumford writes, "Those who use machinery because they are incapable of facing the stream of life and directing it, those who seek order in automations because they lack the discipline and courage to achieve order in themselves, *become the victims of their instruments* and end by becoming mere attachments to a mechanical contrivance" (italics added).[30]

Today, our technological culture has achieved greater heights with its latest machine—the computer, which has become indispensable in facilitating and advancing how we live in a digital age. Indeed, this digital age surrounds our entire existence. So what about our place of living and our environment, which are equally essential for sustaining our future well-being? We are transitioning from a reliance on traditional planning, architecture, and landscape architecture perspectives to visions of the rise of virtual cities. How will this technological movement affect our existing cities? And how will such a transition affect people and alter our understanding of our human habitat as well as the environment? "Traditional urban patterns cannot coexist with cyberspace. . . . Community doesn't have to depend on propinquity. Links among people are formed in hitherto unimaginable ways," suggests professor of architecture and media arts William Mitchell.[31] New avenues of awareness and analysis will open if we acknowledge, as Mitchell says, that "digital communication also remakes the traditional rhythms of daily life."[32]

---

29. David Schafer, "Time Is Not on Our Side," in *Ecohumanism*, ed. Robert B. Tapp (Amherst, N.Y.: Prometheus Books, 2002), 160; emphasis original.

30. Lewis Mumford, *City Development: Studies in Disintegration and Renewal* (New York: Harcourt, Brace, 1945), 46. The original essay appeared in 1934 and was reprinted in the 1945 edition.

31. William J. Mitchell, *e-topia: "Urban Life, Jim—But Not as We Know It"* (Cambridge, Mass.: MIT Press, 1999), 3, 7.

32. Ibid., 4.

FIGURE 3.1. Lewis Mumford self-portrait, July 1919.
(Lewis Mumford Collection, Monmouth University Library. Used With permission.)

Charting a Direction

Mumford was born in Flushing, New York, on October 19, 1895, and he died in Amenia, New York, on January 26, 1990. His literary output during such a long lifetime is nothing less than incredible: thirty books and more than a thousand essays, articles, and reviews. Much of his work is still in print today. In 1938, following the publication of *The Culture of Cities*, a forty-three-year-old Mumford appeared on the front cover of *Time* magazine, straddled in the embrace of a tree. He had already published his first book, *The Story of Utopias* (1922), as well as *Sticks and Stones: A Study of American Architecture and Civilization* (1924), a biography of Herman Melville (1929), *The Brown Decades: A Study of the Arts in America* (1931), and *Technics and Civilization* (1934), among several other publications.[33] So for *Time* to present a fairly comprehensive review of *The Culture of Cities* was not surprising, since Mumford had clearly established himself as a notable intellectual. (Interestingly, in that review article, he is continually referred to as "Author Mumford.") *Time*'s critical assessment makes the point that "Lewis Mumford has displayed a unique capacity for sensing and understanding the advanced thought, the advanced craftsmanship of his time, reconciling its contradictions in a persuasive synthesis."[34] Such an assessment would prove true as measured by his total literary output.

A CRUCIAL ASPECT of understanding and appreciating Mumford's thought revolves around his deepest concern: that we must not allow the advancement of technology to supplant our humanity. To Mumford, such an error would have the consequential result of altering—perhaps irrevocably—the traditional and essential elements of our humanness. Besides, an "organic system" just works better than a mechanical one. He drove this point home when he once again was called on to offer the final commentary at a conference. The event was the "Challenge for Survival Symposium," sponsored by the New York Botanical Garden and Rockefeller University in April 1968. In his remarks, Mumford asserted that "our present lack of ecological balance is largely due to the fact that our technology, in overcoming our organic limitations and increasing, by an enormous factor, the amount of energy at our disposal, has none of the self-limiting and self-correcting devices that organic systems have developed."[35]

While editing the extensive correspondence between Mumford and his mentor, Geddes, from 1915 to 1932, professor of English Frank Novak gleaned unique insights to Mumford's thinking. "The essential quality of Mumford's thought," he concludes, "is more akin to a religious faith—emphasizing certain moral values and an intuitive understanding—than a rigorously formulated, logically cohesive philosophy."[36] Novak continues,

---

33. Many years later, in the introduction to a bibliography of his published works, Mumford writes, "What a writer has written and *not* published is in some ways even more revealing than what he has finally thought fit to expose. . . . Yet somehow they give a certain substance and definition to what has gone into print." Lewis Mumford, introduction to *Lewis Mumford: A Bibliography, 1914–1970*, by Elmer S. Newman (New York: Harcourt Brace Jovanovich, 1971), xviii.

34. "Art: Form of Forms," *Time*, April 18, 1938, 42.

35. Lewis Mumford, "Survival of Plants and Man," in *Challenge for Survival: Land, Air, and Water for Man in Megalopolis*, ed. Pierre Dansereau (New York: Columbia University Press, 1970), 226.

36. Frank G. Novak, *The Autobiographical Writings of Lewis Mumford: A Study in Literary Audacity* (Honolulu: University of Hawaii Press, 1988), 45.

"Mumford's fundamental outlook is characterized by a cosmic inclusiveness, an emphasis on discovering the meaning and value of human experience, and a belief in the sacredness of life in all its organic manifestations."[37] We can discern a true cosmology in Mumford's thinking and writing: "Every transformation of man, except that perhaps which produced neolithic culture, has rested on a new metaphysical and ideological base; or rather, upon deeper stirrings and intuitions whose rationalized expression takes the form of a new picture of the cosmos and the nature of man."[38] He was not religious in a formal sense and did not identify with any religious persuasion. Professor Miller maintained that Mumford "did not believe in God as an actual spirit or being; 'God' was his own expression for his unshakable belief that there is a hidden purpose in nature."[39]

STICKS AND STONES (1924), Mumford's first book that engaged American culture, "was devoted to architecture, which he considered the most important of the social arts," according to Miller.[40] He continues that Mumford's three principle concerns—architectural criticism, regional planning, and American cultural history—became "interlinked aspects of a program of cultural renewal that established him in the 1920s as an independent moral force on the American Left."[41] Mumford's critique is strong and to the point: "Scarcely any element in our architecture and city planning is free from the encroachment, direct or indirect, of business enterprise."[42] The human endeavors of architecture, landscape architecture, and city planning (as well as regional planning) need to be understood as organic, and they need to capture a human spirit that cannot be set aside as communities grow and develop. This emphasis captures a critical essence of Mumford's ecohumanism. For Mumford, this emphasis relies not on some mystical notion of human progress but rather on the knowledge and recognition that people, places, and environment are inextricably a part of a holistic pattern of human progress. "All organic change partakes of creation," he believes, since this takes place "not through the investigation of mechanical sequences, . . . but through the observation of purposive action in man's own creative acts."[43]

---

37. Ibid.
38. Lewis Mumford, *The Transformations of Man*, ed. Ruth Nanda Anshen (New York: Harper and Brothers, 1956), 231.
39. Miller, *Lewis Mumford*, 561.
40. Ibid., 168.
41. Ibid.
42. Lewis Mumford, *Sticks and Stones: A Study of American Architecture and Civilization* (New York: Boni and Liveright, 1924), 159.
43. Lewis Mumford, *The Conduct of Life* (New York: Harcourt, Brace, 1951), 136.

The broader concern that pervades his entire life's output is the issue of how we are compromising our basic humanity as a result of our increasing reliance on the "machine." This theme has reverberated through the ages, and Mumford's continued warnings have acute relevance today. "By turning our environment over to the machine," he writes in 1924, "we have robbed the machine of the one promise it held out—that of enabling us to humanize more thoroughly the details of our existence."[44] Mumford is not against the machine—even though he never drove a car, he did use a typewriter. Yet he insists that we need only elevate the role of the machine as a complement to human existence and endeavor, not the other way around. In this regard, he differentiates between art and technics: "Art is that part of technics which bears the fullest imprint of the human personality; technics is that manifestation of art from which a large part of the human personality has been excluded, in order to further the mechanical process."[45]

A closer look at the development of the machine through history brings him to the point of evaluating its social and environmental impacts and results, which are "more disturbing than the prophets of mechanical progress were willing to admit; from the beginning of the fifteenth century blasted landscapes, befouled streams, polluted air, congested filthy slums, epidemics of avoidable disease, the ruthless extirpation of old crafts, the destruction of valuable monuments of architecture and history—all these losses counterbalanced the gains."[46] Such a position, based on his deep study and interpretation of history, would provide the environmental movement that coalesced in the 1960s, with Mumford its star. He offers "a personal view of human history and an emphasis on personality in the shaping of history while centering around the transformation between human societies and their natural environments."[47]

Mumford's conception of economics complements his social philosophy. As "the quantitative bias of modern economic theory and practice originated in a mechanistic worldview," according to professor of history Kenneth Stunkel, Mumford's "economic thought has been swayed by an antiquated mechanical world picture that undermines human interests."[48] As a result, "there is no number crunching in his books, no econometric analysis of interest rates, consumer indexes, labor productivity, or gross domestic

44. Ibid., 166.

45. Lewis Mumford, *Art and Technics* (New York: Columbia University Press, 1952), 21.

46. Lewis Mumford, *The Myth of the Machine: Technics and Human Development* (New York: Harcourt Brace Jovanovich, 1966), 293.

47. Jamison and Eyerman, *Seeds of the Sixties*, 89.

48. Kenneth R. Stunkel, "Vital Standard and Life Economy: The Economic Thought of Lewis Mumford," *Journal of Economic Issues* 40, no. 1 (2006): 116, 115.

product," which would be expected in conventional economic assessments.[49] Mumford's economic model would replace "megatechnics, its seemingly endless resourcefulness in concocting technocratic answers to human problems," with a new model—"biotechnics . . . the first step toward passing from power to plentitude."[50] So for Mumford, "once an organic world picture is in the ascendant, the working aim of an economy of plentitude will be, not to feed more human functions into the machine, but to develop further man's incalculable potentialities for self-actualization and self-transcendence, taking back into himself deliberately many of the activities he has to supinely surrender to the mechanical system."[51]

HAVING BEEN BORN before the turn of the twentieth century, Mumford was, as he called himself, "a child of the city." He states in his autobiography, "Since I have spent no small part of my life wandering about cities, studying cities, stirred by their activities, this original envelopment by the city constitutes an important clue to my life."[52] Yet the country also had its pull, as he spent the summers between 1903 and 1908 on a farm in Vermont. He would later recall, "Those summers, with their round of rural activities, left such a sharp imprint that I have drawn on them ever since."[53]

One aspect of Mumford's life that is not commonly known is that he was quite the artist. His "first real awakening to Modern Art," he explains, "did not come until 1915 when, in the Boston Museum of Fine Arts, I was dazzled by the dancing broken colors of Monet's canvases, and began making small water color drawings in the same fashion."[54] Professors Vincent DiMattio and Kenneth Stunkel have discovered and assembled a Catalogue Raisonné of 321 sketches, watercolors, and drawings, plus 16 photographs that are now in the custody of Monmouth University. They describe the pieces as "small in scale, but [they] are notable in the landscapes and cityscapes for their handling of space. The media are usually colored pencil, crayon, and watercolor, materials easily carried in Mumford's knapsack during hikes in city and countryside."[55]

---

49. Ibid., 115.
50. Lewis Mumford, *The Myth of the Machine: The Pentagon of Power* (New York: Harcourt Brace Jovanovich, 1964), 347, 395.
51. Ibid., 395.
52. Mumford, *Sketches from Life*, 4–5.
53. Ibid., 86.
54. Mumford, *My Works and Days*, 211.
55. Vincent DiMattio and Kenneth R. Stunkel, *The Drawings and Watercolors of Lewis Mumford* (Lewiston, N.Y.: Edwin Mellon Press, 2004), 5.

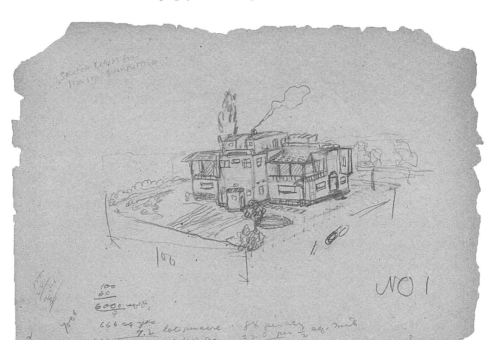

FIGURE 3.2. Lewis Mumford, sketch for a house design, 1918.
(Lewis Mumford Papers, Kislak Center for Special Collections, University of Pennsylvania.
Copyright © 1918 by Elizabeth M. Morss and James G. Morss. Used by permission.)

Mumford's wife, Sophia, writes of her husband, "For as far back as I can remember him, Lewis sketched as he thought—constantly. . . . The sketching was as instinctive as the writing. It was Lewis's way of talking to himself."[56] Mumford himself found that his art—and that of others—served an essential cathartic purpose: "The work of art is the visible, potable spring from which men share the deep underground sources of their experience. Art arises out of man's need to create for himself, beyond any requirement for mere animal survival."[57]

Of course, Mumford is best known for his extensive writings, which required an intellectual mind that craved discovery and a disciplined lifestyle that would get results. Wojtowicz has recounted how Mumford worked:

---

56. Sophia Mumford, preface to *The Drawings and Watercolors of Lewis Mumford*, by Vincent DiMattio and Kenneth R. Stunkel (Lewiston, N.Y.: Edwin Mellon Press, 2004), 1.
57. Mumford, *Art and Technics*, 16.

Mumford's daily routine could be considered almost monkish in its ascetic self-discipline. An early riser, he would spend most mornings at his desk writing. In the more leisurely afternoons, he would work in his garden, take long walks, or catch up on his correspondence. His evenings were often devoted to reading in preparation for the next morning. He looked for ways to improve himself, as for example, when he taught himself to write more legibly while in his late fifties. If at times he seemed aloof, even to his children, this intense focus on his writing was absolutely essential for him to be productive.[58]

Mumford was a classic empiricist, relying on observation coupled with extensive reading and contemplation to learn about the ways we shape our habitat. As time would prove, and as his many writings attest, Mumford developed strong views on the ecological impact of urban expansion. Miller writes, "Comparing the city to a living biological organism, Mumford argued that when it grew too large it disrupted its symbiotic relationship with its surrounding territory, destroying the ecological balance that originally prevailed between city and country in the first stages of urbanization."[59]

Wojtowicz relates that Mumford traveled to Europe in the spring of 1932 to conduct research and "to examine recent architectural developments, and in particular the new Siedlungen. Mumford's travels were extensive, taking him to England, Scotland, France, the Netherlands, Germany, and Austria."[60] Always the acute observer, Mumford would find that the experience made him turn away from the burgeoning international style that was becoming increasingly popular in Europe and America. Wojtowicz points out, "Significantly, Mumford's sketches from this trip reveal a growing fascination with medieval architecture and town planning, rather than an abiding interest in modern architecture."[61]

From this beginning interest in the early medieval town, Mumford would later write, "Though surrounded by a wall, it was still part of the open countryside."[62] More to the point of perpetuating such a design, he held that the medieval town reflected "organic planning," which "does not begin with a preconceived goal: it moves from need to need, from opportunity to opportunity, in a series of adaptations that themselves become increasingly coherent and purposeful, so that they generate a complex, final design,

---

58. Wojtowicz, *Lewis Mumford and American Modernism*, 4.
59. Miller, *Lewis Mumford*, 197.
60. Wojtowicz, *Lewis Mumford and American Modernism*, 95.
61. Ibid., 96.
62. Lewis Mumford, *The Culture of Cities* (New York: Harcourt, Brace, 1938), 42.

hardly less unified than a pre-formed geometric pattern."[63] Could this appreciation of the organic have served as a model for how twentieth-century America should develop?

To a great degree, such a perspective was the springboard of Mumford's life pursuit, as he would ask, "If there are favorable habitats and favorable forms of association for animals and plants, as ecology demonstrates, why not for men?"[64] As a pillar of his ecohumanism, he maintains that "people, their occupations, their workplaces and living places, form inter-related and definable wholes."[65] The idea of balance and its variations needs to be understood, since this concept "involves the utilization of a variety of ecological groupings and a variety of human responses: balance and variety are the two concepts, in fact, which help one to define a region of cultural settlement."[66]

MUMFORD FIRST READ GEDDES'S PAMPHLETS in 1915 and referred to him as "master" during their thirty-year correspondence and friendship. Mumford absorbed Geddes's teaching about the environment, ecology, and planning; after reading the master's *Cities in Evolution* (1915), he would proclaim that this work "performed the most valuable service that any single book could have performed: it taught the reader, in simple terms, how to look at cities and how to evaluate their development."[67] Geddes opened Mumford's mind to the idea of the physical environment and social environment existing as one.

This recognition of physical and social environments as a composite, or two parts of the whole, informs Geddes's analysis of human settlements in *Cities in Evolution*. According to sociologist Marshall Stalley, "He believed it essential to view the city in the context in which it exists . . . so a city can be understood only with reference to the region in which it is located, the history of its people, and the social and physical forces affecting and being affected by it."[68] This concept gave rise to the administration of a "regional survey" prior to any planning—in essence, a study of the city or the region before planning it. The extent and purpose of the regional survey as described by Geddes would frame Mumford's methodological approach to regional planning. In his first book, *The Story of Utopias* (1922), Mumford

63. Lewis Mumford, *The City in History: Its Origins, Its Transformations, and Its Prospects* (New York: Harcourt, Brace and World, 1961), 302.

64. Mumford, *The Culture of Cities*, 302.

65. Ibid.

66. Ibid., 314.

67. Lewis Mumford, *The Human Prospect*, ed. Harry T. Moore and Karl W. Deutsch (London: Secker and Warburg, 1956), 106.

68. Marshall Stalley, *Patrick Geddes: Spokesman for Man and the Environment* (New Brunswick, N.J.: Rutgers University Press, 1972), 107.

advocates for the regional survey: "The aim of the Regional Survey is to take a geographic region and explore it in every aspect. . . . [I]t emphasizes . . . the natural characteristics of the environment, as they are discovered by the geologist, the zoologist, the ecologist—in addition to the development of natural and human conditions in the historic past, as presented by the anthropologist, the archeologist, and the historian." In short, Mumford concludes, "the regional survey attempts a local synthesis of all the specialist 'knowledges.'"[69] (Ultimately, this very approach would become the cornerstone in the development of ecological and human ecological planning by Ian McHarg, as I illustrate in subsequent chapters.)

The linchpin of Geddes's conceptual thinking that Mumford would embrace was the trilogy "Place, Work, Folk." It positions Geddes as a synthesizer of observation and thought rather than as a specialist, who would confine a specific discipline to a set role and a set function. Geddes "take[s] the three elements basic to social life anywhere, at any time—Place, Work, and Folk— and link[s] them with their respective sciences: geography, economics, and anthropology," which ensures their interrelatedness.[70] In the purest sense, the importance of Geddes to Mumford was his standing as a "generalist with interdisciplinary interests."[71]

Geddes's approach to understanding cities and regions was predicated on viewing a system of interacting environmental and human elements. Planning theorist Nigel Taylor concludes that "Geddes's ideas remained marginal to the mainstream of town planning thought throughout the first half of the twentieth century, which continued to be dominated by architectural ideas. And so by the 1960s, against the background of a design-based view of planning, the systems view struck many planners as novel, even revolutionary."[72] Mumford the disciple would keep the Geddes systems view in the forefront through his prodigious writings on city and regional planning.

After analyzing the correspondence between Geddes and Mumford, Novak concludes, "What Geddes taught Mumford about how to study cities remained an important influence throughout his long career. The 'method and outlook' Geddes advocated provided a model of 'how to look at cities, how to interpret their origins, their life, their cumulative history, their

---

69. Lewis Mumford, *The Story of Utopias* (New York: Boni and Liveright, 1922), 279.

70. Philip Boardman, *Patrick Geddes: Maker of the Future* (Chapel Hill: University of North Carolina Press, 1944), 402.

71. Helen Meller, *Patrick Geddes: Social Evolutionist and City Planner* (London: Routledge, 1990), 318.

72. Nigel Taylor, *Urban Planning Theory since 1945* (London: Sage Publications, 1998), 62.

PATRICK GEDDES
26 - VII - 23

FIGURE 3.3. Drawing
of Patrick Geddes by
Lewis Mumford, 1923.
*(Lewis Mumford Collection,
Monmouth University Library.
Used With permission.)*

potentialities.'"[73] Mumford believed that all aspects of the environment—communities, cities, and regions—are governed by organic rules of growth related to their function. If those limits are exceeded, then we invite catastrophe. Modern technology must be subordinated to human needs rather than be thought of in purely economic terms.

Geddes was insistent on "his own particular theory of knowledge," and Mumford acknowledged his intellectual debt to his predecessor, yet he also formulated "his own approach to analyzing cities, past, present, and future."[74] Mumford was especially influenced by Geddes in his formative years, between 1915 and 1925; he would later write that Geddes had "left [his] mark on my whole life." However, he would add, "Geddes's greatest gift to me was to deepen and reinforce the foundations that other minds had already laid, while he gave me courage to build an original structure with new materials in a different style: radically different, necessarily, from his own."[75]

73. Frank G. Novak Jr., *Lewis Mumford and Patrick Geddes: The Correspondence* (London: Routledge, 1995), 25.

74. Meller, *Patrick Geddes*, 302.

75. Mumford, *Sketches from Life*, 158.

IN HIS 1902 PUBLICATION, *Garden Cities of To-Morrow*, Ebenezer Howard proposes a type of development that would offer the advantages and opportunities of the city *and* the country. Such a city in the country—a Garden City— would ensure limits on its size with a greenbelt to contain the settlement pattern. Attracted to its self-sustaining entities, Mumford saw this approach as a means to reconcile humans to their social and natural environments. "In short," Mumford writes, "Howard attacked the whole problem of the city's development, not merely its physical growth but the interrelationship of urban functions with the community and the integration of urban and rural patterns, for the vitalizing of urban life on the one hand and the intellectual and social improvement of rural life on the other."[76]

Howard's Garden City spurred a movement that intrigued Mumford and made him a strong advocate for their development on the American scene. His attraction to the Garden City "as the foundation for a new cycle in urban civilization" was predicated on the idea that "the means of life will be subservient to the purposes of living, and in which the pattern needed for biological survival and economic efficiency will likewise lead to social and personal fulfillment."[77]

Coupled with his advocacy of the Garden City as a viable means to plan and develop regions, Mumford's approach to the concept of regionalism and planning would become the key ingredients in shaping his ecohumanism.

Mumford's Ecohumanism in Regional Planning

In his writings, Mumford continually seeks a balance between humans and the environment. He identifies "the new mutation" as a "re-polarization of the existing creeds and ideologies and methodologies, which now function at cross-purposes, [that] could take place under one condition: through the appearance of a new concept of space and time, of cosmic evolution and human development."[78] He continues, "Now the new polarizing element is the concept of the person: the last term in the development of the organic world and the human community."[79]

If *ecohumanism* is a compounding of the reality of ecology as it governs the natural world and natural systems and *humanism* represents a value structure

---

76. Lewis Mumford, "The Garden City Idea and Modern Planning," in *Garden Cities of To-Morrow*, by Ebenezer Howard, ed. F. J. Osborn (Cambridge, Mass.: MIT Press, 1965), 35.

77. Ibid., 40.

78. Mumford, *The Conduct of Life*, 240.

79. Ibid., 241.

that promotes human needs and concerns, then Mumford's analysis of regionalism and support for regional planning certainly represent such a direction. His theme for a new direction—or "renewal"—is fairly straightforward and emphasizes "the resurgence of life, the displacement of the mechanical by the organic, and the re-establishment of the person as the ultimate term of all human effort. Cultivation, humanization, co-operation, symbiosis: these are the watchwords of the new world-enveloping culture."[80]

DURING THE 1920s AND 1930s, Mumford would secure his place in American planning history by pushing the idea of regionalism into the public agenda. In his introduction to a 1925 issue of *Survey Graphic* devoted to the subject of regional planning, Mumford describes "two Americas," the first being the original settlements and the second including a series of migrations. The first migration involved seeking land through "the clearing of the continent" to make way for the many communities that would develop. The second migration consisted of the "great flow of population . . . from the countryside and from foreign countries into the factory town that in effect would promote industrial production." The third migration found its "magnet" in the financial center that accelerated the growth and consolidation of the banking, insurance, and advertising interests. The fourth migration was the "technological revolution," which had the cumulative impact of making "the existing layout of cities and the existing distribution of population out of square with our new opportunities." "Fortunately for us," he writes, "the fourth migration is only beginning: we may either permit it to crystallize in a formation quite as bad as those of our earlier migrations, or we may turn it to better account by leading it into new channels."[81] What Mumford clearly saw was the beginning of the suburbanization of the region, the dilution and eventual annihilation of a traditional American way of life that he wished to see maintained. This increasing reality of the twentieth century would be a direct result of advances made under the aegis of the new technological culture.[82]

---

80. Lewis Mumford, *The Condition of Man* (New York: Harcourt, Brace, 1944), 399.

81. *Survey Graphic* 7 (May 1925): 130–133. Mumford later incorporated this essay as "Preface: The Fourth Migration" in *The Urban Prospect* (New York: Harcourt, Brace and World, 1968), ix–xx.

82. Professor of architecture and urban planning Robert Fishman recognizes Mumford's historic migration trends and argues that "the fourth migration to suburbia and beyond is now finally ebbing, and a fifth migration is now underway . . . in what I call the *reurbanization* of those inner city districts . . . that had been most devastated during Mumford's fourth migration" (emphasis original). Robert Fishman, "The Fifth Migration," *Journal of the American Planning Association* 71, no. 4 (2005): 358.

The genesis and growth of regionalism between 1920 and 1945 have been extensively discussed by historian Robert Dorman, who cites the analysis of regionalist and folklorist Benjamin Botkin, who in turn called it a vital and practical force in American life. Botkin maintained that regionalism might become a new ideology, since it would conserve, select, integrate, and interpret cultural values and social thought.[83] Mumford agreed and vigorously worked to impart this understanding of regionalism and the necessity of regional planning.

In July 1931, Mumford gave an address to the Round Table on Regionalism at the University of Virginia, wherein he proclaimed that "the recognition of the region as a fundamental reality is part of the achievement of modern human geography. . . . [I]t has a natural basis and is a social fact."[84]

Mumford accepted the reality of regionalism with the unbridled insistence that planning must be done: "Genuine planning is an attempt not arbitrarily to displace reality, but to clarify it and to grasp firmly all the elements necessary to bring the geographic and economic facts in harmony with human purposes."[85] He defined regional planning as "the conscious direction and collective integration of all those activities which rest upon the use of the earth as site, as resource, as structure, as theater."[86]

A contemporary analysis of region-focused planning reviews historic definitions and current approaches, including Mumford's description. In their work *Regional Planning in America*, Ethan Seltzer and Armando Carbonell argue that "there may be less distance than we think between the so-called utopian idealists of the early twentieth century and our contemporary results-oriented pragmatists."[87] The emphasis on regional planning today, they maintain, "is carried out over a territory . . . that share[s] enough characteristics to assert its existence as a region. Fundamentally, rather than planning within boundaries, regional planning addresses issues across boundaries."[88] This perspective gives Mumford's conception of the region and regional planning some additional depth, since he understood

---

83. See Robert L. Dorman, *Revolt of the Provinces: The Regionalist Movement in America, 1920–1945* (Chapel Hill: University of North Carolina Press, 1993), 151.

84. Mumford's entire address is included in *Planning the Fourth Migration: The Neglected Vision of the Regional Planning Association of America*, ed. Carl Sussman (Cambridge, Mass.: MIT Press, 1976), 199–208; the quotation is at 202–203.

85. Mumford, *The Culture of Cities*, 376.

86. Ibid., 374.

87. "Planning Regions," in *Regional Planning in America: Practice and Prospect*, ed. Ethan Seltzer and Armando Carbonell (Cambridge, Mass.: Lincoln Institute of Land Policy, 2011), 9.

88. Ibid.

the importance of the relationship of the interdependent parts and how they relate to the whole.

Mumford outlines four stages that regional planning requires, beginning with Geddes's insistence on the regional survey as a "first-hand visual exploration and by systematic fact-gathering, [of] all the relevant data on the regional complex." The second stage is "the critical outline of needs and activities in terms of social ideals and purposes." The third stage "is that of imaginative reconstruction and projection. On the basis of known facts, observed trends, estimated needs, critically formulated purposes, a new picture of regional life is now developed." This becomes the regional plan. The fourth stage involves community engagement and acceptance and "its translation into action through the appropriate political and economic agencies." In Mumford's vision, the "plan undergoes a readaptation as it encounters the traditions, the conventions, the resistances, and sometimes the unexpected opportunities of actual life."[89]

AN APPLICATION of the Garden City concept would provide a compass for how a region could be planned and ultimately developed. Mumford saw the Garden City as a way to adapt regional planning on a human scale, control growth, and create a workable balance among various land uses from residential to commerce, from agriculture to industry. Promoting the Garden City notion in America required a new emphasis to address regional planning, which gave rise to the Regional Planning Association of America (RPAA) in 1923, a group of people representing architecture, planning, and business. However, Mumford, forester Benton MacKaye, architect Clarence Stein, and housing advocate Catherine Bauer Wurster could be considered the critical nucleus. Each brought complementary skills to their shared mission to advance the planning of regional cities, not just the planning of city regions. Mumford would later write that despite "how few we were, how diverse our cultural interests and our professional qualifications, how experimental our approach, and how modest our personal claims . . . [i]n spirit we answered Aristotle's definition of a good society: 'a community of equals, aiming at the best life possible.'"[90]

The RPAA's focus was a deep concern about the nature and extent of regional expansion. Its members "critically assess[ed] the new urban order, a social system they called *metropolitanism* because, among other things,

---

89. Mumford, *The Culture of Cities*, 376–380.
90. Mumford, *Sketches from Life*, 339–340.

FIGURE 3.4. Lewis Mumford and Benton MacKaye at an early gathering
of the Regional Planning Association of America, Netcong, New Jersey, May 1923.
*(Clarence S. Stein Papers, #3600, Division of Rare and Manuscript Collections,
Cornell University Library.)*

this form was too big and too congested to function as a city."[91] Mumford
was increasingly committed to challenging the growth of the technological culture, which was seemingly on a path to untie the traditional bonds
that an ecologically based community offered. As a result, the concept of
regionalism would unite Mumford's advancement of three ideas: "'*neotech-
nics*'—the adaptation of new technologies for the purpose of restoring the
natural environment; *organicism*—the restoration of nature's influence on
culture through literature, architecture, and the built environment; and
community—the recovery of human-scaled, civic-minded social order."[92]

Mumford's thesis is that a region is an organic network, with the city or
cities within its geographical bounds functioning along the lines of Howard's Garden City parameters—principally, to limit growth and expansion.
Effectively, Mumford writes, "the problem of regional planning is to revive
or create regional cities in permanent relationship with the countryside,
instead of turning into agglomerations."[93]

Mumford's RPAA-era writings frame what could be considered "the

91. Sussman, *Planning the Fourth Migration*, 6; emphasis original.
92. Mark Luccarelli, *Lewis Mumford and the Ecological Region: The Politics of Planning*
(New York: Guilford Press, 1995), 22.
93. Lewis Mumford, "The Theory and Practice of Regionalism," *Sociological Review*
20, no. 1 (1928): 31.

first environmental argument against the metropolis in urban literature," as he compares "the city to a living biological organism."[94] Compatible with the laws of ecology, he proposes that if a city grows too large, it will disrupt "its symbiotic relationship with its surrounding territory, destroying the ecological balance that originally prevailed between city and country in the first stages of urbanization."[95] Focusing on the region when planning could solve many current ills: "It is time that we came to terms with the earth, and worked in partnership with the forces that promote life and the traditions that enhance it."[96]

The RPAA's philosophy of regionalism, according to professor of urban history Stanley Buder, rested on Mumford and MacKaye and was "done in a way which set the RPAA on a course apart from the American Planning establishment."[97] This situation has been confirmed by American planning history chronicler Mel Scott, who remarks that "Mumford's hope for a 'renewal' of the larger region, embracing farmland and forest as well as village and city, seemingly was hardly shared, though in another decade city planners would be more receptive to his views."[98]

Mumford and MacKaye believed that "existing communities might be radically reshaped, great cities dramatically shrunk and restructured, [and] smaller communities economically redirected and vitalized."[99] I argue that their intellectual partnership reached its zenith with MacKaye's publication of his "philosophy of regional planning." Mumford's introduction to MacKaye's seminal work supports his assertion that the "city is the first victim of the metropolitan flood," or, as it is characterized, "the invasion of metropolitanism."[100]

MacKaye had a deep and abiding respect for the New England hill village as a "pronounced example of a unit of humanity—a community—a definite 'living together.'"[101] For MacKaye, such an urban form represented a structural and cultural symmetry. Like Mumford, MacKaye was a cham-

---

94. Miller, *Lewis Mumford*, 197.

95. Ibid.

96. Mumford, "The Theory and Practice of Regionalism," 140.

97. Stanley Buder, *Visionaries and Planners: The Garden City Movement and the Modern Community* (New York: Oxford University Press, 1990), 169.

98. Mel Scott, *American City Planning since 1890* (Berkeley: University of California Press, 1969), 251.

99. Buder, *Visionaries and Planners*, 169.

100. Lewis Mumford, introduction to *The New Exploration: A Philosophy in Regional Planning*, by Benton MacKaye (New York: Harcourt, Brace, 1928), xix.

101. Benton MacKaye, *The New Exploration: A Philosophy of Regional Planning* (New York: Harcourt, Brace, 1928), 59. A paperback edition was published in 1962 by the Appalachian Trail Conference and the University of Illinois Press.

pion of regional planning, and he challenged planners to "uncover, reveal, and visualize." This mandate was essential, since "planning is two things: (1) an accurate formulation of our own desires—the specific knowledge of what it is we want; and (2) an accurate revelation of the limits, and the opportunities, imposed and bequeathed to us by nature."[102]

The RPAA dissolved in 1933. The group made an impression, yet its collective efforts did not have a measurable and lasting impact. Mumford would later lament, "The fact is we dispersed and none of us were as good after as we were together."[103]

The Garden City settlement undoubtedly influenced the design of a number of communities following Sunnyside (1924), in Queens, and Radburn (1929), fifteen miles from Manhattan in New Jersey, both by architects Clarence Stein and Henry Wright. The RPAA understood that change was "inevitable and often beneficial but also requir[ed] controls to guarantee that it enhanced humane values of civilization."[104] An emphasis on regional planning would not completely go away but would evolve as the metropolitan area—in America and elsewhere—began to be further shaped by urban and suburban expansion and development. Never one to sit on the sidelines, Mumford continued to write and allowed his critical viewpoints to be presented and debated. After all, he was becoming the American spokesperson for ecohumanism.

With the publication of *The Culture of Cities* in 1938, "Mumford was at the peak of his influence as an urban thinker."[105] It was also a time when planners were addressing the need for a new settlement pattern and developing plans for greenbelt towns (Greenbelt, Maryland; Greenhills, near Cincinnati, Ohio; and Greendale, near Milwaukee, Wisconsin) based on Howard's Garden City principles that would offer a "planned integration of residential community functions, . . . each attaining a moderately high density in a spacious setting."[106]

IT WAS PERHAPS a stroke of fate that the American Institute of Planners asked Mumford to write and narrate a film to be presented at the 1939 World's Fair in New York City. The resulting landmark documentary film, *The City*, has been described as "a wonderfully rich statement of the faith that the proper

---

102. Ibid., 147.
103. Sussman, *Planning the Fourth Migration*, 43.
104. Buder, *Visionaries and Planners*, 179.
105. Miller, *Lewis Mumford*, 366.
106. Blake McKelvey, *The Emergence of Metropolitan America, 1915–1966* (New Brunswick, N.J.: Rutgers University Press, 1968), 92.

environment could shape better communities. . . . His role was to move the film from the level of mere entertainment to incisive public commentary."[107] *The City* (with a musical score by Aaron Copland) moves from scenes of a New England village, a mill town, a city, and finally a new town, all with the purpose of recapturing the essence of living in well-planned communities in the regional milieu. Mumford's commentary endorses the current planning direction to build sustainable neighborhoods, picking up the RPAA's emphasis on "the importance of a planned environment in the process of socialization."[108] In a way, the film was also a propaganda piece to promote Mumford's push for planned regionalism, to improve the public's understanding of city and regional planning, and to solidify the mission of its sponsor, the American Institute of Planners.

MUMFORD'S ENDURING WRITINGS and critical assessments provide ample evidence to secure his legacy as a first-rate contributor to historic-cultural analysis. Additionally, professional planners in Britain and America have acknowledged their debt to Mumford. In 1946, the Royal Town Planning Institute presented him with the Ebenezer Howard Memorial Medal and named him an honorary member. The American Planning Association followed suit by designating Mumford a "Planning Pioneer" in 1989. His impact on American planning practice has been described this way: "For one thing, he has forced his ideas on us with a tenacity that we might envy and emulate. He has compelled us to think comprehensively. . . . He has challenged us to see beyond the limits of our immediate constraints to a larger view. . . . He has rooted the profession in the rich literary and aesthetic traditions of our country."[109] All in all, Mumford was not just a major force in the world of ideas but an inspiration and mentor to others to ensure that those ideas would be carried on.

Mumford's all-embracing ecohumanism approach to planning as a specific theory and method had its strongest practical proponent in Artur Glikson and its strongest educational proponent in Ian McHarg. Mumford's influence would become evident in the work of both men in much the same way as Geddes's work influenced Mumford. In fact, it was through Mumford that Glikson and McHarg became acquainted with the ecological

---

107. Howard Gillette Jr., *Civitas by Design: Building Better Communities, from the Garden City to the New Urbanism* (Philadelphia: University of Pennsylvania Press, 2010), 45, 52.

108. Ibid., 53.

109. David A. Johnson, "Lewis Mumford: Critic, Colleague, Philosopher," *Planning* 49, no. 4 (1983): 14.

thinking of Geddes, which emphasized that every city and region is unique and that cultural evolution is a reflection of their unique attributes.[110]

The regional survey method would become commonly applied to many cities and regions. Glikson's work—especially its debt to Mumford—has not received the recognition it deserves or that McHarg's work would later achieve.

GLIKSON WAS BORN IN KOENIGSBERG, GERMANY, in 1911. After receiving a diploma in architecture from the Technische Hochschule at Berlin-Charlottenburg in 1935, he immigrated to Palestine (under British mandate at the time). For ten years following the establishment of the state of Israel in 1948, he served in several principal capacities as a government planner and architect. Of note, Glikson led the planning team to undertake a master plan for Kiryat Gat, the central town in the newly formed Lakhish region, as well as several other regional plans. In 1964, he joined the professional team tasked with preparing a comprehensive development plan for the island of Crete.

The importance of Glikson's work as an architect and planner is that he "evolved a comprehensive and holistic body of thought based on a twin set of interests."[111] His first interest was a "humanist approach [that] reflected his interest in people in whom he saw not only a rich and endless variety but also a common identity: people with the same problems, the same pains, and the same joys all over the world." His second interest was to appreciate "the complexity of forms and species [that] evolved by the forces of nature that created diverse environments and life forms uniquely adapted to their specific location."[112]

It has been said that Glikson's "planning philosophy crystallized due in

---

110. Actually, McHarg's earliest encounter with the work of Geddes dates to a correspondence course he took in 1944 while still in military service. The course, "The Background of Planning," was designed by Jaqueline Tyrwhitt (1905–1983), a British town planner, landscape architect, editor, and educator who "stimulated the mid-century revival of interest in Geddes's ideas." Ellen Shoshkes, "Jaqueline Tyrwhitt Translates Patrick Geddes for Post World War Two," *Landscape and Urban Planning* 166 (October 2017): 15. See also Ian L. McHarg, *A Quest for Life: An Autobiography* (New York: John Wiley and Sons, 1996), 56.

It is my assessment that even though McHarg learned of Geddes through this correspondence course, the real impact of his thinking did not have a lasting impact until McHarg came under the influence of Mumford at the University of Pennsylvania.

111. Rachel Wilkansky, "From Regional Planning to Spatial Planning: The Sources and Continuing Relevance of Artur Glikson's Planning Thought," *Journal of Architectural and Planning Research* 21, no. 2 (2004): 127. I should point out that this entire issue of the *Journal of Architectural and Planning Research* is themed "Artur Glikson and the Making of Place: A Look at His Lasting Impact on Planning and Architecture."

112. Ibid.

large measure to his deep friendship and continuous professional dialogue with Lewis Mumford, which lasted until Glikson's death in 1966."[113] In addition, the works of MacKaye, Aldo Leopold, and Geddes influenced his evolving planning and design philosophy. In "The Planner Geddes" (originally published in 1954), Glikson writes, "Planning, for Geddes, represented the unity of practical knowledge and skill with social ideals for a positive use of natural conditions and human potentialities." He continues with a discussion of the classic Geddes trilogy: "Planning, nevertheless, is only a part of a threefold social action based on the recognition of the factors of society (or folk), economics (or work), and town and region (or place). . . . These three activities should be coordinated with no clear dividing lines between them."[114]

Glikson's description of the classic Geddes notion of the regional survey had a particular relevance and importance in how such a survey would be used—especially later in McHarg's planning and design work. In Glikson's words, "A survey of a town or region does not mean merely a listing of facts, but an insight into the essence of social interrelations, as well as the relations between the society, its sources of livelihood and its habitation." Glikson's conclusion would become a central focus of his work: "As the Survey progresses, the planner begins sensing clearly the characteristics of regional life . . . [and must] make a wise selection of the factors whose investigation should yield the richest harvest."[115]

When Mumford first met Glikson, they became "friends at first sight." And Mumford quickly realized that Glikson's emphasis on "ecological aspects [was] where his ideas were more penetrating and profound than those of most of his contemporaries."[116] Mumford saw in Glikson a rare opportunity to form a close bond that would promote ecohumanism in real-world applications. After all, Glikson was in the trenches, as one might say, planning and designing new town developments in the burgeoning state of Israel to accommodate its growing population during the 1950s. In retrospect, Mumford writes, "from Artur Glikson's career one thing clearly emerges. He was primarily concerned, not to display technical virtuosity or superficial esthetic originality, but to provide a setting that would do justice

---

113. Shmuel Burmil and Ruth Enis, "An Integrated Approach to Landscape Planning," *Journal of Architectural and Planning Research* 21, no. 2 (2004): 141.

114. Artur Glikson, *The Ecological Basis of Planning*, ed. Lewis Mumford (The Hague: Martinus Nijhoff, 1971), 49.

115. Ibid., 48.

116. Lewis Mumford, ed., introduction to *The Ecological Basis of Planning*, by Artur Glikson (The Hague: Martinus Nijhoff, 1971), xvi.

to the complexities of nature and the varied needs of human life."[117] He was, according to Mumford, "a pioneer in sociological planning."[118]

As immigrants streamed into Israel, the accepted practice was to place them in housing complexes based on their countries of origin, effectively segregating them from veteran Israelis who had been in the country prior to statehood. Glikson saw this policy as a detriment in creating a holistic community living environment, especially since population assimilation was a national goal. His approach was to establish an "experimental neighborhood" that would acknowledge and give primacy to integrating social needs and cultural expressions:[119] "His experimental neighborhood was conceived as a means of addressing the need to not only house new immigrants but also to do so in a way that facilitated their transformation into productive and socially responsible Israeli citizens."[120] The neighborhood that Glikson wanted to create would "be stimulated by the economic and social diversity of its residents" as well as a mix of housing units that differed by size and spatial distance, largely reflecting varying immigrant attitudes and cultural differences.[121] Glikson formalized this concept in what he called the *Integral Habitational Unit*, which would promote "Unity in Variety . . . by creating mixed residential units, representative of a wide range of variations in the population [with the hope] to foster urban community development and arrive at new composite urban structures."[122]

Mumford clearly saw in Glikson's approach to planning a holism and "a departure from the single-factor analysis, the mechanistic oversimplifications, and the unbalanced activities that are now undermining the very basis of organic existence, to say nothing of human culture."[123] Glikson demonstrated in his planning and design projects that, for example, land use planning and landscape architecture cannot be separated and must combine beauty with function: "Just as in architecture the functional syntheses found for a variety of programmatic requirements have to be elevated to functional quality; so the useful and the beautiful must be fused."[124]

---

117. Ibid., xxi.

118. Ibid., vii.

119. Glikson's proposal is strikingly similar to what American planner Clarence Perry had proposed in 1929 as incorporated in the Radburn plan as the "neighborhood unit," wherein the elementary school would serve as the design nucleus to achieve a socially compact community.

120. Robert W. Morans, "Neighborhood Planning: The Contributions of Artur Glikson," *Journal of Architectural and Planning Research* 21, no. 2 (2004): 119.

121. Ibid., 115.

122. Glikson, *The Ecological Basis of Planning*, 111–112.

123. Mumford, introduction to Glikson, *The Ecological Basis of Planning*, vii.

124. Glikson, *The Ecological Basis of Planning*, 43–44.

Glikson can be considered an early proponent of seeking a synchronicity between ecology and humanism in addressing development issues and pressures. His success in doing so can be measured by historians, but he did pioneer a way of thinking that moved from vision to practice.

Mumford's Ecohumanism in Education

Geddes's influence on Mumford's early understanding of cities and regions would seal the direction of his life's work, but another aspect of the Geddes-Mumford relationship would also have a lasting impact and principally shape his evolving goal of embedding ecohumanism in education. Miller explains the extent of that influence: "It was not Geddes the city planner and sociologist that Mumford was most strongly drawn to; it was Geddes the educator and activist, who called for the development of the total person, of all our capacities for reason and calculation, passion and poetry, mental work and full-bodied living. Geddes's writing—and his personal example—helped Mumford chart a new direction for his life."[125]

Considering the breadth of Geddes's adventurous and fertile mind, it seems inevitable that his interests would expand into education, especially his favorite disciplines: geology, geography, economic history, and the natural and social sciences. Moreover, he was convinced that conventional education was not really providing a comprehensive educational experience. He believed that education should go beyond classroom lectures and required examinations. Geddes "wanted to concentrate on stimulating interest, inspiring enthusiasm, and thus increasing the potential creativity of every student. . . . This meant that there had to be practical activities such as laboratory work and field studies."[126] Accordingly, he transmitted to Mumford two key educational precepts: the indispensable value of learning by observation and the necessity of learning through an interdisciplinary lens.

However, Mumford would expand Geddes's educational philosophy that encompassed ecology and humanism. In his autobiography, Mumford recalls that when he discovered Geddes's writings, "I myself was . . . a somewhat premature student 'activist,' full of rebellion against the formal requirements of a fixed curriculum. . . . To be honest, I seethed with many of the same inner hostilities that broke out collectively during the widespread student rebellions of the 1960s."[127] Mumford would continually tackle that ever-present issue of technology and how our increasing reliance on the "machine" erodes

125. Miller, *Lewis Mumford*, 57.
126. Meller, *Patrick Geddes*, 93.
127. Mumford, *Sketches from Life*, 156.

the humanity that we, as a species, need for our sustenance and survival. This reality would spill over into his assessment of the state of education.

Never willing to shy away from making his views known, Mumford assailed the "social responsibilities of teachers" and the inadequacy of the educational process when he spoke before the Commission on Teacher Education of the American Council on Education in August 1939. The most important change needed in education to meet the current challenge, he said, was "a change from the metaphysics of the machine, derived from the needs and interests of capitalism, to the metaphysics of the organism, directed to the needs and interests of the co-operative social order that [was] now emerging."[128] Once again, he brought to the forefront the work of Geddes, suggesting that the regional survey would secure that synthesis between philosophy and science and be "the introduction to orderly knowledge [coming] directly from the student's observation of, and participation in, the activities of man and nature."[129] The ultimate value of the regional survey "itself [was as] a program of acting and doing, as well as knowing," and since it was "a study of social processes and activities, it [would] lead inevitably to critical reevaluations, and finally to the formation of policies, plans, and projects that will alter the existing situation."[130]

Mumford's critique of accepted educational pedagogy did not change much over the next twenty-five years. He expressed his displeasure with the educational system when he gave the opening address to the nineteenth National Conference on Higher Education in April 1964. Here, Mumford proclaimed that the basic problem with education was that the "processes of automation into every department of our lives . . . proceed more rapidly than ever with the automation of knowledge." He challenged the audience of educators to "bring back, as essential to the further development of life, the complex organic components, above all the full human personality, that we have too peremptorily repressed and rejected."[131] Hard hitting and to the point, he must have provoked some uncomfortable feelings as he said, "The current belief in mechanical quantification without constant human qualification makes a mockery of the whole educational process."[132]

---

128. Lewis Mumford, "The Social Responsibilities of Teachers," in *Values for Survival: Essays, Addresses, and Letters on Politics and Education* (New York: Harcourt, Brace, 1946), 147. This address was originally published in *Educational Record* 20 (October 1939): 471–499.

129. Ibid., 151.

130. Ibid., 153–154.

131. Lewis Mumford, "The Automation of Knowledge: Are We Becoming Robots?" *Vital Speeches of the Day* 30, no. 14 (1964): 442.

132. Ibid., 444.

TWO PIVOTAL IDEAS can be ascribed to Mumford's ecohumanism in education: "New World" ideology on the one hand and "One World" humans on the other. When he gave the closing statement at the Conservation Foundation's April 1965 conference, he pleaded for "the need for re-education of ourselves so as to get on top of a technological system that is destroying both organic variety and human choice." He continued to directly challenge the status of education: "In educational terms, this means that we must provide a curriculum aimed not at producing more technicians, more engineers, more mathematicians, more scientists, but at producing more whole men and women. In a word, the conservation of natural resources means nothing less than the conservation of human potentialities."[133]

To Mumford, "New World education" was "the fabrication of Mechanical Man: one who will accept the mechanical world picture, who will submit himself to mechanical discipline, in thought and act will enlarge the empire of the machine."[134] In a cultural evolutionary sense, this view can be ascribed to the Enlightenment as it fashioned the scientific revolution, highlighted by the application of new methods of observation and experimentation to understand the laws of nature. It also was manifest in the aim of European exploration to find and eventually settle a "new world."

The concept of a "One World" human challenges humankind "to create a new self . . . [that will] take as its province the entire world, known and knowable, and will seek, not to impose a mechanical uniformity, but to bring about an organic unity, based upon the fullest utilization of all the varied resources that both nature and history have revealed to modern man."[135]

IN 1976, the first work assessing Mumford's role in advocating for a truly transformative philosophy of education was published. In compiling his important and carefully prepared analysis, David Conrad, professor of educational foundations at the University of Vermont, explored Mumford's intellectual output, conducted several interviews with him, and maintained a correspondence that spanned a decade. Conrad's conclusion that "implications for education in Mumford's philosophy are vast" establishes Mumford as a key person to articulate a new and visionary education.[136] He looks at

---

133. Lewis Mumford, "Closing Statement," in *Future Environments of North America*, ed. F. Fraser Darling and John P. Milton (Garden City, N.Y.: Natural History Press, 1966), 728.

134. Mumford, *The Condition of Man*, 259.

135. Mumford, *The Transformations of Man*, 179.

136. David R. Conrad, *Education for Transformation: Implications in Lewis Mumford's Ecohumanism* (Palm Springs, Calif.: ETC Publications, 1976), 4.

Mumford's goal of achieving the "One World" human as another phase in historic transformations, "undergoing regeneration and entering into fresh integrations. The communal pattern of village and family group, a feature of archaic man, becomes strengthened and renewed in cooperatives and neighborhood organizations—not as isolated communal forms but as local units in a worldwide cooperative."[137] Mumford's idealism notwithstanding, inventing a new universal transformation of cultural values does have applicability if one focuses on the role and purpose of education. Incremental steps may be needed, but the immediate and long-range impacts of educating for a "world community" have urgency and legitimacy.

The two key points of emphasis to glean from Mumford's ecohumanism are interdependence and self-renewal. We might think of interdependence in the sense that Leopold stressed that we are all part of a "world" community, not apart from it. Here, we find the notion of ecology has special relevance, since all organisms relate to the environment; we are in no small measure the perpetuators of an environment that will either sustain us or cause our demise. On the other hand, individual and collective self-renewal can be a relevant way to think of how we should shape our social institutions and community bonds. Such a normative perspective can give us a clearer understanding and appreciation for establishing communities that serve the complexities of human needs.

Mumford's drive to make cities and regions more humane provides a direction for an educational focus and, more specifically, for curriculum innovation. As Conrad argues, "Educators might take his suggestion to focus upon the planning and designing of totally new communities as well as explore the problems and promises of present urban areas."[138] For Conrad, the most valuable tool for educators is "Mumford's notion of regional survey as an intensive study of one's region [that] can be used by educators at all levels and in virtually all discipline areas."[139]

HAVING JUST COMPLETED HIS SERVICE in the British Army during World War II, twenty-six-year-old Major Ian L. McHarg was ready to start his education. In the fall of 1946, he traveled to America and enrolled in the School of Design at Harvard University to study landscape architecture and city planning. Since he was a bit older than most matriculating students, he would be referred to today as a *returning student*, someone returning for

---

137. Ibid., 141.
138. Ibid., 167.
139. Ibid.

a university education after a hiatus for work, personal reasons, or military service.

McHarg was critical of his experience at the Harvard Graduate School of Design and found "that the instincts were splendid and the energy and commitment admirable, but there was a notable absence of wisdom. Yet this quality existed in the person of Lewis Mumford. He came each year, gave marvelously thoughtful lectures, diagnostic and prescriptive, but he was seen as aberrant."[140] This first encounter with Mumford would prove life-changing for McHarg, as subsequent chapters illustrate. Mumford would eventually fulfill the mentor role for McHarg as Geddes had for Mumford. Mumford's influence would lure McHarg from conventional landscape architecture to become an ecological planner and designer who eventually would garner international recognition.

McHarg's career journey began soon after he arrived in Philadelphia in the fall of 1954, ready to begin teaching in the Graduate School of Fine Arts (today the School of Design) at the University of Pennsylvania. Mumford had been a member of the faculty since 1951 in the Department of City and Regional Planning in the Graduate School of Fine Arts, and the two became reacquainted, this time not as teacher and student but as colleagues.

Miller writes that "Mumford was in demand on college campuses because he was a riveting speaker and an accomplished classroom teacher. As a lecturer he exuded strength and power, and an almost Olympian certainty."[141] In 1951, Mumford had joined the faculty in the Department of Land and City Planning (later the Department of City and Regional Planning) in the Graduate School of Fine Arts at Penn. According to Wojtowicz, Mumford taught only in the fall so that he could spend time on his research and writing, and he "offered courses primarily in urban history, contemporary architecture and civic design. One of Mumford's primary goals was to reacquaint students with architectural history and its critical importance in the design process."[142]

Mumford would teach at the University of Pennsylvania from 1951 to 1956 and from 1959 to 1961. He was named professor emeritus at Penn in

---

140. McHarg, *A Quest for Life*, 83.

141. Miller, *Lewis Mumford*, 458. Over the years, Mumford had a number of appointments as a visiting professor or scholar, including at Brandeis University, Dartmouth College, Harvard University, the Massachusetts Institute of Technology, North Carolina State College, Stanford University, and the University of Pennsylvania.

142. Robert Wojtowicz, "Lewis Mumford," in *The Book of the School: 100 Years, the Graduate School of Fine Arts of the University of Pennsylvania*, by Ann L. Strong and George E. Thomas (Philadelphia: University of Pennsylvania, 1990), 160–161.

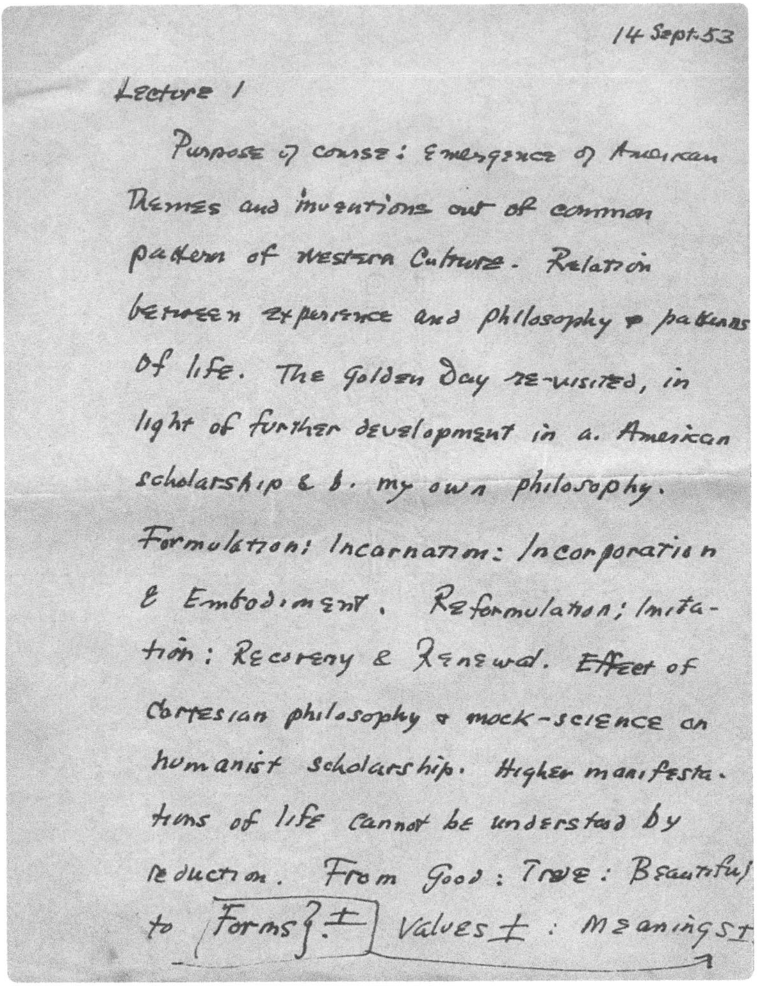

14 Sept. 53

Lecture 1

Purpose of course: Emergence of American Themes and inventions out of common pattern of Western Culture. Relation between experience and philosophy & patterns of life. The Golden Day re-visited, in light of further development in a. American scholarship & b. my own philosophy.

Formulation: Incarnation: Incorporation & Embodiment. Reformulation; Imitation: Recovery & Renewal. Effect of Cartesian philosophy & mock-science on humanist scholarship. Higher manifestations of life cannot be understood by reduction. From Good: True: Beautiful to Forms? ± Values ± : Meanings ±

FIGURE 3.5. Lewis Mumford, first lecture notes, American Forms and Values course, University of Pennsylvania, September 14, 1953.
(Lewis Mumford Papers, Kislak Center for Special Collections, University of Pennsylvania. Copyright © 1953 by Elizabeth M. Morss and James G. Morss. Used by permission.)

1975, on his eightieth birthday. After 1954 (when McHarg arrived at Penn), the two colleagues would solidify their intellectual bond (see Part III).

Ultimately, the Mumford-McHarg association would serve as the crucial step in moving ecohumanism to a new level, beginning with McHarg's development of a theory and method of ecological planning and later human ecological planning. McHarg's evolving graduate curriculum at Penn, with its emphasis on ecology in regional planning and landscape architecture, would also secure his legacy in education.

PART II

PLANNING AND DESIGN

The Fusion of Theory and Practice

4

Ian McHarg's Theory
and Method of Ecological Planning
and Design

W E CAN THINK of ecohumanism as a philosophy that justifies
planning and designing with the goal of moving toward an
ecological culture. This mind-set is what Lewis Mumford
sought and what Ian McHarg accomplished. This chapter begins with various definitions of planning. It then moves to an explanation of McHarg's
approach to planning and design, including the key aspects for understanding his *theory of ecological planning*—(1) the underlying principles of ecological planning, (2) the difference between ecological planning and ecological
design, (3) the fusion of ecological planning and regional planning, and (4)
the transition from ecological planning to human ecological planning—and
a description of the *ecological planning method*.

There is a direct correlation between McHarg's theory and method of
ecological planning and how the graduate education curriculum was shaped
at the University of Pennsylvania (Penn). The educational thrust would be
to inculcate ecology into regional planning and landscape architecture (see
the comprehensive discussion in Part III).

What Kind of Planning?

City and regional planners have perhaps as many definitions of planning as
there are ways in which people attempt to understand the present and project
the future. The history of planning theory and the practice of planning have

provided certain guidelines for or definitions of what planning is, should be, and ought to accomplish. Countless books and articles have discussed the concept of planning and molded it into a conceptual definition for theory and a working definition for use in practice. I argue that a cognitive process of planning, as a human endeavor to manage or effect change in the future, has remained constant over time. However, what has changed is the manner in which planning is done, and that relates directly to how it is defined, to accomplish a specific end.

Perhaps one of the most fruitful ways to approach the question of *what is planning?* is to recall the typology established by planning theorist John Friedmann. He maintains that planning is related to intellectual traditions that come and go, with bits and pieces of one captured or modified by another. Friedmann links knowledge to action in defining four major traditions of planning, including social reform, social mobilization, policy analysis, and social learning. These have paved the way for an enunciation of not just one but three definitions of planning that are each underscored by two operative terms: *social guidance* and *social transformation*. Friedmann's three definitions of planning can be concisely stated as (1) planning attempts to link scientific and technical knowledge to actions in the public domain, (2) planning attempts to link scientific and technical knowledge to processes of social guidance, and (3) planning attempts to link scientific and technical knowledge to processes of social transformation.[1]

Planning theorist Ernest Alexander cites a number of historic and evolutionary trends that he brings together in the hope of advancing an "acceptable synthesis" of what planning is—and should be. According to Alexander's understandable perspective, "Planning is the deliberate social or organizational activity of developing an optimal strategy of future action to achieve a desired set of goals, for solving novel problems in complex contexts, and attended by the power and intention to commit resources and to act as necessary to implement the chosen strategy."[2] Two questions to test the relevancy of this definition are whether (1) this is a meaningful and manageable description of what planning is and (2) this is what planners do. In a general sense, the answer to both questions is yes, since the evolution of planning has been a discipline (a field of study) and a profession (a vocation of practice). Yet Alexander's broad-brush, all-inclusive definition does not account for the incredible impact that a wide range of intellectual and pragmatic influences

---

1. John Friedmann, *Planning in the Public Domain: Linking Knowledge to Action* (Princeton, N.J.: Princeton University Press, 1987), 38.

2. Ernest R. Alexander, *Approaches to Planning: Introducing Current Planning Theories, Concepts and Issues* (Philadelphia: Gordon and Breach Science Publishers, 1992), 69–73.

have had in shaping how planning has attempted to invent, synthesize, or formulate an ideal future condition for people, their places, and the environment. Moreover, this broad-brush definition does not address changing professional and societal perspectives on what planning should be. The unique challenge, in theory and in practice, in formulating or adjusting a definition (or definitions) of planning is how to fuse different disciplinary approaches to problem identification and problem solving under this general rubric. For example, in the second edition of his classic text *Land Use Planning*, F. Stuart Chapin writes that "land use planning is part of this larger process of city planning,"[3] which emphasized a shift from the designer-craftsman notion of planning to the embodiment of a scientific approach to planning. Thirty years later, in the fourth edition of Chapin's text, this description of planning is vastly expanded to encompass a number of changes: (1) "incorporating microcomputer technology in the organization and analysis of information and the presentation and evaluation of plans," (2) the "integration of plan and action," (3) "extension of the planning process beyond advance planning to development management and problem solving," and (4) "the evolving governmental context for local planning, which features greater state influence and more attention to the consistency between plans and action, and between local and regional plans."[4]

A brief sampling of some of the perspectives that have appeared in the planning literature during the last four decades to define *planning* represent a potpourri of approaches that have emphasized a rational, comprehensive, and technical view. For example, Alan Altshuler proposes that the function of a master plan or comprehensive plan is "to guide the deliberations of specialist planners."[5] Martin Meyerson and Edward Banfield distinguish between *comprehensive* planning, where "the most important ends are to be attained," and *partial* planning, where "some but not all of the most important ends are to be attained or only . . . ends of subordinate importance are to be attained."[6] On a different theme, Britton Harris views planning as "essentially anticipatory decision-making."[7] In a standard introductory text,

---

3. F. Stuart Chapin Jr., *Land Use Planning*, 2nd ed. (Urbana: University of Illinois Press, 1966), vi.

4. Edward J. Kaiser, David R. Godschalk, and F. Stuart Chapin Jr., *Urban Land Use Planning*, 4th ed. (Urbana: University of Illinois Press, 1995), xiv.

5. Alan A. Altshuler, *The City Planning Process: A Political Analysis* (Ithaca, N.Y.: Cornell University Press, 1965), 299.

6. Martin Meyerson and Edward C. Banfield, *Politics, Planning, and the Public Interest: The Case of Public Housing in Chicago* (New York: Free Press, 1955), 313.

7. Britton Harris, "New Tools for Research and Analysis," in *Urban Planning in Transition*, ed. Ernest Erber (New York: Grossman, 1970), 197.

John Levy proposes that "planning in its generic meaning is a ubiquitous activity" that shares a common denominator—among its meanings—as "a conscious effort to define systematically and think through a problem to improve the quality of decision making."[8] Finally, Michael Brooks strips away the embellishments to define planning, "quite simply, as the process by which we attempt to shape the future."[9]

However one defines planning philosophically or intellectually and however one pursues planning in practice, one aspect of understanding what planning is has to do with making it a relevant endeavor that addresses defined problems, with implementable solutions that can be realistically achieved. Moreover, whether one assumes a generalist or specialist view of planning, one of the most significant defining issues has been what kind of planning is most applicable in addressing the exigencies of society and projecting a future condition for people. Under such schemes as social enhancement, systems analysis, political power, physical design, economic cost-benefit analysis, resource allocation, and growth management, planning and its many components have, in most instances, aimed at projecting a better future. If we stipulate this understanding, then the important question becomes what knowledge we need to be acquired to make planning work in the world of reality—a reality that can be projected as an ought-to-be for the future. As history has shown, we have seen planning move from the traditional design of cities and the creative design of urban and nonurban spaces to the provision of social service delivery systems at the federal, state, and local levels. We have also seen the evolution of all sorts of planning: land use planning, environmental planning, social planning, public policy planning, economic development planning, advocacy planning, and even virtual reality planning.

If we think about the elementary concept that lies at the root of the definition of planning, I suggest that it is an activity of human consciousness to determine optimal relationships of people to their places and to their environment. People form bonds and structure those bonds in the form of settlements—villages, towns, cities, and regions. People also need and use resources—air, water, and land. People express social and cultural values and create governmental and other institutions to better their lives. Thus, with the inevitable association of people to people, to their places,

---

8. John M. Levy, *Contemporary Urban Planning*, 5th ed. (Upper Saddle River, N.J.: Prentice Hall, 2000), ix.

9. Michael P. Brooks, *Planning Theory for Practitioners* (Chicago: Planners Press, American Planning Association, 2002), 9.

and to their environment, the concept and use of planning become essential and purposeful functions to maximize the benefits of those relationships while minimizing the negative consequences that might damage those relationships.

This perspective on planning is consistent with McHarg's approach.

McHarg's Theory of Ecological Planning

Generally, the development of ecological planning in America was influenced by the changing points of view from the 1930s through the 1950s concerning how humans not only respond to but also rely on environmental resources. In a comprehensive account of the profusion of ecological approaches, Forster Ndubisi argues that three significant aspects have established the parameters of ecological planning: (1) the continued evolution of ecological ideas, (2) the translation of ecological ideas into planning and the articulation of ethical principles that govern humans' use of the land, and (3) the refinement of techniques for the application of ecological ideas to planning efforts.[10] Two principles form the focus of ecology as the basis of planning. First, following from the perspective of the biological sciences, the concept and definition of ecology state that all organisms, including plants, animals, microorganisms, and people, are interdependent and exist in complex relationships with their environment. Second, planning is predicated on elements of understanding, establishing, modifying, or projecting these relationships among people and between people and their environment.

McHarg would develop his theory of ecological planning within this frame. The principal thrust of McHarg's contribution is that we must design with nature in mind to ensure the most beneficial living environment for our immediate and long-term survival. Put in this context, ecological planning becomes the means for meeting humanity's continuing process of adapting to a living environment. This process of adaptation recognizes the undeniable relationship between all living organisms and their environment. As a result, this inextricable interdependence must be not just understood but promoted as the underpinning of all land use planning and development. Simply put, the underlying theme is that ecological planning offers the best hope for people to achieve the maximum social, economic, and environmental benefits in designing their present and future towns, cities, and regions. Therefore, to achieve this end, ecological planning is

---

10. Forster Ndubisi, *Ecological Planning: A Historical and Comparative Synthesis* (Baltimore: Johns Hopkins University Press, 2002), 16.

FIGURE **4.1.** Ian McHarg, self-portrait, circa 1954.
(Ian McHarg Papers, The Architectural Archives, University of Pennsylvania.)

McHarg's alternative to his contemporaries' prevailing emphasis on a rational, comprehensive planning model.

McHarg's "notion of planning" stems from "two fundamental characteristics of natural processes: creativity and fitness." Creativity, he holds, "provides the dynamics that govern the universe," while fitness derives "from Darwinian notions about how organisms adapt and survive."[11] When planning is linked to ecology, the goals and purposes become subject to the resources of the place, and "ecological planning" becomes an instrument for revealing the "interacting and dynamic natural systems having

---

11. Ian L. McHarg, "Ecological Planning: The Planner as Catalyst," in *To Heal the Earth: Selected Writings of Ian L. McHarg*, ed. Ian L. McHarg and Frederick R. Steiner (Washington, D.C.: Island Press, 1998), 140.

intrinsic opportunities and constraints for human use."[12] Underscoring his philosophy of planning and design is the essential premise that McHarg would continually describe as *ecological determinism*, the title of a paper he presented in 1965 at the Conservation Foundation conference that discussed the "future environments of North America." Like many of McHarg's pronouncements, his characterization of ecological determinism was presented in a straightforward and self-evident manner. The framework of his staunch viewpoint was simply that the "understanding of natural process is of central importance to all environmental problems and must be introduced into all considerations of land utilization."[13]

The principal work that represents the McHargian concept and use of ecological planning is *Design with Nature*. It begins with the proclamation, "The world is a glorious bounty" and ends with the prospect, "In the quest for survival, success and fulfillment, the ecological view offers an invaluable insight. It shows the way for man who would be the enzyme of the biosphere—its steward, enhancing the creative fit of man-environment, realizing man's design with nature."[14] The influences on McHarg's ecological determinism were multiple and varied. They found an essential justification in a biophysical understanding of how the "fittest" organisms—including humans—survive (in light of Charles Darwin's observations) and how the organism will find the "fittest" available living environment to meet its needs (as Lawrence Henderson explains).[15] To McHarg, the idea of ecological determinism—or as he often calls it, the *ecological imperative*—could evolve quite logically from this biophysical understanding and would have direct and inevitable "implications of natural processes upon the location and form of development."[16]

McHarg MAKES AN IMPORTANT DISTINCTION between *ecological planning* and *ecological design*. Since he held graduate degrees in city planning and landscape architecture, he understood that planning and design are distinctly different yet fill complementary roles, and he would blend the two disci-

---

12. Ibid., 143.

13. Ian L. McHarg, "Ecological Determinism," in *To Heal the Earth: Selected Writings of Ian L. McHarg*, ed. Ian L. McHarg and Frederick R. Steiner (Washington, D.C.: Island Press, 1998), 54.

14. Ian L. McHarg, *Design with Nature* (Garden City, N.Y.: Natural History Press, 1969), 1, 197.

15. Charles Darwin's classic *The Origin of Species* was first published in 1859, and Lawrence Henderson's work *The Fitness of the Environment* first appeared in 1913.

16. Ian L. McHarg, *A Quest for Life: An Autobiography* (New York: John Wiley and Sons, 1996), 40.

plines as he constructed ecological and human ecological planning. In fact, when I once asked him, "How do you think of yourself, professionally?" he responded curtly, "I am a landscape architect and regional planner." Although the disciplines of landscape architecture and city and regional planning may overlap to some extent, they embody different approaches and methodologies in viewing two different parts of the whole; in McHarg's view, the whole becomes the total living and natural environment. McHarg is quite clear about the distinction in a 1990 letter to the editors of *Landscape Architecture*: "I have never viewed and do not now view ecology and design as antagonists. While there is no doubt that I have devoted my life to the development of human ecology as the theoretical basis for landscape architecture and regional planning, this was never meant to displace design, but rather to provide more and better knowledge and to expand the areas of competence in the profession."[17]

In a 1997 essay, he clearly distinguishes between ecological planning and ecological design:

- *Ecological planning* is that approach whereby a region is understood as a biophysical and social process comprehensible through the operation of laws and time. This approach can be reinterpreted as having explicit opportunities and constraints for any particular human use. A survey will reveal the most fit locations and use.[18]
- *Ecological design* follows planning and introduces the subject of form. An intrinsically suitable location, processes with appropriate materials, and forms should exist. Design requires an informed designer with a visual imagination as well as graphic and creative skills. It selects for creative fitting revealed in intrinsic and expressive forms.[19]

AN IMPORTANT ASPECT of McHarg's development of his theory of ecological planning is its fusion with an understanding of the concept of *region*, which would become the basis of his *regional planning*. In this context, we can rely on the categorization of *region* offered by professor of planning Melville Branch, who has examined the myriad dimensions of how regional space is organized. For our purposes, we can generalize two types of regional space:

---

17. Ian L. McHarg, letter to the editors, *Landscape Architecture* 80, no. 4 (1990): 8.

18. Ian L. McHarg, "Ecology and Design," in *To Heal the Earth: Selected Writings of Ian L. McHarg*, ed. Ian L. McHarg and Frederick R. Steiner (Washington, D.C.: Island Press, 1998), 195.

19. Ibid.

"physical regions" and "institutional regions." According to Branch, "These regions may be used for description, basic research, operational analysis, or decentralized management. In most cases they represent or reflect realities of the physical world, with boundaries that may be adjusted to coincide with jurisdictional boundaries established by man. They may also represent special designations for purposes unrelated to any physical characteristic or institutional jurisdiction."[20]

Chapter 2 provides an overview of the empirical planning approaches of Patrick Geddes, Ebenezer Howard, Lewis Mumford, Benton MacKaye, and Artur Glikson, among other intellectual and design traditions with established philosophical bases that either directly influenced McHarg or are compatible with his enunciation of ecological planning. Mumford's important influence on McHarg is his definition of regional planning as containing four "stages."[21] The first "stage" is the survey—originally Geddes's idea—as the means to disclose, "by first-hand visual exploration and by systematic fact-gathering, all the relevant data on the regional context."[22] The second "stage in [regional] planning is the critical outline of needs and activities in terms of social ideals and purposes."[23] The third "stage" Mumford calls "imaginative reconstruction and projection," and, "on the basis of known facts, observed trends, estimated needs, [and] critically formulated purposes[,] a new picture of regional life is now developed."[24] In the final "stage, the plan undergoes a re-adaptation as it encounters the traditions, the conventions, the resistances, and sometimes the unexpected opportunities of actual life."[25] MacKaye pushes Mumford's "stages" to more directly connect human ecology and regional planning. MacKaye distinguishes between the region "as a unit of environment" and "planning [as] the charting of activity . . . affecting the good of the human organism; its object is the application or putting into practice of the optimum relation between the human and the region. Regional planning in short is applied human ecology."[26]

---

20. Melville C. Branch, *Regional Planning: Introduction and Explanation* (New York: Praeger, 1988), 97.

21. Frederick Steiner has written that Patrick Geddes's approach, which was advanced by Lewis Mumford and later accepted by Ian McHarg, "contends that a region represents an entity that can be understood by an examination of its parts. The components include physical, biological, social, and cultural phenomena." Frederick Steiner, *Human Ecology: Following Nature's Lead* (Washington, D.C.: Island Press, 2002), 97.

22. Lewis Mumford, *The Culture of Cities* (New York: Harcourt, Brace, 1938), 376.

23. Ibid.

24. Ibid., 378.

25. Ibid., 380.

26. Benton MacKaye, "Regional Planning and Ecology," *Ecological Monographs* 10, no. 3 (1940): 351.

A composite of the Mumford–MacKaye descriptions of regional planning establishes the link between environment and humans by cementing ecology to human ecology in the context of regional planning. However, as McHarg was developing the ecology-based regional planning curriculum at Penn in the early 1960s, he seemed to be more interested in the ecological approach to regional planning. Only later, when human ecological planning was developed, did he move closer to MacKaye's applied human ecology as regional planning.

In a 1963 paper, McHarg writes that the "criteria for land-use planning . . . should be based upon an understanding of the natural processes in the region."[27] In his autobiography, McHarg makes the point even clearer: "My wholehearted endorsement of ecology . . . was directed toward its application. I was firmly committed to ecology as the scientific foundation for landscape architecture, but I also submitted that it could perform invaluable services if employed in environmental and regional planning."[28]

From McHarg's own account, it is clear that because he originally perceived regional planning as ecological planning, that became the essence of the regional planning program created at Penn, as subsequent chapters show.

ONE ASPECT OF McHARG'S THEORY that is not widely recognized is his deliberate transition from *ecological planning* to *human ecological planning* following the publication of *Design with Nature* in 1969. In response to certain critically acclaimed omissions, and in a bid to receive a substantial grant to expand the academic curriculum in regional planning at Penn, McHarg initiated a new iteration of ecological planning to include culture. With this move, he effectively folded human ecology into his theory of ecological planning. For our purposes, the key evolutionary variable to identify is his desire to correct what may be considered a deficiency in his original ecological planning theory:

When the term [ecological planning] is compounded into "human ecological planning" the region is expanded into a physical, biological, and cultural region wherein opportunities and constraints are represented in every realm. Geophysical and ecological regions are identified as cultural regions in which characteristic people pursue

27. Ian L. McHarg, "Regional Landscape Planning," in *To Heal the Earth: Selected Writings of Ian L. McHarg*, ed. Ian L. McHarg and Frederick R. Steiner (Washington, D.C.: Island Press, 1998), 96.

28. McHarg, *A Quest for Life*, 191.

means of production, develop characteristic settlement patterns, have characteristic perceptions, needs and desires and institutions for realizing their objectives.[29]

McHarg's Planning Method

The indispensable technique that McHarg developed to make his theory of ecological planning a usable form is the *ecological planning method*. To construct a practical method for planners, McHarg developed a straightforward use of data and information that would become a two-step process. First, an assemblage of natural resource and physical features characteristics is portrayed as mapped layers in what would become known as the "layer cake."

Each layer represents a component of the natural and physical environment and includes, among others, the mapping of bedrock geology, surficial geology, groundwater hydrology, geomorphology, surficial hydrology, soils, vegetation, wildlife, land use, and climate.[30]

Each layer is then superimposed on each other to show the composite information and how each component of data relates to each other. McHarg was less concerned with each individual layer than with how they interact to form the natural landscape pattern.

The diagrammatic arrow in Figure 4.2 represents the time element (or causal theory) that is directly related to the interaction of the layers over time. For example, bedrock geology (the oldest phenomenon) must be understood before soils (a later phenomenon).

The second task in the method is a four-step procedure to determine which areas in any given locale or on any given site are suitable for specific kinds of development. The locations containing the most propitious (i.e., suitable) factors for development would require less human adaptation to create habitats; therefore, development in these locations—based on natural resource constraints—would cause the fewest negative impacts on the environment. This essential inventory of natural resource information and data allows the suitability of a subject land area to be determined.

The suitability analysis determination has often been considered analogous to McHarg's conception of planning, and therefore ecological planning really stops here. Frederick Steiner proffers, "The ecological planning meth-

---

29. Ian L. McHarg, "Human Ecological Planning at Pennsylvania," in *To Heal the Earth: Selected Writings of Ian L. McHarg*, ed. Ian L. McHarg and Frederick R. Steiner (Washington, D.C.: Island Press, 1998), 144.

30. In the "layer-cake" model, climate does not fit as neatly as the other components. For example, macroclimate forces influence geology, hydrology, and geomorphology, while microclimate is more related to soils, vegetation, and land use.

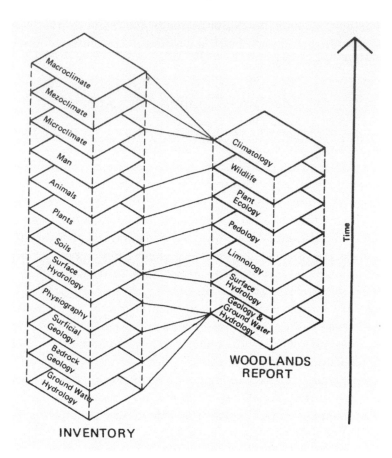

FIGURE 4.2. "Layer Cake Representation of Phenomena,"
prototype model for ecological planning, 1971–1974.
(Ian L. McHarg, A Quest for Life: An Autobiography
[New York: John Wiley and Sons, 1996], 258.)

od is primarily a procedure for studying the biophysical and sociocultural
systems of a place to reveal where specific land uses may best be practiced."[31]
Even though among some practitioners this method is *de facto* ecological
planning, the McHarg approach recognizes separate parts of an entire process
that begins with inventory through the layer cake and then proceeds to suitability analysis, to planning, and then to design. There is a distinction, since
the ecological planning method is clearly a technique to do the evaluation.

---

31. Frederick Steiner, *The Living Landscape: An Ecological Approach to Landscape Planning*
(New York: McGraw-Hill, 1991), 9.

Planning requires additional steps, including an identification of alternatives, implementation measures, and ongoing administration.[32] Design follows to specifically engage form.

A further iteration to the suitability analysis method evolved in the Medford study in 1974 (see the discussion in Part III). Here, nature's values are juxtaposed with human social values. To make this method operational, Narendra Juneja, one of McHarg's key associates and the author of the study, created a series of "matrices" to show the relationship. The first endeavor was to identify natural phenomena and then to define those phenomena in relation to their "value to society" and "value to individuals." Juneja writes, "This can best be accomplished by interpreting the available understanding of the extant [natural] phenomena and processes in terms of those societal objectives which are clearly definable and about which agreement can be reached by all those affected."[33] See Figure 7.2.

THE UNDERLYING THEME of McHarg's thinking and practice is his indefatigable advocacy for ecological planning, which he embraced with a religious fervor. He exuded a charisma that was exhibited in the classroom at Penn and in many consulting projects that he engaged in worldwide. His singular message, as a professor, landscape architect, and regional planner, was that his philosophy is an *ecological imperative*. It is the prescription for success and survival. Planning and designing with nature are not open to debate or compromise, and the ecological imperative must rule supreme as people continue to build new settlements. Such a strong position, regardless of its intellectual grounding, emotional appeal, or acceptance as a legitimate form of practice, would become the subject of academic criticism and even refutation in certain quarters. This controversy would become evident after the publication of *Design with Nature*, McHarg's milestone contribution to the environmental planning and design literature.

32. Frederick Steiner and Kenneth Brooks, "Ecological Planning: A Review," *Environmental Management* 5, no. 6 (1981): 501.

33. Narendra Juneja, *Medford: Performance Requirements for the Maintenance of Social Values Represented by the Natural Environment of Medford Township, N.J.* (Philadelphia: Center for Ecological Research in Planning and Design, University of Pennsylvania, 1974), 11.

5

Design with Nature

Planning Theory and Critiques

I N 1967, Ian McHarg took a sabbatical from his teaching and administrative duties at the University of Pennsylvania (Penn) to write *Design with Nature*, which was published in 1969. Since its publication, *Design with Nature* has been heralded as one of the most important contributions to understanding the human-environment relationship as we plan, design, and build new towns, cities, and regions. Yet despite the book's popularity among practicing city and regional planners, landscape architects, and architects, McHarg's theory of ecological planning was not accepted by the academic wing of the profession as a legitimate or meaningful pursuit.

The first critical reviews of *Design with Nature* appeared in scholarly journals, for the most part, and they were concerned with specific elements of the theory and the method of ecological planning. The rejection of ecological planning by planning theorists and critical reviewers—most of them also academics—highlights a paradox of McHarg's work: simply put, while it was not accepted by planning theorists as normative planning theory, ecological planning as proffered in *Design with Nature* was wholeheartedly embraced by planners in practice.

The later *Design with Nature* critiques were advanced on several fronts. McHarg had his personal detractors. He had a dynamic personality and was criticized for exaggeration; he was also charged with being dogmatic in his representation of the ecological imperative. The relevance of ecological planning was also challenged—was it a method of planning, or was it just a method of inventorying?

Finally, a powerful critique was aimed at the epistemological foundation of ecological planning that referred to a biophysical model of the environment. Critics charged that there was no inclusion of cultural and human use values relative to how humans adapt to the environment or, for that matter, adapt the environment for human use. This last critique would play an important role in the emergence of human ecological planning as it became integrated into the regional planning curriculum at Penn (see Part III).

The Rejection of Ecological Planning as Normative Planning Theory

What was the theorist's response to ecological planning immediately after the publication of *Design with Nature*? And, more important, why was ecological planning not accepted as normative planning theory? British philosopher and town planner Nigel Taylor has described normative planning theory as comprising two elements: how planning *should be approached* and a theory of the kinds of environments that planning *should seek to create*.[1] This approach presupposes that *ethical* or *value* perspectives and functional realities become essential variables of normative planning theory. McHarg's ecological planning did not convince planning theorists that it was worthy of their acceptance, especially as a break from the dominant tenets of the rational-comprehensive model, which dominated planning thought in the 1960s and 1970s.

To begin, we should turn to a 1971 article titled "The 'New' Environmentalism: An Intellectual Frontier." Authors George Hagevik and Lawrence Mann make a distinction between the "old" environmentalism, "understood as design determinism writ large on the socioeconomic screen," and the "new" environmentalism composed of several social, economic, information, and management subsystems. They stress the need to recognize "that environmental planning is one kind of socioeconomic planning."[2] Surprisingly, the subject of ecological planning as well as any reference to McHarg and *Design with Nature* are noticeably absent from the body of the article and the references.

The first important work on planning theory to be published after *Design with Nature* includes a 1978 article by McHarg titled "Ecological Planning:

1. Nigel Taylor, *Urban Planning Theory since 1945* (London: Sage Publications, 1998), 22.
2. George Hagevik and Lawrence Mann, "The 'New' Environmentalism: An Intellectual Frontier," *Journal of the American Institute of Planners* 37, no. 4 (1971): 274, 278.

The Planner as Catalyst." Editors Robert Burchell and James Hughes of Rutgers University acknowledge that this article delineates "the functional roles and tasks of planning within an even more tightly defined sector of the planning spectrum—ecological planning."[3] Their description of McHarg's contribution continues: "Rationality, a systems orientation, and non-biased, apolitical perspective dominate the McHargian tenets of environmental planning."[4]

The inclusion of McHarg's work in a planning theory text gained the attention of academic theorists, if not their allegiance. Many years later, Frederick Steiner would write, "Throughout his academic career, McHarg continued to rub up against the 'orthodox' city planning tradition, frequently irritating planning theorists but also influencing and changing their ideas about planning."[5]

Notwithstanding the above examples, there seems to have been almost a total failure among theorists to discuss McHarg's direct and rather uncomplicated approach to planning. McHarg wanted to pave a new direction for planning and design. Acceptance by theorists or at least some of the leading thinkers in the discipline would have been helpful in this aim. However, the "conversations" among planning theorists, as Ernest Alexander writes, continues to search for a "response to the breakdown of the rational paradigm."[6] Moreover, Alexander pleads, "If a paradigm is revealed as flawed to the point that it becomes useless for any conceptual or practical purposes, look for another."[7] For the most part, theorists did not view *Design with Nature* as an available alternative.

Certainly one of the most productive and admired planning theorists is John Friedmann, whose 1987 work *Planning in the Public Domain* describes the major traditions in planning theory. Friedmann is chiefly concerned with social theories of planning and how knowledge is linked to action. Yet, somewhat surprisingly, he does not even mention ecological planning—although McHarg's *Design with Nature* is cited in a footnote. Alex-

---

3. Robert W. Burchell and James W. Hughes, introduction to *Planning Theory in the 1980's: A Search for Future Directions*, ed. Robert W. Burchell and George Sternlieb (New Brunswick, N.J.: Center for Urban Policy Research, Rutgers University, 1978), xxiv. The article was later published in Ian L. McHarg and Frederick Steiner, eds., *To Heal the Earth: Selected Writings of Ian L. McHarg* (Washington, D.C.: Island Press, 1998), 139–141.

4. Ibid., xxv.

5. The assessment is part of Steiner's essay "Planning the Ecological Region," which appears in McHarg and Steiner, *To Heal the Earth*, 89.

6. Ernest R. Alexander, "After Rationality, What? A Review of Responses to Paradigm Breakdown," *Journal of the American Planning Association* 50, no. 1 (1984): 65.

7. Ibid.

ander's 1992 planning theory text declares, "As of this writing 'ecological planning' does not seem to be catching on as a popular concept either among planning theorists or practitioners, nor does anyone seem to see it as a wave of the future."[8] Ecological planning certainly challenged the scientific world view that valued rationality and technology above ecological interconnections. It is not unrealistic conjecture to say that many planning theorists probably viewed ecological planning, to paraphrase Doug Aberley, as a weed in the "Cartesian Garden."[9] In the twenty-fifth-anniversary edition of *Design with Nature*, published in 1992, McHarg acknowledges his disappointment with mainstream planning theorists' lack of discussion of ecological planning as normative planning theory: "I have one deep dissatisfaction. The theory presented in *Design with Nature* was never reviewed. I had presented the material on many occasions. . . . [I]t had elicited some surprise but also approbation. But in print it elicited no responses whatsoever."[10]

I suggest three reasons why McHarg's *Design with Nature* did not receive recognition as an important contribution to planning theory. First, the planning theory community itself was in somewhat of an intellectual dilemma. How could they reconcile a rational comprehensive planning model—the dominant view in the late 1960s through the 1970s—predicated on natural resource constraints, which rational planning could not control?

Second, McHarg developed his method (centered on the layer-cake analysis) to correspond with his theory. This approach in itself was a rather dubious undertaking for most planning theorists, who often had difficulty proposing operational models for their own theories. From another perspective, it could be argued that McHarg consciously tried to confront the perennial difficulty in reconciling theory and practice. Whatever the reason, McHarg's ecological planning did not convince important planning theorists that such a direction was worthy of further explication, dialogue, and ultimate acceptance as normative planning theory.

A final reason why ecological planning may have failed to achieve a standing in the universal community of planning theorists can be ascribed to their intellectual interests: they were simply neither attuned to nor con-

---

8. Ernest R. Alexander, *Approaches to Planning: Introducing Current Planning Theories* (Philadelphia: Gordon and Breach Science Publishers, 1992), 106.

9. Doug Aberley, "Weeds in the Cartesian Garden: The Context of Ecological Planning," in *Futures by Design: The Practice of Ecological Planning*, ed. Doug Aberley (Gabriola Island, Canada: New Society Publishers, 1994).

10. Ian L. McHarg, *Design with Nature*, 25th anniv. ed. (New York: John Wiley and Sons, 1992), v.

cerned with biological science and environmental thinking as the essential foundation of planning, as McHarg was.[11] Their preoccupation was with the social science and public policy aspects of planning, so, for the most part, calls for ecological planning fell on deaf ears. Perhaps the concept of ecological planning was not intellectually challenging enough—it was just too pragmatic. Perhaps it did not fully account for the myriad social and political movements with which planning theory of the 1960s, 1970s, and 1980s had become enamored. In all fairness to those who pursue planning theory, I recognize it has experienced shifts since the 1970s and 1980s—for example, by reaching out more to include sustainability as a theoretical and practical element that is subsumed in the discipline and practice of planning.

Perhaps in the final analysis, as described by urban designer Jonathan Barnett, planning theorists simply "reacted to the evident failure of their theories . . . by condemning society, and by indulging in escapist fantasies."[12]

An interesting parallel exists between planning theorists' lack of acceptance of McHarg's ecological planning and what Ebenezer Howard faced when he published *Garden Cities of To-Morrow* in 1902. Although McHarg's work found a wide-ranging, eager, and accepting audience—principally, practicing planners and designers—Howard's proposals for a new town in the country, the Garden City, initially went unread within the first year or two of its publication. Howard's earliest greatest advocate, Frederic Osborn (who had been the planner for the first two British Garden Cities, Letchworth in 1904 and Welwyn in 1920), observes, "More explicable is the neglect of the book and its thesis in academic circles, notably those of sociology and economics. It is not read in those circles because it is too easy to read. . . . [I]t does not seem a serious contribution to thought. It has been disregarded as a mere popularization. But in fact its analysis is original, shrewd, and sound, and its proposals are realistic and important."[13]

Similarly, Steiner, who co-edited with McHarg his essential writings before and after *Design with Nature* appeared, clearly states McHarg's contribution to theory: "Design with nature is an elegant theory. Both simple and direct, it is much a proposition as a principle. Design with nature is a normative theory, an ideal to be achieved. A process is suggested to reach that goal."[14]

---

11. See, for example, Ramón Margalef, *Perspectives in Ecological Theory* (Chicago: University of Chicago Press, 1968).

12. Jonathan Barnett, *An Introduction to Urban Design* (New York: Harper and Row, 1982), 8.

13. Frederic J. Osborn, *Green-Belt Cities* (New York: Schocken Books, 1969), 25.

14. McHarg and Steiner, *To Heal the Earth*, 5.

The First Critical Reviews of *Design with Nature*

In his autobiography, McHarg writes, "The book [*Design with Nature*] was very well reviewed; indeed there were several hundred reviews, with only one bad criticism. I was accused of prostituting science."[15] Indeed, the work was highly acclaimed, receiving much praise, complimentary remarks, and expressions of support. Yet a number of critical reviews did raise some salient issues that impeded the acceptance of ecological planning as a new contribution to planning theory.

It is not my intent here to present all the reviews. Rather, I have evaluated the critical assessments as they address a fundamental question: is the critical review intellectually worthy of providing a more in-depth or meaningful understanding of ecological planning, as is the thesis of *Design with Nature*, to either advance theory or augment practice? If the answer is in the affirmative, then I accept that the critical assessment has merit and consequently dismiss the usual nit-picking professional jealousy and occasional sarcasm that may be found in some so-called critical reviews.

McHarg's construction of ecological planning as embodied in *Design with Nature* received its first series of critiques on several fronts: (1) it is elitist in its orientation, (2) its philosophy is confusing, (3) the method is unsystematic and incomplete, (4) it ignores the ecology of the city, (5) there is a need to incorporate political and moral values, (6) the treatment of population growth is vague, and (7) it does not address the economic allocation of land resources. Let's examine each of these critiques.

The Charge of Elitism

Two planning professors at the University of California at Berkeley wrote the first review of *Design with Nature*, which appears in what was then the *Journal of the American Institute of Planners*. To Burton Litton and Martin Krieger, it is a "beautiful book," sensitive to the need to strengthen "the scientific basis for design." However, "it is, unfortunately, also elitist and technocratic in orientation at a time when these values are being seriously questioned."[16] The reviewers point out that people in less-developed countries have a greater need for food and work than for a "natural landscape."

---

15. Ian L. McHarg, *A Quest for Life: An Autobiography* (New York: John Wiley and Sons, 1996), 206.

16. Burton R. Litton and Martin Krieger, "Review of *Design with Nature*," *Journal of the American Institute of Planners* 37, no. 1 (1971): 50.

Questioning of the Philosophy

Litton and Krieger assail the philosophy of McHarg in the following way:

> The philosophical sections seem rather confusing on first reading. . . .
> On repeated reading and rumination, it becomes apparent that this is
> McHarg's way of elaborating on the complex elements making up an
> ecological viewpoint—and suggesting implications for a prospective
> environment.[17]

A review of *Design with Nature* by Robert McClintock, of Columbia University, is quite positive but finds that McHarg's critical assessment of the Judeo-Christian tradition comes down to an individual perspective on history: "Although McHarg is not at his best in the history of ideas, it matters little. Whether one agrees or disagrees with his historical interpretations does not determine whether one can be moved by his vision of nature."[18]

McHarg's position relative to the impact of the Judeo-Christian tradition in imbuing a Western attitude concerning land and nature values is a crucial point in his philosophy that plays into his justification for ecological planning. McClintock perhaps offers the most apt response when he says, "The real strength of [McHarg's] position lies in the fact that his chosen route to the goal [of ecological planning] is not the only one possible. As a result, many of us who are not ready to give up our humanism or theism for his naturalism may still eagerly agree, for reasons of our own, with his conviction that the nature of design is to Design with Nature."[19]

An Unsystematic and Incomplete Method

"There are deep problems with his technique," according to Litton and Krieger, who stress that "McHarg's ideas of what we should know are quite unsystematic." They argue that McHarg's use of ecology is "piecemeal and ad hoc" and that he "prostitutes scientific knowledge in an attempt to make it a justification for his ideas." On this point, they conclude that McHarg does not provide a "suitably powerful technique for achieving his aims."[20] However, Litton and Krieger do call McHarg "inspired" and concede that "the problem

---

17. Ibid., 51.
18. Robert McClintock, "Review, *Design with Nature*," *Main Currents in Modern Thought* 7, no. 4 (1971): 135.
19. Ibid.
20. Litton and Krieger, "Review of *Design with Nature*," 51.

of a design method, such as his, is that it must convert those who are inspired but not geniuses into competent practitioners."[21]

In 1971, Michael Laurie—a former student of McHarg's and a professor of landscape architecture at the University of California at Berkeley—wrote a brief review in *Landscape Architecture* in which he proclaims, "I don't believe *Design with Nature* sets out to provide a method. If it does it is clearly incomplete."[22] Later Laurie asks, "Why is he not describing a method? Tell us what to do and how to do it. But that is not the intention, nor should it be."[23] McHarg's work, he concludes, should properly be seen as representing certain values.

Ignorance of the Ecology of the City

Litton and Krieger take issue with what they consider "the limited ecological technology . . . that ignores some emerging aspects of the ecology of the city." They consider the organization of information and knowledge and education to be more vital resources than the organization of biological systems.[24]

The Need to Incorporate Political and Moral Values

Planning involves political issues as well as ecological issues, according to Litton and Krieger. They stress, rather sardonically, that poor people "will [not] see planning heavily influenced by ecology any more desirable, than planning heavily influenced by a *beaux arts* tradition."[25] As a result, they call for a design approach that represents "political and moral values . . . so that those who are not of the profession can participate in the design process."[26]

In addressing this issue, Laurie says, "McHarg's work should properly be seen as representing certain values and an approach specific to a particular time and place." He continues, "We must develop and be equally sure of our own values. . . . Methods are easy. Values are very hard to articulate, let alone hold consistently. This is what McHarg is about and it is for this that we should be grateful."[27]

---

21. Ibid., 52.
22. Michael Laurie, "Scoring McHarg: Low on Method, High on Values," *Landscape Architecture* 61 (1971), 206.
23. Ibid., 248.
24. Litton and Krieger, "Review of *Design with Nature*," 51.
25. Ibid.
26. Ibid., 52.
27. Laurie, "Scoring McHarg," 248.

Vague Treatment of Population Growth

Within their highly positive review, Diane Ringger and Forest Stearns, of the University of Wisconsin, make one critical point: "McHarg is vague in treating the problem of population growth. Likewise he fails to take into account how our economy and natural resources will be able to support the people he is planning for. It is unclear to us, for example, how New York City will support thirty million people."[28]

The Economic Allocation of Land Resources

Andrew Gold, a professor of economics at Trinity College in Hartford, argues that even though "nature provides the matrix within which human decisions must be made," McHarg's construct of ecological planning does not resolve the "economists' problem of how scarce land resources should be correctly allocated."[29]

Using a market analysis methodology that prefers a "comparative advantage" to allocate land uses rather than McHarg's use of "absolute advantage," Gold carries out his critique "to show that McHarg's method is incomplete and may lead to wrong results."[30] After performing a series of straight-line diagramatics of the type that often pervade economic analysis, Gold concludes, "The McHarg scheme fails to recognize that it is 'intrinsic suitability' in conjunction with the values people place on the use of 'intrinsically' suitable land that should determine the correct allocation [of land uses]."[31]

Of course, we must remember that as an economist, Gold is chiefly concerned about productivity and value as intrinsic suitability variables that can exclude other potentially desirable intrinsically suitable variables. For example, he posits the following: "One can show that private decisions may not lead to socially optimal results—city uses may spoil recreational water use through pollution, or agricultural feedlots may poison city water supplies, but that is another matter. We know that private decisions will not yield socially optimal results for beauty, quiet, and other amenities but that, too, is another matter."[32]

---

28. Diane L. Ringger and Forest Stearns, "Nature's Landscape Architect," *Ecology* 51 (1970): 1110.

29. Andrew J. Gold, "Design with Nature: A Critique," *Journal of the American Institute of Planners* 40, no. 4 (1974): 284.

30. Ibid.

31. Ibid., 286.

32. Ibid.

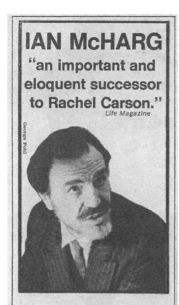

IAN McHARG
"an important and eloquent successor to Rachel Carson."
Life Magazine

"He is now the nation's most visible apostle of using ecology for planning," says *Time Magazine.* "DESIGN WITH NATURE, his new book, clearly shows that the main obstacle to saving the U.S. landscape is ignorance."

"DESIGN WITH NATURE demonstrates how the new knowledge of ecology can and must be applied to actual environments," writes *Wolf von Eckhardt,* architecture critic of the *Washington Post.* "It may well be one of the most important books of the century, a turning point in man's view and treatment of his environment."

Lewis Mumford says: "Here are the foundations for a civilization that will replace the polluted, bulldozed, machine-dominated, dehumanized, explosion-threatened world that is even now disintegrating and disappearing before our eyes. In presenting us with a vision of organic exuberance and human delight, which ecology and ecological design promise to open up for us, McHarg revives the hope for a better world."

DESIGN WITH NATURE

214 pages • 11" x 11" • 300 photographs, drawings, diagrams, plans and maps, many in color • Second printing • $22.50 at all booksellers

THE
NATURAL HISTORY
PRESS
a division of Doubleday & Company, Inc.; publisher for The American Museum of Natural History.

FIGURE 5.1. Advertisement for *Design with Nature* in *Saturday Review,* February 21, 1970. *(Ian McHarg Papers, The Architectural Archives, University of Pennsylvania.)*

Later Critiques

While the first reviews of *Design with Nature* assail specific points of McHarg's theory and method, later critiques involve other salient issues that have had a greater impact on the understanding, utilization, and acceptance of ecological and human ecological planning. These assessments include (1) how to define political circumstances, (2) exaggerated claims of originality, (3) dogmatic adherence to environmental determinism, (4) the difference between ecological inventorying and ecological planning, and (5) the absence of a cultural or human perspective.

Political Circumstances

In her review of *To Heal the Earth: Selected Writings of Ian L. McHarg* (1998), Wendy Kellogg, of Cleveland State University, provides generally favorable comments on the selected writings, all of which exemplify McHarg's development of ecological planning before and after *Design with Nature.* She writes, "An important missing part of this retrospective is an account of some of the challenges McHarg has faced and how he and his associates overcome them."[33] She is particularly concerned with the "political

33. Wendy A. Kellogg, "Review of *To Heal the Earth: Selected Writings of Ian L. McHarg,*" *Journal of the American Planning Association* 65, no. 3 (1999): 336.

circumstances" that were involved with the many projects that are presented as case studies. Kellogg asks, "What strategies did he use to convince decision makers and clients that the ecological approach was important?"[34] The Kellogg review is especially timely, since McHarg's professional and academic work spanned a period of almost four decades, beginning in the 1950s—a period that witnessed many changes in the development and political acceptance of environmentally based land use regulations and laws at the local, state, and national levels.

Exaggerated Claims of Originality

Some of McHarg's most vociferous critics have been professional and allied colleagues, especially in the discipline of landscape architecture but also to a lesser degree in city and regional planning. The heart of collegial criticism is that McHarg often exaggerates his contributions and that he did not invent all of what he says he did. In addition, it has been argued, his attitudinal penchant is nothing less than dogmatic. The most dramatic critique with regard to each of these charges is written by Anne Whiston Spirn, a student of McHarg's from 1973 to 1977 and his successor as chair of the Department of Landscape Architecture and Regional Planning at Penn, serving from 1986 to 1993. Spirn writes:

> McHarg ignored precedent when he asserted, as he has many times, "I invented ecological planning in the 1960s" ("Ecology and Design," in *Quest for Life*). The importance of McHarg's contribution is not diminished when seen in the context of work by others such as Phil Lewis, [G.] Angus Hills, and Artur Glikson, who pursued similar ideas from the 1950s and early 1960s, not to mention many prior figures such as Patrick Geddes and Warren Manning. This tradition was not acknowledged . . . when I was a student, . . . nor did we draw from it in our work at Wallace, McHarg, Roberts and Todd during that period. Though both department and firm made numerous innovations, there were also many reinventions.[35]

---

34. Ibid.

35. Anne Whiston Spirn, "Ian McHarg, Landscape Architecture, and Environmentalism: Ideas and Methods in Context," in *Environmentalism in Landscape Architecture*, ed. Michel Conan (Washington, D.C.: Dumbarton Oaks Research Library and Collection, 2000), 102.

In the above quotation, "Ecology and Design" refers to a paper that McHarg presented at a 1992 symposium at Arizona State University. The paper was first published in 1997 and again the following year in *To Heal the Earth*.[36] In his autobiography, McHarg gives a somewhat belated accolade to Charles Eliot (1859–1897), a Harvard-trained landscape architect who performed what arguably could be called the first ecological inventory on Mount Desert Island, Maine, in 1880. McHarg refers to him as the "innovator, inventor of what we would now call ecological planning" and adds that he "was destined to become the major figure in the field of the environment in the United States."[37] McHarg further acknowledges that he is a "strong advocate" of Eliot, whom he characterizes as "the founding father" of ecological planning.[38]

McHarg also writes in his autobiography, "I invented 'intrinsic suitability,' a device [the layer-cake model] to identify and array both propitious and detrimental factors for all land uses. . . . I believe that this was the first demonstration of a device to establish fitness for prospective land uses, and it has held up well."[39] McHarg is very clear about who did what. For example, he acknowledges G. Angus Hills, a Canadian forester and planner, as the person who "conceived of 'carrying capacity,' a measure to determine suitable factors, notably for agriculture and forestry." However, McHarg's objectives were different: "I was interested in developing a method to locate the 'most fit' environments for all prospective land uses."[40]

While working in the office of Frederick Law Olmsted, Eliot—the same person whom McHarg recognizes as the progenitor of ecological planning—actually was the first to overlay maps to show the "essence of landscape." Even though the initial process was rudimentary, according to Professor Forster Ndubisi, "it would later become one of the most powerful techniques for systematically documenting and evaluating natural and cultural data."[41]

The relevant point is not who was the first to use a particular technique or method but rather *how* the technique was used and *what* its sustaining im-

---

36. Ian McHarg's "Ecology and Design" was first published in George F. Thompson and Frederick R. Steiner, eds., *Ecological Design and Planning* (New York: John Wiley and Sons, 1997), 321–332, and later in McHarg and Steiner, *To Heal the Earth*, 194–202.

37. McHarg, *A Quest for Life*, 358.

38. Ibid., 360.

39. Ibid., 330.

40. Ibid.

41. Forster Ndubisi, *Ecological Planning: A Historical and Comparative Synthesis* (Baltimore: Johns Hopkins University Press, 2002), 12. For additional historic perspectives, see Carl Steinitz, Paul Parker, and Lawrie Jordan, "Hand-Drawn Overlays: Their History and Prospective Uses," *Landscape Architecture* 66 (1976): 444–455.

pact was, if any. He did not originate the overlay method, but McHarg was the first to use it in a new and unique way that could be readily adapted into professional practice. So it is true that the overlay "concept was not original with McHarg," as landscape architect William Thompson points out, but "it took McHarg to turn an old refrain into an environmental call to arms."[42] Likewise, George Thompson and Frederick Steiner have written, "He was not the first to blend art and science, and design and planning"; yet he "is still the revolutionary mind and spirit in the [landscape architecture] profession's collective memory."[43]

Dogmatic Adherence to Environmental Determinism

Even though "McHarg's *Design with Nature* led to fundamental changes in the teaching and practice of landscape architecture," according to Spirn, his claim that "science is the only defensible authority for landscape design . . . [proves] particularly damaging to discourse and practice."[44] Spirn continues, "Such aggressive overstatements no longer advance the field, and have provoked equally dogmatic reactions from those who seek to promote landscape architecture as an art form."[45]

On its face value, such a critique—whether it be directed at McHarg or anyone else—might appear to have merit. However, when extended to include the important contributions of those who have made an impact on the use of a discipline or a body of legitimate knowledge in practice, such a critique loses its punch.

The history of any discipline includes points of view or logically deduced positions that have their supporters and opponents. Whether nature is real in a scientific sense or is a contrived metaphor in an artistic sense is of interest in philosophical discussions and does contribute to the establishment of a design or planning perspective.

But beyond any stated philosophical perspective lies the challenge to address a reality of shaping a total human environment and how to better understand that total environment. If designers and planners are fully dedicated to that end, concerns surrounding the question of dogma-

---

42. William Thompson, "A Natural Legacy: Ian McHarg and His Followers," *Planning* 57, no. 11 (1991): 14.

43. Thompson and Steiner, introduction to *Ecological Design and Planning*, 3.

44. Anne Whiston Spirn, "The Authority of Nature: Conflict and Confusion in Landscape Architecture," in *Nature and Democracy: Natural Garden Design in the Twentieth Century*, ed. Joachim Wolschke-Bulmahn (Washington, D.C.: Dumbarton Oaks Research Library and Collection, 1997), 256.

45. Ibid.

tism about any particular perspective seem to grow dimmer in a real-world context.[46]

Ecological Inventory or Ecological Planning

In the early 1980s, Brenda Lee, of the Institute for Environmental Studies at the University of Toronto, wrote that McHarg's method "is primarily an information synthesis; it analyzes spatial relationships and organizes information. Its only guidelines relate to human use: ecosystem potential for use and the effects of use."[47] While it is true that McHarg's approach is heavily dependent on an ecological inventory, the question still remains: does it constitute ecological planning? To explore this issue, I begin with the most recent intellectual contribution made to the understanding of the various approaches to ecological planning and then look at some of McHarg's own work. Additionally, this question arises in the context of the regional planning curriculum at Penn (see Part III).

In his comprehensive historical analysis of the development of ecological planning, Ndubisi offers a definition that emphasizes ecological planning as "a way of mediating the dialogue between human actions and natural processes. . . . It is a view of the world, a process, and a domain of professional practice and research. . . . It is also a recognized activity of federal, state, and local governments."[48] Ndubisi concludes his analysis with the perspective that "fundamentally, ecological planning is more than an approach or

---

46. It is not my intent to engage in a debate on this issue, but I do harbor the view that, philosophical discourse notwithstanding, the ultimate test of the validity of a particular persuasion lies in its acceptability to others who either incorporate it into their own views or adapt its methods in practice. For example, in their introductory essay to an excerpt from *Design with Nature*, Richard LeGates and Frederic Stout write, "Since publication of *Design with Nature*, an entire field of environmental impact analysis and planning has developed. Thousands of planners have read McHarg and incorporated his approach into their environmental impact statements, studies, and plans. Physical city planning of all kinds incorporates environmental values to a much greater extent than before *Design with Nature*." Richard LeGates and Frederic Stout, eds., *The City Reader* (London: Routledge, 1996), 132.

47. Brenda J. Lee, "An Ecological Comparison of the McHarg Method with Other Planning Initiatives in the Great Lakes Basin," *Landscape Planning* 9 (1982): 158.

48. Ndubisi, *Ecological Planning*, 5. Ndubisi develops a typology that includes six approaches to ecological planning: (1) the first landscape suitability approach (up to 1969), (2) the second landscape suitability approach (after 1969), (3) the applied human ecology approach, (4) the applied ecosystem approach, (5) the applied landscape ecology approach, and (6) assessment of landscape values and landscape perception. McHarg's theory and method fall principally in the first landscape suitability approach and the applied human ecology approach.

a method. It is a world view for managing our relations with the land to ensure that the ability of future generations of the 'biotic community' to meet their needs is not sacrificed by current human actions."[49] Ndubisi's treatment of ecological planning is a carefully presented evolution of the several approaches that he discusses. Moreover, it clearly shows that there is not just one way to do ecological planning.[50] This analysis is consistent with and complementary to the view that planning theorist Seymour Mandelbaum has promoted previously, arguing that it is impossible to have a general theory of planning, since "a general theory must generate a set of propositions which relate all the necessary categories of processes, settings, and outcomes."[51] He advocates a mode of theorizing that is a process, not a product: "Its worth lies in the tension it generates against practice rather than its unique claim to validity."[52]

If we weave Ndubisi's conclusion that emphasizes multiple paths for defining ecological planning with Mandelbaum's conclusion that there can be no single general theory, we should push the investigation and ascertain McHarg's portrayal of ecological planning as a precursor to determine whether it is inventory or planning. This path allows an understanding of where McHarg fits into this continuum of approaches to ecological planning.

A sampling of McHarg's writings and projects during the period 1965 to 1997 draws a distinction between inventory and planning. The 1964 report "Plan for the Valleys" (for the Green Spring and Worthington Valleys in Baltimore County) consists of "two forms," including the "technical report" and "five concepts" that would "have a wider relevance as conceptual tools for planning for metropolitan growth."[53] In a subsequent article, McHarg asserts that the "maps of intrinsic suitability" were "not a plan."[54] In essence, a four-step process begins with understanding "nature as process insofar as the natural sciences permit," continues with a revelation of "casualty," and is followed by an interpretation of "natural processes as resources,

---

49. Ibid., 240.

50. A more comprehensive assemblage of scholarly works over the last one hundred fifty years may be found in Forster O. Ndubisi, ed., *The Ecological Design and Planning Reader* (Washington, D.C.: Island Press), 2014.

51. Seymour J. Mandelbaum, "A Complete General Theory of Planning Is Impossible," *Policy Sciences* 11, no. 1 (1979): 67.

52. Ibid., 70.

53. Ian L. McHarg, "Plan for the Valleys vs. Spectre of Uncontrolled Growth," in *To Heal the Earth: Selected Writings of Ian L. McHarg*, ed. Ian L. McHarg and Frederick Steiner (Washington, D.C.: Island Press, 1998), 272.

54. Ian L. McHarg, "An Ecological Method for Landscape Planning," in *To Heal the Earth: Selected Writings of Ian L. McHarg*, ed. Ian L. McHarg and Frederick Steiner (Washington, D.C.: Island Press, 1998), 214–215.

to prescribe and even to predict for prospective land uses," and finally by producing "a plan."[55]

Two other notable projects highlight the incorporation of this procedure. The first involved the highway route selection method used for a study (completed in 1965) of a section of I-95 between the Delaware and Raritan Rivers in New Jersey. The second was the ecological planning study done for the Woodlands in Texas, a new town completed in 1973. In the latter case, after finishing the suitability analysis, an "overall plan" was proposed to locate "the best areas for development, including high and low-density residential, commercial, recreational, municipal, industrial and open-space land uses . . . derived from the inventory of the landscape."[56]

McHarg's use of the inventory of the natural resource base as a predecessor to actual planning is the first step in a two-step process that demarks a logical framework to do planning. Hills takes the same approach when he writes, "Landscape planning is a hierarchical complex of a number of investigations . . . [that] constitute the basis for the formulations in the next order in the hierarchical progression at the apex of which is the land use plan."[57] An obvious conclusion to this discussion is that no ecological planning can occur without the ecological inventory.

The Absence of a Cultural or Human Perspective

Design with Nature is predicated on a biophysical approach to determining fit environments for human use. The notion of human-user values in juxtaposition to the constraints posed by understanding natural suitability variables did not initially enter McHarg's prescription for ecological planning, but this perspective would later change.

In Lewis Mumford's introduction to *Design with Nature*, he expresses great praise not only for the landmark position of the work but also for McHarg himself. Mumford calls McHarg "an inspired ecologist" and proclaims that "McHarg's emphasis is not on either design or nature by itself, but upon the proposition **with,** which implies human cooperation and biological partnership" (bold in original).[58] Mumford continues, "So, too, in

---

55. Ibid., 215.

56. Ian L. McHarg, "A Case Study in Ecological Planning: The Woodlands, Texas," in *To Heal the Earth: Selected Writings of Ian L. McHarg*, ed. Ian L. McHarg and Frederick Steiner (Washington, D.C.: Island Press, 1998), 254.

57. G. Angus Hills, "A Philosophical Approach to Landscape Planning," *Landscape Planning* 1 (1974): 341.

58. Ian L. McHarg, *Design with Nature* (Garden City, N.Y.: Natural History Press, 1969), viii.

embracing nature, he knows that man's own mind, which is part of nature, has something precious to add that is not to be found at such a high point of development in raw nature, untouched by man."[59] A close reading of Mumford's depiction of *Design with Nature* suggests that this interpretation goes beyond what McHarg intends. I further contend that Mumford truly wants McHarg's work to serve a wider frame—to go beyond embracing simply a natural environment to embracing a human environment as well. Essentially, this introduction serves as Mumford's call to McHarg to transition from a strict reliance on natural systems ecology to a combined natural-human systems ecology—the critical dimension of ecohumanism.

I conclude that in this introductory statement, Mumford challenges McHarg to make *Design with Nature* more than it is. To be sure, it includes chapters that deal with the human impact on the environment, the exploitation of the environment for personal pleasure, the destruction of the environment through insensitive development, the general lack of recognition of the importance of the environment for human use as a resource, and the condemnation of Western attitudes toward nature. Yet Mumford seems to be testing the waters by framing McHarg's approach as one that encompasses a human ecology along with a biophysical ecology.

In the twenty-fifth-anniversary edition of *Design with Nature*, published in 1992, McHarg confesses to "one significant omission . . . [that] social systems were neglected."[60] Human ecological planning emerges as the next iteration in McHarg's development of ecological planning. He expresses a concise view of this change that stems from a recognition of human ecology and how to incorporate it into human ecological planning. McHarg writes, "Ecology must be extended to include man. Human ecology can then be defined as the study of the interactions of organisms (including man), and the environment (including man among other organisms)."[61]

To McHarg, human ecological planning encompasses physical, biological, and cultural elements. Thus, as he describes it, a three-step process underscores human ecological planning:[62]

---

59. Ibid.

60. McHarg, *Design with Nature*, 25th anniv. ed., v.

61. Ian L. McHarg, "Human Ecological Planning at Pennsylvania," in *To Heal the Earth: Selected Writings of Ian L. McHarg*, ed. Ian L. McHarg and Frederick Steiner (Washington, D.C.: Island Press, 1998), 143.

62. Ibid., 144.

1. "Geophysical and ecological regions are identified as cultural regions in which characteristic people pursue means of production, develop characteristic settlement patterns, have characteristic perceptions, needs and desires and institutions for realizing their objectives."

2. "Hypothetical future alternatives are derived from expressed needs and desires of groups. These are matched against the physical, biological, and cultural resources."

3. "Preferred hypothetical futures can be derived for each group with its associated value system."[63]

Although McHarg's work has been subject to further discussion, debate, criticism, and even modification by others over time, the importance of the evolution of ecological planning to human ecological planning is the most significant advance made by McHarg himself. Steiner explains its practical impact: "Human ecology dominated the Penn Department of Landscape Architecture and Regional Planning research agenda throughout the 1970s."[64] In an earlier paper, Steiner, Gerald Young, and Ervin Zube remark that "McHarg has advanced well beyond his theoretical-methodological conceptualization of 1969 and has responded to criticisms raised at that time (Krieger and Litton 1971). He has developed a theory of human ecological planning that is central to the curriculum and its content."[65]

An understanding of McHarg's penchant and strong—or, as some claim, unwavering—predilection for environmental sanctity would become the crucial underpinning of his development of the ecological planning curriculum at Penn. His long career there opens a new door to understanding the legacy he established in environmental planning and education.

---

63. Ibid.

64. Ian L. McHarg, "Planning the Ecological Region," in *To Heal the Earth: Selected Writings of Ian L. McHarg*, ed. Ian L. McHarg and Frederick Steiner (Washington, D.C.: Island Press, 1998), 91.

65. Frederick Steiner, Gerald Young, and Ervin Zube, "Ecological Planning: Retrospect and Prospect," *Landscape Journal* 7, no. 1 (1988): 37.

PART III

ECOLOGY AND HUMAN ECOLOGY IN PLANNING AND DESIGN EDUCATION

*A History of an Interdisciplinary Curriculum,
1936–2000*

6

The Academic Environments at
Harvard and the University of Pennsylvania,
1936–1968

THE PURPOSE OF CHAPTERS 6–10, which tell a story unto themselves, is to follow and document the key graduate curriculum that
serves as a model to further an educational legacy for the ecological
culture. The educational career of Ian McHarg becomes the focal point for
this legacy, since he would be the key person to carry out Lewis Mumford's
mission to initiate an educational component predicated on ecohumanism.
Of singular importance is that Mumford's influence on McHarg's curriculum development is the very essence of the man's approach to acquiring
knowledge. Mumford sought balance, comprehensiveness, an understanding of wholeness in human cultural endeavors, and a genuine reliance on
an interdisciplinary blending of historic facts, ideas, and results. He wrote
in 1915, "Knowledge does not consist in knowing the things you know; it
consists in knowing the things you don't know."[1]

McHARG WAS EXPOSED to two principal academic environments that
would, each in their unique way, provide the fertile caldron for intellectual
growth. The first was Harvard University, during his student years between
1946 and 1950. After graduating from Harvard, McHarg taught his first
courses at the Royal College of Art in Edinburgh and the Glasgow School
of Art between 1950 and 1954. However, the University of Pennsylvania

---

1. Lewis Mumford, *My Works and Days: A Personal Chronicle* (New York: Harcourt
Brace Jovanovich, 1979), 30.

(Penn) would serve as his life-long base, from his arrival as a new faculty member in 1954 until his death in 2001. Penn's intellectual environment provided the impetus that would allow him to develop his thinking about ecological planning and design.

In his autobiography, McHarg acknowledges the shortcomings of his graduate study at Harvard—especially the dearth of instruction in the natural sciences—and states unabashedly that Penn allowed him "to complete the education that Harvard so expensively denied me."[2]

Penn's academic environment was a powerful force on McHarg. It opened new vistas to satiate his inquisitiveness and continued desire to learn, understand, and formulate conceptual meanings of environmental knowledge. This aim became his life-long quest.

The academic milieu's structure would serve as the conduit for his learning. Clearly, as he became more exposed to ideas and methods, the notion of interdisciplinary cooperation and interaction would provide the most important pedagogical perspective that McHarg embraced and advanced. This perspective, focusing on a collaboration of the disciplines of architecture, landscape architecture, and city planning, was implemented at Harvard and continued and advanced at Penn under the leadership of Dean G. Holmes Perkins after his arrival in 1951. This pedagogical relationship allowed McHarg to make innovations in environmental education, with Mumford's unequivocal support. As is evident in subsequent chapters, McHarg's unique contribution is his expansion of the interdisciplinary collaboration beyond the three base disciplines to incorporate first the natural sciences and later the social sciences. Indeed, it could be hypothesized that without such a collaborative and supportive academic environment, the interdisciplinary curriculum that McHarg championed in ecological planning probably would not have evolved as it did. Indeed, Mumford's influence would be direct and decisive.

The Academic Environment at Harvard University, 1936–1950

The Harvard Graduate School of Design was established in 1936 and united the three disciplines of architecture, landscape architecture, and city and regional planning. Dean Joseph Hudnut is credited as the intellectual force to effect such a unification, which he conceptually developed during his previous post at Columbia University. Hudnut served as professor of the

---

2. Ian L. McHarg, *A Quest for Life: An Autobiography* (New York: John Wiley and Sons, 1996), 82.

history of architecture at Columbia from 1926 until he was appointed dean of the School of Architecture at Columbia in 1934. In just over a year, Hudnut transformed the curriculum at Columbia from a traditional *stylistic* (historical) perspective to an *organic* (practical) perspective in the training of architects. As he writes in a 1934 report, the *organic* perspective "begins with the belief that the approach to the study of architecture is best made through the practice of architecture."[3]

Although principally remembered for bringing the renowned Bauhaus architect Walter Gropius to Harvard in 1937, Hudnut's enduring contribution was that he gave the Graduate School of Design "its modern pedagogical direction, and he continued to oversee its curriculum and staffing for the next seventeen years."[4]

After his arrival as chairman of the Department of Architecture, Gropius taught a studio course in the spring of 1937. He was assisted in the studio by Perkins, whom Hudnut noted "is very popular with the students and is generally in sympathy with your work."[5] Born in Cambridge, Massachusetts, in 1904, Perkins matriculated at Harvard, where he earned a master of architecture degree in 1929. Afterward, he taught briefly at the University of Michigan until he was invited back to Harvard to become a member of the faculty in the Graduate School of Design. Although Perkins's academic and professional penchant was architecture, he clearly recognized the value of moving planning education to a stronger position in the curriculum. He was acutely aware of the 1943 assessment done by his faculty colleague John Merriman Gaus, who advocated "a plan for the development of instruction in regional planning at Harvard."[6] Gaus was unequivocal in his urging that planning become a mainstay of the curriculum along with architecture and landscape architecture. In a text for the graduate school, he writes, "In the preparation of architects and landscape architects for the work to be done in the years ahead, the contributions of city planning have become essential."[7] By 1945, Perkins was named chair of the Department of City and Regional Planning, in which Charles Dyer Norton was a professor; they transformed

---

3. Cited by Judith Oberlander, "History IV 1933–1935," in *The Making of An Architect 1881–1981: Columbia University in the City of New York*, ed. Richard Oliver (New York: Rizzoli, 1981), 120.

4. Jill Pearlman, "Joseph Hudnut's Other Modernism at the 'Harvard Bauhaus,'" *Journal of the Society of Architectural Historians* 56, no. 4 (1997): 452.

5. Anthony Alofsin, *The Struggle for Modernism: Architecture, Landscape Architecture, and City Planning at Harvard* (New York: W. W. Norton, 2002), 134.

6. Joseph Hudnut, foreword to *The Graduate School of Design and the Education of Planners*, by John Merriman Gaus (Cambridge, Mass.: Harvard Graduate School of Design, 1943), 3.

7. Ibid., 38.

the planning curriculum to stand shoulder to shoulder with that of architecture and landscape architecture. Effectively, Perkins was key in making the interdisciplinary approach work at the Harvard Graduate School of Design.

In his comprehensive history of the Harvard Graduate School of Design, Anthony Alofsin argues that this approach was "elegant in its simplicity" for training "a modern practitioner of architecture, landscape architecture, or city and regional planning" by offering a core curriculum of "four closely integrated courses taught in the first year to all students by an interdepartmental team of instructors."[8] Moreover, Alofsin assesses the pedagogical integration that flourished from 1945 to 1950 as having unprecedented impact:

> Judging from the professional success of its students and its role as a model for other schools, the [Graduate School of Design] reached an apogee in this period. The students who attended during this fruitful time ultimately became a *Who's Who* of American and international architecture, landscape architecture, and planning, some of them among the most successful practitioners of the twentieth century. . . . As teachers, they passed on the ethos of the Harvard training to their students and in the programs they created and implemented.[9]

From 1943 until after the end of World War II, the Harvard Graduate School of Design offered an accelerated program to admit students who had not completed their bachelor's degrees "to allow veterans to return to the workplace more quickly."[10] This program allowed McHarg to enter Harvard in the fall of 1946 after serving in the British Army during the war and retiring with the rank of major. By his own admission, McHarg's "academic credentials were meager," and he held no bachelor's degree.[11] With Perkins as his adviser, McHarg immediately became immersed in the seminars and courses in this "new world," where "the common denominator was not valor, but intellect."[12] McHarg was educated in this milieu, and, as later years would prove, he would become one of the prime beneficiaries of the interdisciplinary academic innovations that Hudnut had established at Harvard.

McHarg's own assessment of his student experience would become an important factor in the development of his pedagogical philosophy as a

---

8. Alofsin, *The Struggle for Modernism*, 196.
9. Ibid., 202.
10. Ibid., 198.
11. McHarg, *A Quest for Life*, 66.
12. Ibid.

teacher. For example, in his autobiography, McHarg reflects on the positives and negatives of his educational experience at Harvard, where he earned three degrees: the bachelor of landscape architecture (BLA; 1949), the master of landscape architecture (MLA; 1950), and the master of city planning (MCP; 1951).

McHarg WAS ESPECIALLY CRITICAL of three aspects of his Harvard education. First, he believed that the graduate program in landscape architecture did "not engage the mind, far less challenge it."[13] City planning, on the other hand, did challenge the mind. He found that the "planning studios, conducted by practitioners from public agencies and private firms, were excellent examples of professional education."[14]

Second, he held that while the "instincts" at the Harvard Graduate School of Design "were splendid, and the energy and commitment admirable[,] . . . there was a notable absence of wisdom. Yet this quality existed in the person of Lewis Mumford. . . . He warned of the dangers of deifying technology, [and extolled] the necessity of giving primacy to human values."[15] Graduate school provided McHarg's first direct encounter with Mumford, who would later become his principal mentor when they served on the faculty of the Graduate School of Fine Arts at Penn.

Finally, his course of study did not include any exposure to the natural sciences or ecology, since engineering was more compatible with the designs of modernism and current technology: "Modern architecture had a deep antinatural content. . . . Nature, if considered, was believed to provide the podium for the building and, perhaps, its backdrop. . . . Natural science, particularly environmental science, was never considered."[16]

Several of McHarg's student notebooks from his early days in the Harvard program (1946–1947) give an insight on the fashioning of his thinking regarding land and the environment. While taking a course taught by landscape architect Norman T. Newton—who had succeeded Henry Vincent Hubbard, the pioneering landscape architect and planner at Harvard—McHarg writes, "Second to man & his environment in importance as material of design comes the land."[17] Another entry written during a course with geographer Edward L. Ullman reads, "Environment is a factor

---

13. Ibid., 71.
14. Ibid., 77.
15. Ibid., 83.
16. Ibid., 85.
17. Ian McHarg's Student Notebooks, Harvard University, 1946 or 1947, 109.I.B.2.2. Ian L. McHarg Collection, The Architectural Archives, University of Pennsylvania. Subsequent citations reference McHarg Collection, AAUP.

FIGURE **6.1.** Lewis Mumford, 1940.
(Lewis Mumford Collection, Monmouth University Library. Used With permission.)

equally important to culture and adaptations to a new environment will influence culture, while culture will influence any course of action when confronted by environmental problem[s]."[18] Although these sketchy notes do show that McHarg was introduced to the relationship of land, environment, and culture, it would be several decades before the conceptual and practical incorporation of this relationship emerged in a pedagogical model for human ecological planning.

18. Ibid.

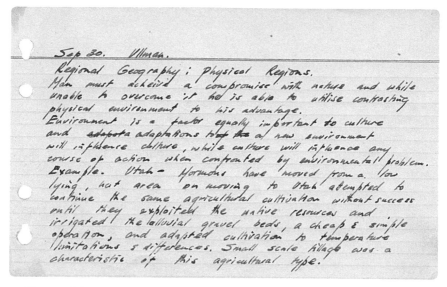

FIGURE 6.2. Ian McHarg, student notebook, Harvard University, 1946 or 1947. *(Ian McHarg Papers, The Architectural Archives, University of Pennsylvania.)*

A significant experience of McHarg's education at Harvard was that "the culminating requirement for both landscape architecture and city planning was a thesis."[19] Specifically, it was a "collaborative thesis" predicated on the influence of "radical European modernism [that] believed in the interdependence of the design arts, the role of design as a social art, the vision of collaboration as a process and technique, and the conception of modern design as an attitude involving a rational, analytical approach to problem solving."[20] In addition to McHarg, representing landscape architecture and city planning, the team included three architecture graduate students: William Conklin, Robert Geddes, and Marvin Sevely. The team members selected the redevelopment of Providence, Rhode Island, as their project's focus, wrote their own thesis statement, conducted field work, and finally presented their project to a jury of Gropius and his colleagues in June 1950. Many years later, McHarg would recount in his autobiography how valuable the collaborative thesis had been, especially since "it had posed a real problem, and the advisors, the actual functionaries engaged in seeking solutions, were of high caliber."[21]

---

19. McHarg, *A Quest for Life*, 87.
20. Alofsin, *The Struggle for Modernism*, 206.
21. McHarg, *A Quest for Life*, 91.

McHarg's First Teaching Assignments, 1950–1954

After completing his education at the Harvard Graduate School of Design, McHarg returned to Scotland. His first teaching experience came when he was invited to present a course in landscape architecture for architects at the Royal College of Art in Edinburgh. A similar course would also be offered at the Glasgow School of Art. The latter had an especially rich tradition of coalescing the arts and crafts design movement with the developing interest in modernism, especially under the influence of architect, artist, and designer Charles Rennie Mackintosh (1868–1928).

McHarg's papers in the Architectural Archives at Penn include a copy of the syllabus for Landscape Architecture, consisting of ten lectures taught during the 1953–1954 school year, as well as a copy of his "Introductory Lecture" and handwritten notes for a lecture on "Plant Materials." These documents give a sense of McHarg's initial teaching approach, with subject matter that spans from landscape design history to technical information to the process of design. Five of the ten lectures are devoted to the development of landscape design in various cultures from ancient Egypt to modern times—including the Renaissance, Chinese and Japanese design, and the English picturesque tradition. From the historical perspective, his notes read, "My intention in examining the landscape architecture of past epochs is not to burden you [the student] with obscure and irrelevant information. I do this because I believe that the solution to a problem, be it valid, contains an important lesson. A solution does not lose its value because it has been used before."[22]

Keeping in mind that his teaching role was to acquaint architects with the principles of landscape architecture, McHarg includes in his "Introductory Lecture" an early formulation of his interdisciplinary thinking, albeit focused on landscape architecture. He tells his students that a principle of "functionalism" is used to design the "modern house. . . . [F]rom a useful disposition of space and structure—may we not then discover analogous disciplines in the design of outdoor space?"[23] McHarg continues that a "series of disciplines I believe can provide the objective basis for a modern landscape architecture."[24] In McHarg's context, "disciplines" include "de-

---

22. "A Course of Ten Lectures in Landscape Architecture: Introductory Lecture," n.d., 3, 109.I.B.1.18. McHarg Collection, AAUP.
23. Ibid., 12.
24. Ibid.

termination of use areas, their size, orientation, structural or plant division, their constituent materials, circulation, the provision of shade, shelter, privacy, sound insulation, areas for active recreation, areas for passive recreation, [and] *the interrelationship of the parts to the whole.*"[25]

In his early years as a teacher, McHarg was acutely aware that functional relationships of the site—the focus of landscape architecture at the time—comprised a set of parts that must be interrelated to form the entirety. This valuable beginning perspective would later evolve into an ecological inventory—the identification of the functional or structural elements of a total environmental perspective.

He taught at Glasgow for three years, and his "lectures improved annually, as did my confidence as a teacher," he recalls in his autobiography. "I had never before considered teaching as a serious profession, but, clearly, it had charms."[26]

McHarg's Early Years at the University of Pennsylvania, 1954–1959

The collaborative dream at Harvard ended as tensions between Hudnut and Gropius mounted. Faculty retirements and departures became noteworthy, the most significant being the move by Perkins in 1951 to the University of Pennsylvania to become dean of the School of Fine Arts and chair of the Department of Architecture. He was hired by Penn president Harold Stassen and brought a viewpoint "shaped by the social philosophy of Lewis Mumford and the reforming ideals of Ebenezer Howard, [which] were given form by the architectural precepts of Walter Gropius."[27] At Penn, Perkins "proved to be a strong, vigorous dean, bringing rapid and dramatic change."[28] He restructured the curriculum at the graduate level so that it effectively became a transplant from Harvard of the shared academic offerings for the Departments of Architecture, Landscape Architecture, and Land and City Planning (as it was then called at Penn).

For the first year, all students took the same courses, regardless of their undergraduate backgrounds. In retrospect, Martin Meyerson, a former student of Perkins's who would come to Penn as associate professor of city

---

25. Ibid; emphasis added.

26. McHarg, *A Quest for Life*, 112.

27. Ann L. Strong and George E. Thomas, *The Book of the School: The Graduate School of Fine Arts of the University of Pennsylvania* (Philadelphia: University of Pennsylvania, 1990), 133.

28. Ibid., 134.

FIGURE 6.3. Dean G. Holmes Perkins, Graduate School of Fine Arts,
University of Pennsylvania, June 1966.
(Ian McHarg Papers, The Architectural Archives, University of Pennsylvania.)

planning in 1952 and later become president of the university (1970–1981),
commented "that the visions of interdepartmental collaboration Perkins had
absorbed at Harvard under Hudnut and Gropius were carried out more fully
at the University of Pennsylvania than at Harvard."[29]

By his own account, Perkins had to play "certain tricks" to make his
vision work at Penn. One of his most successful "tricks" was the way he
formed juries in all three programs: "The jury members—I picked them
every time—I made sure that on every jury you had somebody from each
one of the areas. It made them argue with each other . . . as part of the education of the students."[30]

---

29. Alofsin, *The Struggle for Modernism,* 230.
30. G. Holmes Perkins, interview with the author, October 15, 2002.

After Perkins assumed his duties at Penn, he decided to include landscape architecture within the Department of Land and City Planning. There had been a Department of Landscape Architecture at one time, but it had been suspended during the previous decade. Perkins hoped to create an independent focus for landscape architecture, and his offer to McHarg of the position of assistant professor to teach "city planning, but charged with the responsibility of developing a department of landscape architecture," would make the reality possible.[31]

McHarg began his tenure at Penn in the fall of 1954, and one of his first charges was to introduce a curriculum in landscape architecture. He recalls, "I had no office, no secretary; there were no students, no budget. The first year was devoted exclusively to designing a new curriculum, raising scholarship funds, recruiting a student body, and creating a new department."[32] According to Perkins, "It was his job to make landscape architecture a separate program,"[33] which occurred with the 1955 establishment of the Department of Landscape Architecture.

McHarg's initial appointment was as assistant professor to teach city planning and landscape architecture. As a junior member of the Department of Land and City Planning, McHarg found himself in the company of whom he would later characterize as the "entire leadership of the planning movement."[34] Perkins had assembled a brilliant faculty (as listed in the 1954–1955 *Bulletin* of the School of Fine Arts) that would undeniably distinguish Penn. The faculty included Robert Mitchell as chairman, William Wheaton, Martin Meyerson, Blanche Lemco van Ginkel, Charles Abrams, Edmund Bacon, John Dyckman, Chester Rapkin, Anatole Solow, and Lewis Mumford.[35] For McHarg, this appointment would be the beginning of a developing intellectual, collegial relationship with Mumford. And it would become ever clearer that Mumford's influence would carve out a prime direction for McHarg's nascent notions of ecohumanism. Mumford obviously saw something unique in his new university colleague when he inscribed a copy of his book *The Brown Decades* (1931) to McHarg in December 1955: "For Ian McHarg, with high hopes for his own contribution to the American Townscape."

31. McHarg, *A Quest for Life*, 118.
32. Ibid., 135.
33. Perkins, interview.
34. Strong and Thomas, *The Book of the School*, 139.
35. "School of Fine Arts, 1954–1955," *University of Pennsylvania Bulletin* 54, no. 9 (1953): 20.

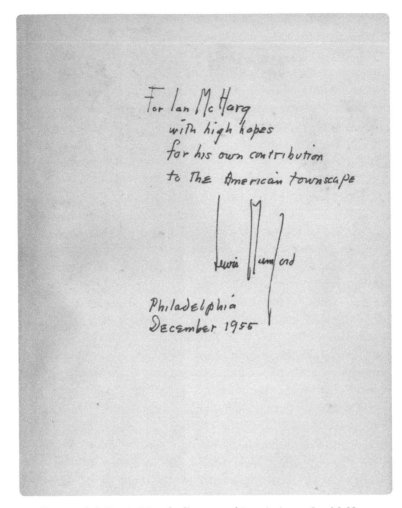

For Ian McHarg
with high hopes
for his own contribution
to The American townscape

Lewis Mumford

Philadelphia
December 1955

FIGURE 6.4. Lewis Mumford's personal inscription to Ian McHarg
in his book *The Brown Decades,* December 1955. *(Ian and Carol McHarg Collection,
The Architectural Archives, University of Pennsylvania.)*

THE INSTITUTE FOR URBAN STUDIES, established in 1951, was allied to the
Department of Land and City Planning, with advisory faculty from across
the university, including the Fels Institute and the Sociology, Economics,
Political Science, and Engineering Departments. The institute was "the first
venture of the School of Fine Arts into [urban] research"[36] and included
faculty and graduate students. By the mid-1950s, the institute staff included
additional luminaries in the planning field, such as Herbert Gans, William

36. Strong and Thomas, *The Book of the School,* 168–169.

Grigsby, and Britton Harris. Wheaton served as the director of the institute, and McHarg was a member of the research staff.

In *The Book of the School*, Ann Strong and George Thomas remark, "Though theory and curriculum provide direction, it is on the selection of faculty that a school rises or falls. . . . In an era presumed to have little use for history, Perkins's first position was offered to the historian and social critic, Lewis Mumford."[37] When asked years later about the intellectual role that Mumford played, Perkins remarked that in the beginning years of the program, "All of us at that stage were very much under the general influence of Mumford. He provided the breadth of interest that we were really looking for. When McHarg first came, he was only talking about landscape gardening and the exposure to people like Mumford expanded his breadth."[38] Meyerson commented that as a "lecturer [Mumford] exuded strength and power, and an almost Olympian certainty. The supremely self-assured tone that left so many of his readers flat could be impressive on the podium. He was, as his teaching colleagues testified, 'a force,' 'a presence.' He took hold of a class or a public audience and established complete control."[39]

In the Department of Land and City Planning, McHarg's first courses included Introduction to Design for City Planning, which analyzed terrain and appropriate types of design solutions as well as elements of general site layout.[40] In landscape architecture, he presented two courses. One course, Landscape Architecture and Planting Design, focused on site planning, engineering calculations, "and the development of planting plans." A second course, Landscape Architecture, concentrated on two "problems[,] of which one is in collaboration with students of city planning on the design of a new town."[41]

The curriculum in landscape architecture was pedagogically oriented to train practitioners to work with city planners and architects in offering "those services whereby the earth's surface is molded [*sic*] for human use and enjoyment."[42] At the basic level, in pursuing the bachelor of landscape architecture, the student would concentrate on a combination of "personal field" investigations and "successive drafting room courses" to bring together "as an indissoluble unity a concept of space, structure, and materials which grows out of the needs of man and his resources."[43]

---

37. Ibid., 135.

38. Perkins, interview.

39. Meyerson made these comments in 1987, as cited by Donald L. Miller, *Lewis Mumford: A Life* (New York: Weidenfeld and Nicolson, 1989), 458.

40. "School of Fine Arts, 1954–1955," 20.

41. Ibid., 32.

42. Ibid., 29.

43. Ibid., 31.

For the 1955–1956 school year, McHarg's teaching expanded to include three new courses: Landscape Construction, Municipal and Highway Engineering, and History of Landscape Architecture, which he co-taught with George Tatum, assistant professor of the history of art.[44] Other faculty during this academic year included John M. Fogg Jr., professor of botany; John W. MacGuire, assistant professor of architectural engineering; and Ralph Koliner, assistant professor of civil engineering.[45]

The pedagogical statement of the Department of Landscape Architecture that appears in the 1955–1956 School of Fine Arts *Bulletin* is slightly modified from the previous year's and reflects for the first time either the authorship of McHarg or at least his preferences for the structure of the curriculum: "The emphasis of landscape architecture has changed. . . . [W]hile still concerned with the private garden, the direction has turned more towards the design of open space in housing, urban space, municipal parks and playgrounds, national and state parks."[46] The statement continues that the landscape architect must "re-examine his techniques, disciplines and materials and evolve a new body of principle."[47] Although the representation of the academic program relies on the "study of plant materials" and the discipline of "landscape engineering," the department's statement stresses that central to training in landscape architecture is design—"the synthesis of function and material which is art."[48]

McHarg's papers at the Penn Architectural Archives include a handwritten manuscript that may be his initial report assessing the first few years of the curriculum in landscape architecture. Composed in 1956, it is addressed to "Mr. President, Officers, Ladies and Gentlemen" of the university. McHarg states, "This fundamental unity of the three professions in large part influences the character of the program in Landscape Architecture. This program is not a distinct entity, divorced from its partners. It is not a dependent of architecture, botany or horticulture[;] it is rather an equal partner and collaborator with its indivisible fellow [disciplines of] architecture and planning."[49] In the same "report," he summarizes the number and characteristics of the earliest student enrollments:

---

44. "School of Fine Arts, 1955–1956," *University of Pennsylvania Bulletin* 55, no. 7 (1954): 33–34.

45. Ibid., 32.

46. Ibid., 28.

47. Ibid.

48. Ibid., 29.

49. "Report on the Curriculum of Landscape Architecture" (1956), 109.II.E.1.3. McHarg Collection, AAUP.

With a student enrollment of one undergraduate student in 1954 the student body has grown to 14 in 1955 and 20 in the current year. No applications were received in 1954, 32 in 1955 and 70 in 1956. . . . Certain distinctions in this curriculum distinguishes [*sic*] it from others. The student body's multi-national representation points to a growing international reputation: Australian, American, Dutch, English, Scottish, [and] Turkish students are represented.[50]

The years 1957 and 1958 would prove to be important turning points for McHarg and the evolving curriculum. First, the Department of Landscape Architecture received its accreditation from the American Society of Landscape Architects in January 1957. Next, the department "became independent of [the Department of] Land and City Planning."[51] Finally, the first outside peer review of the department's staff and curriculum was conducted by Newton, chairman of the Department of Architectural Sciences and professor of landscape architecture at Harvard University.

Newton lauds Perkins and McHarg in his evaluation: "The building of the department to its current strength and liveliness in but a little over three years is a notable achievement, for which virtually the entire credit, in the opinion of the present reviewer, is due to the insight and interest of the Dean and to the unremitting energy of the Chairman."[52] In his assessment of the faculty, Newton addresses "one possible inadequacy: the fact that the regular staff has not had as great accumulative total of experience in the professional practice of landscape architecture."[53] His remedy is to either add a person "of considerable professional practice" or "to encourage—or indeed to require—members of the present staff to engage in professional landscape architectural practice."[54] Newton further makes several observations concerning course content, of which two in particular merit mention. The first concerns instruction in the history of landscape architecture, taught by Tatum, an art historian. In Newton's view, "In the case of students aspiring to be designers rather than to be historians or art-critics, study of their profession's past is likely to gain in a creative dimension if it is

---

50. Ibid.

51. Strong and Thomas, *The Book of the School*, 139.

52. Norman T. Newton, "A Report on the Department of Landscape Architecture, the School of Fine Arts: University of Pennsylvania," March 17, 1958, 1. Newton's "Report" was later shortened and incorporated in "Summaries of Survey Reports by 'Outside' Consultants and by 'Inside' Committees," *The Educational Survey of the University of Pennsylvania*, June 30, 1958, 109.II.E.1.11. McHarg Collection, AAUP.

53. Ibid., 3.

54. Ibid., 3–4.

guided by an able interpreter who is himself trained in their profession."[55] The second comment reflects the interdisciplinary perspective that Perkins and McHarg shared in establishing the curriculum: the course Architecture and City Planning "serves a noteworthy function in bringing together students from the several design professions for an invaluable early view of the comprehensiveness of the arts of design and of the close interrelationship among them."[56]

The major recommendation of Newton's report concerns the structure of the curriculum: he strongly believes that the training of landscape architects (as well as architects and city planners) "is most effectively done at the graduate level after receipt of the A.B. degree."[57] After analyzing the four curricula paths available for the education of landscape architects at Penn, he recommends "that a six-year curricular structure, to include both the A.B. and the professional degree, be adopted."[58] Essentially, this change would make the MLA degree attainable in three years plus a summer session.

In 1957, McHarg achieved recognition from his peers when he was promoted to associate professor. In 1958, "with new faculty appointed in all departments, new curricula established, doctoral programs approved, and research opportunities for faculty and graduate students increasing, the School was renamed the Graduate School of Fine Arts."[59] For the 1958–1959 school year, the pedagogical statement for McHarg's Department of Landscape Architecture broke away from the seemingly confining approach of the previous years, exhibiting a new temperament—and, indeed, a new direction: "One of the most conspicuous failures of 20th century western society has been the environment created. Squalor and anarchy are more accurately descriptive than are efficiency and delight. . . . Despoliation of landscape, the accretion of ugliness as cities are inevitable consequences of such values."[60] This bluntness, which clearly reflects McHarg's growing interest in environmental realities, shows that the department was embracing a new educational philosophy. In this regard, the graduate curriculum was "dedicated to the search for a body of principle and a formal expression for design in open space by which the landscape architect can make

---

55. Ibid., 4.
56. Ibid., 5.
57. Ibid., 10.
58. Ibid., 10–11.
59. Strong and Thomas, *The Book of the School*, 136.
60. "Graduate School of Fine Arts, 1958–1959," *University of Pennsylvania Bulletin* 58, no. 10 (1958): 92.

a significant contribution to the creation of a superior social and physical environment."[61]

The Department of Landscape Architecture would now focus on offering "special opportunities and facilities" to link the teaching curriculum with actual "field projects." Contacts were established with a number of agencies in Philadelphia, including the National Park Service, city planning agencies, redevelopment authorities, and park and recreational agencies. Within the university, the department developed contacts with the Botany Department, the Morris Arboretum, and the various engineering schools. In addition, the Institute of Urban Studies provided an opportunity for research in landscape architecture.[62]

Although the course offerings in the curriculum for the 1958–1959 and 1959–1960 school years did not shift appreciably from the preceding few years, a new awareness was clearly taking hold under McHarg's leadership. He curated a small, but talented faculty, with each member offering a particular specialty; among them were Fogg, a botanist and the director of the Morris Arboretum; George E. Patton and B. Michael Brown, landscape architects; and Karl Linn, with a background in agronomy and psychology. McHarg would later write in his autobiography that Linn "might well be the most stimulating and original of all the teachers of landscape architecture during the history of the Penn landscape architecture program. . . . [H]e was a powerful teacher and practitioner."[63] A sense of why McHarg was impressed by Linn is revealed in a 1959 faculty memo concerning the curriculum. Linn begins, "Since most of the students are graduates of some form of design training, not necessarily landscape architecture, our task will consist not only in educating but also in reeducating."[64] Moreover, he cautions his colleagues, "the pitfall of a landscape architectural curriculum that is over influenced by planners is that one gets excited about large scale projects, statistics, and abstracts to the extent that one becomes a social worker of landscape architecture rather than an artist of landscape architecture."[65] Linn's assessment is consistent with the city planning profession's movement away from its traditional design-oriented perspective to a rational comprehensive and systems approach.

---

61. Ibid., 92–93.

62. Ibid., 93.

63. McHarg, *A Quest for Life*, 138, 139.

64. Karl Linn, memorandum to McHarg, Fogg, Patton, Brown, and Shepheard, April 2, 1959, Subject: Curriculum of Landscape Architecture, Department of Landscape Architecture, University of Pennsylvania, 1, 109.II.A.1.51. McHarg Collection, AAUP.

65. Ibid., 3.

FIGURE 6.5. Penn-Rockefeller Conference on Urban Design Criticism, January 1959. Participants pictured (left to right): William L. C. Wheaton, Lewis Mumford, Ian McHarg, J. B. Jackson, David A. Crane, Louis I. Kahn, G. Holmes Perkins, Arthur Holden, unidentified member of Dean Perkins's staff, Catherine Bauer Wurster, Leslie Cheek Jr., Mary Barnes, Jane Jacobs, Kevin Lynch, Gordon Stephenson, Nanine Clay, and I. M. Pei. *(Ian McHarg Papers, The Architectural Archives, University of Pennsylvania.)*

Landscape Architecture and Regional Planning, 1960–1968

Around 1960, the Department of Landscape Architecture began to move in a McHarg-inspired direction that would plant the seeds for a new ecological planning curriculum. Finding sources of financial support was essential if the department was to grow and prosper. The earliest funding support came from the Rockefeller Foundation, a modest grant of $6,000 for the 1956–1957 school year and another for the 1957–1958 school year to establish a clearinghouse for professional information. The Rockefeller Foundation increased its support for the 1958–1959 and 1959–1960 school years by awarding $36,000 for creative research. Among McHarg's papers at the Penn Architectural Archives is what appears to be a generic funding request proposal, written in McHarg's style and soliciting additional funds ($15,000 to $18,000 per year) to support the department's progress. What is most interesting about this document is that it clearly enunciates the educational path that McHarg envisioned.

The document states, "The character of the Landscape Architecture program is believed unique. Unlike most others elsewhere, it seeks out and

hand-picks its students; none comes unrecommended."[66] As to the curriculum, we find that McHarg was establishing two elements: (1) the Penn program "has kept its hand in horticulture; it has not subordinated flowers to concrete"; and (2) the curriculum in "Landscape Architecture [is] a freely expressive art, aspiring to evoke a vibrant response in those it envelops. Unlike any other, it grounds the student firmly in human ecology—the reaction of the body and mind to environmental stimuli of all sorts."[67]

"Man and Environment," 1959–1963

In the fall of 1959, McHarg began teaching a new course, Landscape Architecture, Man and Environment. The course was aimed at exploring "the scientific view of creation, religious attitudes to environment, the interaction of environment on man, of man on environment and the quest for an

---

66. "Landscape Architecture: A Program to Project Its Influence on an Increasingly Urban Society," University of Pennsylvania, n.d. (The presentation of certain data suggests that this was written in 1960 or 1961.) 109.II.E.1.22. McHarg Collection, AAUP.
   67. Ibid., 10–11.

ethic for man and environment."[68] In his autobiography, McHarg describes this course as "the most powerful act I initiated. . . . I originated the conception and was the impresario."[69] The course had more far-reaching consequences than simply providing a learning requirement for matriculating students—it was a learning mechanism for McHarg himself. It brought him into contact with and under the intellectual influence of many of the outstanding thinkers and recognized experts of the time in the natural, physical, and social sciences as well as theology. In fact, the structure and content of Man and Environment would become the intellectual backbone for the development of the future ecological planning curriculum.

The first offering of Man and Environment was presented as a four-part course, with each part augmented to explore an interrelated set of issues, concerns, and problems. Part 1 examined The Scientific View of Creation and included such notable guest lecturers as Dr. William M. Protheroe ("Cosmic Creation"), Dr. Horace G. Richards ("Geological Change"), and Dr. Robert MacArthur ("Ecology"). Part 2 examined Religious Attitudes to Man and Environment. Here, McHarg introduced the major world religions, each represented by a theologian or scholar. Lectures addressed primitive attitudes, Judaism, Islam, Christianity, Tao, Shinto, Confucius, and Zen Buddhism. Part 3, titled Environment-Man: Man-Environment, delved into such perspectives as "The Social Anthropologist" (Dr. Loren Eiseley), "The Psychologist" (Linn), "The Geographer" (Dr. Lester Klimm), and "The Botanist-Ecologist" (Fogg). Part 4 of the course was titled An Ethic for Man and Environment and included presentations on "Law and Environment" (Professor Clarence Morris), "Landscape Architecture as an Ethic" (Linn), and "An Ethic for Man and Environment" (Professor Paul Sears).[70]

McHarg has described how the course was presented and how it would provide a springboard for collateral undertakings:

> Most of the lectures were given by guest speakers; I introduced and concluded each segment. All other lectures were provided by visiting professors. The subjects were the scientific conceptions of matter, life, and man; the views of God, man, and nature in the major philosophies and religions, and, last, an examination of the interaction of man and nature, mainly ecological. This became the forum for my

---

68. "Graduate School of Fine Arts, 1960–1961," *University of Pennsylvania Bulletin* 60, no. 5 (1960): 30.

69. McHarg, *A Quest for Life*, 140.

70. Syllabus for Man and Environment, L.A. 530 (1959), 109.II.E.3.9. McHarg Collection, AAUP.

FIGURE 6.6. Loren Eiseley and Lewis Mumford, May 22, 1963.
(Lewis Mumford Papers, Kislak Center for Special Collections, University of Pennsylvania.
Copyright © 1963 by Elizabeth M. Morss and James G. Morss. Used by permission.)

continued education for a quarter of a century. It, in turn, begat the television series for CBS entitled *The House We Live In* and provided much of the scientific basis for *Design with Nature*, written in 1967, which in turn propagated the movie *Multiply and Subdue the Earth*.[71]

The House We Live In could be considered a companion intellectual venture; it became a popular weekly television series produced by WCAU-TV in Philadelphia (a CBS affiliate) during 1960 and 1961. Bringing together a blue-ribbon assortment of scholars, philosophers, and theologians who represented a number of disciplines and perspectives, McHarg interviewed "many of the world's leading thinkers about human-environment relationships, focusing largely on religious, ethical, and philosophical issues."[72]

---

71. McHarg, *A Quest for Life*, 140.
72. Ibid., 162.

Lewis Mumford was the eighth interview in the second series, which took place on an early spring Sunday in March 1961. It would prove to be a prescient experience for McHarg:

McHARG: Lewis Mumford, this is a great and proud moment for me to have you as a guest on *The House We Live In*, the inquiry into man and environment. You have been the oracle for man and environment for 35 years, the leading philosopher in this field, the man best advised in the Western world on urbanization and the development of its resources. May I say again how wonderfully proud and happy I am to have you here and I await listening to you with great, great pleasure, Lewis Mumford.

MUMFORD: Professor McHarg, you and I are old friends and I don't like to have an oracle stand between us and our friendship, so please feel the liberty to interrupt me as often as you find the need for it and keep this from being an ordinary standardized university lecture. Have you ever read Lawrence Henderson's *The Fitness of the Environment*?

McHARG: No, I am afraid not.

MUMFORD: Well, very few people have, so there is no shame in that, but it is a very important book . . . [where] he made an analysis of the physical and chemical properties of the earth, the disposition of the elements and the way they behaved toward each other. He found that the earth was favorably disposed toward life. This is almost a heretical conclusion for a great many people, who had thought of the earth as being hostile to life, of life being in a perpetual struggle against the earth.[73]

Several years after this revelation, McHarg consolidated his thinking as he structured his theory of ecological planning predicated on the notion of fitness and synthesizing ideas from Charles Darwin and Lawrence Henderson. In a 1968 essay, McHarg writes, "We can use 'fitness' both in the sense that Henderson employs it, and also in Darwinian terms. Thus the environment is fit, and can be made more fitting; the organism adapts to fit the environment."[74]

---

73. Interview with Lewis Mumford by Ian L. McHarg, *The House We Live In*, WCAU-TV, Philadelphia, March 26, 1961, 109.II.B.2.8. McHarg Collection, AAUP.

74. Ian L. McHarg, "Values, Process and Form," in *To Heal the Earth: Selected Writings of Ian L. McHarg*, ed. Ian L. McHarg and Frederick R. Steiner (Washington, D.C.: Island Press, 1998), 67.

Over the years that Man and Environment was taught, the subjects and the cast of invited guest lecturers changed. McHarg sought to push the limits of scientific, humanistic, cultural, and religious thinking to comprehend people's relationship to the environment. Specifically, the course "placed ecology at its center, but broadened the area of inquiry into a larger biophysical environment, and, not least, included human attitudes toward the environment."[75]

In 1963, McHarg presented "Man and Environment" as a chapter in a book edited by Leonard Duhl, *The Urban Condition.* This contribution is McHarg's "first serious theoretical writing," according to Frederick Steiner, who characterizes it as a "tremendous leap in scale. He changed his focus from small-scale urban concerns to a larger regional vision."[76] By McHarg's account, "This involvement encouraged me to introduce another course, entitled 'Ecology of the City,' in an attempt to focus ecologists, ethologists, and epidemiologists on the problems and remedies of the urban plight."[77]

In the 1964–1965 school year, McHarg taught Ecology of the City for the first time. The course description is succinct, promising "an examination of the city as a complex of physical and biological systems amenable to analysis through the insights of ecology."[78] In his autobiography, McHarg offers the following assessment: "'Man and Environment' was immensely successful, growing to 250 students. 'Ecology of the City' never achieved great success. It was clear that scientists were not attracted to the city."[79]

Wallace-McHarg Associates, 1963–1964

David A. Wallace and McHarg had been classmates at Harvard, and they renewed their friendship when Wallace joined Penn's city planning faculty in 1962.

In 1963, Wallace was asked to create a plan for the Green Spring and Worthington Valleys, an unspoiled, upper-income area in rapidly developing Baltimore County in Maryland. Many years later, he would recall, "Although I already had a number of [consulting] clients in my budding practice at Penn, I had no employees except students working part-time,

---

75. McHarg, *A Quest for Life,* 158. See also pp. 155–162 for the evolving list of subjects and guests that McHarg recruited over the years that the course was offered.

76. Ian L. McHarg and Frederick R. Steiner, eds., *To Heal the Earth: Selected Writings of Ian L. McHarg* (Washington, D.C.: Island Press, 1998), 6, 10.

77. McHarg, *A Quest for Life,* 141.

78. "Graduate School of Fine Arts, 1964–1965," *University of Pennsylvania Bulletin* 64, no. 5 (1963): 45.

79. McHarg, *A Quest for Life,* 141.

and realized that the assignment would require a variety of disciplines. I needed help."[80] Wallace had served on a jury in one of McHarg's classes and was impressed by the "new ecological emphasis in the landscape program."[81] Thus, Wallace-McHarg Associates was formed. Two years later, two early employees of the consulting practice, William Roberts and Thomas Todd, would form the nucleus of a new partnership, Wallace, McHarg, Roberts and Todd (WMRT). McHarg's participation in this consulting partnership would continue for the next sixteen years, until he resigned in 1979.

In 1964, the completed *Plan for the Valleys* addressed the critical question with a clear prescription for planning:

> If indeed uncontrolled growth inevitably destroys, what principles can preserve natural beauty and determine the appropriate locations and character of development? In order to answer this question an analysis was made of natural processes, geology, ground and surface water, flood plains, soil types, topography, and vegetative cover. This physiographic analysis provided conservation principles for development.[82]

This plan represents McHarg's first application of ecology in a professional planning project.

Developing the Regional Planning Curriculum, 1963–1967

With the advent of the 1964–1965 school year, the Department of Landscape Architecture offered two "areas of concentration": one in civic design and the other in regional land planning, both in conjunction with the Department of City Planning. For the latter, the Department of Landscape Architecture would "design curricula for selected students interested in Regional Problems."[83]

However, McHarg's increasing preoccupation with ecology and the natural sciences was driving him to institute some significant revisions to the curriculum. Initially, he was interested in applying ecology to landscape architecture, spurred on by new (although short-lived) hires to the faculty, including landscape architect Lewis Clarke and ecologist William Martin. But that perspective changed.

---

80. David A. Wallace, *Urban Planning/My Way: From Baltimore's Inner Harbor to Lower Manhattan and Beyond* (Chicago: Planners Press, 2004), 78.

81. Ibid.

82. Wallace-McHarg Associates, *Plan for the Valleys* (Philadelphia: Wallace-McHarg Associates, 1964), 3.

83. "Graduate School of Fine Arts, 1964–1965," 40.

The turning point came with the appointment of Nicholas Muhlenberg, a resource economist, as assistant professor of landscape architecture in 1963. Muhlenberg had served on the faculty of Pennsylvania State University and before that the University of California at Berkeley. He held a master's degree in forestry from the University of Michigan, a master's degree in economics from Yale University, and a doctorate in resource economics from the Yale School of Forestry. Muhlenberg's impact would be decisive and far-reaching, as recounted by McHarg: "Muhlenberg was the first faculty member in the Graduate School of Fine Arts who was informed in ecology and familiar with the literature and many of the scientists. . . . Nick gave direction to our tentative exploration. Here was a body of knowledge that must be incorporated into the curriculum. Here at last was the theoretical basis for the practice of landscape architecture. . . . He would be our intellectual leader."[84]

Because of Muhlenberg's academic background and breadth of knowledge in ecology and natural resources conservation, McHarg asked him to design a natural sciences curriculum in regional planning. When questioned about how he started, Muhlenberg stated, "McHarg had the broad concept; I was leaned on to structure the curriculum."[85] As a point of departure, Muhlenberg analyzed the curricula in forestry and natural resources conservation at Yale University, the University of Michigan, and the University of California at Berkeley. When asked why he choose these three schools, he commented, "Each of these schools were powerhouses in their regions: Yale in the East, Michigan in the Midwest, and Berkeley in the West. Next, there were astonishing people at each one of them—Paul Sears at Yale, Stanley Cain at Michigan, and Henry James Vaux at Berkeley, among many others. Finally, each of these schools was heavily supported by the Ford Foundation to develop strong curricula in 'resources for the future,' that emphasized resource conservation."[86]

As Muhlenberg fashioned the multidisciplinary approach with a strong natural resource component that would ultimately become the heart of Penn's regional planning program, he sought out successes at these three schools. For example, Cain, chairman of the Department of Conservation

---

84. McHarg, *A Quest for Life*, 172. Lenore Sagan, McHarg's longtime administrative assistant, said in an October 16, 2002, interview with the author that "Mr. McHarg thinks [*sic*] that Dr. Muhlenberg is the smartest person on our faculty. He thought he [Muhlenberg] was a genius."

85. Nicholas Muhlenberg, interview with the author, October 18, 2002, and follow-up, January 11, 2003.

86. Ibid. The Ford Foundation would later underwrite the regional planning program at Penn.

in the School of Natural Resources at the University of Michigan, described such a curriculum as giving "special emphasis to what we think is an important and growing area of usefulness to persons with training in natural resources and conservation; this is the broad field that includes watershed management, area development, and regional planning."[87] As Cain further described it, the key to the multidisciplinary construction of a curriculum is to build "a faculty with a diversity of professional backgrounds; the present small staff can point to biology, ecology, education, public administration, economic geography, and economics as areas of special competence."[88]

The Conservation Foundation provided financial support for the initial research. After four months of investigation, Muhlenberg reported, "The outlook for a program in regional land planning seems reasonably assured."[89] He further outlined three basic objectives: first, "to focus attention on the biological parameters of planning. The second is to design curricula which would be consistent with the first objective, and the third, although considerably less important, is to find a name for this proposed program."[90] The name did emerge in an undated paper written for the faculty by McHarg with an annex by Muhlenberg—probably shortly after the submission of Muhlenberg's 1964 report to the Conservation Foundation. In this paper, McHarg writes, "Conservation is not a profession but rather an ethical view of man and nature. . . . I suggest that this movement requires a body of professionals who are ethically conservationists, but who are professional natural scientist-planners. I suggest that the profession of regional land planning be created to fill this need at least in part."[91]

In February 1964, McHarg and Muhlenberg wrote "Regional Land Planning," a paper that offers the essence of the proposed curriculum that would train practitioners in the new profession "tentatively titled Regional Land Planning."[92] They propose specific parameters for the disciplinary structure for faculty recruitment and student training for this new curriculum: the physical sciences considered central would be geology and hydrology; in the biological sciences, botany, zoology, and ecology would be central.

---

87. Stanley A. Cain, "The Conservation Program at the University of Michigan," in *Resource Training for Business, Industry, Government*, by Natural Resources Study Committee (Washington, D.C.: Conservation Foundation, 1958), 29.

88. Ibid.

89. Nicholas Muhlenberg, "Report to the Conservation Foundation," January 20, 1964, 109.II.E.1.27. McHarg Collection, AAUP.

90. Ibid.

91. Ian L. McHarg (with annex by Nicholas Muhlenberg), "Natural Sciences and the Planning Process" (n.d.), 109.V.D.1.8. McHarg Collection, AAUP.

92. Ian L. McHarg and Nicholas Muhlenberg, "Regional Land Planning," February 24, 1964, 4, 109.II.C.86. McHarg Collection, AAUP.

Moreover, they suggest, "ecology is considered to present the conceptual framework for the inclusion of all of the physical and biological sciences. Indeed, the description of the conceptual basis of this prospective profession might well be Ecological Determinism."[93] McHarg and Muhlenberg outline a provisional curriculum with three phases. The first would include courses concerned with planning, the second would include courses in the natural sciences, and the third would be "composed of the case study courses in Regional Land Planning directed towards problem solving."[94]

On June 19, 1964, McHarg sent details of the regional land planning curriculum to his friend and mentor Mumford. Mumford responded on June 30, offering unqualified support and optimism for future prospects: "Your new curriculum delights me. It will fill in a big hole in our computer-oriented planning curricula. What is more, if the New York State plan that [Governor Nelson] Rockefeller has just announced goes through[,] your students will have careers assured them."[95] Mumford's continuing support was crucial in keeping McHarg on track as the ecology-based graduate curriculum evolved.

Muhlenberg's regional planning curriculum (emphasizing the natural sciences) first appeared during the 1965–1966 school year. This was also the academic year when the Department of City Planning became the Department of City and Regional Planning. Regional planning, as a program of study, was now "offered cooperatively by the Department of Landscape Architecture and the Department of City Planning in the Graduate School of Fine Arts and the Department of Regional Science in the Wharton School, under the general guidance of an interdepartmental committee."[96] The pedagogical statement of the department's philosophy that explained the curriculum and related academic engagements appears under the heading "Department of Landscape Architecture and Regional Planning" in the *Bulletin* for the 1965–1966 school year. Consistent with the department's expansion to include regional planning, the program is described as being "directed towards the training of Regional Planners based upon the natural sciences, [and] satisf[ying] an important deficiency in the field of planning by developing spokesmen for physical and biological processes."[97]

---

93. Ibid., 5.

94. Ibid., 9.

95. Lewis Mumford, letter to Ian L. McHarg, June 30, 1964, 109.II.A.2.65. McHarg Collection, AAUP.

96. "Graduate School of Fine Arts, 1965–1966," *University of Pennsylvania Bulletin* 65, no. 3 (1964): 49. The program advisers were McHarg, Muhlenberg, and Gerald A. P. Carrothers, chairman of the Department of City and Regional Planning.

97. Ibid., 50.

The faculty included, among others, Peter Shepheard, visiting professor of landscape architecture; Anthony Walmsley, assistant professor of landscape architecture; and Jack McCormick, lecturer on botany.[98]

This new regional planning curriculum consisted of "two streams[,] with a common core of planning courses." One "stream" was based on student preparation in the natural sciences, while the other was based on preparation in the social sciences. Both culminated in the master of regional planning (MRP) degree after two years of full-time study.[99] The MLA degree was also offered as the advanced professional degree in that field. The department's complete course offerings were detailed under the two fields of landscape architecture and regional planning, with graduate courses listed in the "related professional fields" of architecture, biology, botany, city planning, geology, regional science, and zoology.[100]

For the following three school years, beginning in 1966–1967, the department's regional planning program evolved slightly into two subcurricula picking up the two "streams" approach of natural science and social science. In this manner, the regional planning emphasis broadened its appeal by welcoming students who had backgrounds (i.e., bachelor's degrees) in a field in the natural sciences or in the social sciences. In the case of the latter, "students entering the Regional Planning program through the Department of City and Regional Planning are required to develop a thorough grounding in the social sciences with emphasis in a selected area (e.g., economics, political science, regional science)."[101]

Ecology became the "unifying discipline," and consequently, "studies of the environment of necessity had to be inter- and multidisciplinary."[102] Indeed, McHarg's efforts were beginning to be recognized beyond Penn. In a February 1966 letter to McHarg, Eugene Odum, professor of zoology at the University of Georgia and author of the acclaimed *Fundamentals of Ecology*, writes, "I am naturally elated that you are finding a basic ecological approach useful in practical landscape planning. . . . I am glad you are assuming leadership in pushing ecology at the University of Pennsylvania. I believe the large eastern universities are now in the mood to make up for lost time in this area."[103]

---

98. Ibid., 44.

99. Ibid., 49.

100. Ibid., 53–56.

101. "Graduate School of Fine Arts, 1966–1967," *University of Pennsylvania Bulletin* 66, no. 4 (1965): 30.

102. McHarg, *A Quest for Life*, 173.

103. Eugene P. Odum, letter to Ian L. McHarg, February 7, 1966, 109.II.A.1.75. McHarg Collection, AAUP.

A 1967 Ford Foundation grant in the amount of $500,000 expanded the faculty and supported the move into regional planning with a concentration on the natural sciences. Initially, McHarg recommended that potential students have a background in the various environmental sciences (physical or biological) that could be expanded and augmented through an examination of contemporary problems,[104] and he recruited an interdisciplinary faculty to advance this teaching approach. McHarg was especially delighted when he retained the renowned South African botanist and ecologist John F. V. Phillips to be visiting professor of ecology during the first semester of the 1966–1967 academic year. Many years earlier, in developing a holistic theory of ecology, Phillips had coined the term *biotic community* as his key conceptual base.[105] During his appointment, Phillips wrote a brief paper that outlines the first internal critical look at the department—its curriculum, staffing, and funding for equipment. Like so many others, Phillips had come under the spell of McHarg's personal magnetism: "Professor McHarg, the Department, and the University itself, so far have gained an enviable reputation through the exposition of the ecological approach—almost wholly due to Professor McHarg himself—through his consistent enthusiasm and eloquence."[106] Among a number of suggestions he makes regarding the curriculum, staffing, and needed equipment, Phillips argues, "The University cannot afford to do anything but work for the best possible fulfillment of the objectives and philosophy of the [ecological approach]. The influence of this upon the history of landscape architecture and regional planning in this country could be profound and the credit to the University could be, accordingly, massive and far-reaching."[107]

The Institute for Environmental Studies

In *The Book of the School*, Ann Strong and George Thomas point out that Dean Perkins's "emphasis on the unity of education and research reached a fitting conclusion in 1965 with the creation of the Institute for Environmental Studies, into which were merged the Institute for Urban Studies and the Institute for Architectural Research. The name was appropriate, given

---

104. McHarg, *A Quest for Life*, 191.
105. See John Phillips, "The Biotic Community," *Journal of Ecology* 19, no. 1 (1931): 1–24.
106. John F. V. Phillips, "Some Thoughts Regarding Landscape Architecture and Regional Planning at the University of Pennsylvania" (1966), 1, 109.II.E.1.39. McHarg Collection, AAUP.
107. Ibid. See also John Phillips, "Ecology and the Ecological Approach," *Via 1* (Philadelphia: Graduate School of Fine Arts, University of Pennsylvania, 1968), 17–18.

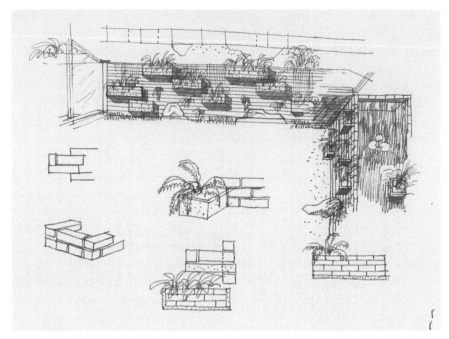

FIGURE 6.7. Ian McHarg, landscape doodle, spring 1965.
(Ian McHarg Papers, The Architectural Archives, University of Pennsylvania.)

the growing importance in the School and in the nation of environmental issues."[108] Its specific function was "to carry on a continuing program of study and research focused on the nature and control of man's environment, considered to be the concern common to all teaching divisions of the Graduate School of Fine Arts."[109]

The institute was established to engage in a diverse research agenda that would incorporate the interests from the three professional departments: the Department of Architecture, the Department of City and Regional Planning, and the Department of Landscape Architecture and Regional Planning. By 1967, the following "research groups" were in place to conduct wide-ranging projects that could influence McHarg's curriculum: Studies on Legal Aspects of Planning and Development Control (chaired by Strong), Research on Natural Sciences in Landscape Architecture and Regional Planning (chaired by Muhlenberg), Planning Sciences (chaired by Harris), Regional Planning Studies (chaired by David E. Boyce), and Transportation Research (chaired

108. Strong and Thomas, *The Book of the School*, 148.
109. "Graduate School of Fine Arts, 1966–1967," 48.

by Anthony Tomazinis).[110] The first director of the institute came from the Department of City and Regional Planning, Gerald A. P. Carrothers, professor of city planning. He was followed by Michel Chevalier, and in 1970, Strong, professor of city and regional planning, became the institute director.

In a 1967 memorandum to Perkins, McHarg proposes "that a Center for Ecological Research in Planning and Design be created within the Institute."[111] This center would serve as the principal research group that produced the ecological planning study done for Medford, New Jersey, in 1974.

The Dawning of the Golden Age of Ecological Planning

Reliance on the ecological perspective as the basis of a regional planning curriculum would continue to accelerate after 1967 and would culminate in a comprehensive and complete cross-fertilization of disciplines in the natural, physical, and social sciences that would provide the essential preparation for a new generation of regional planners and designers. In fact, the curriculum would serve as a kind of laboratory to nurture and advance what would become known as the "McHarg Method," a method of ecological inventory and planning that would determine the location or suitability for certain land uses for a particular site or an entire region.

The first publication that contains a comprehensive presentation of the regional planning curriculum (undated, but probably done in 1967) is a brochure titled *An Ecological Approach to Regional Planning*. Its statement of purpose is clear and to the point and would be the guiding credo in the years ahead: "The program in regional planning . . . is based upon the premise that planning requires the contribution of those who understand nature as process, responsive to laws, constituting a value system, proffering opportunities but with inherent limitations, and that such understanding is derived from the natural sciences and is integrated by ecology."[112] A unique aspect of the regional planning curriculum was its lecture courses "responsible for presenting the basic evidence and planning methods" and a series of four planning studios that focused on case studies to apply the planning data and methods in a problem-solving context.[113]

---

110. "Graduate School of Fine Arts, 1968–1969," *University of Pennsylvania Bulletin* 68, no. 5 (1967): 50–53.

111. Ian L. McHarg, memorandum to Dean G. Holmes Perkins, August 31, 1967, 109. II.E.1.42. McHarg Collection, AAUP.

112. *An Ecological Approach to Regional Planning: A Graduate Program at the Department of Landscape Architecture and Regional Planning*, Graduate School of Fine Arts, University of Pennsylvania (1967), 4, 109.IV.C.23. McHarg Collection, AAUP.

113. Ibid., 12.

As the 1968–1969 academic year began, the regional planning program was firmly established with new faculty and an expanded curriculum. In the next school year, the ecological program in regional planning would increase in recognition and in its student body. It would not be long before the Penn graduate program in ecological planning would become well known as a unique interdisciplinary curriculum. In many ways, it would be the standard bearer in the environmental education of planners and landscape architects, who would spread McHarg's philosophy and technique of ecological planning throughout the world.

7

The Ecological Planning Curriculum, 1969–1973

THE REGIONAL PLANNING CURRICULUM at the University of Pennsylvania (Penn) predicated on ecology, was, to a large degree, spurred on by the changing attitudes toward the environment. The 1970s have been popularly called the environmental decade, fostered by a growing awareness that human activities were having destructive effects on the natural environment.[1] Ian McHarg became nationally recognized as one of the most eloquent faces of this accelerating movement. Several elements account for his increasing recognition and stature, all of which would directly influence the development of the ecological planning curriculum as well as the attraction of students to Penn.

Furthermore, the early 1970s saw the beginnings of a trend to develop curricula in the environmental sciences at a number of American colleges and universities. Although it was not new, an environmental sciences perspective with an emphasis on human ecology was considered the next

---

1. Beginning in 1969, in response to the heightened concern of the American people for environmental protection, Congress enacted more than a dozen major environmental statutes, the most important of which were the National Environmental Policy Act (1969), the Clean Air Act (1970), the Federal Water Pollution Control Act (1972), the Coastal Zone Management Act (1972), the Resource Conservation and Recovery Act (1976), the Surface Mining Control and Reclamation Act (1977), and the Comprehensive Response, Compensation, and Liability Act, known as the Superfund Law (1980). These laws shifted primary responsibility for environmental protection from the states to the newly created Environmental Protection Agency.

progressive step in curriculum evolution from the focus on conservation education that relied on the biologically based natural sciences, forestry, and wildlife conservation. In a 1968 symposium, where Lewis Mumford gave the concluding remarks, Canadian plant ecologist Pierre Dansereau proclaimed, "The crying need for a 'new science' of environmental study, with ecology at its core and medicine at all of its outlets, is now being met by a few institutions of higher learning."[2] He called on universities to be more than "diploma factories" by providing leadership "towards a better understanding . . . of whole environments."[3] The individuals whom Dansereau hoped would usher in this emphasis would be "gifted coordinators [who] have something to ordain and they are bound to collaborate with workers in several fields who are themselves specialists, and possibly narrow ones. . . . The truly gifted make up in depth what they may lack in breadth, and by shifting their gaze, they develop range."[4] McHarg also participated in that symposium, which provided yet another podium from which he could add his voice to the growing awareness of environmental issues facing the nation. And this 1968 symposium took place the year before he published *Design with Nature*.

Design with Nature, 1967–1969

During the winter of 1966, McHarg wrote to Dean G. Holmes Perkins to formally request a sabbatical "to write a book on ecological principles for Architecture, Landscape Architecture, City and Regional Planning." "As you know," he continues, "I have been increasingly preoccupied with ecology, both as a science and as a point of view." He adds, "The publication of this is my first priority."[5] The sabbatical was granted, and McHarg spent the next academic year working at home to prepare the manuscript.

McHarg recalls in his autobiography that as his work progressed, he "was growing more and more frightened. The book was becoming presumptuous, as the evidence I was compiling was impelling me to make greater and greater denunciations and claims . . . but here I was questioning prevailing values, methods, and processes, not only at the regional and national levels,

---

2. Pierre Dansereau, ed., "Megalopolis: Resources and Prospect," in *Challenge for Survival: Land, Air, and Water for Man in Megalopolis* (New York: Columbia University Press, 1970), 12.

3. Ibid.

4. Ibid., 13.

5. Ian L. McHarg, letter to Dean G. Holmes Perkins, February 7, 1966, 109.II.E.1.38. Ian L. McHarg Collection, The Architectural Archives, University of Pennsylvania. Subsequent citations reference McHarg Collection, AAUP.

but on a global scale."[6] He concluded that he needed help: "The wisest man I have ever known was Lewis Mumford. I decided to present my predicament to him."[7] In early 1967, he sent Mumford the draft of his manuscript titled "A Plan for Nature in Man's World."

How many others McHarg sent the early manuscript to is not known. However, he did send a copy to his friend and former faculty member Jack McCormick, the first ecologist in Penn's Department of Landscape Architecture, whom McHarg described as "a brilliant and irascible fellow." In a letter to McHarg dated February 8, 1967, McCormick writes, "My general feeling is disappointment. I know McHarg and admire him. But he sounds like a pompous ass in this writing. . . . More than your personal reputation rides on anything you publish. . . . This book, as presently conceived and written[,] would not be a monument—it would be a tombstone. . . . [S]crap the manuscript and begin anew."[8]

Yet Mumford's letter dated January 31, 1967, provides a radically different perspective:

> And first of all, let me say that you've opened up a noble theme, one for which you are better qualified than anyone else that I know or have come across in print; and if you are a little dismayed, if not panicked and discouraged by the difficulties you are already aware of, be assure[d] that this is a normal state for a writer, and will remain with you, in all probability, to the end.[9]

Mumford's support and encouragement were crucial: "But above all, don't be discouraged. You have made a good start."[10]

Design with Nature was published in 1969 and immediately received approbation from a number of reviewers.[11] *Time* magazine claims, "Though McHarg is only one of several such pioneers, he is now the nation's most vis-

6. Ian L. McHarg, *A Quest for Life: An Autobiography* (New York: John Wiley and Sons, 1996), 201–202.

7. Ibid., 202.

8. Jack McCormick, letter to Ian L. McHarg, criticism of *A Plan for Nature in a Man's World*, February 8, 1967, 109.II.B.1.9.1. McHarg Collection, AAUP. See also McHarg, *A Quest for Life*, 282.

9. Lewis Mumford, letter to Ian L. McHarg, January 31, 1967, 109.II.A.2.65. McHarg Collection, AAUP.

10. Ibid.

11. Since the critical academic reviews of *Design with Nature* are covered in Chapter 5, the discussion here focuses on the relationship of *Design with Nature* to the regional planning curriculum.

ible apostle of using ecology for planning."[12] Noted ecologist-biologist Frank Fraser Darling wrote to McHarg shortly after *Design with Nature*'s publication. Darling had been a participant in McHarg's Man and Environment course and in 1969 was the director of research and vice president of the Conservation Foundation. He readily foresaw that McHarg's work would have influence outside the curriculum: "This is a book for anybody interested in a design for living and I do hope it will reach far beyond the landscape architects and ecologists. . . . Let me rejoice with you in this moment."[13]

Mumford's supportive and optimistic introduction to *Design with Nature* holds testament to the strength of his relationship to McHarg, which would continue to grow stronger. To affirm his appreciation, McHarg presented an inscribed copy to Mumford: "With limitless admiration, gratitude & affection—Ian"[14] In a letter, Mumford responds, "What a fine book your 'Design with Nature' is, dear Ian[,] and how pleased I am with your inscription. I predict it will have a long and fruitful life. Though you didn't know Patrick Geddes in the flesh, you are in fact his best disciple, and I am the only the link that binds you two Scots together."[15]

Design with Nature stands as the hallmark in presenting McHarg's theory and method of ecological planning. As he states in his autobiography, it is his "single most powerful identification."[16] *Design with Nature*'s impact was fast and furious, and it raised McHarg from "obscurity and [gave] prominence to my person and my views."[17] In fact, McHarg saw the prescriptive direction from *Design with Nature* as having a direct bearing on the curriculum: "[I] concluded very early that introduction to the ecological method should be the foundation of the curriculum and should be presented to students upon entry."[18]

George Thompson and Frederick Steiner have written that in *Design with Nature*, "McHarg reminded us—and taught a new generation of scholars, students, and practitioners—that landscape architecture involves art and science, nature and culture, city and region, the public good as well as the need to make a living. His tone was revolutionary, and oriented heavily toward

12. "The Land: How to Design with Nature," *Time*, October 10, 1969, 70.

13. Frank Fraser Darling, letter to Ian L. McHarg, May 18, 1969, 109.II.B.1.14. McHarg Collection, AAUP.

14. Mumford's inscribed copy of *Design with Nature* is in the Lewis Mumford Collection at Monmouth University, which is the depository of Mumford's personal library.

15. Lewis Mumford, letter to Ian McHarg, May 27, 1969, 109.II.A.2.65. McHarg Collection, AAUP.

16. McHarg, *A Quest for Life*, 206.

17. Ibid., 175.

18. Ibid., 198.

the use and implementation of ecological design and planning—so much that a good portion of the field resented the seeming dismissal of art as a viable part of the profession."[19] However, under McHarg, landscape architecture—as art—was being modified to rest on an ecological premise. The momentum was accelerating, and McHarg was becoming the undaunted promoter for ecological planning, especially as the audience expanded beyond the academic halls of Penn.

Two Pivotal Nonacademic Ventures, 1969–1970

In addition to the publication of *Design with Nature*, two important events propelled McHarg's growing national recognition: the film *Multiply and Subdue the Earth*, his second major public media venture, and the first celebration of Earth Day in April 1970. Moreover, McHarg's involvement in these events outside the strictly academic milieu where he was an administrator and teacher directly influenced the curriculum's focus on ecology and how it was marketed to potential students.

McHarg recounts in his autobiography that *Design with Nature* "propagated the movie *Multiply and Subdue the Earth*."[20] Not yet fifty years old when the film was released, he describes himself and the impact of the film this way: "There I was, with a full head of brown hair, a bushy moustache, energetic, given to hyperbole and colorful language. Although [the film is] almost thirty years old it remains remarkably topical. It seems that we have learned little."[21] Austin Hoyt produced the film for WGHB in Boston, and McHarg served as the main participant and commentator. It allowed him to present to a wide viewing audience a number of projects that he had participated in that were based on the concept of ecological planning—*Plan for the Valleys* in Baltimore County, the ecological study for the twin cities Minneapolis–St. Paul, and *Sea Storm and Survival*, for the New Jersey coastal community, Harvey Cedars.[22]

McHarg's message of environmental concern and the essential need to embrace an understanding of ecology in the planning of human settlements was beginning to reach an empathetic and curious public, with potential students eager to learn more. The time was ripe for a new national focus.

Barry Commoner writes, "The environment has just been rediscovered

---

19. George E. Thompson and Frederick R. Steiner, eds., *Ecological Design and Planning* (New York: John Wiley and Sons, 1997), 3.

20. McHarg, *A Quest for Life*, 141.

21. Ibid., 205.

22. Ibid., 204–205.

Staff photo by Greg Clarke

FIGURE 7.1. Ian McHarg, Earth Day lecture,
University of Delaware, April 20, 1970.
(University of Delaware Archives and Records Management. Used with permission.)

by the people who live in it. In the United States the event was celebrated in April 1970 during Earth Week. It was a sudden, noisy awakening. . . . Everyone seemed to be aroused to the environmental danger and eager to do something about it."[23] As one of the organizers of the celebration in Philadelphia, McHarg describes it as "an exciting time . . . the great and unexpected efflorescence in environmental sensitivity."[24] He addressed a crowd numbering in the thousands, bringing a strong and powerful message to raise awareness of the technological threat to our future survival. During Earth Week, McHarg accepted many invitations to speak on college and university campuses, spreading the word and solidifying his public persona as an intellectual force to be reckoned with, especially as an educator di-

23. Barry Commoner, *The Closing Circle: Nature, Man, and Technology* (New York: Alfred A. Knopf, 1971), 5.

24. McHarg, *A Quest for Life*, 208.

recting the development of what would become the preeminent graduate program to train ecologically oriented planners.

The Ecological Planning Curriculum, 1969–1972

A 1981 retrospective review states, "As the environmental decade influenced academic institutions, many university departments and programs added the prefix 'environmental' to their course and program names. But very little change occurred in the course content. In order for ecological knowledge to be linked to action, fundamental changes are necessary."[25] It singles out McHarg and the University of Pennsylvania as having "been primarily responsible for developing an ecological approach for community, regional, and resource planning."[26]

In the 1968–1969 academic year, the Graduate School of Fine Arts curriculum in regional planning was available through either the Department of City and Regional Planning or the Department of Landscape Architecture and Regional Planning. It consisted of two "streams," with a common core of planning courses. In the Department of City and Regional Planning, the focus was "with the locational pattern and relationships of residential and work places and other urban activities, the systems of transportation and public utilities, the production of housing and urban physical renewal programs and the three dimensional quality of the physical environment."[27] In the Department of Landscape Architecture and Regional Planning, the emphasis was "based on the premise that planning requires the contribution of those who understand nature as process, responsive to laws, constituting a value system, proffering opportunities but with inherent limitations, and that such an understanding is derived from the natural sciences and is integrated by ecology."[28] The principal distinction was that in the Department of City and Regional Planning, planners were trained in the social sciences, while McHarg's program trained planners in the natural sciences and ecology.

The growing stature of ecology's infusion into planning and landscape architecture as well as McHarg's increasing public personality were directly reflected in the Department of Landscape Architecture and Regional Planning's pedagogical statement as it began the 1969–1970 school year. This year would see the critical legitimization and advancement of the ecological

---

25. Frederick Steiner and Kenneth Brooks, "Ecological Planning: A Review," *Environmental Management* 5, no. 6 (1981): 495.

26. Ibid., 496.

27. "Graduate School of Fine Arts, 1968–1969," *University of Pennsylvania Bulletin* 68, no. 5 (1967): 18.

28. Ibid., 39.

planning curriculum at Penn. The curriculum advanced in two discernible directions: landscape architecture and regional planning.

The department's pedagogical statement asks landscape architects, "What is the role of landscape architecture as we confront despoliation, anarchy and the inhibition to the spirit represented by the modern city?"[29] The answer is self-evident: "In the search for a scientific basis of Landscape Architecture, this Department holds that ecology is the single integrative science which permits both diagnosis and prescription. . . . Ecology provides the single indispensable basis for landscape architecture and regional planning."[30] Ecology is not only indispensable but also "vital in the search both for understanding form in nature and the creation of form. . . . The ecological method allows one to understand form as an explicit point in [the] evolutionary process."[31]

In the 1969–1970 school year, the Department of Landscape Architecture and Regional Planning curriculum for the first time described "An Ecological Program in Regional Planning." According to Perkins, McHarg brought the landscape architecture curriculum "to life, especially through the regional [planning] perspective."[32] In a very poignant way, the curriculum served as an intellectual call-to-arms: "The urgent need for a profession of Regional Planners is self-evident. For proof it is enough to look at the countryside, the metropolis and the city. There could hardly be a more propitious time for such an examination—on the eve of the Bi-Centennial, a time for re-appraisal and new resolution."[33]

In the 1970–1971 academic year, the "Description of the Curriculum" for landscape architects in the Department of Landscape Architecture and Regional Planning was more cogently presented than it had been earlier, clearly delineating the three major subject areas:

- The first consisted of the biological sciences, "with an emphasis on botany, ecology, plants and design."
- The second consisted of the physical sciences, "notably geology and engineering."
- The third "contain[ed] history and theory."[34]

---

29. "Graduate School of Fine Arts, 1969–1970," *University of Pennsylvania Bulletin* 69, no. 5 (1968): 31.

30. Ibid.

31. Ibid.

32. G. Holmes Perkins, interview with the author, October 15, 2002.

33. "Graduate School of Fine Arts, 1969–1970," 37.

34. "Graduate School of Fine Arts, 1970–1971," *University of Pennsylvania Bulletin* 70, no. 7 (1969): 33.

By the 1971–1972 school year, the course offerings in the progression of study were prescribed for landscape architects, first in a workshop course followed by a studio; regional planners began with a seminar course followed by a studio. This approach allowed the weaving together of a common set of core courses to be taken by students in both fields. These "core courses" would evolve further as the curriculum was modified during the next several years, eventually becoming the 501 Studio. One of the key advantages of a curriculum with an interdisciplinary faculty is the richness and the breadth of the subject matter that such a variety of courses can offer. On the other hand, this assumption presupposes that the courses have been designed to offer engaging and challenging learning experiences. To accomplish this goal, designing the individual courses in the curriculum was left to the faculty.

According to Arthur Johnson, a soil scientist and geologist who joined McHarg's faculty in the mid-1970s, "As long as the bases were covered and people were competent to do their job [in teaching the students], McHarg left the work to the faculty to design their courses—there was a great deal of latitude."[35]

During the 1972–1973 academic year, the department added anthropologists David and Vera-Mae Fredrickson and Yehudi Cohen as visiting faculty. Cohen's initial course, Social Processes, was designed to "explore the varieties of adaptive strategies in human societies."[36] To a great degree, this faculty expansion would be the pedagogical predecessor that would eventually advance the curriculum from ecological planning to human ecological planning.

THE FIRST COURSE that used computers to facilitate the use of ecological resource data was taught in 1969 by E. Bruce MacDougall, the first geographer on the faculty. MacDougall's course, Computer Programming for Spatial Problems, was aimed at the application of "common computer languages to computer graphics, computer mapping and the processing of map data."[37] McHarg had a strong interest in the adaptation of computer methods to ecological planning, since "the conception of large-scale ecological inventories has always been dependent on computer capability."[38]

Even though spatial computation was evolving and geographic information systems (GIS) were still in early stages of development, MacDougall

---

35. Arthur Johnson, interview with the author, December 3, 2002.
36. "Graduate School of Fine Arts, 1972 1973," *University of Pennsylvania Bulletin* 72, no. 6 (1971): 58.
37. "Graduate School of Fine Arts, 1970–1971," 68.
38. McHarg, *A Quest for Life*, 366.

and Lewis Hopkins (a graduate student who received his doctorate from Penn in 1975 and later joined the first landscape architecture faculty at the University of Illinois) developed a computerized route-selection model for a highway project. The consulting firm Wallace, McHarg, Roberts and Todd was hired by the Delaware Department of Transportation to design a process to select a highway route in 1973. McHarg would later write that this project served as his "initiation into computerized ecological planning."[39] While the importance of this application was to underscore the value of using digitized data in suitability analysis (as contrasted with the hand-overlay technique), a somewhat murky future lay ahead for the curriculum's incorporation of the important advances in GIS technology.

A list of the faculty during the 1972–1973 academic year, the zenith of the ecological planning curriculum, follows:[40]

Ian L. McHarg, MLA, MCP, *professor of landscape architecture and regional planning, chairman*

Peter Shepheard, BArch, *professor of architecture and environmental design, dean of the Graduate School of Fine Arts*

Nicholas Muhlenberg, MF, MA, PhD, *associate professor of regional planning*

William H. Roberts, DipArch, MLA, *associate professor of landscape architecture*

Anthony J. Walmsley, BArch, MCD, MLA, *associate professor of landscape architecture*

Yehudi Cohen, PhD, *visiting associate professor of landscape architecture and regional planning*

Robert Giegengack, PhD, *assistant professor of geology*

Ronald B. Hanawalt, PhD, *assistant professor of regional planning*

Robert Hanna, BArch, MLA, *assistant professor of landscape architecture*

Narendra N. Juneja, BArch, MLA, *assistant professor of landscape architecture*

Michael Levin, PhD, *assistant professor of landscape architecture and regional planning*

E. Bruce MacDougall, PhD, *assistant professor of landscape architecture*

Arthur Sullivan, PhD, *assistant professor of regional planning*

John F. Collins, MLA, *lecturer in landscape architecture*

---

39. Ibid., 339. The project, *Outer Wilmington Beltway Corridor Study*, was completed in 1973.

40. "Graduate School of Fine Arts, 1972–1973," *University of Pennsylvania Bulletin 72*, no. 8 (1971): 8.

David M. DuTot, MLA, *lecturer in landscape architecture*

Ruth Patrick, PhD, *lecturer in landscape architecture*

Jack McCormick, PhD, *lecturer in landscape architecture*

Raymond T. Schnadelbach, BArch, MLA, *lecturer in landscape architecture*

David A. Fredrickson, PhD, *visiting lecturer in landscape architecture*

Vera-Mae Fredrickson, MA, *visiting lecturer in landscape architecture*

BUT WERE STUDENTS attracted to this intellectual adventure? "There was a surfeit of applications to the department," according to McHarg. "Many candidates had Ph.D.'s, and even more had master's degrees before admission. We regulated the numbers: sixty landscape architects, sixty regional planners. . . . Standards were very high, as was enthusiasm."[41] Johnson explains:

> The reason that the students were attracted to the program was that this curriculum was fashioned to be put into action. When the students completed the program and left college—they left wanting to change the system. There were enemies of nature and we kind of knew who they were. One of the things that McHarg was very able to do was to find the environmental villains. It always gave students comfort to know that there was a contest, and that the good guys were always smarter than the environmental villains were, and you could always get them in the end. McHarg's ideas were broad enough to do the job, and they were marketed with superb skill.[42]

Students entering the curriculum were given several options of study, based on their background preparation. Students with a social science bachelor's degree pursued a three-year program; students with a bachelor's degree in geology or biology studied for two years. In both cases, a graduate professional degree of master of regional planning (MRP) was the final award. However, all students fell under the spell of the following dictum: "We need planners who are competent . . . who are instinctively activists and wish to engage in social processes. This is the most challenging adventure, and it is in this spirit that your interest in the study of regional planning is sought."[43]

The curriculum's integrative structure was unique in higher education. Students would proceed "through the curriculum towards a competence

---

41. McHarg, *A Quest for Life*, 213.

42. Johnson, interview.

43. "Graduate School of Fine Arts, 1969–1970," 39.

in these areas. Their synthesis is obtained in a sequence of case studies. This begins with regional problems emphasizing the importance of natural processes to planning. The next consideration is social process in planning. Subsequent case studies are directed towards the resolution of social problems in the context of natural processes through planning and design. The final exercises are conducted at the project scale, emphasizing design, and are realized in working drawings and specifications."[44]

Ecological Planning, Research, Design, and Applied Opportunities, 1970–1973

In the early 1970s, a number of opportunities for research and the application of that research to real-world problems became important adjuncts to McHarg's curriculum in the Department of Landscape Architecture and Regional Planning, which was now firmly predicated on ecology. Three changes are particularly noteworthy, since they would have not only essential research-practical correlations but also important impacts on the curriculum.

Center for Ecological Research in Planning and Design: The Medford Study

Since the Institute of Environmental Studies was the established "research arm" of the Graduate School of Fine Arts, the Center for Ecological Research in Planning and Design would be ascribed a new level of visibility and importance. For several years, the center had been the "research group" for the Department of Landscape Architecture and Regional Planning. By the 1972–1973 academic year, the center was formally described as the "research arm" of the department, "whereby the faculty and graduate students may synthesize the perceptions of their individual sciences in the description, analysis, and prescriptions of whole natural systems, and whereby data, interpretation and method for ecological planning can be elaborated and improved."[45] Two projects were underway: the digitizing of maps from

---

44. Ibid.

45. "Graduate School of Fine Arts, 1972–1973," *University of Pennsylvania Bulletin* 72, no. 6 (1971): 30–31. See earlier in this chapter for a list of most of the faculty of the Department of Landscape Architecture and Regional Planning in 1972–1973. The disciplines represented in the center and their associated faculty were limnology (Ruth Patrick), geology (Robert Giegengack), hydrology (Seymour Subitzky), soil science (Ronald Hanawalt), plant ecology (Michael Levin), animal ecology (Robert Snyder), regional planning (Arthur Sullivan), quantitative methods (Bruce MacDougall), resource economics (Nicholas Muhlenberg), and landscape architecture (Narendra Juneja and Robinson Fisher).

ecological data for the Oak Ridge National Laboratory and an ecological study for Medford Township, New Jersey, with a population of ten thousand, located twenty miles from Philadelphia.

The Medford study began in 1971 after a meeting between McHarg and township officials who were concerned about the seemingly uncontrolled development that was threatening their community. Although McHarg was the principal investigator of the ensuing study, along with the faculty of the center and a number of graduate students, Narendra Juneja was the deputy principal investigator for the planning portion. Juneja had immigrated to the United States from India in 1963 to study at Penn, receiving a master of landscape architecture (MLA) degree in 1965. He was considered by many to be brilliant, and he would play an increasingly important role in the regional planning curriculum, becoming one of McHarg's key confidants. Juneja authored the Medford ecological study, which consisted of a natural resources and historic resources inventory of the township as well as an assessment of "social values." It also presented a series of suitability analyses for different types of development (e.g., rural, urban, and suburban).

The principal means of incorporating "social values" into the study came about through an extensive public participation program and a concerned citizenry. Arthur Palmer, the member of the study team specifically responsible for drafting environmental ordinances, observes "that the level of public understanding of the problems involved in changing from random development to controlled development [was] reasonably well understood, as well as changing from a philosophy of economic values to a philosophy of environmental values."[46] Figure 7.2 illustrates the use of the matrix for hydrology.

The study's unique thrust was to establish through inventory data and analysis a defensible position on which the township could adopt ecologically based ordinances to regulate and control new development. McHarg writes in the introduction that the ecological study was "oriented not to the preparation of a plan, but to the formulation of ordinances. . . . This is a landmark study [if] . . . the people of Medford . . . will assume the power to control and regulate growth through ordinances. . . . America awaits an example of intelligent and effective planning."[47]

The Medford study, which was finally published in 1974, became per-

---

46. Arthur E. Palmer, *Toward Eden* (Winterville, N.C.: Creative Resource Systems, 1981), 172.

47. Ian L. McHarg, introduction to *Medford: Performance Requirements for the Maintenance of Social Values Represented by the Natural Environment of Medford Township, N.J.*, by Narendra Juneja (Philadelphia: Center for Ecological Research in Planning and Design, University of Pennsylvania, 1974), 3.

Phenomenon	Value to Society				Value to Individuals																																
					High Productivity for Extract Agriculture							Forest			Minimum Foundations			On-site Costs for Maintenance				Water Supply			Maximum Desirability for Location								Activity			
HYDROLOGY	Inherently Hazardous to Human Life	Hazardous to Human Life and Health by Specific Human Actions	Irreplaceable Unique or Scarce Resource	Vulnerable Resource Requiring Regulation to Avoid Social Costs	Sand	Gravel	High-Value Crops	General Crops	Pasture	Fruits	Special Produce	Timber	Pulp	Firewood	Paved Surfaces	Light Structures	Heavy Structures	Site Drainage	Paved Surfaces	Lawns, Playgrounds, etc.	On-Site Sewage Disposal	Domestic Use	Industrial Use	Irrigation	Favorable Microclimate	Topographic Interest	Long Views	Sense of Enclosure	Water-Related Views	Vegetation Diversity	Wildlife Diversity	Historic Association	Educational	Fishing	Swimming	Canoeing Boating
Streams and Lakes — Good Quality		●2		●3							●														●●	●			●●				●●	●		
Poor Quality		●2		●3a							●														●●	●			●●				●●			
Quality Unknown		●2		●3							●														●●	●			●●		●		●			
Wetlands		●2		●4							● C															●			●							
Flood-Prone Area	●1			●5																						●			●							

1 Subject to inundation by 100-year frequency probability flood
2 Easily vulnerable to pollution locally and from adjacent lands
3 Degradation of resource will lead to loss of recreation value.
3a Already enriched water, easily vulnerable to further pollution locally and from adjacent lands
4 Alteration of environmental conditions will result in loss of flood storage capacity.
5 Any obstruction will result in alteration and degradation of stream behavior.

FIGURE 7.2. Matrix of hydrology values to society and individual values in Medford study, 1974.
(Center for Ecological Research in Planning and Design, Department of Landscape Architecture and Regional Planning, University of Pennsylvania, 1974.)

haps the single-most-important product of the Center for Ecological Research in Planning and Design. In 1989, McHarg suggested a "re-examination" in a return to Medford with colleagues Jon Berger and John Radke to propose a digitizing of the entire ecological inventory, which did not happen.[48] Nonetheless, the Medford study established an important threshold for future planning studies.

In his autobiography, McHarg claims that the study "became the bible for the township and remains so to this day. It affected the creation of the Pinelands Preserve, was a model for the 1990 New Jersey State Plan, and was employed as the basis for many other studies, including Lake Austin, Texas, and Sanibel, Florida."[49]

Design of the Environment Program

In 1973, a new program offered an interdisciplinary undergraduate liberal arts major in the School of Arts and Sciences. It also served as an undergraduate preprofessional program for those intending to pursue graduate study in architecture and landscape architecture. Dean Peter Shepheard created

48. McHarg, *A Quest for Life*, 286.
49. Ibid., 287.

the Design of the Environment Program with the objective "to foster an understanding of the centrality of the natural environment in the creation of humane man-made environments."[50] The first director was Robert Hanna, who had degrees in architecture from the University of Washington and landscape architecture from Harvard. Hanna had first met McHarg when he taught a studio of city planners and landscape architects at Harvard in 1966 and had been an assistant professor of landscape architecture in McHarg's department since 1969. Hanna recruited Laurie Olin, his former fellow student at the University of Washington, to the faculty in 1974. Hanna and Olin were fellows of the American Academy in Rome, affiliations that McHarg promoted as evidence of their design acumen.

The program's emphasis was "on studio work based on design projects for buildings and landscape[,] supported by lectures dealing with [the] natural and man-made environment."[51] It served as an important academic bridge, connecting the graduate program in the Department of Landscape Architecture and Regional Planning to undergraduate studies. Moreover, the undergraduate Design of the Environment program was geared toward recruiting bright students interested in art, architecture, and ecological design. This program provided basic design instruction to environmentally interested or qualified candidates who otherwise could not be admitted into the design side of the department because of design deficiencies in their background.

Wallace, McHarg, Roberts and Todd, 1965–1973

The establishment of Wallace, McHarg, Roberts and Todd (WMRT) created a valuable and almost indispensable link between the curriculum in the Department of Landscape Architecture and Regional Planning and real-world applications. McHarg writes of the relationship:

> Ideas were developed at the university, wherein was the repository of knowledge in the sciences, and their application was accomplished by WMRT. Data generated by the office were more accurate, the methods more precise. Hypotheses were tested and if successful, were immediately incorporated into teaching. Through this method, research and

---

50. Ann L. Strong and George E. Thomas, *The Book of the School: The Graduate School of Fine Arts of the University of Pennsylvania* (Philadelphia: University of Pennsylvania, 1990), 256.

51. "Graduate School of Fine Arts, 1975–1976," *University of Pennsylvania Bulletin* 75, no. 6 (1974): 11.

development continued. Every project, either in the department or at the office, was seen as a research investigation.[52]

WMRT not only provided the base for the reciprocity of ideas and theories, and the "testing" of those ideas and theories in practice, but also served as an important employer for students and for other faculty who would consult on projects that required their special expertise. The firm's philosophy as a private consulting practice embraced the same interdisciplinary collaborative approach to projects that was embodied in the Graduate School of Fine Arts—to synthesize the practice of architecture, landscape architecture, and city and regional planning.[53]

With McHarg serving as partner-in-charge, several projects undertaken by the firm between 1965 and 1973 provided substantial impetus to the evolution of ecological planning. They also became some of what McHarg would later describe as his "proudest accomplishments."[54] In 1965, *A Comprehensive Highway Route Selection Method Applied to I-95 between the Delaware and Raritan Rivers* for Princeton, New Jersey, was based on a mapping of climate, geology, hydrology, soils, vegetation, and wildlife. According to McHarg, "This was the genesis of environmental impact assessments, and the Interstate-95 study was probably its earliest exercise."[55] The Potomac River Basin study completed in 1966—in partnership with the American Institute of Architects and the University of Pennsylvania—included the first use of the layer-cake technique to compile the ecological inventory. The 1969 landmark *Ecological Study for Twin Cities Metropolitan Region, Minnesota* was the first comprehensive ecological regional assessment of its kind.

Between 1971 and 1973, WMRT was engaged to undertake the ecological inventory, site planning, and design for the Woodlands New Community

---

52. McHarg, *A Quest for Life*, 213. A complete listing of projects completed during McHarg's consulting association between 1963 and 1964 with Wallace and McHarg and between 1965 and 1980 with Wallace, McHarg, Roberts and Todd may be found in *A Quest for Life*, 393–399.

53. Beginning in the late 1970s, and to a lesser extent, the Mid-Atlantic office of the National Park Service played a similar role to WMRT. A compilation is included in Frederick R. Steiner, ed., *The Essential Ian McHarg: Writings on Design and Nature* (Washington, D.C.: Island Press, 2006), 139–146.

54. Specifically, these included the Woodlands New Town, Pardisan, and the Comprehensive Plan for Environmental Quality. See McHarg, *A Quest for Life*, 206.

55. Ibid., 187. The National Environmental Policy Act of 1969 Section 102(2) requires, for example, that for "every federal action," an environmental impact statement . . . be prepared that will "utilize a systematic, interdisciplinary approach which will insure the integrated use of the natural and social sciences and environmental design arts in planning and decision making which may have an impact on man's environment."

in Houston, Texas. The planning approach for the determination of land uses and densities was based on the geohydrological properties of the soils that defined natural drainage areas. This method to guide development would not increase runoff, would not lower the water table, and would promote aquifer recharge. Richard Nalbandian (who held a master's degree in geology from MIT) became the key staff person, as he calculated the water budget and, according to McHarg, "participated in the design for the new town urban hydrology, which worked with incandescent success."[56] The 1973 study *Towards a Comprehensive Plan for Environmental Quality* was completed in association with the American Institute of Planners (now the American Planning Association) for the U.S. Environmental Protection Agency. In it, McHarg proposed that a national ecological inventory be undertaken and that forty ecological laboratories be created for each of the physiographic regions in the nation. This proposal would set the stage for 1992's *Prototype Data Base for a National Ecological Inventory*, which would use computer capability. Finally, between 1973 and 1975, WMRT (working with the Mandala Collaborative) received a major commission to plan a massive environmental park in Tehran, Iran, that would be known as Pardisan. The park, which would be unparalleled worldwide, would emphasize education, recreation, and conservation, integrating the natural and social sciences with art and architecture. In McHarg's words, "The metaphysical view represented in Pardisan is the unity of man and nature. . . . Implicit in this proposition is a commitment to the understanding of whole systems and thus to the holistic science of ecology."[57]

Such endeavors clearly enhanced Penn's curriculum, as students and faculty benefited from challenging opportunities to work in the "laboratory" of applying the principles of ecological analysis and planning.

Changes at the University, 1970–1973

In the early 1970s, some changes and a new reality at the University of Pennsylvania directly affected McHarg's department. The first change took place in 1970, when Martin Meyerson succeeded Gaylord Harnwell as president of the university. Meyerson had had an accomplished career in academia and came to Penn in 1951 at the invitation of Dean Perkins to

---

56. Ibid., 221. A comprehensive account of the planning and building of the Woodlands may be found in George T. Morgan Jr. and John O. King, *The Woodlands: New Community Development, 1964–1983* (College Station: Texas A&M University Press, 1987).

57. The Mandala Collaborative/Wallace, McHarg, Roberts and Todd, *Pardisan: Plan for an Environmental Park in Tehran* (Philadelphia: Winchell Press, 1975), 6.

join the city planning faculty. Although Meyerson's academic focus leaned heavily on the social and policy analysis aspects of a rational, comprehensive planning perspective, he would become very supportive of McHarg and his ecologically based regional planning curriculum.

The second change occurred in 1971, when Perkins retired as dean of the Graduate School of Fine Arts. Meyerson eagerly pursued Peter Shepheard to succeed Perkins. Trained as an architect at the University of Liverpool—for many years the leading architecture program in Britain—Shepheard's strong interest in nature eventually led him toward landscape architecture. He had been a visiting professor in McHarg's department since 1957, so he knew the faculty and, most importantly, shared Perkins's view of the unity of architecture, landscape architecture, and city and regional planning. With Shepheard's acceptance of the position (he would serve from 1971 to 1979) and Meyerson's new role as president of the university, McHarg found himself in a very advantageous position. Nicholas Muhlenberg said simply, "McHarg could do anything he wanted."[58]

The new reality that Shepheard as well as all departments in the Graduate School of Fine Arts faced was that "by the University's calculations, the Graduate School of Fine Arts was awash in a sea of red ink."[59] The word came down from the president's office that all graduate schools would have to be "financial responsibility centers."[60] This new reality would affect not just the administrative functioning of the Department of Landscape Architecture and Regional Planning but its curriculum as well, particularly its ability to hire new faculty.

AS AN ACADEMIC OFFERING in graduate education for professional planners and designers, the ecological planning curriculum was prospering as the 1972–1973 school year drew to a close. Robert Hanna provided this overview:

> What Ian did more than anything else in addition to raising our consciousness about ecology was to develop a method that made decisions and information explicit, as he always said, "replicable," so that you didn't have to take it on faith. You could go back over the evidence and examine it and draw your own conclusions, in a more or less rational way. The problem is that ultimately it's never rational; it assumes a judgment, it assumes values. In this sense his quest could never be totally realized. A lot of people thought it [the

---

58. Nicholas Muhlenberg, interview with the author, October 18, 2002.
59. Strong and Thomas, *The Book of the School*, 253–254.
60. Ibid., 253.

ecological method] ought to be an absolute scientific method that was achievable.[61]

During the mid-1970s, McHarg's program was observed for a year by J. H. Giliomee, visiting from the University of Stellenbosch in South Africa. He would later write that this experience allowed him to become "thoroughly acquainted with, and to evaluate, the ecological planning method developed and taught in that department."[62] Giliomee was impressed and convinced "that ecological planning has put urban and regional planning on a much higher level as a scientific discipline, and it is difficult to understand why it is not even mentioned in some recent textbooks on the subject. It completely breaks away from what is still prevalent in a great deal of modern planning."[63]

A final point made by Giliomee corroborates and extends Hanna's observation: "The method is replicable in the sense that any planner working with the same data should come up with basically the same result. . . . What the method does not do is to indicate who the users will be, or how many of them—this is a function of the socio-economic dynamics of the region."[64] Giliomee called for what he referred to as a "convergence in a final synthesis" of ecological planning and socioeconomic planning.[65]

The ecological planning curriculum would soon take on an added dimension. Human ecology would move into the forefront and become the basis for a restructuring of McHarg's regional planning program. This shift would open the door to the transition of ecological planning into human ecological planning, a development that would greatly expand the curriculum's scope and breadth.

---

61. Robert Hanna, interview with the author, January 9, 2003.
62. J. H. Giliomee, "Ecological Planning: Method and Evaluation," *Landscape Planning* 4 (1977): 185.
63. Ibid., 190.
64. Ibid., 191.
65. Ibid.

8

The Human Ecological Planning
Curriculum Is Established, 1973–1979

THE ECOLOGICAL PLANNING CURRICULUM's formal incorporation of a *cultural* or *human* perspective would become a logical—and pragmatic—evolution in Ian McHarg's Department of Landscape Architecture and Regional Planning at the University of Pennsylvania (Penn). Two events were the real impetus behind the shift. First, McHarg's 1969 publication *Design with Nature* was criticized for its lack of human dimension; as a response, he added the first anthropologists to the faculty in 1971, including Yehudi Cohen, David and Vera-Mae Fredrickson, and Martin Silverman. Cohen's appointment was particularly noteworthy, since he would teach the first courses addressing social process in McHarg's department. Cohen earned a doctorate in anthropology from Yale University and had taught at Columbia University, Northwestern University, the University of Chicago, and the University of California at Davis before becoming professor of anthropology at Rutgers University.

Second, a significant grant from the National Institute of Mental Health (NIMH) provided funding to expand the curriculum to engage in social and health issues under the aegis of ecological planning. The NIMH grant permitted the hiring of additional key faculty, including Jon Berger, Setha Low, and Dan Rose. As a result, course offerings were expanded under the disciplinary rubric of cultural anthropology, more specifically referred to as "environmental anthropology" and "medical anthropology." These events would effectively shape and transform the curriculum into human ecological planning over the next several years.

The Period of Transition, 1973–1974

Although the pedagogical statement of the ecological planning curriculum did not change, Yehudi Cohen's presence as a visiting professor in the department offered it a new dimension. He was known in the academic world for his editing of a three-volume series, *Man in Adaptation*, between 1968 and 1971. This milestone work in cultural anthropology includes more than 106 essays focusing on understanding cultural anthropology as "cultural evolution"—a sequential change in the organization of social relations over time—and how that change makes the habitat a more fit place to live. The pedagogical emphasis in the curriculum, which would complement the contributions of the natural and physical scientists, was the history of cultural development from the human perspective. Cohen's contribution was to address human predilections toward use of the immediate environment, explaining how attitudes and values have become institutionalized as sanctioned patterns in how humans use their environment.[1] The notion of cultural adaptation would become the intellectual foundation for McHarg's transition from ecological to human ecological planning.

In the 1974–1975 academic year, Cohen taught a new course, User Preference in Living Patterns, that concentrated on the "principles that govern people's affiliations with each other in urban and suburban localities through exploration of the circumstances under which members of different ethnic groups and occupational groups live side by side and the consequences of living in different kinds of localities for people's self-definition."[2]

The National Institute of Mental Health Grant

In his autobiography, McHarg recounts a June 1973 telephone call from Richard Wakefield of the Center for Studies of Metropolitan Problems of the NIMH: "He had a proposition. Ecological planning had developed very well and was efficacious, he said, but it concentrated on physical and biological science. Could it not be extended to include social science and people? Moreover, could it not focus on planning for human health and well-being? This seemed reasonable but difficult. . . . Wakefield persisted: surely there were compatible views within the social sciences that could

---

1. Yehudi Cohen's three edited works included *Man in Adaptation: The Biosocial Background* (1968), *Man in Adaptation: The Cultural Present* (1968), and *Man in Adaptation: The Institutional Framework* (1971).

2. "Graduate School of Fine Arts, 1974–1975," *University of Pennsylvania Bulletin* 74, no. 5 (1973): 60. In the 1975–1976 school year, Cohen's "Social Process" course would be retitled Man in Adaptation.

transform ecology into human ecology and enrich planning."[3] Wakefield's inducement was to offer a substantial grant. The McHarg-Wakefield connection actually predated the telephone call. Wakefield had received a master of city planning (MCP) degree at Harvard in 1950; he and McHarg were contemporaries in the program, headed by G. Holmes Perkins. Wakefield had an impressive history of public service; resource economist Gerald F. Vaughn has said of his career, "His vision and activities focusing on human values, world futures, and the environment were extraordinary and have proven to be enduring contributions."[4]

The NIMH was the principal federal agency concentrating on behavioral science and cultural and social problems related to mental health. Consistent with these interests, it had funded the establishment of the Center for Urban Ethnography at Penn in 1969 and would now venture into new territory with essential funding to underwrite McHarg's nascent human ecological planning curriculum.

The proposal that was finally submitted to the institute was predicated on an approach that would extend the physical and biological process model of ecology to embrace a synthesis that would include human cultural traditions and adaptations. According to McHarg, "We determined to use adaptation as the unifying theme"[5] for this model of interdisciplinary cooperation. The Department of Landscape Architecture and Regional Planning's grant amounted to $500,000 over a multiyear period starting in 1974. The grant primarily facilitated expanding the faculty in the department to develop the curriculum in human ecological planning.

IN 1973, the addition of key faculty members with backgrounds in anthropology and regional planning would help provide the intellectual strength needed to move the curriculum into human ecological planning. The first was Jon Berger, who had graduated from the regional planning program with a master of regional planning (MRP) degree in 1972 and was appointed lecturer in the Department of Landscape Architecture and Regional Planning. Berger had a bachelor's degree in history, had served in the Peace Corps in Africa, and would earn a doctorate in city and regional planning from Penn in 1984. He brought to the department extensive multicultural fieldwork experience. One of the research fellows at the Penn Center for

3. Ian L. McHarg, *A Quest for Life: An Autobiography* (New York: John Wiley and Sons, 1996), 268–269.

4. Gerald F. Vaughn, "Sheffield's Richard P. Wakefield: Advocate for Human Values, World Futures, and the Environment," *Historical Journal of Massachusetts* 32, no. 2 (2004): 213.

5. McHarg, *A Quest for Life*, 269.

Urban Ethnography from 1969 to 1973 was Dan Rose, who would receive a doctorate in anthropology from the University of Wisconsin in 1973. In 1974, Rose accepted an appointment as assistant professor in the Department of Landscape Architecture and Regional Planning. Another appointment made in 1974 was Setha Low as a lecturer in McHarg's department. She had an academic background in medical anthropology and would earn a doctorate from the University of California at Berkeley in 1976.

With new faculty to bolster the social-cultural dimension in the ecological planning program, the progression toward human ecological planning could begin. McHarg's portrayal of the situation in the department during the 1970s is clear and to the point: "Penn had not only a unique group of physical, biological and social scientists, but an exceptional design team as well. The personnel were at hand to accomplish the revolution [to] human ecological planning."[6]

Pedagogical and Practical Underpinnings of the Regional Planning Curriculum

As the curriculum in human ecological planning began its development in earnest starting around 1974, it seems valuable to lay out the basic precepts of the theory and the methods that served as its pedagogical and practical underpinnings. In this manner, we can begin to understand the evolving relationships between the intellectualizing and the actual—between the world of academe and the world outside—and the elements that would shape the changing curriculum.

I should point out that even though I discuss the basic elements of McHarg's prescription—or "model"—for human ecological planning within the 1973–1979 time frame, it was not so succinctly laid out during this period. McHarg's first comprehensive published statement defining human ecological planning did not appear until his 1981 article in *Landscape Planning*, "Human Ecological Planning at Pennsylvania." The second important source, as a complement to this first article, is McHarg's 1996 autobiography, *A Quest for Life*. However, the following discussion relies on McHarg's representation of human ecological planning in the 1981 article, since it is, in my view, his best statement.

MCHARG'S CONCEPT of human ecological planning "is based on the premise that all social and natural systems aspire to success. Such a state can be described as 'syntropic-fitness-health.'" The next step in his "model" is to

---

6. Ibid., 229.

understand "the process of interaction between the landscape and the people who inhabit it [that] provides a basis for assessing opportunities and constraints afforded by the environment and the needs and desires of the population which can be combined to present alternative futures." The bridge between ecology and human ecology is crucial to place McHarg's definition of human ecological planning in perspective. As he argues, "Ecology has been used to integrate the sciences of the biophysical environment. If we extend ecology by adding ethology, we introduce the subject of behavior as an adaptive strategy." This definition is further extended to include ethnography and anthropology, which permit "the study of human behavior as adaptation. If, finally, we extend into medical anthropology and epidemiology[,] we can close the cycle by examining the natural and human environment in terms of human health and well-being."

McHarg links "planning" to "ecological" so that ecological planning becomes "an instrument for revealing regions as interacting and dynamic natural systems having intrinsic opportunities and constraints for all human uses." Consequently, "preferred hypothetical futures will be proffered by locations where all or most propitious factors exist with none or few detrimental ones for any and all prospective uses."

When McHarg compounds the term into "human ecological planning," it expands the region "into a physical, biological, and cultural region [where] opportunities and constraints are represented in every realm." This expansion is accomplished by identifying "geophysical and ecological regions . . . as cultural regions in which characteristic people pursue means of production, develop characteristic settlement patterns, [and] have characteristic perceptions, needs and desires and institutions for realizing their objectives." The essence of the planning component takes form as "hypothetical future alternatives" that have been derived from expressed needs and desires of people and "are matched against the physical, biological, and cultural resources." Finally, "preferred hypothetical futures can be derived for each group with its associated value system." This essential definition of human ecological planning would be fostered in the pedagogy of the curriculum.[7]

The leap to fully operationalize specific methods of human ecological

---

7. Ian L. McHarg, "Human Ecological Planning at Pennsylvania," *Landscape Planning* 8 (1981): 109–110. This article also appears in Ian L. McHarg and Frederick Steiner, eds., *To Heal the Earth: Selected Writings of Ian L. McHarg* (Washington, D.C.: Island Press, 1998), 142–155.

McHarg did not particularly care for the term "human ecological planning," which was reputedly proposed by Jon Berger and Dan Rose; he thought that it was a "cumbersome and graceless title." He expressed hope that the "human" descriptor could eventually be abandoned in favor of reverting to "ecological planning." Ibid., 110.

planning relied on ascertaining user values, principally people's perceptions, by doing an ethnographic history of a place. Berger commented, "Ian insisted on using a historical approach. He used to say, 'chronology reveals causality.' To some extent he was right, [but] to some extent he was wrong."[8]

Rose and Berger presented their first joint statement regarding this approach in 1974.[9] Rose became the prime intellectual mover to fully enmesh what he called "environmental anthropology" into the theory of human ecological planning. This inclusion would become the chief variable by which to evaluate and shape the human element of ecological planning. The use of ethnography in planning analysis was explained as a technique to gather information about a region by asking questions of ordinary citizens, professionals, business owners, and so forth. The information received was treated as equally true, no matter who the informant was, and became part of a "'folk model,' a summary of the particular respondent's view of the world." Thus, the "planner's expertise consists of assembling and synthesizing more perspectives on reality than anyone else."[10]

In his doctoral dissertation, Berger distinguishes the primary field techniques to define what he refers to as an environmental ethnography for landscape planning: an "environmental ethnography is a cluster of field techniques to inventory, analyze, and interpret the many cognized models [of the users] of the landscape. It results in an applied field report that synthesizes the scientist's model of the landscape—the operational model—with the user's view of place—the cognized model."[11]

Two projects began in 1973 in McHarg's department that effectuated the theory of human ecological planning and cemented ethnography as the critical field method. In essence, their focus would facilitate the development of field methods and techniques that would directly influence the human ecological planning academic curriculum. Rose and Berger were the principal investigators in both projects.

Under the NIMH grant, Rose and Berger began field work in Hazleton, Pennsylvania. Rose was especially interested in explaining what he called "puzzling social phenomena generated by ethnographic methods" in a study of a depressed coal-mining region in northeastern Pennsylvania that was experiencing full employment during the energy crisis in the 1970s.

---

8. Jon Berger, interview with the author, November 27, 2002.

9. Dan Rose and Jon Berger, *Human Ecology in the Regional Plan* (Philadelphia: Department of Landscape Architecture and Regional Planning, University of Pennsylvania, 1974).

10. Ibid., I-18–I-19.

11. Jon Berger, "Environmental Ethnography for Landscape Planning" (Ph.D. diss., University of Pennsylvania, 1984), 260. Rose was Berger's dissertation supervisor.

Although theirs was not a planning study per se, several lessons from their field work can be applied to the use of human ecological planning regarding how people interface with natural systems.[12]

Rose and Berger instituted what they called a "regional human ecological reconnaissance" to note the recurrence of various settlements and land use patterns and to perform household interviews to determine how people used their environmental resources on a day-to-day basis.[13] The reconnaissance's goals were to map the region as an "interactive-natural social space; and to identify the cultural core, the interface between nature and culture."[14] The important thrust of their work was to "suggest that planning be thought of as a device to alert citizens to the possibilities of creating the kind of environment they want" rather than be confined to a growth model that relied on projecting present economic trends.[15] The underlying premise of this perspective was that "it is at the level of preferences and decisions, not values, that the action of individuals may be empirically predicted."[16]

They performed this case study in a rapidly growing area of Chester County in southeastern Pennsylvania. The study team wanted to know "who would be the future users of the land, what would be their needs and desires, and how potential plans could be implemented."[17] The approach used in Kennett was different from the one used in McHarg's 1974 Medford project. This time, as Berger explained, no reliance was placed on public meetings. More personal and informal discussions took "place in such settings as club rooms of volunteer fire companies, farmer's kitchens, Quaker meeting houses, and so on, leaving formal public meetings as places [solely] for conducting business."[18]

The theory of applied human ecology, as subsumed in human ecological planning, was solidified in the Kennett Square project. One important dimension that emerged was that "the applied human ecology approach complements and goes beyond the citizen participation programs employed largely as a result of large Federal programs, including environmental

---

12. Ultimately, a book was produced from their efforts. See Dan Rose, *Energy Transition and the Local Community: A Theory of Society Applied to Hazleton, Pennsylvania* (Philadelphia: University of Pennsylvania Press, 1981).

13. Rose and Berger, *Human Ecology in the Regional Plan*, I-5–I-9.

14. Rose, *Energy Transition and the Local Community*, 10.

15. Rose and Berger, *Human Ecology in the Regional Plan*, 1-22.

16. Setha M. Low and Richard D. Walter, "Values in the Planning Process," *Ekistics* 49, no. 292 (1982): 59.

17. Jon Berger, "Toward an Applied Human Ecology for Landscape Architecture and Regional Planning," *Human Ecology* 6, no. 2 (1978): 180.

18. Ibid., 184–185.

regulations."[19] The method that emerged and that would be worked into the curriculum had a special strength "in eliciting the interior viewpoint of citizens and identifying the local community as part of a social system adapting to a natural environment."[20]

As the integral component in making human ecological planning work, part of the ethnographic analysis is predicated on what Rose called the tenuous position of the planner: it is "exacerbated because he has neither a single institutional home base nor an established constituency."[21] Moreover, the planner's role can be made more effective through an "integrated form of thinking" that understands the working complexity and relationship between natural and human ecosystems.[22] A few years later, Low would summarize the role of ethnography as "a method, and approach and a strategy for dealing with the local community in relation to cultural landscapes."[23] Thus, "it will increase our understanding of that landscape and suggest ways in which that landscape can be interpreted, preserved and maintained."[24]

An Interdisciplinary Curriculum in a Multidisciplinary World, 1974–1979

In his first cogent statement on the interdisciplinary-multidisciplinary connection, McHarg calls for "a New Mandate . . . that the GSFA [Graduate School of Fine Arts] must now be at once multidisciplinary and interdisciplinary."[25] The thrust of his thinking continues:

The foregoing requires two types of interaction[:] the first, interdisciplinary between the sciences, arts and professions of the environment. The other between those preoccupied with different scales of prob-

---

19. Dan Rose, Frederick Steiner, and Joanne Jackson, "An Applied Human Ecological Approach to Regional Planning," *Landscape Planning* 5 (1978/1979): 259.

20. Ibid.

21. Dan Rose, "Resource Competition in the Kennett Region of Pennsylvania," *Landscape Planning* 8 (1981): 176.

22. Ibid., 178–179.

23. Setha M. Low, "A Cultural Landscapes Mandate for Action," *Cultural Resources Management Bulletin* 10, no. 1 (1987): 30.

24. Ibid.

25. This concept is advanced in a handwritten draft titled "Some Thoughts on the Future of the Graduate School of Fine Arts," February 12, 1978, 109.II.E.1.87. Ian L. McHarg Collection, The Architectural Archives, University of Pennsylvania. Subsequent citations reference McHarg Collection, AAUP. As I contend later in this chapter, McHarg prepared this draft document as a statement about the Graduate School of Fine Arts when he was a candidate for dean of the school.

lems from the individual building of space to region and nation. Yet one further kind of integration is necessary. This begins with problem identification, formulation of research, completion of research, application of conclusions to real problems, testing and closing the cycle, introduction of experience with interaction. [These] last objectives should be accomplished by two [means]. The first is the undertaking of research by faculty and students. The second in the transmission of experience by professional practitioners who are members of the faculty.[26]

Of course, the key pedagogical foundation would rest on ecology: "Ecology is a systems view of life. Systems analysis identifies an end product and determines the process necessary to achieve the objective. Ecology has no end product, there is only process."[27]

Several months later, McHarg consolidated his views for Provost Eliot Stellar: "I propose that the University of Pennsylvania create a unique new institution entitled 'The School for the Human Environment.' . . . The faculty of this new school would be distinguished by their commitment to ameliorating the human environment, their commitment to integration, interdisciplinary and multi-disciplinary teaching and research, and, finally, their commitment to human ecology as the theoretical basis of their collective endeavors."[28]

Berger reflected on the connection between the concepts of interdisciplinary and multidisciplinary as promoted by McHarg:

The curriculum was multidisciplinary, but McHarg was asking the student to be interdisciplinary, that is replicable—it can be done over and over again. Interdisciplinary means that you extract relevant information from multidisciplines, to create something out of the multidisciplines—a picture of a place. This is the crux of the regional planning program. McHarg wanted to be interdisciplinary in a multidisciplinary world.[29]

A portrayal of McHarg's use of information and knowledge in this multidisciplinary world came from Arthur Johnson:

---

26. Ibid.
27. Ibid.
28. Ian L. McHarg, letter to Provost Eliot Stellar, August 16, 1978, 109.II.E.1.88. McHarg Collection, AAUP.
29. Berger, interview.

One of the things that I think is a credit to McHarg's way of looking at it [the various disciplines] is that he pigeonholed everything.
To him there was a geologist, a surficial geologist, a soil scientist, a
hydrologist, an ecologist, and each of these were pigeonholes, and I
don't think he knew a great deal about what went on inside of these
disciplines. But he knew that if a person wanted to understand how
natural systems worked, that the way to do that was to tap each of
those different disciplines.[30]

Arthur Palmer, who entered the curriculum when he was sixty-two,
had a law degree from Yale, and had been a special assistant to the secretary
of war under Franklin Roosevelt, provides a more personal description of
the interdisciplinary nature of the program: "One of the many valuable
traits of Mr. McHarg and his department was the creation, through sheer
conviction and determination, of an inter-disciplinary competence among
his faculty and its associates. . . . To lift the blinders and have each scientist
appreciate the contributions of the other is an exercise in force and diplo-
macy as well as wisdom."[31]

During October 1979, the Board of Landscape Architectural Accreditation of the American Society of Landscape Architects visited Penn for
its periodic review of McHarg's department. In its assessment, the visiting
team states, "Overall, the MLA program of the University of Pennsylvania
may be best characterized as outstanding."[32] Moreover, among a number
of "strengths" identified is "a departmentally-funded faculty comprised of
designers and scientists from several disciplines effectively collaborating in
interdisciplinary teaching. The high levels of expertise, enthusiasm, and
dedication of this faculty are remarkable."[33]

Another contemporary presents this view of McHarg and his work at
Penn during this period: "McHarg is a combination of iconoclast, guru, and
synthesizer. In the last role, he is probably one of the few genuinely interdisciplinary thinkers around. He has brought an extraordinary range of disci-

---

30. Arthur Johnson, interview with the author, December 3, 2002.

31. Arthur E. Palmer, *Toward Eden* (Winterville, N.C.: Creative Resource Systems,
1981), 196. In his dedication to McHarg, Palmer writes, "The experience was one of the
most important of my life because of the content of the course, the new way of looking
at the world around us, and the experience of participating in McHarg's thinking and
acting." Ibid., ii.

32. [Department of Landscape Architecture and Regional Planning, University of Penn-
sylvania] Board of Landscape Architectural Accreditation, American Society of Landscape
Architects, Donald F. Behrend, Paul Baerman, and Chester Volske, "Report of Visiting
Team," October 7–10, 1979, 1, 109.II.A.2.7.2. McHarg Collection, AAUP.

33. Ibid.

plines into his department."[34] McHarg's overriding concept of incorporating an ecological view more than any other factor made his interdisciplinary approach so important.[35] Nicholas Muhlenberg simply stated, "McHarg was an innovative genius."[36]

The most important effort to implement the interdisciplinary curriculum began with the introduction of the regional planning program during the 1965–1966 academic year. R.P. 501 Regional Planning became the department's foundation course that would later serve the "interdisciplinary studio," as McHarg called it, and would be offered for the next two decades.[37] The first modification appeared during the 1971–1972 academic year, when a new course sequence of 501 and 502 was established for the landscape architecture and the regional planning programs. The 501 Studio became generally known as the core course that first provided a base level of knowledge and then examined specific situations or case studies to apply that knowledge. As the curriculum evolved during the next decade, the core course and its subsequent studio course were initially titled L.A. 501 Workshop and L.A. 502 Studio for landscape architects. For regional planners, the courses were initially called R.P. 501 Seminar and R.P. 502 Studio. The final evolution in this interdisciplinary emphasis in the curriculum would come in the 1981–1982 school year, when the 501 Studio would become the "Common Core" for landscape architects and regional planners. This final iteration is discussed in Chapter 9.

Some New Pedagogical Engagements, 1975–1978

The regional planning degree was becoming "more popular than the M.L.A. as McHarg's ecology-grounded faculty gained strength; and enrollment of women and foreign students steadily increased."[38] In fact, by the 1975–1976 academic year, courses in regional planning were offered by the Department of City and Regional Planning in addition to those in the Department of

---

34. Constance Holden, "Ian McHarg: Champion for Design with Nature," *Science* (New Series) 195, no. 4276 (1977): 379.

35. As a functional approach to graduate education, this was true, according to Robert Hanna, despite the "incredible internal squabbling among various members of the faculty, suspicions, jealousies, and so forth." Robert Hanna, interview with the author, January 9, 2003.

36. Nicholas Muhlenberg, interview with the author, October 18, 2002.

37. McHarg, *A Quest for Life*, 226.

38. Ann L. Strong and George E. Thomas, *The Book of the School: The Graduate School of Fine Arts of the University of Pennsylvania* (Philadelphia: University of Pennsylvania, 1990), 254.

Landscape Architecture and Regional Planning. As the curriculum evolved into human ecological planning, two important inclusions accentuated this transition: (1) the initiation of a method to account for social values as a deliberate part of the design process and (2) the establishment of a health program in human ecological planning.

LOW'S COURSE Aspects of Community Life examined "specific subjects such as health, education, cultural ecology and social values."[39] Its main purpose— as was Low's role in the department—was to get social science into landscape architecture to help students understand place. In a sense, this inculcation of social value perspectives into the design process would parallel the inclusion of ethnographic methods in regional planning.

Several years after Low and Robert Hanna conducted a studio in 1977— a design project that was aimed at renovating the green space and landscape plan at the university—Low would crystallize an approach of using social methods applicable to design projects.[40] Her premise was that "the human ecological approach to planning and design is concerned with the creation of an explicit and replicable method by which to evaluate the sociocultural values of residents of a region."[41] After practicing different methodological approaches, Low concluded that "design is neither a linear nor an additive sequence but rather a recursive process. . . . The studio method therefore evolved into a series of recursive stages in which a number of methods and techniques could be employed based on the nature of the site or design problem."[42]

THE NOTION THAT HEALTH is an important variable in discerning environmental fitness for humans was not new for McHarg. In *Design with Nature*, he addresses the issue by asking, "Where is the environment of health— physical, mental and social? There is the environment of the creative and the fit. Where is the environment of pathology? There is the environment of the

---

39. "Graduate School of Fine Arts, 1975–1976," *University of Pennsylvania Bulletin* 75, no. 6 (1976): 60.

40. President Martin Meyerson had provided funding at the urging of Dean Peter Shepheard and McHarg. A design team comprising Laurie Olin, Carol Franklin, Colin Franklin, Narendra Juneja, Rolf Sauer, Leslie Sauer, and several graduate students produced the Landscape Architecture Master Plan (LAMP). A major component of the plan "transformed College Green into Blanche Levy Park and created the pedestrian spine of Locust Walk." Strong and Thomas, *The Book of the School*, 257, 190–191.

41. Setha Low, "Social Science Methods in Landscape Architecture Design," *Landscape Planning* 8 (1981): 137.

42. Ibid., 138.

destructive and the misfit, or perhaps better, there is the destructive misfit of social and physical environments."[43]

Since the NIMH grant's purpose was "to create a curriculum in human ecological planning directed to human health and well-being," the obvious need was the inclusion of a teaching and research capability in the areas of medical anthropology and epidemiology. During the 1976–1977 school year, the first course in Health Planning was offered in the regional planning program, and by the following school year, a new concentration had been defined: Health Program in Human Ecological Planning. According to the program's description, a "new health professional, a human ecological health planner," would be trained to understand "health, the environment, and/or the health consequences of environmental and social change."[44]

The thrust of this new program was aligned with the department's interdisciplinary strength and was "based upon human ecology and medical anthropology, holistic in its integration of natural and social factors and interdisciplinary in its examination of human health strategies as they are mediated by culture."[45] As such, the program integrated "an ecological and sociocultural understanding of health with training in the ecological planning method."[46]

NEW COURSES WERE ADDED to the landscape architecture and regional planning programs for the 1977–1978 academic year that began to expand the department's offerings under the rubric of human ecological planning and health planning. Low designed the course Social Organization of Communities as "the second offering within the anthropological sequence [the first being Cohen's Man in Adaptation] for landscape architecture and regional planning students."[47] In addition, the health planning concentration was strengthened by two additional courses taught by Low: (1) Anthropology and Community Health and (2) Ecology of Health. Anthropology and Community Health was a seminar that emphasized the "sociocultural aspects of the study of health and disease, [the] social organization of health care, social structure and disease, symptom as symbol, and [the] cross-cultural comparison of medical systems."[48]

---

43. Ian L. McHarg, *Design with Nature* (Garden City, N.Y.: Natural History Press, 1969), 188.

44. "Graduate School of Fine Arts, 1977–1978," *University of Pennsylvania Bulletin 78*, no. 9 (1977): 35.

45. Ibid., 34.

46. Ibid., 35.

47. Ibid., 79.

48. Ibid., 81.

Rose offered three new courses. Human Ecology and Theory of Applied Human Ecology each focused on "a unified model of man-land relationships."[49] Rose's third course, Ideas of Social Space, was aimed at understanding "the way places are used and symbolized."[50] Each of these new courses contributed to the achievement of McHarg's goal of completing the curriculum's transition to human ecological planning.

Ominous Portents: Cracks in the Mirror, 1978–1979

As the 1970s came to a close, Dean Peter Shepheard resigned. A national search for a replacement began, and a number of candidates were given final consideration, including McHarg.[51] Two pieces of correspondence in McHarg's papers in the Penn Architectural Archives support his elevation to the deanship of the Graduate School of Fine Arts. The first is a letter from Anthony R. Tomazinis, professor of city and regional planning, to university president Martin Meyerson, saying that he had "just heard that the name of Ian McHarg is being discussed seriously in connection with the Deanship of GSFA."[52] Tomazinis had emigrated from Greece and had received an MCP from the Georgia Institute of Technology. He had been a faculty member, specializing in transportation, in Penn's Department of City and Regional Planning since receiving his doctorate there in 1963. Tomazinis sent a copy of his letter to McHarg with the following notation: "I just hope you will say yes. I know that from all the names I heard mentioned, you have the best chances of unifying the school and of advancing it to its proper place of eminence. Let me hope that they will be wise enough to draft you."[53]

The second is a memorandum to Provost Stellar from Peter McCleary, representing the faculty of architecture. After reviewing each of the final candidates, McCleary writes:

> Ian McHarg is the only candidate with both an international reputation and a multi-disciplinary stance. McHarg's "architecture as a science" attitude (to Ian as "design with nature")[,] when combined with Penn's tradition through [Louis] Kahn of "architecture as the mother

---

49. Ibid.
50. Ibid.
51. In addition to McHarg, the other candidates were Gerald A. P. Carrothers, Lee G. Copeland, William Lacey, and Edward Logue.
52. Anthony R. Tomazinis, letter to President Martin Meyerson, February 8, 1978, 109.E.1.87. McHarg Collection, AAUP.
53. Ibid.

art" and through [G. Holmes] Perkins as "urbanism," will prove to be an exciting future for all concerned. In summary, Ian McHarg is our outright first choice.[54]

Despite these recommendations, Lee G. Copeland ultimately became the new dean in 1979. Copeland had received master of architecture and master of city planning degrees from Penn and would serve as dean until the early 1990s.

In the late 1970s, a public policy shift was beginning to emerge from the federal government. The strong environmental leadership exerted during the 1960s and 1970s was curtailed as new governmental initiatives "encouraged entrepreneurship without either social or ecological responsibility"; this change in world view inevitably had an impact on attracting students interested in pursuing ecological planning.[55]

IN 1979, MCHARG WAS forced to resign from Wallace, McHarg, Roberts and Todd (WMRT). McHarg's resignation followed a major project that the firm had begun in 1973, a plan for an environmental park in Iran known as *Pardisan*. The firm had established an office in Tehran, and Narendra Juneja had supervised the preparation of the master plan. But after the fall of the shah during the Iranian revolution in 1979, WMRT was not able to collect its substantial fee for consulting services, and the other members held McHarg personally liable.[56]

In his 1996 autobiography, McHarg writes that from a personal and professional perspective, the resignation "robbed me of a fascinating practice that I have been unable to resurrect."[57] It was, as he describes it, a "major loss," particularly the "wonderful staff who had worked with me for decades. These people were among my closest friends, allies, and colleagues. Together we had developed and applied ecological planning."[58]

It was widely recognized that "WMRT and the Landscape Architecture Department were largely indivisible. McHarg, [William] Roberts, Narendra Juneja and others moved between the classroom and office, using the university as a platform to formulate and test ideas then applied in the firm's

54. Peter McCleary, memorandum to Provost Eliot Stellar, July 31, 1978, 109.II.E.1.87. McHarg Collection, AAUP.

55. Strong and Thomas, *The Book of the School*, 279.

56. The events are described in McHarg, *A Quest for Life*, 290–296. My focus here is not to present the business issues between McHarg and his partners but rather to concentrate on how McHarg's leaving the firm affected the Penn curriculum.

57. McHarg, *A Quest for Life*, 333.

58. Ibid., 296.

professional projects and ultimately offered as studios."[59] Anne Whiston Spirn assesses McHarg's role with the firm: "For eighteen years, the creative tension between theory as developed at Penn and practice as pursued at McHarg's firm led to innovations in method. When McHarg's practice [with WMRT] ended, his ideas and methods, as he articulated them, ossified. But the issues they raise and the challenges they pose are part of his legacy, and they continue to be worked out by others."[60]

This event would have significant personal reverberations. As Muhlenberg remembered, "McHarg was deeply disappointed by his friend, David Wallace, who he thought would intervene in his favor—he didn't. Ian became depressed, and that showed in everything—his work, his teaching, his lecturing, the whole thing. That experience pulled the rug from under Ian."[61] McHarg's friend and former partner Wallace offered the following perspective: "McHarg used the firm and the firm's projects to advance student work. When he resigned, it [the firm] stopped being a source of power and influence over the students."[62]

AFTER E. BRUCE MACDOUGALL—the only member of the faculty skilled in doing computerized spatial analysis—left the department in 1974, several years passed before the curriculum would include any course in computer mapping or geographic information systems (GIS). McHarg was a fervent supporter of improving the curriculum's computer classes, especially as the hand-drawn overlay mapping for suitability analysis was not as efficient or accurate as computer mapping. For four to six academic years, the department provided no instruction in computer-based spatial mapping.[63]

McHarg was constantly on the move, especially during the 1970s, traveling throughout the world to give speeches and consult on assignments, yet his attention to student recruitment and success in the program remained a high priority. "His first loyalty was to the students. The students could do no wrong," according to Lenore Sagan, McHarg's longtime administrative

---

59. Strong and Thomas, *The Book of the School*, 116.

60. Anne Whiston Spirn, "Ian McHarg, Landscape Architecture, and Environmentalism: Ideas and Methods in Context," in *Environmentalism in Landscape Architecture*, ed. Michel Conan (Washington, D.C.: Dumbarton Oaks Research Library and Collection, 2000), 112.

61. Muhlenberg, interview.

62. David A. Wallace, interview with the author, December 20, 2002.

63. The *Bulletins* for the 1975–1976 and 1976–1977 academic years list the course that E. Bruce MacDougall taught (Computer Programming for Spatial Problems), but no instructor is indicated, and I have not been able to ascertain that anyone actually taught the course. For the next four academic years, from 1977–1978 through 1981–1982, the department's course listings do not show any offerings in computer-based spatial mapping or GIS.

assistant, who joined the department in 1965.[64] However, in the classroom, "McHarg was a terrible teacher. He basically created chaos," remarked Rose. "He taught more by provocation, not by mentoring. He would come in [to the studio] with a new idea each week."[65] Rose continued, "McHarg worked on two levels: the intellectual and the methodological. It was that middle level—the studio—McHarg didn't know how to do that."[66] On the other hand, as Arthur Johnson recalled, "When he lectured, he was extremely entertaining, and his style never changed. It was a great marketing style [to attract students]."[67]

McHarg's gifts as a passionate and persuasive advocate for ecological planning were formidable, and this commitment shaped his mission to create the interdisciplinary curriculum in human ecological planning—which he did. In the final analysis, McHarg was a unique blend of theoretician and practitioner, and his contribution as a teacher should not be judged solely on the basis of his classroom performance. Rather, his strengths and accomplishments allowed him to formulate and promote an educational curriculum, one that others would continue.

Dan Rose shared how McHarg felt about the curriculum: "I asked Ian, 'You have made a lot of contributions, but what do you see as your most enduring contribution?' He said, 'The curriculum in the Department of Landscape Architecture and Regional Planning.' He saw that as the monument to himself. 'But,' I said, 'curricula are like building your house on sand, because the next generation can come in and modify it.' But he was adamant about that; he was very proud of his accomplishment."[68]

As the 1970s ended, McHarg was still consolidating the gains made in securing the place of the interdisciplinary human ecological planning curriculum as an important achievement in environmental and planning education. In 1979, McHarg, Johnson, and Berger published a case study of The Woodlands, Texas, New Town project—undertaken almost a decade earlier through WMRT—that outlines the entire ecological planning process. Their undaunted conclusion was that "ecological Planning as it is described here is sound in practice as well as in concept."[69] Nonetheless, signs indicated that the human ecological planning program at Penn was beginning to lose momentum.

---

64. Lenore Sagan, interview with the author, October 16, 2002.
65. Dan Rose, interview with the author, January 16, 2003.
66. Ibid.
67. Johnson, interview.
68. Rose, interview.
69. Arthur H. Johnson, Jonathan Berger, and Ian L. McHarg, "A Case Study in Ecological Planning: The Woodlands, Texas," in *To Heal the Earth: Selected Writings of Ian L. McHarg*, ed. Ian L. McHarg and Frederick Steiner (Washington, D.C.: Island Press, 1998), 263.

9

Increasing Disarray and
the Loss in Momentum, 1980–1985

IAN MCHARG'S STATURE and prominence as an educator and as the prime mover on the national and international scenes to fuse ecology with planning continued. In 1980, he was suggested as an "outstanding candidate" to be chairman of the landscape architecture program at Virginia Polytechnic Institute and State University in Blacksburg, but he declined. In 1983, he was nominated as dean of the College of Design and Planning at the University of Colorado, but again, he declined.[1] In 1983, the University of Pennsylvania (Penn) Graduate School of Fine Arts held a symposium and reunion highlighted by the theme "The Design of Fitting Environments." McHarg, who was the keynote speaker, remarked in part, "It is clear that our professions emphasize different roles within overall adaptive strategies. Regional planners and landscape architects emphasize selection of fit environments; architecture and project-scale landscape architecture emphasize modification to enhance fitness; city planning is much concerned with development of social strategies, modification of the problem solver's behavior to solve environmental problems."[2]

1. Correspondence relevant to the "outstanding candidate" nomination, 1980, 109.I.A.1. Ian L. McHarg Collection, The Architectural Archives, University of Pennsylvania. Subsequent citations reference McHarg Collection, AAUP. Correspondence relevant to the nomination of deanship, letter to Lance Wright, 1988, 109.II.A.2.100. Ibid.

2. "The Design of Fitting Environments," GSFA Symposium and Reunion, *Penn in Ink* (Special Supplement to the Annual Review of the Graduate School of Fine Arts, University of Pennsylvania, Fall 1983), May 13–15, 1983, 2, 109.V.D.4.54. McHarg Collection, AAUP.

McHarg's intellectual prowess did not escape notice in the professional association he was a member of, the American Society of Landscape Architects (ASLA).[3] By 1984, he was being considered for the ASLA Medal, the society's highest award. McHarg's colleague, Professor Julius Gy. Fábos, from the University of Massachusetts, writes in a poignant recommendation: "As a world traveler and lecturer myself, I have met many landscape architects and planners, most of whom have read McHarg's book, *Design with Nature*. All of these people were familiar with the name Ian McHarg and had used his planning and design approach and ideas. Is there any other landscape architect alive today who can claim such global influence?"[4] McHarg was selected as the award recipient; Darwina Neal, the president of the ASLA, writes in a congratulatory letter, "Certainly, your impact on the profession and the public has been an international one—not only in educating new professionals, but also in the breadth of your practice, writings and lectures."[5]

At Penn, the gains that characterized the curriculum's success would be consolidated, but signs indicated that the momentum was beginning to slow. Change was in the making. In a direct way, changes outside the university would have a decided impact on the human ecological planning curriculum, and 1985 would mark McHarg's last year as chairman of the Department of Landscape Architecture and Regional Planning.

Changes outside the University Affecting the Curriculum

The 1980s witnessed the shifting of certain national environmental priorities that would directly influence educational programs generally and McHarg's focused ecological planning approach specifically, especially in regional planning. Consequently, critical external factors emerged that would affect the curriculum: (1) new policies affecting national environmental priorities, (2) the realities of the job market, (3) declining enrollment, and (4) changing student attitudes.

The environmental thrust of the 1970s had focused on addressing the most obvious manifestations of pollution in the air, in the water, and on the land, but the 1980s would herald a different concern. Now, all branches and

---

3. He had achieved the distinction of Fellow of the American Society of Landscape Architects (FASLA).

4. Julius Fábos, letter to Whom It May Concern, ASLA Medal, March 27, 1984, 109. II.F.1. McHarg Collection, AAUP.

5. Darwina L. Neal, letter to Ian L. McHarg, June 22, 1984, 109.II.F.1. McHarg Collection, AAUP.

levels of the government would evaluate "the acceptability of costs associated with environmental protection."[6] Even though environmental issues and concerns would not diminish, Ronald Reagan's administration firmly established a cost-benefit philosophy that would affect not only regulatory formation and implementation but also the national consciousness toward the environment. One very tangible result of this change was in the job market, primarily for city and regional planners.

In 1981, the renowned 701 local planning program, originally initiated as part of the Housing Act of 1954, ceased functioning from a lack of presidential support and congressional funding. The same was true for the Section 208 program, which had been part of a nationally mandated area-wide (i.e., regional) water and wastewater treatment planning policy. The formerly lucrative job market for planners throughout the country in local, county, and state agencies in the 701 and 208 programs began to show signs of decline, although students graduating with "environment" in their degrees, including environmental planning, did find work. In states with strong environmental laws and growing populations, such as Washington, Oregon, Arizona, Colorado, and Florida, jobs remained plentiful.

However, the new national environmental focus combined with new economic realities hit hard, as Dan Rose explained:

> With the decline of 208 planning . . . there was a fundamental shift away from clean air, clean water to chemistry and law as the dominant professions that would be running the American environment, from the standpoint of the perspective of the U.S. government. What it meant, then, is that there was a complete collapse of jobs in the job market. . . . [W]ith a collapse in the demand for regional planners, there was a collapse in enrollment. So with the shift back to landscape design [in the 1980s], it was brought about by national environmental policies and economics.[7]

The "collapse in enrollment," as characterized by Rose, was typical for planning programs throughout the country. As Ann Strong and George

6. Walter A. Rosenbaum, *Environmental Politics and Policy* (Washington, D.C.: Congressional Quarterly Press, 1985), 22.

7. Dan Rose, interview with the author, January 14, 2003. Setha Low's view was similar, but from a different perspective. She believed that "the economic times influence[d] the kinds of projects and the amount of science [that would be] used in design. When the economy really bombed [in the 1980s], . . . there was a contraction in the public sector and [in] any kind of social methodology and practice. We moved back to Beaux-Arts design, and art became important." Setha Low, interview with the author, January 31, 2003.

FIGURE **9.1.** Ian McHarg meeting with students, with Frederick Steiner
facing him, University of Pennsylvania, 1983. *(Photograph by Przemyslaw Wolski.
The Architectural Archives, University of Pennsylvania.)*

Thomas observe, "The department [of Landscape Architecture and Regional Planning], as was true of many planning programs, saw a decline in
the 1980s in the number of applicants who wished to become planners."[8]

Concomitant with declining enrollment was the changing attitude of
the students. Arthur Johnson analyzed this situation: "The students of the
'80s and '90s had a different attitude [from the students] of an earlier decade.
The former group was more motivated to learn. The latter group wanted to
acquire the skills that would be marketable to have careers of lifestyle comfort rather than to change the system."[9] Jon Berger agreed that during the
1980s, "The students changed. They were less interested [in commitment
to the environment] and more interested in making money."[10]

Each of these changes, taken collectively, would have a direct relationship
to declining student enrollments, particularly in Penn's regional planning
program, the primary academic purveyor of human ecological planning.

8. Ann L. Strong and George E. Thomas, *The Book of the School: The Graduate School of
Fine Arts of the University of Pennsylvania* (Philadelphia: University of Pennsylvania, 1990),
282. The peak years in the regional planning program were between 1973 and 1977. By
the 1980–1981 academic year, enrollments were beginning to show a fairly steep decline.

9. Arthur Johnson, interview with the author, December 3, 2002.

10. Jon Berger, interview with the author, November 27, 2002.

Modifying the Pedagogical Statement and Joint Degree Programs, 1981–1985

As the 1981–1982 academic year began, the Department of Landscape Architecture and Regional Planning radically modified its pedagogical statement for the first time since the 1969–1970 school year. The alteration was substantial, perhaps, in part, to promote a program that was experiencing declining enrollments.

The statement opens with a *tour de force*: "The Department of Landscape Architecture and Regional Planning is widely regarded as the pioneer of ecological planning and the major center for its continued development."[11] The statement makes a number of salient points relevant to landscape architecture and regional planning. The emphasis is on uniting each of these elements and mutually reinforcing the incorporation of human ecology—the most important pedagogical objective.

Furthermore, the statement professes that "the undisputed distinction in ecological planning has overshadowed the department's distinction in design. . . . However, the aspiration is to train informed designers who understand places and people, and look to both for program, plan, design, and form. Human ecological planning is now well developed and assured, [but] ecological design is at an early stage of development. Its evolution is a challenge which faculty and students have accepted as the main thrust in the evolution of landscape architecture."[12] The reinforcement theme, for both disciplines, is that "the underlying assumptions which characterize the department, its teaching, and research are that both landscape architects and regional planners are applied human ecologists seeking to assist individuals and institutions in adaptation; the selection and modification of their environments to enhance their success, health, and well-being."[13]

The pedagogical statement also includes a description of the disciplinary affiliation of the faculty, which "provides the major explanation for [the department's] distinction. It is unique in that it comprises physical, biological, and social scientists, architects, landscape architects, and city and regional planners."[14] The representation of the faculty in the list below demonstrates the breadth of the intellectual resources that were involved with the regional planning and landscape architecture programs in the early 1980s:[15]

---

11. "Graduate School of Fine Arts, 1981–1982," *University of Pennsylvania Bulletin* 82, no. 1 (1980): 22.

12. Ibid.

13. Ibid.

14. Ibid., 23.

15. Ibid., 78.

Ian L. McHarg, MLA, MCP, *professor, chairman*

David M. DuTot, MLA, *lecturer in landscape architecture*

Carol Franklin, MLA, *adjunct assistant professor of landscape architecture*

Robert Giegengack, PhD, *associate professor of geology*

Robert Hanna, BArch, MLA, FAAR, *associate professor of landscape architecture and environmental design*

Arthur Johnson, PhD, *associate professor*

John C. Keene, BA, JD, MCP, *associate professor of city planning*

Narendra N. Juneja, BArch, MLA, *associate professor*

Setha Low, PhD, *assistant professor*

Nicholas Muhlenberg, PhD, *associate professor of regional planning*

Laurie D. Olin, B.Arch., FAAR, *assistant professor of landscape architecture and environmental design*

Stephen H. Putman, PhD, *associate professor of regional planning*

Daniel Rose, PhD, *assistant professor*

Leslie Sauer, BS, *lecturer in landscape architecture*

Sir Peter Shepheard, CBE, BArch, *professor of architecture and environmental design*

Thomas Siccama, PhD, *visiting lecturer in landscape architecture*

Peter Skaller, *assistant professor of landscape architecture*

Nathan Sullivan, MLA, *lecturer in landscape architecture*

Anthony J. Walmsley, BArch, MCD, MLA, *associate professor of landscape architecture*

ONE WAY IN WHICH the department consciously expanded in the 1980s was the creation of a joint degree program with other disciplines. The goal was to provide greater flexibility for landscape architecture or regional planning majors, so they could broaden their matriculation through allied specializations. Yet it could be speculated that an additional reason for expanding the curriculum was to combat the reality of declining enrollments. Under this assumption, offering joint degrees was a practical necessity to keep the regional planning program functional. In addition to the Health Program in Human Ecological Planning offered within the Department of Landscape Architecture and Regional Planning, joint degree programs were established in three additional areas. One of these, a joint program between McHarg's department and the Department of Architecture, had already been operational for some time. Additionally, although they were not part of a joint degree program, the Department of City and Regional Planning admitted students from McHarg's regional planning program to pursue their doctorates.

During the 1982–1984 school years, two new joint degree programs were formally announced. One joined regional planning with civil engineering. The emphasis of this program was on environmental planning and environmental engineering, with John D. Keenan as the program's adviser.[16] The second was called Regional Planning and Law, offering in cooperation with the law school. This program's adviser was John C. Keene, a member of the Department of City and Regional Planning and a strong proponent of McHarg's interdisciplinary approach. Keene had a law degree from Harvard University and a master of city planning (MCP) degree from Penn, and he focused his research and teaching on exploring ways in which law, planning, land use policy, and environmental policy interact. The program's pedagogical statement indicated that "environmental law is now a significant specialization and exponents who combine the scientific expertise contained in the Regional Planning program with competence in law confront a challenging and fruitful career."[17] Unfortunately, the regional planning and law program attracted only a few students.

During the 1984–1986 school years, the curriculum in the department was consistent with that of the previous period (1982–1984), and the gains that had been consolidated remained virtually intact.

The 501 Studio: Common Core of the Curriculum, 1981–1984

The primary educational vehicle for human ecological planning in the department would become the studio, a more pragmatic, project-oriented approach than the seminar or lecture format of most courses. It has been written that "the studio was largely abandoned in American planning education during the 1960s, but was retained at [the University of] Pennsylvania in regional planning, as well as in city planning and urban design. . . . [T]he workshop format involves 'learning by doing' and should not only be retained but emphasized in an applied field like planning."[18]

The 1981–1982 school *Bulletin* once again emphasizes the complete infusion of ecological planning in the landscape architecture and regional planning programs: "All students who join the department are required to take L.A/R.P. 501, a studio in human ecological planning. This consumes half of the student's time in the first term and will introduce the theoretical basis employed by the department and demonstrate its application to a plan-

---

16. "Graduate School of Fine Arts, 1982–1984," *University of Pennsylvania Bulletin* 83, no. 1 (1982): 25.

17. Ibid.

18. Frederick Steiner, Gerald Young, and Ervin Zube, "Ecological Planning: Retrospect and Prospect," *Landscape Journal* 7, no. 1 (1988): 37.

FIGURE 9.2. A 501 Studio field trip to Hawk Mountain, Pennsylvania, September 30, 1983. Seated toward the left, Ian McHarg; seated and pointing at the center, Robert Giegengack; standing toward the right (with beard), James Thorne. *(Photograph by Frederick R. Steiner. The Architectural Archives, University of Pennsylvania.)*

ning process."[19] The *Workbook* used in the 501 Studio in 1981 explains that the purpose of the studio was "to define core values on the landscape. The focus will be on natural processes and social processes. *No law, economics, or design* will be taught."[20] So the 501 Studio was intended to acquaint all students with the basics of the ecological inventory. A key aspect of the 501 Studio during the early 1980s was its emphasis on field observation. Every Friday, the studio class would board a bus and visit a site, where lectures occurred and students took notes, shot photographs, or sketched. In dramatic ways, this field-based learning contrasted with other modes of learning planning and design, especially those that were more directed toward analysis through geographic information systems (GIS) programs. In GIS-oriented classes, students typically became glued to their computer screens.

19. "Graduate School of Fine Arts, 1981–1982," 24.

20. *Workbook: Core Course LARP 501* (Department of Landscape Architecture and Regional Planning, University of Pennsylvania, Fall 1981), 1; emphasis original.

IN 1981, NARENDRA JUNEJA, one of the principal faculty members of the 501 Studio and a close associate of McHarg's, died suddenly. With this event, the curriculum lost one of its most respected and strongest advocates, and McHarg was greatly moved. He would later describe Juneja as "my good right hand. We developed a deep affection and marvelously complementary roles. Narendra knew what I could do, what I could not, and what he could do or cause to be done. It was a most gratifying relationship . . . never to be replaced."[21] With Juneja's death, McHarg approached Jon Berger about reorganizing the studio as a "Common Core" that would be required for landscape architects and regional planners. Berger had a reputation for being assertive, brash, bright, and a strong supporter of McHarg and ecological planning. He brought a "crew boss attitude to running the studio; he knew how to get a project from the start to the end," according to Rose, a close colleague who played a major role in teaching the studio.[22] The full faculty who taught the redesigned Common Core, the 501 Studio, included Berger, Robert Giegengack, Arthur Johnson, McHarg, Nicholas Muhlenberg, Dan Rose, and Jorge Sanchez-Flores.

In Rose's view, the full "integration of field work with academic work" finally cemented the curriculum's interdisciplinary approach.[23] But Berger admitted that the studio's "first time around" was difficult, although it improved in the second year. As he later recalled, "501 was the backbone of the curriculum, but there was never any focus; the rhetoric far surpassed the reality."[24]

Johnson provided extensive remarks about the 501 Studio, which he said was designed "to teach concepts."[25] He believed that the studio experience worked very well for students who were eager to learn, especially those who did not have a strong background in the natural sciences. But the key to the evolution of the studio and the experience it would provide was McHarg's notions of teaching and learning. Johnson explained an important dimension of how the core curriculum took shape: "McHarg did not differentiate very much between teaching and learning. They are very different things;

---

21. Ian L. McHarg, *A Quest for Life: An Autobiography* (New York: John Wiley and Sons, 1996), 218.

22. Dan Rose, interview with the author, January 16, 2003. After Berger resigned from Penn in the 1982–1983 school year, Frederick Steiner became the studio coordinator for a year, and then McHarg assumed leadership again. See McHarg, *A Quest for Life*, 226.

23. Ibid.

24. Berger, interview.

25. Johnson, interview.

that students learn by doing, by listening; they learn by making maps, by seeing things. Teaching is where a person goes through a bunch of things, and the student is supposed to learn what the teacher teaches. To a certain extent the 501 [Studio] was a reflection of teaching."[26]

The 501 Studio created a kind of intellectual tension. As Johnson pointed out, "501 taught them [the students] what information to use for planning purposes; courses allowed them to learn about a subject matter and to learn how the pieces fit together."[27] The logic of such an approach could be questioned, since one could argue that course work, as the purveyor of knowledge, ought to precede the application of that knowledge in a particular situation or context. I asked Arthur Johnson how one could apply a supposed body of knowledge that, practically and intellectually, one does not have. Johnson responded:

> From a purely logical point of view, you might say that it is better to know something before you start to use the information. But human brains do not work in a linear fashion. You can always go backwards and forward; and you can go back many years and retrieve important concepts and apply them today. And, as long as you are in touch with the information, you can keep your brain running. You can learn, over the course of a semester, the principles that you applied before you really knew what you were doing. You can do that, and it comes out ok.[28]

After completing the 501 Studio, landscape architects proceeded to L.A. 502, taught by McHarg, John Coe, Hanna, Low, Muhlenberg, and Anthony Walmsley. The *Bulletin* describes the course this way: "The second semester of the initial year sees the landscape architects and the regional planners sharing common lecture courses but having independent studios. The differences are principally a matter of scale and emphasis."[29] The primary distinction was that regional planners "work on larger scales and utilize a higher discrimination of scientific data than do the landscape architects."[30]

Concomitant with the initiation of the 501 Studio as the Common Core, the curriculum in the landscape architecture and regional planning programs was restructured to present the courses as "modules" that would follow the

---

26. Ibid.
27. Ibid.
28. Ibid.
29. "Graduate School of Fine Arts, 1982–1984," 17.
30. Ibid.

Common Core. According to Nicholas Muhlenberg, "It was a period of experimentation; people were trying different things, and many times, nobody knew what they were doing."[31] The structural integration of the Common Core and modules would continue into the near future.

At the very heart of ecological and human ecological planning is the ecological inventory. After assessing the evidence, I believe that McHarg did make a clear distinction between *inventory* and *planning*, with inventory coming first. Therefore, his parameters indicated to perform the ecological inventory and then do ecological planning. However, in such a schema—especially when it becomes a usable method in actual projects—one could argue that the planning element is not really a creative exercise in the allocation of proposed land use patterns. Rather, planning becomes a perfunctory activity that requires no particular skill, since the inventory in effect determines the plan. Or, in another sense, by its very determination of the most propitious areas for development, the inventory becomes a substitute for the plan. This interpretation cannot be dismissed. Yet a more plausible reason for McHarg's emphasis on the ecological inventory is that the information derived from the layer cake was more closely aligned with his goal of achieving an interdisciplinary composite analysis.

In reviewing the role of the 501 Studio in the curriculum during the 1980–1985 school years, it is fair to explore the relative degrees of importance accorded inventory and planning and their respective levels of strength in the curriculum. The question to ask is whether, as taught to graduate students in the Department of Landscape Architecture and Regional Planning, ecological (and later human ecological) planning was more inventory than planning. The answer can be found by reviewing how the 501 Studio, described by Berger as "the backbone of the curriculum," was presented.[32]

To begin, I have reviewed the department's pedagogical statement from the 1969–1970 academic year, when the ecological planning curriculum was firmly established in the regional planning program. The inventory-planning interface's future direction is clear: the natural sciences and the planning process would be integrated through the principles of ecology. The pedagogical statement contains two points that indicate the curriculum's direction. First, it states, "There is an urgent need at the moment for the contribution of *natural science planning* as an enlargement and complement of the *planning process*." Next, it reads, "We need more and better knowledge

---

31. Nicholas Muhlenberg, interview with the author, October 18, 2002, and follow-up, February 7, 2003.
32. Berger, interview.

FIGURE **9.3.** Ian McHarg explaining the "layer cake" at Osaka University
of the Arts, Japan, June 1, 1971 (Harvey A. Shapiro, translator).
(Photograph courtesy of Harvey A. Shapiro. William J. Cohen personal collection.)

of the operation of the physical and biological process in order that we may
predict and formulate choice."[33]

In the department's sequence of course offerings, Regional Planning
(R.P.) 503 involves "elementary exercises, . . . emphasizing the use of natural science techniques in the *planning synthesis*; data are generated for use in
planning decisions."[34] This course is followed by R.P. 512, Case Studies in
Regional Planning, for the "review and analysis of regional planning activities, giving special attention to *methods of implementation.*"[35]

At the next level, R.P. 601, Regional Planning, covers the following: "*Regional plans are made* for more complex areas in studies utilizing the joint skills
of natural sciences, within the perspective of the social sciences."[36] A second
course, R.P. 602, Regional Planning, includes the following activity: "*A joint
regional plan is made* for an extensive area. . . . [E]ach student's work is reviewed
as an individual *terminal project within the perspective of the general plan.*"[37]

In the original ecological planning curriculum, inventory and planning

33. "Graduate School of Fine Arts, 1969–1970," *University of Pennsylvania Bulletin* 69, no.
5 (1968): 39; emphasis added.

34. Ibid., 68; emphasis added.

35. Ibid; emphasis added.

36. Ibid; emphasis added.

37. Ibid; emphasis added.

were two distinct steps, with the latter building on the former. But how did those distinctions fare over time, at least with regard to the department's pedagogical statement? By the 1973–1974 school year, a "Plan of Study" was set out in the department's description of the "Ecological Program in Regional Planning." This study plan outlines the requirements for the degree, including an understanding of the "principles of geology, ecology, and *the planning method*, and demonstrat[ion of] this understanding with *case studies*."[38] This academic year can be identified as the transition period when the ecological planning curriculum was solidifying its move toward human ecological planning. Course offerings were modified; R.P. 501 became a "Seminar," and R.P. 502 became a "Studio," of which the *Bulletin* says, "*Exercises in planning* are conducted, emphasizing the various natural science *techniques in the planning synthesis*."[39]

By the 1977–1978 academic year, the course sequences for the regional planning and landscape architecture programs were on a parallel track. The regional planning seminar and studio sequence coincided with the L.A. 501 Workshop that "analyze[d] sites . . . [using] the human ecological planning method."[40] The final curriculum iteration came (as discussed earlier in this chapter) in the 1981–1982 school year, when L.A./R.P. 501 became the Common Core studio for all students entering the landscape architecture or regional planning program.

With the fusion now complete, the curriculum's Common Core was set to engage inventory and planning, but in different ways. According to Johnson, "The preparation of the inventory became the heart of the Studio: six weeks for natural features, six weeks for the cultural analysis, and three weeks to manipulate the information to do the suitability analysis."[41] It is accurate to say that the Common Core was confined to ecological inventory and analysis, for planning was not introduced until the next course in sequence, R.P 502, Regional Planning Studio, in which "students undertake a complex planning problem which draws upon the data and method employed in L.A./R.P. 501, but augments this with considerations of law and implementation."[42] For the first (and only) time, the regional planning faculty of Berger, Johnson, and Rose was augmented by John Keene, who added land use and environmental law to the curriculum.

---

38. "Graduate School of Fine Arts, 1973–1974," *University of Pennsylvania Bulletin* 73, no. 5 (1972): 37; emphasis added.

39. Ibid., 61; emphasis added.

40. "Graduate School of Fine Arts, 1977–1978," *University of Pennsylvania Bulletin* 77, no. 9 (1977): 79.

41. Johnson, interview.

42. "Graduate School of Fine Arts, 1981–1982," 91–92.

The Common Core description that appears in the 1982–1984 *Bulletin* is revised and expanded, this time incorporating a planning element. Now the Common Core includes three distinct tasks. First is "a comprehensive examination which focuses on the interactions within natural systems, their evolutionary history, and their dynamic tendencies." This test would take the form of a "method" that would be applied to actual sites. Second, the "human ecology" element is introduced so that a "systematic relationship" can be understood between "place-work-folk" through the completion of an "ethnographic history." Finally, "the common experience concludes with a planning problem . . . [that] consists of locating the objective, whether housing, a park, sewage treatment plant, or other facility, so as to utilize all or most of the propitious factors on the site and none or few detrimental ones."[43]

So was there more inventory than planning in the 501 Studio? The answer is yes, but the evidence demonstrates that the inventory did precede planning and that planning was not entirely eschewed in the Common Core or in the curriculum. For the first school year in which it was presented (1981–1982), the studio was described as essentially involving an inventory. But by the following academic year, the planning element took on a more pronounced role in the studio to become the third in a series of three tasks.

Losing the Momentum: Dilemma and Change, 1982–1985

The growth of McHarg's interdisciplinary human ecological planning curriculum seems to have reached its peak somewhere between 1980 and 1981; during and after this time, a number of factors and indicators emerged that suggest the momentum was waning.

DURING THE 1982–1984 SCHOOL YEARS, the 501 Studio saw computer-based spatial analysis reemerge in the curriculum, ending its hiatus since E. Bruce MacDougall's departure in 1974. This time, the subject was taught in the 501 Studio by Sanchez-Flores, a recent Penn graduate (master of landscape architecture [MLA] 1980 and master of regional planning [MRP] 1981). The Graduate School of Fine Arts purchased computer hardware and software costing $500,000 in the early 1980s, and McHarg wrote to his faculty, "1984–1985 should be that year when fully computerized ecological plan-

---

43. "Graduate School of Fine Arts, 1982–1984," 16.

ning would be taught here."[44] By the 1986–1988 academic years, John Radke was presenting a separate course, Computer Graphics, in the regional planning program, and later he would teach the first course with GIS in its title. McHarg was highly impressed with Radke's capability and contribution. He believed that Radke "engaged with great success in developing computerized ecological planning. Unfortunately, this paragon was little appreciated by Penn, and he was seduced to Berkeley and given appropriate salary, status, and lab."[45]

This comment about Radke highlights a major obstacle that McHarg faced—receiving continued financial support from the university to build a state-of-the-art computer capability to produce spatial graphics and GIS. Technology in the early 1980s was making enormous advances that had the potential to improve the reliability, speed, and accuracy of manipulating inventory data, the basis of ecological planning. Muhlenberg bemoaned the fact that "there was a lack of [continued] support from the administration to provide funding and space for computer hardware. The administration just didn't want to get involved with an expensive undertaking."[46]

FOR THE 1980–1981 ACADEMIC YEAR, the landscape architecture program was expanded to include "four major subject areas," a move that was intended to relate its design emphasis to a human ecological planning component. The program was constructed to include the physical sciences, biological sciences, social sciences (notably ethnography and anthropology), and history and theory. Effectively, "all of the sciences of the environment bec[a]me the basis for planning and landscape architecture design."[47] Robert Hanna, a key member of the landscape architecture faculty, pointed out that one of McHarg's concerns was that "urban design had failed because it never considered the natural environment of cities. Ian was so absolutely right; it's just architecture. It has nothing to do with the organic nature of cities and people and how they interact."[48]

In a way, the overriding reality was that McHarg had finally succeeded

---

44. Letter, "LARP/FACULTY/McHarg," 109.II.E.1.81. McHarg Collection, AAUP. Although the letter is undated, references in the document suggest that it was written in the autumn of 1984. Years earlier, E. Bruce MacDougall had critiqued the accuracy of the overlay maps, thus establishing yet another reason to move vigorously toward developing a computer-mapping capability. See E. Bruce MacDougall, "The Accuracy of Map Overlays," *Landscape Planning* 2 (1975): 23–30.

45. McHarg, *A Quest for Life*, 367.

46. Muhlenberg, interview and follow-up.

47. "Graduate School of Fine Arts, 1980–1981," *University of Pennsylvania Bulletin* 81, no. 2 (1979): 24.

48. Robert Hanna, interview with the author, January 9, 2003.

in fashioning the landscape architecture curriculum to integrate a natural sciences and social sciences perspective as a critical design component. However, one major difficulty would preclude the curriculum's full potential for educating future landscape architect practitioners.

Hanna reminisced that he was hired "to bring a balance between planning and design" and that "one of Ian's ambitions was to create something in the department that had to do with 'adaptive architecture'—that was truly responsive to content and other natural factors. We never quite brought that off."[49] However, Hanna continued, "McHarg really had the best department of landscape architecture in the world. It was largely because of the marriage of the scientifically oriented curriculum and some pretty good planning and design instruction."[50] G. Holmes Perkins was unequivocal in his view that "McHarg rescued landscape architecture as a profession."[51]

McHarg was very clear that the curriculum in landscape architecture should follow an "evolutionary process." That process would contain four steps and would "begin with the recognition of the extraordinary accomplishments of the eighteenth-century landscape tradition, the transformation of an entire countryside, and its development in the nineteenth-century United States with the powerful contributions of Olmsted and Eliot."[52] The next step would see "ecology embraced as the scientific and philosophical basis for the profession. This involved no repudiation of the historic examples; the eighteenth century had employed a rudimentary but effective ecology."[53] The third step would be the "next great leap[,] . . . which led to the expansion of ecology to include people, human ecology."[54] Finally, continuing the "circular quest [would be the] develop[ment of] ecological design. Parallel to these advances has been the effort to develop computerized ecological planning and, ultimately, design."[55]

By his own admission, ecological (or, more properly, human ecological) design never achieved the success that human ecological planning did in the regional planning program, even though the department "had a design faculty beyond compare."[56] Such a situation posed a dilemma for the landscape

---

49. Ibid.

50. Ibid.

51. G. Holmes Perkins, interview with the author, October 15, 2002.

52. McHarg, *A Quest for Life*, 197–198.

53. Ibid., 198.

54. Ibid.

55. Ibid.

56. Ibid., 229. McHarg acknowledges Peter Shepheard, Robert Hanna, Laurie Olin, Carol Franklin, Jon Coe, Anthony Walmsley, A. E. Bye (an annual visitor), and, of course, himself.

architecture program. Setha Low, who brought the human-cultural emphasis to the landscape architecture program, offered the following reason:

> I had to take human ecological planning to the design level, which was different than the planning level. The reason that it did not work as successfully in landscape architecture as it did in regional planning was scale. I think we were doing it, but it's harder at the level of design to see the kinds of impact and trends that Jon [Berger] and Ian were able to see in the geomorphology—in the larger landscape.[57]

Low reiterated that the great difficulty that the landscape architects had in accepting human ecology precepts, in contrast to the regional planners, especially in their field work—the applied aspect of the curriculum—really arose out of the different perspective that each had. She continued, "When the application is at the level of a house garden, it is much more difficult to see the larger ecological trend. We were, conceptually, doing ecological design, but it was much harder to demonstrate it with clarity."[58] In essence, Low's comments illustrate that the theory was sound, but in practice it inevitably broke down; a human ecology element, as envisioned by McHarg in the curriculum, just did not work at the design scale of a small site.

ONE EVENT THAT INFLUENCED THE CURRICULUM between 1980 and 1985 was the phasing out of the Center for Ecological Research in Planning and Design, which had been established in the early 1970s in the Graduate School of Fine Arts (see Chapter 7). The *Bulletin* for the Graduate School of Fine Arts in 1980–1981 shows that the faculty of the center represented the variety of multidisciplines that were the hallmark of the curriculum. McHarg became the center's director, with J. Toby Tourbier as director of research. Tourbier had received an MLA from Penn in 1966 and had served as an adjunct assistant professor in McHarg's department since 1976.[59] Continuing as the research arm of the Department of Landscape Architecture and Regional Planning, the center's four "most recent projects" included (1) an ecological inventory for Buckingham Township, Pennsylvania; (2) the Medford, New Jersey, study; (3) the International Conference on Biological

---

57. Low, interview.

58. Ibid.

59. "Graduate School of Fine Arts, 1980–1981," 25. Other faculty with their specializations included Ruth Patrick (limnology), Robert Giegengack (geology), Nicholas Muhlenberg (resource economics), Narendra Juneja (landscape architecture), Arthur Johnson (soils), Peter Skaller (plant ecology), Dan Rose (ethnography), Setha Low (medical anthropology), and Jon Berger (regional planning).

Water Quality Improvement Alternatives of 1975; and (4) the development of a methodology for coastal zone management for the state of Delaware.[60]

By the following school year, the center listed "several long-term research projects in planning and the natural sciences." These studies emphasizing the natural sciences ranged from acid rain on forested ecosystems in the Northeast to the phytosociology of gypsy moth infestation on sprayed and unsprayed forests. The social scientists were evaluating future land use and resource use in the New Jersey Pine Barrens and the cultural effects on land use patterns in the Brandywine Basin of Pennsylvania and Delaware.[61]

In 1981, Dean Lee G. Copeland proposed creating the Center for Environmental Design and Planning "to expand research and opportunities for the faculty and students of the Graduate School of Fine Arts."[62] With the establishment of this new center to serve the research pursuits for all departments in the graduate school, McHarg's Center for Ecological Research in Planning and Design was phased out.

During the first half of the 1980s, a number of factors caused the curriculum to be continually adjusted. As 1986 began, yet another significant change would take place, this time within the Department of Landscape Architecture and Regional Planning. This shift would usher in the final period of McHarg's human ecological planning curriculum.

---

60. Ibid.
61. "Graduate School of Fine Arts, 1981–1982," 27.
62. "Graduate School of Fine Arts, 1982–1984," 40.

10

Phasing Down of the Human Ecological Planning Curriculum and New Directions, 1986–2000

THIS CHAPTER COMPLETES the history of Ian McHarg's educational curriculum in regional planning and landscape architecture at the University of Pennsylvania (Penn). The first section covers the period between 1986 and 1993 and includes the tenure of Anne Whiston Spirn, who succeeded McHarg as chair of the Department of Landscape Architecture and Regional Planning. During this period, the curriculum's ecological planning emphasis began to embrace an urban perspective, thus diluting its unitary regional planning focus. Moreover, ecological planning played an increasingly less important role as the curriculum's pedagogical center. This shift was compounded by the fact that financial resource scarcity and declining student enrollments influenced the continued viability of the regional planning curriculum.

The second section of the chapter covers the period from 1994 to 2000, when the department significantly revised the curriculum that emphasized the traditional design roots of landscape architecture. The result was that after 1994, the human ecological planning curriculum in the Graduate School of Fine Arts was eliminated. One unavoidable issue that would factor into the department's revised curriculum—or as it was called, the "new curriculum"—was that landscape architecture as a professional discipline had to maintain its accreditation at Penn. To do so, the department prioritized its master of landscape architecture (MLA) program with respect to course offerings, allocation of resources, and appointment of faculty.

A New Chair and a New Emphasis, 1986–1993

On November 20, 1985, Ian McHarg received a letter from Dean Lee G. Copeland noting, "At sixty-five I must resign my role as chairman. I had founded the department in 1955 and had been its chairman for thirty-two years. . . . I saw the role as the instrument for leading growth and development; it was not a chore, rather, my life's work. But it must end."[1]

During the 1986–1987 academic year, McHarg took a sabbatical from Penn to fulfill an appointment as senior visiting professor at the University of California at Berkeley. This was only the second time he had taken a sabbatical, the first being when he wrote *Design with Nature*. When he returned to Penn, now as a professor in the Department of Landscape Architecture and Regional Planning, the curriculum was already beginning to show modification. When asked how the resignation was felt, Nicholas Muhlenberg replied, "What was lost was the spark that Ian provided and the bold concept that he envisioned."[2]

Since Spirn's appointment as associate professor at Harvard was coming to an end and her promotion to full professor was not secure, she returned to Penn and became the new chair of the department. She had been a student in McHarg's landscape architecture program, receiving an MLA in 1974. She had then worked on a number of projects for the consulting firm Wallace, McHarg, Roberts and Todd (WMRT). Her professional and intellectual background has been described as follows: "While *Design with Nature* introduced her to the full scope of the profession of landscape architecture, her own conception of nature and art had been developing through her study of literature, philosophy and art history."[3]

When Spirn took over as chair, a modified direction for the curriculum began to emerge. Two observations provide insights regarding what happened. Lenore Sagan, McHarg's longtime administrative assistant, described Spirn as "a very strong person, very bright, but she wanted to do her own thing."[4] Robert Hanna explained one particular focus that Spirn brought to the department in marked contrast to McHarg: "Anne made a genuine effort to sustain the ideals and philosophy that Ian had established. But Anne's

---

1. Ian L. McHarg, *A Quest for Life: An Autobiography* (New York: John Wiley and Sons, 1996), 367.
2. Nicholas Muhlenberg, interview with the author, October 18, 2002.
3. Ann L. Strong and George E. Thomas, *The Book of the School: The Graduate School of Fine Arts of the University of Pennsylvania* (Philadelphia: University of Pennsylvania, 1990), 264.
4. Lenore Sagan, interview with the author, October 16, 2002.

side of it was to do for the urban what Ian had done for the regional."[5] Spirn's interest was best illustrated through her important contribution to the planning and design literature that had been published just a little more than a year before she became chair of the department. In *The Granite Garden*, she writes, "As a landscape architect and environmental planner, I was trained to design new communities that accommodate both human purpose and natural processes. However, it seemed contradictory to be so concerned with the integration of nature and human activities at the edge of the city and so little concerned with the reclamation of damaged land at its center."[6]

The department's new emphasis was best demonstrated by a new course offered in the landscape architecture program during the 1986–1988 school years. Taught by Spirn, City and Nature: Natural Processes, Human Purpose and Urban Form explored "the interplay between city and nature. It examines historic tradition, current practices, and potential future directions for urban nature and human design."[7] A new avenue was now open, not to abandon ecological planning but to realign it within an urban context.

ON THE SURFACE, one change that appears in the *Bulletin* of the Graduate School of Fine Arts for the school years 1988–1990 can be interpreted as rather innocuous. However, a deeper reading suggests that it is a subtle symbolic indicator of changes to come.

For many years, the *Bulletins* did not contain any photographs of people or places on campus—until the 1975–1976 school year. The *Bulletin* covering that period contains, for the first time, photographs of people and places. For example, a full-page image of Dean Peter Shepheard follows the title page. A half-page "action shot" of McHarg working with a student over a drafting board appears in the section that presents the landscape architecture program.

In the next *Bulletin* (1976–1977), a full-page photograph shows Hanna, McHarg, and Muhlenberg in a contemplative, somewhat iconic pose. In subsequent *Bulletins*, this photograph is accompanied by the following caption: "Ian McHarg, Chairman, Department of Landscape Architecture and Regional Planning, helps graduate students wrestling with planning problems."

---

5. Robert Hanna, interview with the author, January 9, 2003.

6. Anne Whiston Spirn, *The Granite Garden: Urban Nature and Human Design* (New York: Basic Books, 1984), xii.

7. "Graduate School of Fine Arts, 1986–1988," *University of Pennsylvania Bulletin* 86, no. 5 (1986): 49. Spirn also presented a second course in the landscape architecture program called Designed Landscape: Form and Meaning.

FIGURE **10.1.** Robert Hanna, Ian McHarg, and Nicholas Muhlenberg as a
jury in the Department of Landscape Architecture and Regional Planning,
University of Pennsylvania, 1979. *(Ian and Carol McHarg Collection,
The Architectural Archives, University of Pennsylvania.)*

This image served a more significant role than just depicting McHarg
in the foreground, overshadowing his colleagues. It was a conscious and
dramatic reminder of who was in charge. This photograph would appear in
every *Bulletin* for the next decade, until it was dropped from the 1986–1988
Bulletin.[8]

8. The picture would reappear again in the 1993–1995 Catalogue of the Graduate School
of Fine Arts, this time in a gallery format that highlighted the history of the school and included, among others, Lewis Mumford, Louis Kahn, Edmund Bacon, and Martin Meyerson.

No longer being in charge was difficult for McHarg to endure. Dean G. Holmes Perkins remarked that the ecological planning program declined "when he was not in control anymore. The people who took over did not have the vision. The dynamic feel of McHarg and his passion were not carried on."[9] The synergism that had evolved in the department had perhaps been taken for granted by some and not understood by others. This synergism had become manifested through an interweaving of forces—an exemplary interdisciplinary faculty, bright and inquiring students, and an intellectually stimulating environment that pushed everyone to new heights of exploration and creative achievement. At the top, of course, was McHarg, ruling over a domain of his own making. The program was his passion and commitment. But, after 1985, it would be no more.

McHarg and Spirn, each in different ways and styles, were engaged in accomplishing something meaningful. Inevitably, a creative tension emerged, as Muhlenberg explained: "Spirn had a strategy to change the program, even though Ian came in [to classes] to give pep talks. She never had the spark that Ian had. She was fighting Ian and trying to get the reins; and Ian was grabbing them back. The Department was like a two-headed hydra!"[10]

NEITHER THE LANDSCAPE ARCHITECTURE nor the regional planning program changed significantly during the 1986–1988 period. In fact, the pedagogical statement remained virtually intact (with only some minor editorial changes), and the Common Core, the 501 Studio, stayed the same as before, with McHarg still playing a major role in its presentation.

For the first time, two certificate programs were added to the landscape architecture curriculum: one would be an MLA with a certificate in historic preservation, and the other would be an MLA with a certificate in urban design.[11] In addition, a certificate program was being developed in regional planning that would expand opportunities in energy management, appropriate technology, urban design, and historic preservation.[12] A new joint degree program was presented during the 1986–1988 academic years that combined landscape architecture and regional planning; this program was in addition to the already existing joint degree programs uniting regional planning and civil engineering and regional planning and law. Moreover, the health program in human ecological planning was continued under Setha Low.

---

9. G. Holmes Perkins, interview with the author, October 15, 2002.

10. Nicholas Muhlenberg, interview with the author, October 18, 2002, and follow-up, February 7, 2003.

11. "Graduate School of Fine Arts, 1986–1988," 30.

12. Ibid., 31.

In the regional planning program, advisers included Robert Giegengack, Arthur Johnson, Low, McHarg, Muhlenberg, Dan Rose, James Thorne, and Spirn.[13] In regional planning, Rose continued the courses Human Ecology, Applied Human Ecology, and Ideas of Social Space. Although the human ecological planning emphasis remained intact, one development took place that would have a major negative impact on its future.

The lack of support for a geographic information systems (GIS) continued and would become a key element that cemented McHarg's disappointment with the new departmental direction. More important, it would place ecological planning at a distinct disadvantage in not using computer capabilities to perform ecological inventories in the most efficacious way.

John Radke wrote a memorandum to Spirn and McHarg on July 15, 1987, regarding "The Computer Facility Needed to Maintain our Present Teaching Status."[14] Radke is very clear about what was needed to keep the GIS component in the curriculum current. He spells out hardware, software, and personal needs and concludes with what would be an ominous sign: "I have managed to solve some of these problems but my level of frustration increases each day. . . . I have used every resource available to me to insure [sic] that the 501 computer module is a success this fall. . . . I fear that I may have already compromised too much and that once again I will be attempting to teach the 501 module with a handicap."[15]

A few months later, McHarg wrote to Dean Copeland, "I remain determined to establish a Computer lab at Penn. . . . I seek your approval and support for my continued efforts to establish a serious computer competence in the school."[16]

McHarg's disagreement with the dean on this issue did not dissuade him from pursuing a larger goal—to continue to push for the creation of a worldwide, computerized ecological inventory. In May 1987, he joined with Sim Van der Ryn, a professor of architecture at the University of California at Berkeley and the founder of the Ecological Design Institute, to write a brief paper, "GAIA 2000: A Computerized World Model (A Moral Equivalent to Star Wars)" that would serve as the basis to seek funding from the Pew Charitable Trusts for an international conference. McHarg and Van der Ryn are nothing less than prescient in their statement:

---

13. Ibid., 30.

14. John Radke, memorandum to Anne Spirn and Ian L. McHarg, July 15, 1987, 109. II.E.1.114. Ian L. McHarg Collection, The Architectural Archives, University of Pennsylvania. Subsequent citations reference McHarg Collection, AAUP.

15. Ibid.

16. Ian L. McHarg, letter to Dean Lee G. Copeland, September 23, 1987, 109.II.A.2.17. McHarg Collection, AAUP.

The most powerful instrument available to guide private and govern-mental policies as they affect national and planetary security would be a world model. . . . The more difficult task is to develop good predictive models of how the planetary environment works as a whole system—so that the consequences of warming effects resulting from hydrocar-bon pollution, the disruption of the ozone layer, the assault on global climate engendered by desertification and rain forest destruction—and of course nuclear war itself—can be scientifically understood and visu-ally communicated to decision makers and citizens.[17]

Spirn stated adamantly, "Ecological planning would not decline on my watch."[18] Within three years after assuming the chair, she proclaimed that the department's leadership "in the nation and the world . . . [could] be attributed to a particular curriculum and research program that was inter-disciplinary and action-oriented, based on the philosophy of environmen-tal stewardship, and to a series of teacher-practitioners who gave reality to those ideas through professional projects that became landmarks for the profession."[19] However, during the 1988–1990 academic years, certain modi-fications in the curriculum suggested a phasing down of the emphasis on human ecological planning or, at the very least, a dilution of its prominent position in the department.

A major change was the termination of the health program in human ecological planning after Setha Low left the university in 1988. Also dur-ing the 1988–1990 academic years, there was no longer a separate listing of courses for landscape architects and regional planners; all courses in the department were combined under one heading, "Landscape Architecture and Regional Planning." The 501 Studio (or "The Core," as it was now called) remained, as did an array of natural, physical, and social science courses. The first course specifically titled Geographic Information Systems was taught by Radke and covered "the topic of spatial analysis where both theory and application are explored."[20]

McHarg was scheduled to teach several courses, including L.R. 501, The

17. Ian L. McHarg and Sim Van der Ryn, "GAIA 2000: A Computerized World Model (A Moral Equivalent to Star Wars)," May 1987, 109.III.D.35. McHarg Collection, AAUP. This typed manuscript later became the essence of a proposal to the Pew Charitable Trusts dated January 1988 for an international conference "to consider a World Computerized World Ecological Inventory."

18. Anne Whiston Spirn, interview with the author, December 13, 2002.

19. Strong and Thomas, *The Book of the School*, 282.

20. "Graduate School of Fine Arts, 1988–1990," *University of Pennsylvania Bulletin* 86, no. 6 (1988): 57.

Common Core (taught in the fall semester); two modules of 501, Introduction to Ecological Planning and Design (fall semester) and Case Studies in Ecological Planning and Design (fall semester); and a new course that was added for the spring semester, Theory, with the objective "to produce a tentative theoretical basis for environmental planning and design. The method is to select from relevant existing theory of physical, biological and social science and combine these perceptions into a single statement."[21]

Notwithstanding the structure of the curriculum's course offerings, McHarg was continually striving to reinvigorate what he perceived as a loss of momentum in the ecologically based regional planning program. In a 1989 letter to John C. Keene (who was now chairman of the Department of City and Regional Planning and a strong supporter of McHarg's), McHarg writes, "I cannot assure [student] candidates that Pennsylvania offers a GIS based curriculum. I am totally convinced that providing such a curriculum could regalvanize Regional Planning."[22] And in a letter to Spirn later that year, McHarg writes, "I am strongly convinced that the recruitment of regional planners can be accomplished with a single move, to offer and provide a GIS based regional planning curriculum. . . . I would urge, with both passion and energy, that you, the faculty, Chairmen and Dean agree on such a policy as will produce a stronger Department, better able to survive and prosper in the future."[23]

One significant event transpired outside Penn. In 1990, McHarg was contacted by William Reilly, the administrator of the U.S. Environmental Protection Agency (EPA). Reilly had "exhumed [McHarg's] 1974 report ["Towards a Comprehensive Plan for Environmental Quality"] and asked whether the subject should be reexamined."[24] The answer, of course, was yes, and McHarg formed Expert Information Systems, a partnership with colleagues John Radke, Jon Berger, and Kathleen Wallace (another graduate of the regional planning program). Their ensuing report, "A Prototype Database for a National Ecological Inventory," was completed in 1992 with a grant from the EPA. But with the national election and the change of administration in Washington, "the timing of the release of their report in 1992 doomed its implementation."[25]

---

21. Ibid. It is interesting to note that in the course description, "environmental" is the modifying term, not "ecological," as one would have expected.

22. Ian L. McHarg, memorandum to Professor John Keene, June 14, 1989, 109.II.A.2.92. McHarg Collection, AAUP.

23. Ian L. McHarg, letter to Professor Anne Whiston Spirn, Chairman, October 6, 1989, 109.II.A.2.92. McHarg Collection, AAUP.

24. McHarg, *A Quest for Life*, 362.

25. Ian L. McHarg and Frederick R. Steiner, eds., *To Heal the Earth: Selected Writings of Ian L. McHarg* (Washington, D.C.: Island Press, 1998), 270.

McHarg's willingness to take on new challenges while remaining an integral member of the faculty was recognized when President George H. W. Bush presented him with the National Medal of Art in September 1990—the first landscape architect or planner to receive the award. At Penn, his value was recognized as well; McHarg received a letter from Dean Copeland that reads, "You are one of a kind and a giant in your field. You built this Department of Landscape Architecture and Regional Planning into the internationally-recognized program it is today and your continued affiliation will be an honor for the School."[26] In July 1991, McHarg became professor emeritus in the Graduate School of Fine Arts.

A list of the faculty in the Department of Landscape Architecture and Regional Planning during the 1988–1990 academic years, after McHarg had resigned as chairman, follows:[27]

Anne Whiston Spirn, AB, MLA, *professor of landscape architecture and regional planning, chairman, Department of Landscape Architecture and Regional Planning*

Sally Anderson, AB Geology, *lecturer*

Ignacio Bunster, BArch, MLA, *lecturer*

James Corner, BLA, MLA, *lecturer*

David DuTot, MLA, *lecturer*

Carol Franklin, MLA, *adjunct associate professor of landscape architecture*

Susan Rademacher Frey, BA, *lecturer*

Robert Giegengack, PhD, *professor of geology*

John Radke, PhD, *research assistant professor of regional planning*

Daniel Rose, PhD, *associate professor of landscape architecture and regional planning*

Leslie Sauer, BS, *adjunct associate professor of landscape architecture*

Sir Peter Shepheard, CBEBArch, *professor emeritus of landscape architecture and environmental design*

W. Gary Smith, BS, MLA, *adjunct assistant professor of landscape architecture*

David Stonehill, PhD, *adjunct professor of landscape architecture*

Nathan Sullivan, MLA, *lecturer*

James Thorne, PhD, *assistant professor of regional planning; assistant chair, Department of Landscape Architecture and Regional Planning*

Joachim Tourbier, MLA, *lecturer*

---

26. Lee Copeland, letter to Professor Ian L. McHarg, September 6, 1990, 109. II.A.2.24. McHarg Collection, AAUP.

27. "Graduate School of Fine Arts, 1988–1990," 62–63.

Anthony Walmsley, BArch, MCD, MLA, *assistant professor of landscape architecture*

As 1990 MARKED THE CENTENNIAL of the Graduate School of Fine Arts, Dean Copeland proclaimed that the school's mission for the future would "be concerned fundamentally with the quality of life, especially as it is affected by the beauty and usefulness of the built environment, and the continuing health and vitality of the natural environment."[28]

The *Catalogue* (previously known and referred to as the *Bulletin*) of the Graduate School of Fine Arts for the academic years 1991–1993 offers a revised pedagogical statement for the Department of Landscape Architecture and Regional Planning that reflects Dean Copeland's message and clearly prioritizes design in the curriculum. Again, the ecological planning foundation was not abandoned, but design was moving forward as a more engaging pursuit:

> Ecological **values** form the foundation of our curriculum and inform the **knowledge** of science and art our students master. **Design** expresses these values and applies this knowledge; it is a mode of thinking that integrates reflection and invention. Design, as a deliberate act, as both process and product, is at the heart of our curriculum. But values, knowledge, and design are nothing without **craft**—the means by which visions of the future landscape are communicated and realized. Our commitment to sustainability also demands the skills of **cultivation** required to maintain landscape change over time. (Bold in original)[29]

Upon Copeland's resignation, a search for a new dean was undertaken during 1991. In the hope of influencing the selection process, McHarg advocated that the university seek certain qualities in the new dean. A letter to Provost Michael Aiken reads, "It is probably true to say that both Holmes [Perkins] and Martin [Meyerson], among other qualifications, have displayed an extraordinary gift for discerning high promise among young people and perceiving unrecognized merit among older persons. . . . You hold the future of a proud and excellent school in your hands. You can deserve the praise for

---

28. *Graduate School of Fine Arts, 1991–1993*, University of Pennsylvania (n.d.), 1. Beginning with this publication, the citation format changes, as the university dropped the previous volume references for the *Bulletins*, and the publications have variously been referred to as "catalogues" and "publications." I cite these documents as simply *Graduate School of Fine Arts* with the appropriate date(s).

29. Ibid., 25.

its success, but you must bear the shame of its decline."[30] Patricia Conway was ultimately chosen and would serve as dean from 1991 to 1994.

During the 1991–1993 school years, regional planning was still a visible part of the department's curriculum, and the 501 Ecological Planning Studio and Modules were still intact, at least insofar as titled course offerings. But the content and its emphasis were markedly changed, causing McHarg to state the inevitable. A letter to Spirn reads, "It is true that I have stated to faculty and students alike that ecology has dramatically declined at Pennsylvania. This is neither an invention nor a discovery, but merely a statement of fact. . . . I have spent a lifetime helping to create this department. It should cause no surprise to learn of my distress at its dissolution."[31] By the 1993–1995 academic years, the doctorate program in the Department of City and Regional Planning listed as one of nine concentrations ecological planning and environmental design.[32] This was clearly another sign of the further scaling down of an emphasis on ecology in the Department of Landscape Architecture and Regional Planning.

A New Perception: Traditional Strengths and Process, 1994–2000

After Anne Whiston Spirn resigned as chair of the Department of Landscape Architecture and Regional Planning, C. Dana Tomlin, a faculty member and GIS expert, was appointed acting chair in 1993. Tomlin was responsible for completely revising the curriculum, the first such significant change in twenty years. However, the curriculum revisions—that now would be referred to as the "new curriculum"—eliminated what Spirn called the "powerful integrative core" of "tying the teaching of landscape architecture theory, method, and practice to three key concepts of geography, and environmental science and management."[33]

The "new curriculum" would place a greater emphasis on graphic design, archeology, history, and theory.[34] Modifications in the curriculum were on a fast track, and McHarg quickly communicated his disappoint-

---

30. Ian L. McHarg, letter to Dr. Michael Aiken, February 6, 1991, 109.II.A.2.88. McHarg Collection, AAUP.

31. Ian L. McHarg, letter to Professor Anne Whiston Spirn, November 11, 1992, 109. II.E.1.121. McHarg Collection, AAUP.

32. *Graduate School of Fine Arts, 1993–1995*, 35.

33. Anne Whiston Spirn, "Ian McHarg, Landscape Architecture, and Environmentalism: Ideas and Methods in Context," in *Environmentalism in Landscape Architecture*, ed. Michel Conan (Washington, D.C.: Dumbarton Oaks Research Library and Collection, 2000), 104.

34. *Landscape Architecture Prospectus, 1995–1996*, 2.

ment to Tomlin: "It is readily apparent that any reorganization of 501 [the studio] to correspond to a four course unit structure will seriously reduce content."[35]

One of the primary concerns was that the landscape architecture program's accreditation status could be in jeopardy. In December 1994, the Landscape Architecture Accreditation Board reviewed the department's efforts to reshape its curriculum. The board's report praises the department's "challenge and conventions of design and practice, for its incorporation of new and evolving theories of design and for its emphasis on first-hand observation and interpretation of both natural and cultural phenomena."[36]

John Dixon Hunt, a noted landscape architectural theorist and historian (but not a professional landscape architect), succeeded Tomlin as chair of the department in 1994 and immediately developed "plans to lead the Department, with its revised curriculum and its longstanding responsiveness to change, towards a fresh perspective of the scope and role of landscape architecture."[37] The department's pedagogical statement for the academic years 1995–1997 recognizes McHarg's "pioneering contributions to ecological planning and design" but finds it necessary to respond "to changes in the larger cultural and intellectual spheres, especially ideas of nature, creativity, landscape and environment."[38] This revision would be met by offering four types of courses: theory, workshop, studio, and elective. Thus, the "new curriculum" "was designed to draw upon the traditional strengths of landscape architecture at Penn and yet to connect with fresh ideas arising out of changing cultural and social needs on the one hand and a changing faculty on the other."[39]

As PART OF THE "NEW CURRICULUM," the regional planning program also went through a substantial modification and realignment. No longer stressing the theme of human ecological planning, the program became diffused and combined with other university offerings. The updated pedagogical statement drops references to ecological or human ecological planning, explaining the program this way: "The shared responsibility for this program is a direct reflection of its intent: to bring together in an academic setting all three of the major professional roles that students can expect to either assume or encounter in the practice of regional planning. Respec-

---

35. Ian L. McHarg, memorandum to Professor Dana Tomlin, January 26, 1994, 109. II.4.2.25. McHarg Collection, AAUP.

36. *Landscape Architecture Prospectus, 1995–1996*, 2.

37. Ibid.

38. *Graduate School of Fine Arts, 1995–1997*, 31.

39. *Landscape Architecture Prospectus, 1995–1996*, 15.

tively, the three major roles are those associated with environment, development, and management."[40] The program would now be built on three bases: (1) knowledge of natural systems, drawing on courses from the Department of Landscape Architecture and Regional Planning; (2) knowledge of social sciences, economics, and legal matters, drawing on courses from the Department of City and Regional Planning; and (3) knowledge of the business of real estate finance and development, drawing on courses from the Wharton School Real Estate Department.

A growing problem was that as grant money expired, McHarg and the graduate school attempted to retain affected faculty by arranging joint appointments with other schools and departments within the university (e.g., geology, biology, anthropology, public health, and city and regional planning). This system worked for a while, although it led to split loyalties and contention with other deans and left many faculty in a weak and untenable position relative to advancement. A number of faculty either left the department or retired.

Under the "new curriculum," the 501 Studio—specifically, the "Common Core" that had served as the foundation of the landscape architecture and regional planning programs—was refocused, but this time for only students in the landscape architecture program. For the 1995–1997 school years, the 501 Studio is described as follows: "This introductory studio exposes students to the basic principles and practices employed in landscape architectural design, with particular emphasis on the relationship between process and form and the development of visual and manual acuities."[41]

By the 1998–2000 academic years, the regional planning program was jointly "administered" by the Department of City and Regional Planning and the Department of Landscape Architecture and Regional Planning, with Keene from planning and Tomlin from landscape architecture as cochairs.

It was undisputable that the department had finally returned to its traditional roots, espousing the history, theory, and design components of landscape architecture. The curriculum in human ecological planning had been terminated.

In May 2000, James Corner was appointed chair of the department. He had been a student of McHarg's and received an MLA from Penn in 1986. Corner's direction of the landscape architecture curriculum would enhance and further the inclusion of ecology, pushing it in new, contemporary directions and embracing a focus on landscape ecology to depict spatial relationships. This next iteration of the curriculum, building on McHarg's

40. *Graduate School of Fine Arts, 1998–2000*, 41.
41. *Graduate School of Fine Arts, 1995–1997*, 33.

FIGURE 10.2. Anthony R. Tomazinis and John C. Keene,
professors emeriti, Department of City and Regional Planning,
University of Pennsylvania, April 8, 2006.
(The Architectural Archives, University of Pennsylvania.)

pedagogical legacy, would propel landscape architecture education at Penn
to a sustained level of prominence.

McHarg's Final Courses and Tribute, 1996–2000

As professor emeritus, McHarg taught an occasional course after 1994. He
resurrected Man and Environment, the course that in so many ways had
started it all more than three decades earlier. But this time, it was different.
Beginning in the 1996–1997 academic year (and continuing in 1997–1998),
the department offered LARP 765, Man and Environment, which engaged
the traditional McHarg issues: "the evolution of matter, life, and man, and
the attitudes of the major religions toward the environment and the eco-

logical view.["42] Yet this time, the students would not hear live lectures from invited guests, that superlative stream of intellectuals whom McHarg had brought to this forum, such as Lewis Mumford, Erich Fromm, and Margaret Mead. They would not watch the inflections of the speakers, the twists and turns that even luminaries go through when they make presentations. And they would not be able to ask questions, because this time the course content would be transmitted by the film *The House We Live In*, which McHarg had conceived, narrated, and hosted during 1960–1961.

For the 1995–1997 school years, McHarg taught a new course, LARP 744, Human Ecological Planning, which was offered through the Department of Landscape Architecture and Regional Planning and through the Department of City and Regional Planning as CPLN 530. The course was variably described as a "theory course"[43] and as the "Human Ecological Planning Method[,] which Professor McHarg invented, developed, and applied."[44] Beginning in the fall of 1999, Human Ecological Planning was no longer cross-listed as LARP 744, and it was exclusively offered by the Department of City and Regional Planning.

In the spring of 2000, CPLN 530, Human Ecological Planning, was McHarg's last course. Once again, McHarg stood before a packed room of students, lecturing, reminiscing, telling stories, cajoling, and sometimes offending. But he had not lost that "spark," and his mind, his recall, and his wit were as crisp as always. Time and age were beginning to show; he became ill that year and was not able to attend every class.

On April 20, 2000, in celebration of the thirtieth anniversary of Earth Day—a national event that he had helped organize—he was honored with a plaque in Dean's Alley in Meyerson Hall, the home of the Graduate School of Fine Arts.[45] The ceremony cited his accomplishments and his extraordinary legacy as a leader in integrating environmental principles into modern planning practice. Gary Hack, who had been appointed dean of the Graduate School of Fine Arts (now the School of Design) in 1996, gave the dedication for the plaque.

I recall that McHarg was obviously moved by the recognition. Slowly, he sipped champagne and began speaking in a soft, somewhat measured tone that was not his style. Suddenly, as if a breeze had blown in and pumped him up, he quickened his pace, and his voice modulated up to its familiar

42. *Landscape Architecture Prospectus, 1996–1997*, 24.

43. *Graduate School of Fine Arts, 1995–1997*, 33.

44. *Landscape Architecture Prospectus, 1998–1999*, 26.

45. By 2003, the Graduate School of Fine Arts would be renamed the School of Design, or simply PennDesign.

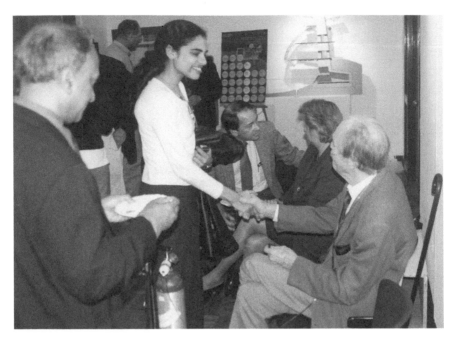

FIGURE 10.3. Reception for the dedication of the plaque honoring Ian McHarg
in Dean's Alley, School of Design, University of Pennsylvania, April 20, 2000.
Participants (from left to right): Alistair McHarg and Deepta Sateesh (standing in the
foreground); William Cohen, Eugenie Birch, and Ian McHarg (seated).
(Photograph by Carolee Kokola. William J. Cohen personal collection.)

pitch. He began to tell stories, which most of us had heard before, but one
can hear his stories over and over and still relish their humor, their serious
purpose, and their moral. That was his skill, and that was the listener's delight. This celebration would be the last time at Penn that McHarg would
be surrounded by those who knew, admired, and appreciated the full value
of his contributions and accomplishments.[46]

He traveled to Tokyo within the week to receive the Japan Prize, award-
ed by the Science and Technology Foundation of Japan. He had been selected in the category of City Planning for his contributions to the promotion
of peace and prosperity of mankind. It was his last honor.

Ian L. McHarg died on March 5, 2001.

---

46. An earlier version of this account appears in William J. Cohen, "Ian McHarg's Triumph," *Planning* 67, no. 5 (2001): 13.

11

A Retrospective Analysis of
the Ecological Planning Curriculum

C AN WE STAND BACK and view the past as a precursor to what we might wish to do in the future? The prognosis to design and implement educational curricula to enhance and promote the concepts contained in ecohumanism is really quite good. But before we embark on such a path, this chapter presents a critical review of the positives and negatives of an actual curriculum based on an ecohumanism approach.

After reviewing the development of the ecological and human ecological planning curriculum, what lessons are to be learned? For four decades, Ian McHarg continually strove to build a legacy around the interdisciplinary approach to planning education and practice. Chapters 6–10 recount shortcomings, disappointments, and even failures. However, these issues are far outweighed by this curriculum's success story—the transformed education of planners and designers who would then continue in the world of practice to make ecological planning operational. The obvious conclusion is that McHarg's Department of Landscape Architecture and Regional Planning unequivocally staked out a new pedagogical and practice direction between 1965 and 1979. So at this juncture, let us stand back and retrospectively assess the curriculum that McHarg firmly believed would be his legacy in environmental planning and education.

Beginning in 1951, under the guidance of Dean G. Holmes Perkins in the Graduate School of Fine Arts, the ties between architecture, city planning, and landscape architecture would be cemented, and the graduate programs would be encouraged to move in new inventive and interdisciplinary directions. When McHarg arrived at the University of Pennsylvania (Penn) in 1954, landscape architecture was part of the Department of Land and City Planning; Dean Perkins tasked him with establishing a separate Department of Landscape Architecture and developing a new curriculum.

By the mid-1960s, with the beginning of a regional planning program and the key addition of Nicholas Muhlenberg to the faculty, the ecological planning curriculum's foundation was set. The entire pedagogical underpinning in the training of regional planners and landscape architects would be based on the notions of what McHarg believed to be ecological (or environmental) determinism. McHarg put into place a curriculum that would challenge students in regional planning and landscape architecture to accept a new practice paradigm. However, one impediment that emerged was that regional planners found the human ecological planning emphasis to be more usable than did landscape architects.

By 1973, the ecological planning curriculum was transitioning into the human ecological planning curriculum, as social and cultural investigations began to assume a larger place in it, particularly through the incorporation of anthropology, ethnography, and medical anthropology into the department's course offerings. A substantial grant from the National Institute of Mental Health (NIMH) underwrote the hiring of new faculty who could adapt human ecology to regional planning and landscape architecture. During the 1973–1974 and 1976–1977 academic years, enrollments in the regional planning program peaked.

During the 1980s, things changed—inside the department and outside Penn—and McHarg's human ecological planning curriculum experienced a loss in momentum. After he retired as chairman of the department in 1985, the human ecological planning curriculum remained essentially intact but was modified to embrace a greater involvement with urban concerns and, in the 1990s, with a revived focus on landscape design.

The pendulum began to swing back toward the traditional roots of landscape architecture, with an increased concentration on history, theory, and design. Concomitant with this trend, the regional planning curriculum was realigned within the Department of City and Regional Planning and no longer was strictly based on human ecological planning. The move away from human ecological planning proceeded slowly at first, as design began to regain an importance in the curriculum in the early 1990s, precipitated by the need to maintain certification by the Landscape Architecture Accreditation Board. Finally, by 1994, a "new curriculum" was fashioned that for all intents and purposes saw the end of human ecological planning as a curriculum emphasis in the Graduate School of Fine Arts. An occasional course taught by McHarg—supported by Anthony Tomazinis, chairman of the Department of City and Regional Planning—from 1992 until the spring of 2000 provided the last vestige of human ecological planning instruction at Penn.

Why, then, the decline? How could a curriculum that had attained such stature with an outstanding interdisciplinary faculty, that had earned a reputation that was coveted by practitioners and academics alike, and that had attracted students from all over the world fall into disfavor? And how could the "inventive genius"—the master of it all—McHarg have fallen from grace? These questions frame the parameters of this chapter.

Clearly—and this point is important—the decline of the human ecological planning curriculum was not precipitated by any single cause or event. A number of factors were at play that were not mutually exclusive and became manifest in a variety of expressions, forms, and dimensions. These can broadly be identified to include (1) McHarg's persona, which exuded a mix of strong leadership, charisma, and an uncompromising attitude embracing an ecological imperative; (2) elements of the interdisciplinary curriculum itself, which experienced many ups and downs through its evolution; and (3) factors and events that occurred outside the university.

McHarg's Persona

McHarg was dynamic, difficult, demanding, brilliant, generous, loyal, and almost foolishly loving and emotional. Through the power of his personality, his presence, and his demeanor, he could inspire many and generate animosity in others. He was such a complex personality that he attracted either unfettered loyalty and admiration or antagonism and downright dislike from friends, colleagues, students, and practically anyone he encountered. Such a persona was at the crux of building the curriculum and eventually becoming a factor in its decline.

Four important aspects can be singled out in a retrospective assessment of McHarg's persona as it relates to his work as an educator and a practitioner of regional planning and landscape architecture.

One cannot avoid examining McHarg's personality when assessing the curriculum. After all, he was a curious combination of positive and negative attributes, and the outward expression of those attributes would rise and fall depending on the situation he was in and to whom he was relating.

Lenore Sagan remarked, "People were very attracted to him—his accent, his charisma—an aura that he perpetuated."[1] Yet Dan Rose remembered the other side of this man, which was on display when McHarg was giving a talk

---

1. Lenore Sagan, interview with the author, October 16, 2002.

in Chester County, Pennsylvania: "He could be extremely insulting, and he just delighted in going in and trashing people in the crowd, some of whom could be his allies."[2] David Wallace, McHarg's colleague and partner in the firm Wallace, McHarg, Roberts and Todd (WMRT), reflected: "Bright, articulate, and domineering, McHarg won most arguments by wearing his opponents down. Not an easy man to be a partner with, he could charm an audience and write like a dream."[3] Muhlenberg provided yet another insight: "McHarg was extraordinarily bright, sensitive, and absolutely trustworthy as a friend—his word was his bond."[4] It makes sense that McHarg's complex persona would be perceived in different ways of acceptance or rejection by the people that he dealt with. Such complexity is revealing and indicative of what sociologist Erving Goffman has noted: "When an individual appears before others[,] he will have many motives for trying to control the impression they receive of the situation."[5]

McHarg was known to be doctrinaire and uncompromising in his view of nature and his adherence to ecological determinism. You had to accept his philosophy; he would not tolerate anything less. He was not open to any reevaluation or reassessment of the philosophical foundation of ecological planning. In fact, this pivotal philosophical tenet would be the focus of his entire career.

McHarg's ecological determinism, first promulgated in the paper he presented at the 1966 Conservation Foundation conference, Future Environments of North America, and later elaborated in *Design with Nature* (1969), became his raison d'être of land use planning and design. One could argue that such a sole reliance was an intrinsic flaw, since no attention was given to existing and planned infrastructure or to social, economic, political, and legal considerations. McHarg had little interest in the economic and governmental institutional processes that influence and control land use planning: in fact, he rejected them. Perhaps this single-mindedness was his Achilles' heel. However, he took a keen interest in politics, forging relationships with President Lyndon Johnson and Lady Bird Johnson, Secretary of the Interior Stewart Udall, and founder of the World Wildlife Fund Russell Train, among others.

Furthermore, McHarg assumed that the rationality of ecological science should prevail in the irrational world of public land use decision making,

---

2. Dan Rose, interview with the author, January 14, 2003.

3. David A. Wallace, *Urban Planning/My Way: From Baltimore's Inner Harbor to Lower Manhattan and Beyond* (Chicago: Planners Press, 2004), xii.

4. Nicholas Muhlenberg, interview with the author, October 18, 2002.

5. Erving Goffman, *The Presentation of Self in Everyday Life* (New York: Anchor Books, 1959), 15.

where ingrained habits, cultural values, and preconceptions have much influence on final policy outcomes.

Frederick Steiner offered another view of McHarg's dogmatism. Originally a student in McHarg's program, where he received a master of regional planning (MRP) degree in 1977 and a doctorate in city and regional planning in 1986, Steiner would coordinate the 501 Studio after Jon Berger left the department in 1983.[6] Steiner's relationship with McHarg was important; he would become the key person to interpret and advance the McHargian construct of human ecological planning. He would also be McHarg's alter ego in the writing of his autobiography, *A Quest for Life*, as well as co-editor of McHarg's writings, *To Heal the Earth*, and later the editor of *The Essential Ian McHarg*. Steiner interpreted McHarg's intellectual posture this way: "Ian had gotten a fair amount of criticism for being an ecological determinist, or a physical determinist, and his reaction to that always was that he had had a lot of social science at Harvard and was not opposed to social science. He was simply trying to advocate for nature to have a more equal standing. He was frustrated until he found anthropology."[7]

However one comes out on this matter, McHarg's outward advocacy convinced many people that he was unbending, and if a significant number of people hold this perception of the man's persona, it must be acknowledged as a factor in forging his legacy in environmental planning and education.

Perhaps no teacher or administrator can fit the ideal. People bring strengths and weaknesses to each of these roles, and McHarg was no different. While Rose accused him of being "a terrible teacher," McHarg's genius, according to Berger, "was [his ability] to get people [the students] together and get them to work on a particular problem."[8] Nonetheless, the power of the curriculum could at times create problems, as Arthur Johnson recalled: "There were always frustrations, mid-semester meetings, and 'miniature revolts' from the students, who felt that there was too much to learn, too much intensity."[9] Despite his dynamism, McHarg was a confusing teacher. It could be surmised that because of his wide range of interests and thinking, he sent students off in many directions. This behavior was not entirely intentional, but it was not unavoidable.

The Department of Landscape Architecture and Regional Planning's administration under McHarg at times seemed to be on a seesaw. There

---

6. Ian L. McHarg, *A Quest for Life: An Autobiography* (New York: John Wiley and Sons, 1996), 226.

7. Frederick Steiner, interview with the author, February 19, 2003.

8. Dan Rose, interview with the author, January 16, 2003, and Jon Berger, interview with the author, November 27, 2002.

9. Arthur Johnson, interview with the author, December 3, 2002.

were constant budget issues related to the enrollment and the number of scholarships available, as Dean Perkins remembered: "McHarg always asked for more than we had available; I was always cutting his budget."[10]

Evidence suggests that McHarg was more committed to the advancement of his curriculum than to compliance with administrative pro forma. In 1969, as he was negotiating to hire E. Bruce MacDougall to advance the computer mapping and geographic information systems (GIS) capability of the department, McHarg ran afoul of the university's hierarchy by offering a higher salary than the university allowed for a starting assistant professor. In a reprimand to McHarg, Provost David Goddard writes, "You have no authority to determine university salaries. . . . I must make it abundantly clear that you may not make salary offers in the future without prior knowledge and approval of your Dean."[11]

McHarg also had to deal with a developing tension between the landscape architects and the regional planners. As Muhlenberg stated, "In the beginning [of the regional planning program], the landscape architects were jealous of the regional planners, who were getting all of the [scholarship] money."[12] One of the great administrative dilemmas that McHarg faced had to do with how the staff worked together. Robert Hanna observed, "The scientific faculty and professional faculty didn't interact a great deal. In the professional faculty, there was a difference of opinion and attitude towards it [the curriculum]."[13]

A number of viewpoints reflect McHarg's style as a leader and administrator in the department and how he related to the faculty and staff. One view was that McHarg wanted to be surrounded by only "yes men" and that he would not tolerate disagreement was fairly common—at least suggested, if not expressed outright. Again, the complexity of McHarg's persona—often displaying contradiction—plays out. Although he had little desire to allow criticism or opposition, he would give unsolicited praise and acknowledgment for contributions to the curriculum or a project.

Anne Whiston Spirn recalled, "Ian was a dictator at school, yet a great boss [at WMRT] who gave credit to all those who worked on a project."[14]

10. G. Holmes Perkins, interview with the author, October 15, 2002.

11. David R. Goddard, letter to Professor Ian L. McHarg, August 18, 1969, 109.II.E.1.42. Ian L. McHarg Collection, The Architectural Archives, University of Pennsylvania. Subsequent citations reference McHarg Collection, AAUP.

12. Muhlenberg, interview.

13. Robert Hanna, interview with the author, January 9, 2003.

14. Anne Whiston Spirn, interview with the author, December 13, 2002. Giving project credit was, and still is, unusual for consulting firms. Bibliographical listings in McHarg's *A Quest for Life* and Steiner's *The Essential Ian McHarg* attest to this recognition.

Johnson provided another dimension of McHarg's administrative and decision-making style: "He made most of the decisions. There was always an opportunity for input. The opportunity for serious input seemed to come one-on-one in that he listened to me more if I was talking to him directly. He was able to get the outcomes he wanted by talking with each of the people, more or less separately, and deflecting things in a way that seemed to fit with what he wanted to do."[15]

A noteworthy element of McHarg's educational philosophy was how he would intervene in selecting students to matriculate in the graduate program, even though—as Sagan remembered—"Dean Perkins always had to see every folder [the student application]; he wrote the letter of admission or rejection. . . . Everybody had to pass muster."[16] According to Muhlenberg, "Ian broke all the rules—he wanted students that he felt could be disciples rather than relying on test scores or grades."[17]

In a 1987 interview, McHarg recalled how he had entered Harvard through the "back door," to pursue graduate studies without even having a bachelor's degree. Many years later as department chairman, he made sure that "there was always a place, a backdoor entrance, for somebody who showed promise and conviction and commitment."[18]

One student who entered the regional planning program in an unconventional way was Peter K. O'Rourke, who held a bachelor of science (BS) in entomology and a master of science (MS) in applied ecology from the University of Delaware. In 1970, O'Rourke traveled to Philadelphia to meet with McHarg and find out about the program. O'Rourke's background impressed McHarg (which included high school teaching), since there was no student currently in the program with an academic background in entomology. McHarg told O'Rourke, "In life there are two ways to get into anything. There is a front door and a back door. The back door is just as good as the front door."[19] One student accepted into the program decided not to attend, so McHarg contacted O'Rourke and instructed him to enroll in the program—he was in through the back door.

In the Graduate School of Fine Arts *Bulletin* covering the 1982–1984 academic years, the Common Core, LARP 501, is described as "the foun-

15. Johnson, interview.

16. Sagan, interview.

17. Muhlenberg, interview.

18. Interview with McHarg by Marshall Ledger, "On Getting the Lay of the Land," *Pennsylvania Gazette* 85, no. 4 (1987): 34. See also 109.V.D.4.63.1. McHarg Collection, AAUP.

19. Peter K. O'Rourke, interview with the author, December 14, 2002. O'Rourke received an MRP from Penn in 1978.

dation for all subsequent instruction. It receives a large allocation of faculty and makes serious demands upon the students who participate. The objectives are original and challenging and the experience is unique."[20]

To a large degree, the 501 Studio would become emblematic of the totality of the educational experience that McHarg offered the students. After all, this was not an ordinary curriculum, and the master was not an ordinary man. As such, the students should be characteristic of the traditional disciple. Yet it was more complex than that. Muhlenberg focused on a deeper motivation: "There was an intent on Ian's part to produce the 'Renaissance man,' and it was successful to a degree, but it didn't work entirely."[21]

The Interdisciplinary Curriculum

A retrospective assessment of the interdisciplinary curriculum that McHarg championed in the Graduate School of Fine Arts, and as presented in previous chapters, brings to light certain pedagogical, methodological, and situational factors that can be judged as contributing to the decline of ecological planning at Penn. The ecological, and later the human ecological, planning curriculum was based on the incorporation of multidisciplinary natural and physical science knowledge that would ultimately embrace the social sciences. Throughout its evolution, the curriculum went through a number of modifications, reflecting the changing emphasis as McHarg described it as he moved from ecological to human ecological planning. The curriculum also experienced problems in providing all that it sought to offer, especially in the area of advancing GIS technology. Even though experimentation with course offerings was highly prized, certain methodological difficulties arose in the actual practice of human ecological planning. The primary difficulty was that the landscape architects were not successful in adapting human ecological planning methods to their site-specific designs. Finally, the possibility was suggested that human ecological planning in the curriculum had reached its apex and was no longer inviting or challenging as "intellectual discovery."

What follows is a summary of the factors that were directly related to various pedagogical and methodological challenges and difficulties that the

---

20. "Graduate School of Fine Arts, 1982–1984," *University of Pennsylvania Bulletin* 83, no. 1 (1982): 16.

21. Muhlenberg, interview. Educating the "Renaissance Man" was not an unheard-of aspiration. In an address on December 8, 1966, Robert C. Weaver, the secretary of the U.S. Department of Housing and Urban Development, called for a "new kind of urban generalist. . . . And it is the universities which must bear most of the burden of producing this new kind of Renaissance Man." Cited in Mel Scott, *American City Planning since 1890* (Berkeley: University of California Press, 1969), 637.

curriculum faced. These encompassed a host of situations, engagements, developments, and modifications presented in Part III.

One trend that becomes particularly noticeable when examining the *Bulletins* and later the *Catalogues* of the Graduate School of Fine Arts is that the curriculum, especially in the regional planning program, was in a constant state of flux. Course offerings changed almost yearly as new courses were presented and others were dropped. As Steiner noted, the curriculum "was adapting all the time; McHarg would come up with an idea that should be pursued."[22]

An important fluctuation involved the presentation of courses devoted to computer mapping, graphics, and GIS. The first course offering computer spatial analysis was given in 1969; it proceeded on an irregular basis and, at times, on a minimal level during much of the life of the curriculum. McHarg repeatedly attempted to improve the situation but was hindered by a lack of funding, equipment, and space.

This hiatus in course work regarding computer mapping and GIS existed from the time MacDougall left the department in 1974 until the 1981–1982 academic year. Even though several doctoral students were proficient in GIS (most notably Meir Gross and Lewis Hopkins) and could assist in providing a technical capability to the department, matriculating students did not receive any formal training until the 501 Studio was reorganized as the "Common Core" during the 1981–1984 school years. In light of the important role that GIS would ultimately perform in improving the efficiency and accuracy of assembling and analyzing natural resource base data and information, its fluctuation in and out of the curriculum during important years in the technology's development undoubtedly had a negative impact on the program.

If one could identify the single course that was the intellectual bedrock of the ecological planning curriculum, it would have to be Man and Environment. First presented by McHarg in the fall of 1959, before the curriculum had been structured around ecological planning, it was structured around lectures from visiting world-known scholars and thinkers in many disciplines and callings. In his autobiography, McHarg calls it "perhaps the most exciting course in the school, if not the university."[23] The uniqueness and dynamism of Man and Environment were truly masterstrokes, yet the course would eventually reach its apex.

Rose assessed the instrumental role of Man and Environment in the curriculum and provided another insight on influencing factors:

---

22. Steiner, interview.
23. McHarg, *A Quest for Life*, 175.

Ian was very proud of the fact that he could get Nobel Laureates to come and talk to the students at Penn. And he was also very proud of the fact that he had hundreds of people in the audience, not all of them drawn from [the Department of] City and Regional Planning and Landscape Architecture. That was a real showpiece for him. He never second-guessed the power of that at all. It was a powerful part of the curriculum after Earth Day, but by 1974, it was beginning to decline in popularity.[24]

Throughout its history, but especially during the period between 1974 and 1987, the curriculum witnessed significant faculty departures. Even though faculty turnover is not unexpected, the departures of five important faculty members—without replacement—were critical to the continued viability of the curriculum. Key events included the following:

- MacDougall's departure in 1974, and lack of replacement, left a void in the curriculum. No one was fully capable of providing a consistent level of instruction in computer-based spatial analysis and GIS during a time of accelerating enrollments and an advancing technology that would eventually revolutionize the hand-drawn overlay mapping of the ecological inventory, thus improving its efficiency and accuracy.
- In 1977, Yehudi Cohen, the cultural anthropologist who had been the principal intellectual precursor of human ecological planning— and, according to Steiner, "a great teacher; he was very special"— left the department and was not replaced, even though anthropologists Dan Rose and Setha Low were members of the faculty.[25]
- Narendra Juneja died suddenly in 1981. He was McHarg's "right-hand man," and as Hanna recalled, "Narendra was McHarg's 'magic marker'; he followed orders and did what McHarg wanted."[26] But Juneja's role should not be minimized. According to Carol Franklin, a friend and colleague in the department (and a former student of McHarg), "He organized color using matrices that were clearly expressive of complex sets of ideas and subtle interrelationships. His maps were beautiful, like works of art."[27] As Spirn said, "Narendra was the key, the glue that kept [the department] together."[28]

24. Dan Rose, interview with the author, January 14, 2003.
25. Steiner, interview.
26. Hanna, interview.
27. Ann L. Strong and George E. Thomas, *The Book of the School: The Graduate School of Fine Arts of the University of Pennsylvania* (Philadelphia: University of Pennsylvania, 1990), 230.
28. Spirn, interview.

- The realignment of Robert Giegengack and Arthur Johnson with the Geology Department also accounted for a significant loss in faculty expertise, since both had been highly respected and admired by the landscape architects and regional planners.
- The trinity that brought the human ecology perspective to the curriculum and became the principal faculty in human ecological planning included Jon Berger, Setha Low, and Dan Rose. The trinity began to break down when Berger left the department in 1983 and was not replaced. With his resignation, the curriculum lost its leading exponent of human ecological planning and the only person who actually was able to make human ecological planning operational as a method of land use planning.[29] Low, who headed the health program in human ecological planning, left the university by 1988 and was also not replaced. Her departure effectively ended this popular concentration in the curriculum. Rose continued teaching in the department until he retired in the late 1990s.

The resignations of Berger and Low had a profound impact on the continuance of the human ecological planning curriculum, particularly since they occurred during the time when the program was beginning to experience declining enrollments. Their departures simply hastened the declining status of the human ecological planning component, especially in the regional planning program.

One of the hallmarks of the regional planning program, as it advanced the use of ecological planning, was the relationship between the teaching of ideas and concepts in the department and the application of those ideas and concepts to practical situations in the "field laboratory"—McHarg's consulting firm, WMRT.

The firm provided a testing ground for theory and an employment base for graduate students as well as faculty. It also "kept [McHarg] current," according to Spirn, and "when he left, it was like a divorce."[30] In his autobiography, McHarg laments the severity of the loss that he felt when he resigned from the firm in 1979. However, his resignation just as severely lessened the vitality of the curriculum and must rank as an important critical factor in the program's decline. No longer would the department have

---

29. Berger's work with John W. Sinton, *Water, Earth, and Fire: Land Use and Environmental Planning in the New Jersey Pine Barrens* (Baltimore: Johns Hopkins University Press, 1985), ranks as an essential step forward in the advancement of McHarg's human ecological planning.

30. Spirn, interview.

such a dynamic and fulfilling outlet where McHarg, faculty, and students could work on actual planning and design projects.

There were methodological difficulties in applying human ecological planning concepts to landscape architecture, and as a result the kind of rapprochement that McHarg had hoped for between planning and design never developed. The regional planners were focusing their analysis on a large scale, and the landscape architects were engaged in site-specific design problems and challenges. The two approaches just could not synchronize under the rubric of human ecological planning as envisioned by McHarg and taught by Robert Hanna, Laurie Olin, and Setha Low.

However, Steiner provided an interesting insight on the frustrations that Low faced in the design studios, as she believed that the scale the landscape architects faced was different and more site-oriented than the broader perspective of the regional planners. Steiner's recalled that the students on the landscape architecture side "did get it" and that McHarg's influence on blending human ecological planning into design did get carried on—it was simply done in a "different representational style, using, for example, computers and photo montage to portray landscapes."[31]

When the 501 Studio became the Common Core of the landscape architecture and regional planning programs in the early 1980s, it was designed to be the pedagogical basis to educate the "Renaissance Man."

However, three crucial disciplines were absent from the *Workbook* that served as the teaching guide for each student. No law, economics, or design courses were taught (although design would be addressed in the 502 sequence and in other courses). This omission alone is indicative of a significant deficiency in the preparation and training of future planners. Additionally, Berger offered several critiques of the studio: (1) "501 was the backbone [of the curriculum], but there was never any focus"; (2) "nobody worked full time on the 501 Studio; it was a part-time endeavor"; and (3) "the rhetoric far surpassed the reality."[32]

A significant variable in the interdisciplinary approach of the entire curriculum had to do with presenting the social sciences in the 501 Studio. As the natural and physical sciences were well represented and integrated into the curriculum for landscape architects and regional planners, the primary emphasis of the social science component was on ethnographic history. It is highly place-specific, but the ethnographic element cannot be mapped in the manner of the layer-cake model. This obstacle in itself raises a question about how one portrays ethnographic data as qualitative information

---

31. Steiner, interview.
32. Berger, interview.

in an inventory process that quantifies an identification of constraints and limitations of natural and physical resources. Rose admitted that the overlay method was inadequate for mapping and representing social values and ethnographic data: "How do you map ethnicity to the land? It became a real challenge."[33] In the final analysis, as a Common Core, the 501 Studio did not fully measure up to what it could have or should have been.

Johnson raised one point that piqued my curiosity and opened a line of inquiry that I could not dismiss: the view that human ecological planning reached its limit and could no longer be characterized by "intellectual discovery." Johnson argued that one reason for the curriculum's decline was the stagnation of the intellectual development of human ecological planning: "How much further could Dan Rose take human ecological planning, and how much further could we take the analysis of the natural features of the landscape? How much further could we take them from where they were in 1985?"[34] According to Johnson, there was not much "intellectual discovery" left to be done, and "academic people live for the intellectual discovery; that's what drives their interest."[35]

When I presented this point to Low, she disagreed: "There was not that kind of limit. Art is more skeptical."[36] Her additional comments are worthy of consideration:

> There was further to go. Art was only looking at the science of it. What Ian hadn't gotten to, and he could have, was all of the [involvement] of conservancies, taxes, and all of the things that John Keene and Ann Strong had talked about, all could have been integrated. All of the regulations and institutions interacted within human ecological systems that Ian didn't include. All could have been integrated; there was a lot farther it could have gone. And the players were standing right there.[37]

Low highlighted another important pedagogical aspect of the curriculum that was omitted in the 501 Studio—namely, law and economics. She stressed that law, including regulations and associated institutional structures, was part of the "human" aspect of the curriculum; had the curriculum combined law with ethnography, it could have moved human ecological planning to "another step."[38]

---

33. Dan Rose, interview with the author, January 16, 2003.
34. Johnson, interview.
35. Ibid.
36. Setha Low, interview with the author, January 31, 2003.
37. Ibid.
38. Ibid.

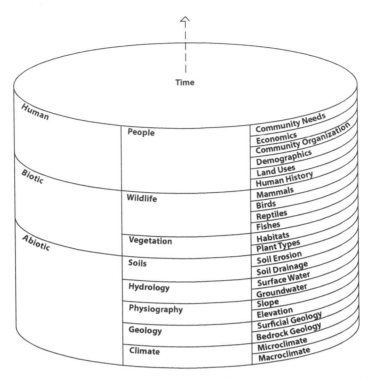

FIGURE 11.1. "Layer-cake" representation to incorporate human ecological planning, 2000. *(Frederick R. Steiner,* The Living Landscape: An Ecological Approach to Landscape Planning, *2nd ed. [New York: McGraw-Hill, 2000], 15.)*

Steiner takes one such "next step" in his 1991 book, *The Living Landscape.* He uses McHarg's ecological planning model and branches out into "a linear yet iterative process" that includes identifying issues, setting goals, undertaking an "inventory and analysis of the biophysical and sociocultural environments," doing suitability analysis, determining future options and developing "a plan for the landscape," continuing "public participation and community education," performing design, and taking into account implementation and administrative considerations.[39] Steiner's contribution sustains Low's position regarding the continued potential for "intellectual discovery." Continuing on such a path just might lay a foundation for a revival of human ecological planning as the basis of a reconstructed or completely new curriculum.

The 2000 edition of Steiner's *The Living Landscape* presents what could be called the second generation of the noted layer cake that would be the

---

39. Frederick Steiner, *The Living Landscape: An Ecological Approach to Landscape Planning* (New York: McGraw-Hill, 1991), x.

essential first step in determining land suitability prior to planning and design by focusing on natural resource and biophysical elements. Steiner expands the original layer-cake model to incorporate the human or cultural element, as depicted in Figure 11.1. This approach could also secure the role and function of human ecological planning.

WHEN MCHARG STEPPED DOWN as chairman of the Department of Landscape Architecture and Regional Planning, the change was immediate and noticeable. The creative tension that developed between McHarg and the new chair, Anne Whiston Spirn, was mostly due to McHarg's emotional response to his new role. "When he stepped down," remembered Muhlenberg, "we had two chairmen—Anne Spirn, who was trying to get famous in her own right, and Ian, who refused to stop coming [to the department]. So there were 'two departments,' Anne's and Ian's. Anne had the budget, so she got the students. It was an emotional split."[40]

With McHarg no longer in the leadership position that he had occupied for more than thirty years yet still on the faculty, the competition for loyalties spawned what Muhlenberg described as "a two-headed hydra," an untenable situation that would affect the viability of the McHarg-structured curriculum.

One of the reasons for the program's decline, according to Steiner, was that "it was misnamed 'Regional Planning.' I think that Ian—partially because of [Lewis] Mumford's influence and partially because it was the right term at the time— chose 'Regional Planning.' But if the program had been named 'Environmental Planning' or 'Ecological Planning,' I think it would have had stronger legs [to stand on]."[41] Steiner believed that "if it had been named what it was, it would have continued to attract [students]."[42] In large measure, as discussed previously, McHarg thought of ecological planning as regional planning. The two go hand in hand; one really cannot be separated from the other. It should be noted that regional planning declined across the nation in the 1980s and that there was no consensus on how, why, or at what scale "regional" should be applied. At Penn, the Department of City and Regional Planning became more city-focused. By 1993, the Regional Science Department, originally started by Walter Isard in 1956, had been eliminated.

SEVERAL SITUATIONS OCCURRED within the Graduate School of Fine Arts that influenced the overall graduate educational experience. First, the de-

---

40. Muhlenberg, interview.
41. Steiner, interview.
42. Ibid.

partment's Center for Ecological Research in Planning and Design was phased out during the 1980–1981 academic year, folded into a new research focus that would serve the entire graduate school. Second, by the 1982–1984 school years, two new joint degree programs were offered with civil engineering and with the law school. While these joint educational ventures would open new graduate study prospects, they also indicate a diffused curriculum that was searching for new levels of relevancy.

The most profound pedagogical change that had occurred by the mid-1990s was the overhauling of the landscape architecture and regional planning programs in the department. After Spirn stepped down as the department chair in 1993, a new pedagogical philosophy attempted to revitalize the design aspects of landscape architecture. Even though regional planning was still offered in the department, primary efforts focused on moving the department's emphasis from the dominant natural science orientation toward a "new curriculum" of history, theory, and design.

By 1994, this "new curriculum" was firmly in place—and human ecological planning no longer existed. The department's pedagogical statement for the 1993–1995 school years proclaims, "Ecological values form the foundation of our curriculum and inform the knowledge of art and science our students master."[43] The next catalogue, covering the 1995–1997 school years, omits any reference to human ecological planning and lists the "new" regional planning program established in 1993 as jointly administered with the Department of City and Regional Planning.

Under chair John Dixon Hunt, the "new curriculum" would be concerned with "connections between design, nature, culture and history."[44] The Department of Landscape Architecture and Regional Planning would finally return to its traditional roots.

External Factors beyond the University

As an approach and method specifically based on an environmental context for planning, ecological planning came to be accepted by many practitioners. These planners identified with the philosophy and practical utility of adapting ecological planning to address real-world problems, principally as it involved an understanding of the limits and constraints inherent in natural resources. For environmental—or ecological—planners, this would become the indispensable first step in a land use planning process. As human ecological planning developed, a method was sought to incorporate an analysis

---

43. *Graduate School of Fine Arts*, 1993–1995, 29.
44. *Graduate School of Fine Arts*, 1995–1997, 31.

and understanding of individual and group values as they represented a unique set of community predilections in the use of land and environmental resources in the planning process.

Many planners who spread the word and practiced the method had been McHarg's students and, in a manner of speaking, thought of themselves as disciples. Robert Yaro (the president of the Regional Plan Association in New York) first heard McHarg speak in 1973 at the Harvard School of Design and would later write the foreword to *To Heal the Earth*. In that essay, Yaro states unequivocally, "McHarg had a particularly profound impact on the nearly two generations of students he taught at the University of Pennsylvania. Many of them became leaders in the design professions as government officials, consultants, and teachers, and most have put Ian's environmental dogma and practices to work in their own careers."[45]

But the reality in spreading the word of the master was not just predicated on emotional and professional allegiance; it was directly correlated to job opportunities—and there were many. The federal government's new national legislation to protect air, water, and land resources trickled down to the state and local levels. Pioneering environmental and growth management laws at all levels of government contained new regulatory procedures and requirements that created an increased demand for planners. Consequently, these changes would also benefit the regional planning curriculum at Penn. Student enrollments increased in the early 1970s, peaked by the middle of the decade, and leveled off until 1980. During the peak period in the 1970s, the number of students matriculating in regional planning surpassed that in landscape architecture. Yet after the 1979–1980 school year, enrollments in the regional planning program dropped precipitously.

Two important factors significantly influenced the decline of the human ecological planning curriculum. These happened outside the department and even beyond the university. The most dramatic direct impact was that because of certain exigencies, enrollments declined, and therefore the program declined.

In the 1980s, priorities toward the environment were redirected from the strong advocacy contained in federal legislation from the previous decade. Less government oversight was replaced with a greater emphasis on private-sector initiatives.

Consequently, the job market for regional planners in many areas of the country began to shrink. This issue became especially noticeable in two major federal grant programs that had created numerous job opportunities

---

45. Robert D. Yaro, foreword to *To Heal the Earth: Selected Writings of Ian L. McHarg*, ed. Ian L. McHarg and Frederick R. Steiner (Washington, D.C.: Island Press, 1998), x.

for planners at the state and local levels, the 701 comprehensive community planning program and the 208 area-wide water and waste water planning program. In essence, this combination of changing federal environmental planning priorities and fewer potential jobs made regional planning less attractive as a course of study to prepare for a career than it had been.

Directly related to declining enrollments was the financial impact on the crucial revenue source for the department and the Graduate School of Fine Arts. Budget and faculty numbers had to be reduced, each of which affected the viability of continuing as in the past. Moreover, scholarships to support graduate study in regional planning were curtailed as well.

As a corollary to declining enrollments, student attitudes changed, moving away from environmental advocacy and toward career security. This trend was perhaps largely due to the private sector's becoming more self-monitoring, with less government regulation. People once thought of as "environmental villains" were recast as environmental partners. Students deciding on career paths picked up on these societal permutations. A job in regional planning that had a strong foundation in human ecological planning just did not offer the promise of a demanding and financially satisfying career.

IN SUMMARY, MULTIPLE FACTORS can be said to have been responsible for the decline of the human ecological planning curriculum. Moreover, it is difficult to conclude whether any one factor, or a selected few factors, determined the decline. Rather, taken in their entirety, the identified personal factors, the evolution of the interdisciplinary curriculum, and the external factors were woven together in a situational and circumstantial tapestry that accounted for the decline of the curriculum.

I have traced the evolution from the beginning to the end of the ecological and human ecological planning curriculum at Penn, and despite everything else, there was an intuitive association between the success of the curriculum—McHarg's vision and genius, the extraordinary multidisciplinary faculty, and the attraction of bright and inquisitive students—and changing, external societal conditions.

I conjecture the possibility of one additional variable—being at the right place at the right time. While such an assertion may be more appropriate in a treatise devoted to metaphysical entanglements, it is nonetheless a real variable. It may not be provable, but then it cannot be fully denied.

So when all the analysis and intellectualizing are finished, only one way may remain to account for the rise and fall of McHarg's curriculum at Penn. I simply conclude that Ian McHarg and the human ecological planning curriculum in the Department of Landscape Architecture and Regional Planning at the University of Pennsylvania were at the right time and at the right place.

PART IV

FUTURE PROSPECTS FOR EDUCATION IN THE ECOLOGICAL CULTURE

12

Ecological Planning

Ian McHarg's Legacy in Practice and Education

OW DO WE MEASURE the impact that one person has on the professional lives of others or, for that matter, on the practice of the planning and design professions coupled with the education of those who embark on such careers? In looking at the career and contributions of Ian McHarg, it is not difficult to find an answer. Inspired by the ecohumanism of Lewis Mumford, McHarg was truly a unique contributor to the practice of landscape architecture and regional planning, the progenitor of using ecological planning in practice and a master at directing the design and implementation of a renowned interdisciplinary graduate curriculum. So, then, can we take these elements of a life's work and see how they mold a legacy in planning and design education that can be applicable to a pedagogical direction for the ecological culture?

Finding an answer has not only merit but also urgency if we are to usher in a relevant refashioning of an educational curriculum for planners and designers in the future. The goal is to simply inculcate ecohumanism in the educational process.

McHarg's Legacy in Practice

It is accurate to say an "environmental conscience" was proffered by landscape architects and planners before McHarg. However, it took the publication of McHarg's *Design with Nature* in 1969 and the celebration of the first Earth Day in 1970 to mobilize that consciousness to a new level in the

FIGURE **12.1.** Gathering of prominent landscape architects of the late twentieth
century, Arizona State University, 1993. Participants standing from left to right:
James Corner, Sally Schaumann, Michael Laurie, Carol Franklin, Metro Vroom,
Laurie Olin, Ian McHarg, and Hamid Shirvani; participants seated from left to right:
Forster Ndubisi, Elizabeth Meyer, and Mark Johnson.
(Photograph courtesy of Frederick R. Steiner. William J. Cohen personal collection.)

practice of planning and design.[1] As discussed in Chapter 5, the release of
Design with Nature was the threshold occurrence that propelled McHarg into
the national and international limelight. Over the years, he received many
honors and accolades, which, if taken alone, would secure his legacy in the
practice of landscape architecture and regional planning. For example, a
1973 *Time* magazine article cites McHarg as the "nation's leading 'ecological
planner.'"[2] And writing more than three decades later, the eminent landscape planner Carl Steinitz proclaims *Design with Nature* to be "probably the
single most influential book in the field of landscape planning."[3]

At a 1993 international symposium exploring the topic "Landscape Ar-

1. See, for example, E. Lynn Miller, "Environmental Conscience before Ian McHarg,"
Landscape Architecture 89, no. 11 (1999): 58–62.

2. *Time*, October 1, 1973, 98. Also mentioned by *Time* as "Earth Movers and Shakers"
are conservationist Laurance S. Rockefeller and developer James W. Rouse.

3. Carl Steinitz, "Landscape Planning: A History of Influential Ideas," *Landscape Architecture* 99, no. 2 (2009): 80.

chitecture: Ecology and Design and Planning," co-hosted by Arizona State University and the Center for American Places, McHarg was one of the principal participants. In George Thompson and Frederick Steiner's introduction to the published papers from that symposium, they acknowledge that "McHarg reminded us—and taught a new generation of scholars, students, and practitioners—that landscape architecture involves art and science, nature and culture, city and region, the public good as well as a need to make a living."[4] Moreover, they point out, *"Design with Nature* laid the groundwork for the emergence of geographic information systems (GIS) and environmental impact assessments, which today dominate practice in both academic and public-policy spheres."[5]

Noted landscape architect and environmental planner Lawrence Halprin's 1996 review of McHarg's autobiography notes that he has "influenced large numbers of people throughout the world and some people in very high places to think in terms of a global morality. For Ian and his students, this is not only a philosophy[;] it is a way of life which he has taught and put into practice."[6]

His greatest international acclaim occurred in 2000, when he was presented with the Japan Prize in the category of city planning for his contribution to the promotion of peace and prosperity of humankind. It should be pointed out that McHarg's ecological planning method was not unfamiliar to the Japanese. Beginning in 1971, Harvey Shapiro, who had studied with McHarg at Penn, began hosting McHarg's many visits to Japan. Writing some years later, Shapiro observes that "interest in the McHargian approach to ecological planning . . . is growing. In its ultimate form, as it continues to be adapted to the complex conditions of Japan, McHarg's method will likely become part of a new approach to landscape architecture that is distinctly Japanese, shaped by the Japanese themselves to fit their own particular needs."[7]

HOWEVER ONE JUDGES the role McHarg had in the evolution of planning and design practice in the twentieth century, one point remains uppermost, as Steiner succinctly states: "Ian McHarg opened a new way for us to see the

---

4. George E. Thompson and Frederick R. Steiner, eds., introduction to *Ecological Design and Planning* (New York: John Wiley and Sons, 1997), 3.

5. Ibid.

6. Lawrence Halprin, "Book Review of *A Quest for Life: An Autobiography*," *Quarterly Review of Landscape Architecture and Garden Design Publications, Land Books* (Winter 1996): 8.

7. Harvey A. Shapiro, "What Happened to the Introduction of the McHargian Method to Japan," *Landscape Architecture* 69 (November 1979): 577.

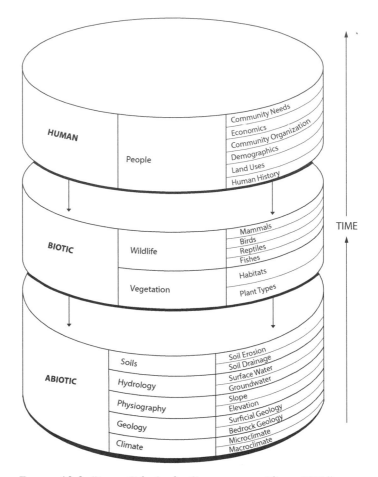

FIGURE 12.2. "Layer Cake in the Contemporary Idiom, 2019."
(Drawing by Charles F. Fifer.)

world. His approach for interpreting the play between natural and cultural systems has become the dominant visualization technology of our time and provides a roadmap for applying ecological information to how we interpret, plan, and shape our surroundings."[8] This assessment is corroborated by planning professor Timothy Beatley and Kristy Manning: "Ian McHarg's *Design with Nature* was particularly influential in changing the way we approach planning and development. . . . The emergence of Geographic Information Systems (GIS) technology, moreover, has enabled McHargian-style environmental analysis to become a commonplace methodological step

---

8. Frederick Steiner, "Healing the Earth: The Relevance of Ian McHarg's Work for the Future," *Human Ecology Review* 23, no. 2 (2017): 75.

in undertaking almost any form of local planning."[9] The use of GIS therefore has become a valuable tool to link databases to maps.

Many people are unaware that the iconic image of the layer cake, which so ably depicted the ecological inventory, has become the modeled representation of information and data that have been advanced by GIS. In its computer-layered approach to arranging data, the layer cake no longer has to be drawn exclusively by hand. Faster and more accurate portrayals of the natural and human resource elements offer a stronger foundation for planning and design. McHarg understood for many years the value that GIS would have for the ecological inventory. As he writes, "The availability of GIS makes inventories a necessity."[10] A third generation of the layer cake captures schematically the use of GIS to undertake the ecological inventory, as shown in Figure 12.2.

AN OVERVIEW of the many consulting projects he was engaged in through his initial association with David Wallace from 1963 to 1964 and then with the firm Wallace, McHarg, Roberts and Todd (WMRT) from 1965 to 1980 offers a sense of the magnitude of his contribution to practice. Although McHarg was directly or indirectly involved in many projects, the following list includes those that I believe to be the most essential to advancing the practice of ecological and human ecological planning:[11]

> 1964. *Plan for the Valleys* (Greenspring and Worthington Valleys, Baltimore County, Maryland): The first incorporation of ecology in a professional planning study
>
> 1965. *Comprehensive Highway Route Selection Method* (Princeton, New Jersey): The first use of environmental and social information to determine a highway route that would be the genesis of the environmental impact statement (EIS)
>
> 1967. *Potomac River Basin:* The first use of the "layer cake" as the basis

---

9. Timothy Beatley and Kristy Manning, *The Ecology of Place: Planning for Environment, Economy, and Community* (Washington, D.C.: Island Press, 1997), 86.

10. Ian L. McHarg, "Natural Factors in Planning," in *To Heal the Earth: Selected Writings of Ian L. McHarg*, ed. Ian L. McHarg and Frederick R. Steiner (Washington, D.C.: Island Press, 1998), 82.

11. The first complete bibliography of McHarg's work, including publications, reports, projects, visual media, profiles, and interviews, appears in his autobiography, *A Quest for Life* (New York: John Wiley and Sons, 1996), 387–405. Frederick Steiner would later expand this listing, which he titles a "Complete Bibliography," to include many publications by others who had written about McHarg and his impact on practice and education. See Frederick R. Steiner, *The Essential Ian McHarg: Writings on Design and Nature* (Washington, D.C.: Island Press, 2006), 131–156.

for the ecological inventory leading to the development of the ecological method

1969. *Twin Cities Region of Minnesota* (Minneapolis–St. Paul): The first comprehensive regional ecological assessment and plan

1973. *Comprehensive Plan for Environmental Quality* (with the American Institute of Planners): The first formal proposal for a national ecological inventory and the establishment of a national ecological laboratory as a precursor to the "Prototype Data Base for a National Ecological Inventory" (1992) using computer capability

1974. *Woodlands New Community* (Houston, Texas): The first determination of land use patterns and densities for a major development based on geohydrological properties

1974. *Medford Township* (New Jersey): The first use of ecologically based performance standards for new development

1975. *Pardisan* (Tehran, Iran): The first planned ecologically based international environmental park, promoting education, recreation, and conservation

A POIGNANT WAY TO GAUGE McHarg's recognition of practice professionals is to look to those whom McHarg himself identified as having accepted and practiced planning and design consistent with ecological principles. In his autobiography, he claims that "Lawrence Halprin, Roberto Burle Marx, A. E. Bye, and Andropogon [are] the most significant landscape architectural designers of the late twentieth century."[12] Moreover, McHarg identifies three landscape architecture and planning firms that had established reputations for infusing ecological planning and design principles in their work: Andropogon, Coe Lee Robinson Roesch, and Jones and Jones.

Established in Philadelphia in 1975, Andropogon Associates comprised principals Carol Levy Franklin, Colin Franklin, Rolf Sauer, and Leslie Jones Sauer. They had an inseparable bond with McHarg and a devotion to the advancement of ecology in the design and restoration of landscapes. Simply stated, their philosophy "shifts the focus from what cannot be done to what can and should be done to develop successful solutions" by bringing "an ecological perspective to problem solving in landscape architecture."[13]

---

12. McHarg, *A Quest for Life*, 125.

13. From an undated firm brochure, *Andropogon Associates, Ltd.* The name *Andropogon* is a common American field grass that is a self-sustaining cover for the gradual return of native forest material and from an ecological viewpoint is a remarkable plant that adapts to stress and change in the landscape.

In McHarg's view, "These landscape architects possess unchallenged primacy in ecological design and restoration."[14] Carol Franklin and Colin Franklin each received a master of landscape architecture (MLA) degree in McHarg's program, and in 1972 and 1982, respectively, were invited to serve as adjunct faculty at Penn; Rolf Sauer earned a master of architecture degree at Penn and joined McHarg's faculty in 1982; Leslie Jones Sauer also became a member of McHarg's faculty, beginning in 1972. In addition to their academic responsibilities, the Andropogon principals also had worked at WMRT.

Coe Lee Robinson Roesch, founded in 1984, had a valuable relationship with McHarg. Jon Coe became an adjunct associate professor in McHarg's department in 1982; Gary Lee and Rodney Robinson each received an MLA at Penn and were appointed adjunct faculty members in 1985; Geoffrey Roesch earned an MLA in McHarg's program in 1977. Most of their firm's work involved planning and designing zoos and aquariums, a unique endeavor that allowed them to raise awareness about wildlife and their supporting habitats.

Grant Jones, a co-founder of Jones and Jones in Seattle, Washington (who holds an MLA from Harvard School of Design), has incorporated ecological design in a wide range of projects for more than three decades. He expressed an unqualified portrayal of McHarg's influence: "The age chose him because he had the largest measure of capacity and desire to break the silence about what we could see was happening to the Earth. He was lifted by a swelling but largely unheard tide. What should interest architects and landscape architects, urban designers and planners is that it was one of them who publicly sounded the alarm, not a scientist or politician."[15]

McHarg's impact on the practice of ecological planning and design has been acknowledged by former students, faculty colleagues, and others working in these professions. In the last published interview with McHarg, landscape architect Laurie Olin proclaims, "Ian's contribution to design and ecology has been enormous. . . . He got much of the world to view the

---

14. Ian McHarg, "Ecology and Design," in *To Heal the Earth: Selected Writings of Ian L. McHarg,* ed. Ian L. McHarg and Frederick R. Steiner (Washington, D.C.: Island Press, 1998), 198.

15. This quotation is from an unpublished manuscript by Grant Jones, "*Design with Nature*: Retrospective Review, 25 Years Later," 2. Although undated, it can be assumed to have been written in 1994. Jones sent it to McHarg, who gave me a copy on May 31, 2000. It may also be found in 109.II.A.4.20. Ian L. McHarg Collection, The Architectural Archives, University of Pennsylvania. Subsequent citations reference McHarg Collection, AAUP.

earth through ecological glasses. A lot of current environmental legislation and methodology is a direct result of Ian's work."[16] James Corner, another of McHarg's successors as chair of the Department of Landscape Architecture and Regional Planning, provides an important perspective: "Too many followers of McHarg simply adopted a methodology for practice, and while most shared his ecological ethics and viewpoint, they failed to grasp the larger conceptual, innovative, and artistic dimensions of what still lies in the potential of ecological concepts."[17] Leslie Jones Sauer recalls that at a surprise seventy-fifth birthday party, virtually all the speakers, including former students and colleagues, described the impact McHarg's teachings had had on them personally: "Every speech was about how he changed their life. Everything they were doing was because of him."[18]

McHarg's Legacy in Education

Since he wished the ecological planning curriculum at Penn to be his lasting legacy, it is fair to ask whether other factors or variables can be identified as securing McHarg's legacy in education.[19] In this regard, three factors can be pinpointed: (1) McHarg's insistence on inculcating the world view at any level of education, (2) parameters to establish a university that would be structured from the beginning to embrace an interdisciplinary pedagogical approach to education, and (3) the distribution of faculty at a wide range of colleges and universities who have either studied with McHarg at Penn or who have been inspired by McHarg to promote or advance ecological planning and design in their own curricula.

IN THE AUTUMN OF 1989, McHarg traveled to Portugal at the invitation of E. Lynn Miller, professor emeritus of landscape architecture at Pennsylvania State University, and Sidónio Pardal, professor of landscape architecture at the Technical University of Lisbon. For six days, Miller and Pardal conducted extensive interviews with McHarg that touched on every aspect of his work.

---

16. Laurie Olin, quoted in Ken Shulman, "The Gospel according to Ian McHarg," *Metropolis* 20, no. 1 (2000): 88–89.

17. James Corner, "The McHarg Event: An Unfinished Project," in *Ian McHarg Conversations with Students: Dwelling in Nature*, ed. Lynn Margulis, James Corner, and Brian Hawthorne (New York: Princeton Architectural Press, 2007), 98–99.

18. Leslie Jones Sauer, quoted in Karen Auerbach, "His Work Continues, Naturally," *Philadelphia Inquirer*, April 20, 1997, B1, B6.

19. At the University of Pennsylvania, the McHarg Professorship Fund was initiated in 1983 through a grant from McHarg's friend George Mitchell. In addition, two student awards have been established as memorials to McHarg's legacy: the McHarg Scholarship and the McHarg Prize.

These interviews were later published with this introduction from Miller: "What effect did he have on education? It was not instant conversion. Most schools started edging toward an ecological approach in the early 70's as the students, who had been mesmerized by Ian in the 60's, began to enter academia and re-examine the way in which landscape architectural design was being taught. . . . By the 1980's McHarg's ecological approach or some variation of it had succeeded in becoming a key part of most landscape architectural programs."[20]

One such academic program that McHarg had a direct role in seeing established and accredited was at Temple University. In 1988, John Collins (who had received an MLA at Harvard University) was appointed chair of the newly formed Department of Landscape Architecture and Horticulture located at Temple's campus in Ambler, Pennsylvania. Collins had been influenced by McHarg's work and had served as a lecturer in Penn's Department of Landscape Architecture and Regional Planning in the early 1970s. In the autumn of 1989, Collins asked McHarg to be the first speaker of "what I hope will be a major lecture series."[21] By 1991, as the Temple department was in the process of applying for accreditation, McHarg transmitted an unqualified position of support to the chair of the Landscape Architecture Accreditation Board: "Professor Collins taught here [at Penn] both offering studios and courses in plants and design. I am familiar with his excellent professional work, and his prize winning accomplishments. . . . [A] very high proportion of his faculty are Penn graduates with whom I am thoroughly familiar. . . . Last year I gave an address at Temple and reviewed the work of the students. I was very impressed. . . . I would rate Temple very high on the scale and recommend that you award unconditional accreditation."[22]

FOR MCHARG, "the ecological view is really the world view. . . . If I had my way, this would become central to the curriculum at every single level of education: kindergarten, lower school, upper school, college, and university."[23] Such a curriculum must also be interdisciplinary—an indispensable McHargian emphasis—stressing "every single human activity.

---

20. E. Lynn Miller and Sidónio Pardal, *The Classic McHarg: An Interview* (Lisbon, Portugal: CESUR, Technical University of Lisbon, 1992), 10–11.

21. John F. Collins, letter to Professor Ian L. McHarg, April 18, 1989, 109.II.A.4.20. McHarg Collection, AAUP.

22. Ian L. McHarg, letter to Thomas Nieman, January 30, 1991, 109.II.A.2.117. McHarg Collection, AAUP.

23. Ian McHarg, "Teaching the Ecological World View," in *Design Outlaws on the Ecological Frontier*, ed. Chris Zelov and Phil Cousineau, 5th ed. (New York: Knossus Publishing, 1997), 310.

. . . The result should be a people, in a place, who understand about natural processes which comprise the environment."[24]

As an adjunct to McHarg's views on education, Thomas Berry, a cultural historian and ecotheologian, has developed a curriculum framework under the rubric "The American College in the Ecological Age." In identifying "human education [as] part of the larger evolutionary process," Berry outlines the content of six courses that would aim to move higher education away from the scientific-technological structure that pervades current curricula. Berry's notions are compatible with McHarg's approach to education and could be blended with an ecological planning and design curriculum.[25] Both of these views share a strong compatibility with Mumford's ecohumanism.

IN THE EARLY 1980s, a unique and not generally known experience opened for McHarg. In the winter of 1984, he traveled to Woodlands, Texas, and joined developer George Mitchell to help celebrate the tenth anniversary of the new community that had been planned by WMRT. Mitchell had an interest in establishing a university campus in the new town and asked McHarg for his advice. In 1982, Mitchell had facilitated the creation of the Houston Area Research Center that became a consortium of the University of Texas, Rice University, Texas A&M University, and the University of Houston engaged in basic, applied, and policy research. What transpired is not documented in McHarg's autobiography but has been uncovered in McHarg's papers in Penn's Architectural Archives. This discovery shows McHarg's thinking on the establishment of an institution of higher learning—from scratch. In 1984, McHarg advised Mitchell "that it would be easier to create a nationally prestigious college than to try to work through the Texas legislature and the university apparatus to create a distinguished university." The masterstroke of his advice was to "identify some twenty distinguished scientists and scholars comprising the range of disciplines required." Specifically, they would include older (around sixty-five years of age) deans, chairs, and terminate professors who, because of university rules (at that time), must resign. "If wisely selected," he continued, "this would provide a faculty with national distinction immediately." This "senior faculty" would then select a "junior faculty" from their most recent doctoral graduates. McHarg believed that "the attraction for the senior faculty would be the challenge of creating a top rank institution,

---

24. Ibid.
25. See Thomas Berry, *The Dream of the Earth* (San Francisco: Sierra Club Books, 1988; repr. 2006), 89–108.

the freedom from the established bureaucracies which inhibit all colleges and universities, and the commitment to excellence." The cycle would be complete, since "the senior faculty should be engaged in the design of graduate and professional curricula from which to create a university."[26] Almost five years would pass before McHarg had another opportunity to recapitulate his advice to Mitchell. This time, Dr. David Gottlieb, director of Institutional Development of the Woodlands Corporation, made contact. He stated that Mitchell was interested in exploring the possibility of establishing a technical college and that McHarg's "thinking on this issue would be very helpful."[27]

McHarg responded with an amplification of his previous comments and added, "Clearly, reductionism has been very beneficial, but it would appear as if interdisciplinary research and models, indeed a more holistic view, is a plausible objective for the next great advance in education. So [faculty] candidates should be committed to major innovation in education, to multidisciplinary research and teaching, in the advancement of a holistic view."[28] McHarg's proposal to establish a college of eminence provides a unique prospect and creative model for the future of higher education. Interestingly, McHarg did not have an earned doctorate himself, yet he had received several honorary doctorates over the years from Amherst College (1970), Lewis and Clark College (1970), Bates College (1978), and Heriot-Watt University in Edinburgh (1998).[29]

THE INCORPORATION OF ECOLOGY into the regional planning and landscape architecture curriculum at Penn alone is sufficient to secure McHarg's legacy in higher education. However, the one variable that gives McHarg's contribution a unique twist is that his influence and impact reached far beyond the academic walls of Penn.

It has been recounted earlier that Penn's Department of Landscape Architecture and Regional Planning attracted not only an international but also an exceptionally smart student body. Students who had had their undergraduate preparation in the social sciences and humanities, physical

---

26. Ian L. McHarg, letter to George Mitchell, December 3, 1984, 109.II.A.2.64. McHarg Collection, AAUP.

27. David Gottlieb, letter to Professor Ian McHarg, September 20, 1988, 109.II.A.2.130. McHarg Collection, AAUP.

28. Ian L. McHarg, letter to David Gottlieb, January 3, 1989, 109.II.A.2.130. McHarg Collection, AAUP.

29. See Frederick Steiner, "Plan with Nature: The Legacy of Ian McHarg," in *Regional Planning in America: Practice and Prospect*, ed. Ethan Seltzer and Armando Carbonell (Cambridge, Mass.: Lincoln Institute of Land Policy, 2011), 25.

and natural sciences, design and fine arts all made their way to McHarg's department to do graduate study in landscape architecture or regional planning, each discipline amply fusing with a pedagogy based on ecology. It is no small consequence that many of the graduates—over three decades—would eventually enter the world of the academy and be the catalysts to establish or perpetuate the McHargian approach to planning and design.[30]

Among the acknowledged accomplishments of McHarg's legacy is the simple fact that his work at Penn influenced so many other academic institutions to adopt an ecological perspective in their educational curricula. The word was spread, principally through former Penn students and faculty colleagues in the Department of Landscape Architecture and Regional Planning but also by many others who were inspired by McHarg's emphasis on ecology as an indispensable intellectual and pragmatic foundation for the education of planners and designers. As these former students, colleagues, and followers of the McHargian approach began to assume teaching and administrative positions in colleges and universities, they confirmed and perpetuated his legacy in education.

A listing of all universities and colleges—in America and beyond—that have directly experienced a McHargian influence in the development of their curricula under the general rubric of environmental, landscape, or ecological planning would be quite extensive. Therefore, a sampling of a number of universities that have been instrumental in adapting ecology or ecological planning in their curricula, whether it be in graduate programs emphasizing landscape architecture, regional planning, or environmental studies, includes College of the Atlantic, Conway School of Landscape Design, Dresden University of Technology (Germany), Harvard University, Massachusetts Institute of Technology, North Carolina State University, Oberlin College, Osaka University of the Arts (Japan), Pennsylvania State University, Rhode Island School of Design, Temple University, Texas A&M University, University of California at Berkeley, University of Georgia, University of Illinois at Urbana-Champaign, University of Massachusetts, University of Oklahoma, University of Texas at Austin, University of Toronto (Canada), University of Virginia, University of Washington, Uni-

---

30. Many of the graduates of McHarg's department earned either an MLA or an MRP and therefore had to matriculate in another department (either at Penn or elsewhere) to earn a doctorate. For example, at Penn, the Department of City and Regional Planning granted the doctorate with a concentration in ecological planning and environmental design that closely corroborated McHarg's curriculum.

versity of Western Australia, Wageningen University (The Netherlands), Washington State University, and York University (Canada).

AT THE UNIVERSITY OF PENNSYLVANIA, McHarg's legacy has received special recognition. In the summer of 2017, the School of Design established the Ian L. McHarg Center for Urbanism and Ecology, an interdisciplinary research center focused on developing practical and innovative ways of improving the quality of life in places most vulnerable to the effects of climate change. The center will be officially launched in conjunction with an international symposium to be held at Penn in June 2019 to honor the fiftieth anniversary of the publication of *Design with Nature*.[31]

Future Educational Prospects for Ecological Planning

It is safe to say that the focus on ecology in evolving curricula in landscape architecture, landscape planning, city and regional planning, and environmental studies programs at many universities and colleges has at last become a reality that many educators have embraced. Ignacio Bunster-Ossa, one of McHarg's students and a principal in his former consulting firm, holds that "from a physical standpoint, regional planning, urban design, architecture, and landscape architecture are the principal world-building disciplines."[32] He continues that we need "a comprehensive, fluid, and hybridized approach to education and practice," which clearly means that ecology is more than just an environmental relationship.[33] Blending and combining—the traditional interdisciplinary approach—are the two necessary ingredients for the future prospects of educating planners and designers who will really make a difference.

The current emphasis in practice and in education to advance sustainability as a critical awareness and achievable goal as we plan, design, and build our places of habitation gives the infusion of ecology in such efforts additional legitimacy. So, what do we do, and where do we go from here in structuring a curriculum, especially at the graduate level, to bring ecologi-

---

31. The initial leadership of the McHarg Center includes Frederick R. Steiner, dean of the School of Design, and Richard Weller, chairman of the Department of Landscape Architecture, serving as co-executive directors. Billy Fleming serves as the Wilks family director.

32. Ignacio Bunster-Ossa, *Reconsidering Ian McHarg: The Future of Urban Ecology* (Chicago: American Planning Association, 2014), 86.

33. Ibid., 87.

cal planning and design into the forefront? But perhaps more specifically, what does the future hold for a curriculum based on the ecohumanism of Mumford as passed on to McHarg?

McHarg was the pioneer, and his insightful work at Penn has indeed set the ground rules. This legacy became very evident at the Shire Conference held at the University of Oregon on July 16–19, 1998. At that conference, a group of distinguished scholars and practitioners came together to explore, examine, and set a future course for ecologically based design and planning curricula. The comprehensive account of the findings and results of the Shire Conference became a collection of papers that was published in 2002 under the title *Ecology and Design: Frameworks for Learning*. The eighteen chapters that compose *Ecology and Design* give us ample evidence and guidance for future educational prospects.

McHarg's influence and importance was cited and acknowledged in almost every aspect that the conference addressed: the indispensability of integrating ecology in planning and design curricula, the creation of an interdisciplinary approach to planning and design in graduate education, the understanding of cultural or human ecology as a companion to understanding natural systems ecology, the value of the studio as an empirical learning experience, and the identification of an ethical obligation that we have to Earth and to ourselves.

The inquiring reader or interested academic should consult *Ecology and Design* for the myriad details of curriculum development that were presented at the Shire Conference. However, I have synthesized the key themes that emerged from that conference to provide a general understanding of how, at that time, the academic community was recommending platforms for the future education of planners and designers. McHarg's prescience is clear.

The following guidelines are exactly that. The suggestion is that, from them, specific courses (whether core, module, studio, required, or elective) that would essentially frame the structure of a graduate curriculum in ecological planning might be developed:[34]

1. The curriculum must be interdisciplinary, with an ability to promote dialogue among natural science, social science, and humanities specializations. This trait will include branching out to incorpo-

---

34. Bart R. Johnson and Kristina Hill, eds., *Ecology and Design: Frameworks for Learning* (Washington, D.C.: Island Press, 2002), 2–6, 146–147. The volume includes significant overlap, and at times repetition, since each chapter has a different set of authors. For simplification, I cite only the pages that include illustrative reference material, rather than the author and the topic of each chapter.

rate new "ecological subdivisions," including conservation biology, landscape ecology, restoration ecology, and ecosystem management. Effectuating the interdisciplinary approach is in the tradition of the McHargian layer-cake ecological inventory.

2. It will emphasize an understanding of "place" as a recognition of the interdependence of culture (including the built environment) and ecosystems. This focus would be consistent with what McHarg evolved as human ecological planning and would promote the understanding of how people relate to place and adapt their immediate environment to fit their needs.[35]

3. It will provide an exposure to environmental ethics that could include a historical iteration of changing human and societal attitudes over time. For example, Aldo Leopold's dictum to change humans' attitude toward the land from conquerors to members of a land community provides an essential linkage to how we should approach planning and design. Likewise, McHarg's insistence on accepting nothing less than an ecological imperative offers a philosophical and practical basis to plan, design, and build. Each of these perspectives, as well as others, needs to be embodied as part of the educational experience.

4. It will be called studio, research workshop, or lab. Each of these terms implies that a valuable learning format for the planning profession involves formulating practical solutions that can be applied in addressing local and regional issues. The emphasis will be on field trips, site visits, and case study examinations, each providing an empirical application of knowledge.[36]

5. It will require students to fine-tune or perfect their oral and written communication as well as visual presentation skills. An understanding of conflict resolution will also play a role in this guideline.

6. Its linkage of academic preparation to practice will become the functional capstone to make planning education valuable and worthwhile.[37]

McHARG'S LEGACY PRESENTS a new challenge to planners and designers as we move to face the urban and regional growth and redevelopment possibilities of the twenty-first century. His lasting legacy—and that of Mumford as well—is that he established the foundation that we can now build on. Our

---

35. Ibid., 306, 399–400.
36. Ibid., 20–21, 406, 415–416.
37. Ibid., 473–491.

path forward needs to recognize that in planning, designing, and building cities and regions, the traditional guideposts of order, form, sense of place, and beauty should not be replaced by computer techniques and tools that could, if overemphasized, become surrogates to human imagination and creativity. So the essence of the challenge to city and regional planners and landscape architects will be to strike out in new yet compatible directions. One such direction—or new synthesis—offers substantial promise to ensure that the fundamental precepts of ecology will remain the soul of planning and designing.

Beginning with a fusion of ecological planning and landscape ecology, current trends are firming up the connections between planning and design. As ecology has stressed the relationship or interaction of humans with the living and nonliving environment, landscape ecology "addresses the interaction of living and nonliving components on a landscape scale."[38] Richard Weller, chair of the Department of Landscape Architecture at Penn, has expressed the importance of this connection: "What is meant by landscape cannot be considered unless one works through what is meant by ecology, and it is perhaps there that we find a new conceptual imagining of landscape, one which landscape urbanist sensibilities apprehend as a hybridization of natural and cultural systems on a globally interconnected scale."[39] These "landscape urbanist sensibilities," according to Steiner, "blur the boundaries between the disciplines traditionally involved in the design and planning of the urban built environment: architecture, landscape architecture, planning, civil engineering, law, historic preservation and real estate."[40] Whatever this new direction is called—landscape ecology, urban ecology, or landscape ecological urbanism—it is a current move to genuinely transform the education of landscape architects and planners to holistically combine an understanding of people, places, and environment in future education. The challenge is not to rely on maintaining strict and separate disciplinary roles but to fully incorporate that interdisciplinary amalgam that educates the person for the future. This, then, will pave the way to develop a curriculum based on ecohumanism as a new and forward vision for the education of planners and designers.

---

38. Anna M. Hersperger, "Landscape Ecology and Its Potential Application to Planning," *Journal of Planning Literature* 9, no. 1 (1994): 16.

39. Richard Weller, "An Art of Instrumentality: Thinking through Landscape Urbanism," in *The Landscape Urbanism Reader*, ed. Charles Waldheim (New York: Princeton Architectural Press, 2006), 73.

40. Frederick R. Steiner, "Living Urban Landscapes," in *On Landscape Urbanism: Center 14, Center for American Architecture and Design*, ed. Dean J. Almy (Austin: University of Texas, 2007), 248.

13

A Future for Ecohumanism
and the Ecological Culture

From Technology to Education

IN APRIL 1968, a group of thirty individuals from ten countries gathered in the Accademia dei Lincei in Rome to discuss the present and future predicament of humans. Out of this meeting—which included scientists, educators, economists, humanists, industrialists, and public officials—came the establishment of the Club of Rome. Its mission was "to foster understanding of the varied but interdependent components—economic, political, natural, and social—that make up the global system in which we all live."[1] Club members stressed that new policy initiatives and actions were needed since "the major problems facing mankind are of such complexity and are so interrelated that traditional institutions and policies are no longer able to cope with them, nor even come to grips with their full content."[2] The focus on the "predicament of mankind" was directed at "poverty in the midst of plenty; deregulation of the environment; loss of faith in institutions; uncontrolled urban spread; insecurity of employment; alienation of youth; rejection of traditional values; and inflation and other monetary disruptions."[3] The first report for the Club of Rome, titled *The Limits to Growth*, was widely hailed as a major breakthrough in assessing global

1. William Watts, foreword to *The Limits to Growth: A Report for the Club of Rome's Project on the Predicament of Mankind*, by Donella H. Meadows, Dennis L. Meadows, Jørgen Randers, and William W. Behrens III (New York: Universe Books, 1972), 9.

2. Ibid, 9–10.

3. Ibid., 10.

issues, although it also had its critics and deniers, especially economists. One recommendation in the report would indeed challenge the nations of the world: to reflect on a new realization that "the quantitative restraints of the world environment and of the tragic consequences of overshoot is essential to the initiation of new forms of thinking that will lead to a fundamental revision of human behavior and, by implication, of the entire fabric of present-day society."[4]

On the fiftieth anniversary of the founding of the Club of Rome, a new report was issued, this time with contributions from thirty-six of its members. With an arresting title beginning with *Come On!*, the latest assessment of the "predicament of mankind" provides up-to-date analysis of the unsustainability of current trends and a recognition of outdated philosophies by proclaiming that "extreme free-market thinking is at the root of the damage humanity is inflicting on the planet."[5] Even more directly, the report addresses eighteen categories, or "basic principles of a new narrative," that include, among others, alternative development strategies, decentralized energy, sustainable agriculture, regenerative cities, climate action, new economic logic, measuring well-being versus gross domestic product (GDP), and education for a sustainable civilization. The urgency in pursuing new directions is directly tied to the report's warning that "humanity is racing with catastrophe. Total system collapse is a real possibility. The evidence of human impact on the planet is undeniable."[6] If anything, the pioneering work of the Club of Rome has laid the foundation for an awareness of and a justification to create a future that will aggressively promote ecohumanism as the essential building block to usher in an ecological culture.

IN 1973, the year after *The Limits to Growth* appeared, Lewis Mumford traveled to Rome to attend a conference convened by a group of international futurists who were concerned with the growing expansion and acceleration of the role of technology in the twentieth century. The Rome Special World Conference on Futures Research focused on discussions and research on alternatives for the world to specifically address human needs. Mumford was invited to address the conference on the subject of technics and human culture, and his foresight provides a suitable beginning for this

---

4. Donella H. Meadows, Dennis L. Meadows, Jørgen Randers, and William W. Behrens III, *The Limits to Growth: A Report for the Club of Rome's Project on the Predicament of Mankind* (New York: Universe Books, 1972), 190.

5. Ernst Ulrich von Weizsäcker and Anders Wijkman, *Come On! Capitalism, Short-Termism, Population and the Destruction of the Planet—a Report to the Club of Rome* (New York: Springer, 2018), 72.

6. Ibid., 101.

final chapter. He concentrated his remarks (later published) on weaving together those themes that had occupied his many years of contemplation and writing—the relationship of technological progress to social change and human development.

He struck a somewhat optimistic note when he proclaimed, "A more organic life-pattern has begun to take possession of our minds, and is laying the foundations for a conception of technology that will do justice to all the dimensions of life, past, present, and possible."[7] Mumford argued that we must "turn to the human organism for self-cultivation and spontaneous expression [to] enjoy the genuine advantages offered by a resourceful technology without allowing ourselves to be imprisoned within the system itself."[8]

I would like to think—and it is strictly conjecture—that Mumford had perhaps a flickering notion that a new mode of thinking and acting would actually happen, perhaps not in his lifetime but certainly in ours. And his remarks at that Rome conference embraced the best of his ecohumanism and established the critical guidepost for the emergence of the ecological culture.

The New *Normal Science* for Technology in the Ecological Culture

The shift from a complete reliance on the technological culture to embracing, incorporating, and promoting the ecological culture is happening right now. This means that all of us—you and I—are currently living in a time of transition toward a Second Enlightenment as the guiding philosophical beacon to the ecological culture. It is important to recognize that this shift does not mean that we need to abandon or minimize the myriad advancements and achievements of the technological culture that have improved the human condition (e.g., in medicine and science). Rather, the emerging ecological culture provides a new thrust and emphasis that singularly relies on the inculcation of ecohumanism in our daily lives; in our planning, designing, and building of communities; in our future technological innovations; and in our educational system.

AT THE CRUX of moving from the technological culture to an ecological culture is how receptive—and adaptable—an economic system based on a free-market capitalistic paradigm will be. Our entrenched American eco-

---

7. Lewis Mumford, "Technics and Human Culture," in *Human Futures: Needs, Societies, Technologies*, The Rome World Special Conference on Futures Research 1973 (Guildford, UK: IPC Science and Technology Press, 1974), 60.

8. Ibid., 62.

nomic system has become a secure venue as it has evolved from the early Enlightenment thinkers and philosophers. Such values as rugged individualism, the dominance of economics that catapults supply and demand, price and profit as the foundation for growth and progress, and the sacrosanct position of private-property rights have not been challenged. Second Enlightenment thinking does not propose that revolutionary overthrow is a realistic option. However, calculated modifications and refinements are.

If I suggest that all economic theory is based not on art or science but on a social-belief ideology, purposed to justify, protect, and sustain the status quo, why should we even think about modifications or refinements? Well, to begin, we find that there is an undying conviction of the supremacy of the market on which to stake our destiny. Milton Friedman, who received a Nobel Prize in 1976, is perhaps the best spokesman for the Chicago School of Economics that promotes the association of a free market with political freedom, the classic American system. Several years ago, he was interviewed about his views. Friedman maintained, "Ecological values can find their natural space in the market, like any other consumer demand. The problems of the environment, like any other problem, can be resolved through price mechanisms, through transactions between producer and consumer, each with his own interests."[9] The fatal flaw in this assertion is that "each with his own interests" does not account for the "interests" of the community and even the planet. The indictment is even stronger when we think about current realities—the profound impacts that communities, regions, and entire continents are experiencing due to climate change coupled with the exponential growth in the world's population.

The ecological culture must have as one of its central values not a neoclassical economic system but a *network system* that places the highest priority on individual, community, and global needs. Daniel Wahl, a consultant, educator, and activist, argues, "On a crowded planet with failing ecosystems we have to learn that out-competing others while destroying the planetary life-support systems is not an evolutionary success strategy. Win-lose games in the long run turn into lose-lose games."[10] Such an assertion is not without recognition by those economists who are more attuned to understanding the relationship between economics and the environment, so there is hope that, if this view is acknowledged, a free-market economic system could promote prosperity without growth. Herman E. Daly, a for-

---

9. Milton Friedman, interview on February 6, 1991, published in Carla Ravaioli, *Economists and the Environment*, trans. Richard Bates (London: Zed Books, 1995), 32.

10. Daniel Christian Wahl, *Designing Regenerative Cultures* (Axminster, UK: Triarchy Press, 2016), 212.

mer senior economist in the environmental department of the World Bank, distinguishes between growth and development: "A growth economy gets bigger, a developing economy gets better."[11] His emphasis is on sustainability: "A sustained steady-state economy does not grow but is free to develop. It is not in any way static, as you might think, but forces us to think of the effects of changes of scale and think in terms of a scale that is ecologically sustainable."[12] Wahl carries the point further when he distinguishes between an *extractive* economy and a *regenerative* economy: "An extractive economy depletes diverse forms of capital in the system and damages the long-term viability, vitality and health of the whole system. A regenerative economy, on the other hand, does more than simply sustain the status quo by refraining from further depletion. It optimizes the whole system rather than maximizing privileged parts."[13]

If we can make a conscious infusion of ecohumanism as a refinement of neoclassical economic theory and practice, we can stand at the threshold of a new form of economics for an ecological culture. Our survival as a species may depend on it.

THE PRINCIPLE OF "THE SURVIVAL OF THE FITTEST" has a rather different meaning than is commonly understood. Charles Darwin's analyses were drawn from extensive observations of how living things interact, relate, grow, and die. What he concluded is that the fittest organisms that are best able to adapt themselves to their environment survive. This biological reality needs to be placed in the context of how we will move from a technological culture to the ecological culture. More and more, the current emphasis on the advancement of technology, still reliant on Enlightenment values, is slowly giving way to a new and irrefutable fact: that our natural resources—and for that matter, all Earth functions—are comingled in an intricate system. This recognition has its basis in what scientist and futurist James Lovelock first described as the *Gaia hypothesis* (now theory): Earth functions as a self-regulating system—it is a living planet. Therefore, "life and its environment are so closely coupled that evolution concerns Gaia, not the organisms or the environment taken separately."[14] This belief, then, becomes our starting point.

An example of how the current technological culture is being altered

---

11. Herman E. Daly, interview on February 16, 1991, published in Ravaioli, *Economists and the Environment*, 59.
12. Ibid.
13. Wahl, *Designing Regenerative Cultures*, 238.
14. James Lovelock, *The Ages of Gaia: A Biography of Our Living Earth* (New York: W. W. Norton, 1988), 19.

and giving way to the ecological culture can be found in the concept of *bio-mimicry*. In 2005, biologist Janine Benyus founded the Biomimicry Institute, whose mission is to nurture and grow a global community of people who are learning from, emulating, and conserving life's genius to create a healthier, more sustainable planet by promoting innovation inspired by nature that has been evolving for billions of years. Specifically, biomimicry allows nature to be the model for new technological inventions by understanding "what works in the natural world, and more important, what lasts."[15] In such a "biometric world," according to Benyus, "we would manufacture the way animals and plants do, using sun and simple compounds to produce totally biodegradable fibers, ceramics, plastics, and chemicals. . . . To find new drugs or crops, we would consult animals and insects that have used plants for millions of years to keep themselves healthy and nourished."[16] Indeed, biomimicry can be a key factor in the new technology that inevitably must be a part of the ecological culture.

Another aspect of technology for the ecological culture involves the contrasting notions of *eco-efficiency* and *eco-effectiveness*, as distinguished by architect William McDonough and chemist Michael Braungart. Simply put, they argue for eco-effectiveness, or doing more with less. The key is that new products should be specifically designed to be reused into new and perhaps different products. This approach furthers the practice of recycling in a manner that will allow products and materials to have an extended life with a planned capability to be reused.[17]

The ultimate test for the survival of the fittest will be how successful the dominant human species will become in advancing a new normal science for the ecological culture. In the realm of technology, the trends, very much influenced by Mumford's ecohumanism, must have the guiding mantra of alternative energy systems, renewable or regenerative systems, and eco-design.

In a historic perspective, planning—whether it is called city, urban, regional, or metropolitan planning—has focused on a common denominator, the community. Moreover, the community has been the subject of planning from two perspectives: as an administrative entity or as a social entity. As a practice, often the two have comingled, and planning has become a process and a substantive engagement. The engagement of planning has

---

15. Janine M. Benyus, *Biomimicry: Innovation Inspired by Nature* (New York: William Morrow, 1997), 3.

16. Ibid., 2–3.

17. See William McDonough and Michael Braungart, *Cradle to Cradle: Re-making the Way We Make Things* (New York: Farrar, Straus and Giroux, North Star Press, 2002).

been directed to address or ameliorate existing community problems and deficiencies on the one hand and to project an optimal future condition or achievable reality on the other. The role of planning has more recently become one of necessity, with new challenges being confronted, including the continuing revitalization of existing communities, the achievement of sustainable communities, and the need to adapt or become resilient to respond to the effects of global and community changes in the natural environment.

THE RISE OF CITY PLANNING as a profession is generally attributed to the World's Columbian Exposition held in Chicago in 1893. Architect and planner Daniel Burnham (1846–1912) became the central figure to direct the visioning, planning, designing, and building of what would become America's quintessential demonstration of architectural, planning, and landscape design excellence as well as modern technological superiority. Burnham's 1909 *Plan of Chicago* secured his role as the "father" of American city planning. The Columbian Exposition (also called the 1893 World's Fair) and the *Plan of Chicago* were planned, designed, and executed to represent a grand scale, and Burnham is often quoted for his famous call-to-arms for the then-burgeoning profession of city planning: "Make no little plans, for they have no magic to stir men's blood and probably themselves will not be realized." But read the rest of what he says: "Make big plans; aim high in hope and work, remembering that a noble, logical diagram once recorded will never die, but long after we are gone will be a living thing, asserting itself with ever-growing insistency."[18] In a rather adroit way, Burnham describes a process of city planning that would firmly establish itself as a planning tradition in thought and action.

But Burnham went beyond planning and designing—he directed and orchestrated the building and construction phase as well. His career represented the complete antithesis to the greatest fear that all planners have—that their plans will be painstakingly researched and beautifully composed but will meet their inglorious fate by sitting on the shelf, never to be implemented.

As time passed, an interesting irony emerged from Burnham's work, identified notably by Mumford. Mumford criticizes the grandeur of baroque planning as "an imperious contempt for human needs" that historically had "no concern for the neighborhood as an integral unit, no regard for family housing, no sufficient conception of the ordering of business and industry themselves as a necessary part of any larger achievement of urban

---

18. Charles Moore, *Daniel Burnham Architect, Planner of Cities*, vol. 2 (Boston: Houghton Mifflin, 1921), 147.

order."[19] And yet, he continues, "there was a measure of deep human insight in Daniel Burnham's famous observation" to "'make no little plans,' for they have no power to stir men's minds [*sic*]."[20]

Burnham is representative of a long line of planning visionaries that also includes Ebenezer Howard, Patrick Geddes, Benton MacKaye, Frederick Law Olmsted, and Mumford, according to planning professor Michael Brooks. He provides a composite view of what it means to have "vision," including "involving as many individuals and groups as possible in the process of dreaming about what might be . . . focusing on all dimensions of the quality of life in our communities . . . dealing creatively and effectively with equity issues . . . [and] having a strong and compelling conception of the good community."[21]

The concept and the emergence of the visionary become essential underpinnings to inculcate ecohumanism in planning for the ecological culture, since it will transcend the typical technician role that has encompassed much contemporary planning in America. Are there visionaries who can fulfill the true mission of planning and secure a future viability for planning to guide community development? Can the charge to "make no little plans" have relevance today and tomorrow? And, finally, will we see a legitimate and essential connection made between planning and design that directly leads to a finished result? Perhaps, in the intellectual tradition of Mumford, we could think of the new visionaries for the ecological culture as a new phase of human organization and development called *ecotechnics*.

Ecohumanism in Planning for the Ecological Culture

The transition from the technological culture to the ecological culture will require a similar transition from traditional planning practice to ecohumanism. Thus, the emphasis will be predicated more on *substance* rather than *process*. All the epistemological ingredients are right there and have been for some time; they just need to be recognized, refashioned and redirected. Sociologists, cultural anthropologists, and human geographers have been in the forefront in analyzing and portraying the community as it connects

19. Lewis Mumford, *The City in History: Its Origins, Its Transformations, and Its Prospects* (New York: Harcourt, Brace and World, 1961), 401.

20. Ibid., 402. Although Mumford's quote is a minor alteration of Burnham's actual words, the meaning is the same.

21. Michael P. Brooks, *Planning Theory for Practitioners* (Chicago: Planners Press, American Planning Association, 2002), 198, 200.

ecological truths to social constructions. For example, a succinct perspective of nature and community can be found in the classic work of sociologist René König, who says, "Ecology and social research are very closely related to each other. This applies to the human community, which is essentially an association of human beings living in spatial proximity and spatially limited."[22]

Moving toward ecohumanism in planning would capture what Mumford has called for: an "age of renewal," when we can "unite to produce a fresh form for every stage of life, and a higher trajectory for life as a whole."[23] For Mumford, this transformation would offer "a fresh release of spiritual energy that will unveil new potentialities."[24] The relevance of such a perspective from a practice point of view envelops the next evolution in the human ecological planning model.

Two variables that often have not been especially prominent—or for that matter, not even included—in traditional planning have emphasized a comprehensive assessment of a community in the area of health and through the discipline of ethnography. I am convinced that these two realms offer the brightest hope for planning in the ecological culture to complete the cycle of compatibility with ecohumanism.

Historically, there is ample justification to incorporate concerns to shape a healthy community environment and to undertake ethnographic analysis to better understand dimensions of community living patterns. As the human ecological planning curriculum emerged and was fully installed between 1973 and 1979 in McHarg's Department of Landscape Architecture and Regional Planning—as fully presented in Chapter 8—health planning and ethnographic analysis became integral components of the new curriculum. In that curriculum, two faculty members played particularly important roles. Setha Low, who had a background in medical anthropology and psychology, and Dan Rose, who had a background in anthropology and ethnography, became the key faculty to offer courses and influence the development of the human ecological planning curriculum.

THE CONCEPT OF THE REGIONAL SURVEY that originated with Patrick Geddes and then was picked up by Mumford does not need to be confined to problems or issues of the natural environment. Geddes was clear that the

---

22. René König, *The Community* (New York: Schocken Books, 1968), 9.

23. Lewis Mumford, *The Transformations of Man*, ed. Ruth Nanda Anshen (New York: Harper and Brothers, 1956), 248.

24. Ibid., 249.

survey needed to go beyond "material buildings" to include "the city's life and its institutions, for of these the builded city is but the external shell."[25] While environmental health is obviously a high (if not the highest) priority, as we move from survey to planning, so too is the challenge to maintain human health and psychological balance, especially as environmental factors might directly influence them. For his part, Mumford recognizes that "in human beings a dynamic balance is the condition of health, poise, sanity; and faith in the creative processes, in dynamics of emergence, in the values and purposes that transcend past achievements and past forms, is the precondition of all further growth."[26]

McHarg was not oblivious to the importance of understanding the importance of health in furthering this aspect of community sustainability. While he was primarily concerned with environmental health, he does point out in *Design with Nature* that "if we can identify the areas of health and disease, we can proceed to associate the factors of the social and physical environment that are identified with both."[27] In a much later discussion of human ecological planning, McHarg shows how his thinking has advanced: "Ecological planning should be health giving. Success in such planning or fitting should be revealed in the existence of healthy communities, physical, biological, and social systems in dynamic equilibrium."[28]

From this perspective, we can discern a current and future direction to inculcate ecohumanism in planning for the ecological culture. In the case of health and well-being, we should look at the insightful work of Hugh Barton, a professor of planning, health, and sustainability. His thesis is simply that there needs to be an understanding of the central focus of planning as how human health and sustainability are directly linked to how we develop human settlements. This approach begins with recognizing "the relationship of one part of city functions to another, to understand the relevance of varied disciplines and professions, and to see the human habitat in a holistic way."[29] Barton becomes more specific as he argues, "By giving pre-eminence to the goals of health, well-being, happiness and quality of

25. The quotation is from Geddes's *Cities in Evolution* (1915), in *Patrick Geddes: Spokesman for Man and Environment*, ed. Marshall Stalley (New Brunswick, N.J.: Rutgers University Press, 1972), 227.

26. Lewis Mumford, *The Conduct of Life* (New York: Harcourt, Brace, 1951), 243.

27. Ian L. McHarg, *Design with Nature* (Garden City, N.Y.: 1969), 188.

28. Ian L. McHarg, "Human Ecological Planning at Pennsylvania," *Landscape Planning* 8, no. 2 (1981): 118.

29. Hugh Barton, *City of Well-Being: A Radical Guide to Planning* (London: Routledge, 2017), 19.

life we provide a sound motivation for spatial planning. . . . Just as engineers provide clear guidance on safe building structures, so planners can offer clear guidelines on healthy towns and cities."[30]

Barton characterizes a moral and ethical obligation for planning to promote "health, well-being and quality of life, for all groups in the population."[31] Concomitantly, he offers seven conclusions on the subject of achieving healthy communities:

- Form and function of human settlements have profound implications for the health of people.
- The history of planning from the earliest times demonstrates that there have been many places designed for well-being.
- The principles of sound city planning apply across countries, cultures, and economic status.
- Those with the power to make land use and infrastructure decisions have a responsibility to ensure that health, well-being, and quality of life provide powerful motives for improving human habitats.
- Professional planners need to accept their moral responsibility and gain knowledge and skills to persuade decision-makers to take appropriate actions.
- Healthy environments can only be achieved if decision-making groups and major investors work collaboratively and together with communities.
- Planning education needs to address these new realities.[32]

ETHNOGRAPHY HAS DEVELOPED from the disciplines of anthropology and sociology as a particular method or a set of methods that a researcher or investigator (the ethnographer) uses to participate in and observe people's daily lives over an extended period of time that are relevant to a specific research focus. As the ethnologist seeks to explain the similarities and differences found in human cultures, the ethnographer seeks to understand the intricate social relationships within a particular culture or subject group. As such, ethnography is "situated between powerful systems of meaning" as it poses questions that define the "boundaries of civilizations, cultures, classes, races, and genders," and it codes and explains the "grounds of col-

---

30. Ibid., 28.
31. Ibid., 270.
32. Ibid., 271–272.

lective order and diversity, inclusion and exclusion."[33] The singular value
that ethnography has in ecohumanism planning rests in its unique quali
tative data-gathering methods (e.g., participant observation) and subsequent assessment of community and how people relate to and shape their
communities.

To a great degree, ethnography is the practicing planner's dream epistemology, since *theory* is not developed through abstract thinking. Rather,
there are no preconceptions or a priori assumptions, and the field methods
are straightforward and without bias. The ethnographic approach, by the
nature of its parameters as a qualitative social research endeavor, must always
be open to developing theory or what has been referred to as "practical
epistemology, [or] how what we do affects the credibility of the propositions
we advance."[34] Consequently, knowledge that leads to theory building is
discovered, not invented.

Setha Low was a member of McHarg's faculty from 1974 to 1988 and
headed the health program in human ecological planning. Since leaving
the University of Pennsylvania (Penn) to join the City University of New
York, she has been involved in ethnographic research that incorporates environmental psychology, especially as it relates to spatial analysis. Her work
demonstrates the indispensable use of ethnography in ecohumanism planning, and since her days at Penn, Low has pushed ethnographic research in
understanding space and place to a new level.

Planning is integrally ingrained with space and place, and as Low points
out, "A basic assumption is that space is socially constructed as well as material and embodied, and the aim is to develop a conceptual framework—
spatializing culture—that brings these ideas together."[35] Place, on the other
hand, is defined as "lived space made up of spatial practices and is phe-
nomenologically experienced, such as the culturally meaningful space of
home."[36] Low's approach to inculcating environmental psychology in her
ethnographic field work emphasizes "the relationship between people and
the material world through the realm of experience and emotion."[37] More-

---

33. James Clifford and George E. Marcus, eds., *Writing Culture: The Poetics and Politics
of Ethnography* (Berkeley: University of California Press, 1986), 2.

34. Howard S. Becker, "The Epistemology of Qualitative Research," in *Ethnography
and Human Development: Context and Meaning in Social Inquiry*, ed. Richard Jessor, Anne
Colby, and Richard Shweder (Chicago: University of Chicago Press, 1996), 57.

35. Setha Low, *Spatializing Culture: The Ethnography of Space and Place* (London: Routledge, 2017), 4.

36. Ibid., 12.

37. Ibid., 25.

over, this leads to understanding of "notions such as place attachment and place identity that conceptualize lived experience as embedded in a person's sense of self and group identity."[38]

A corollary association that combines the two concepts has previously been framed by geographer Yi-Fu Tuan, who maintains that "place incarnates the experiences and aspirations of people. Place is not only a fact to be explained in the broader frame of space, but it is also a reality to be clarified and understood from the perspectives of the people who have given it meaning."[39] Such meaning is probed deeper by human geographer Edmunds Bunkše, as he describes "geographic sensibilities—knowing how to be in a place and how to find one's way in geographic space."[40] To Bunkše, "Geographic sensibilities connect us to the beginnings of life, not just human life but of all life. . . . [They] are primeval and enduring, dormant, atavistic traits imbedded in our bodies and minds."[41] Moreover, they "entail using the senses, the emotions, and the intellect informing relationships with the places and the landscapes that we inhabit."[42]

The value of understanding how people use and inhabit space and place—and what meanings, symbolic or otherwise, they attach—offers a fertile area for ecohumanism planning to inculcate. Such an understanding offers new dimensions in planning for people, places, and environment, from local to global. As Low concludes, "Through ethnographic methods, such as participant observation, in-depth interviewing and other qualitative techniques, a social construction of space analysis can uncover manifest and latent elements of a group's ethos and worldview."[43] Low's work has advanced ethnographic research by identifying a comprehensive perspective of human ecology and the increasingly important role this recognition has in melding nature and culture.

If we acknowledge that Dean Frederick Steiner is correct when he maintains that "culture provides mechanisms to help us organize the complexity that surrounds us," then "we seek to order things as an attempt to make some sense of our surroundings, our interactions with those surroundings, and our

---

38. Ibid.

39. Yi-Fu Tuan, "Space and Place: Humanistic Perspective," in *Philosophy in Geography*, ed. Stephen Gale and Gunnar Olsson (Dordrecht, Holland: D. Reidel, 1979), 387.

40. Edmunds Valdemārs Bunkše, *Geography and the Art of Life* (Baltimore: Johns Hopkins University Press, 2004), 13.

41. Ibid.

42. Ibid., 14.

43. Low, *Spatializing Culture*, 205.

interactions with each other."[44] But Steiner goes further by offering more than just a synthesis: "Both ecology and planning address interrelated systems. *Human* ecology extends how relationships occur in nature to human systems, such as those concerned with managing and planning human affairs."[45] Both Steiner and Low provide a pivotal link that lays down an ecohumanism foundation to underscore planning and design for the ecological culture.

THROUGHOUT HISTORY, visionaries have come from many fields, backgrounds, and interests. Coincidentally, we might find visionaries in places that do not quickly come to mind, such as in the sensual area of sound. In the planning and design professions, we would be hard pressed to find any evidence showing that sound plays any role in our work (except, for example, in measuring decibel levels as part of a land use impact analysis). Yet the intricate construction of musical sounds has had a rather arresting influence in one particular situation and on one individual.

It began with a masterful composition by Johann Sebastian Bach (1685–1750): the *Well-Tempered Clavier*, a collection of two series of preludes and fugues (forty-eight all together) in each of the twelve major and twelve minor keys composed for the solo keyboard (the clavier).[46] What Bach—a musical visionary—did was change and advance the established tonal system, a system that allowed some notes to be in perfect tune while others were not, by making major and minor keys *well-tempered* as a means to achieve a greater and more appealing musical harmony. This discovery is fine for musical history, but an intriguing question does come to mind: Would the genius of this great baroque composer have its impact on not only musical theory and performance but also other areas?

Bach's creative advance in the musical genre has stood the test of time and is revered today as a threshold of musical accomplishment. Interestingly, we find that it has also reappeared in a completely different context more than two hundred fifty years later: "The *Well-Tempered Clavier* was composed to align our highest human aspirations with the sublime harmony of nature. It is a model of the task we have today in designing and reshaping our cities," writes Jonathan Rose, a planner, investor, and developer.[47]

---

44. Frederick Steiner, *Human Ecology: How Nature and Culture Shape Our World* (Washington, D.C.: Island Press, 2016), 20. An earlier edition is titled *Human Ecology: Following Nature's Lead* (Washington, D.C.: Island Press, 2002).

45. Ibid., 24; emphasis original.

46. Bach's *Well-Tempered Clavier* consists of two "books" of twenty-four compositions each. The first book was finished in 1722, and the second was completed in 1742.

47. Jonathan F. P. Rose, *The Well-Tempered City: What Modern Science, Ancient Civilizations, and Human Nature Teach Us about the Future of Urban Life* (New York: HarperCollins, 2016), xii.

Rose has a background in psychology and philosophy (a bachelor's degree from Yale University) and earned a master's degree in regional planning in McHarg's curriculum at Penn. In 1989, he founded Jonathan Rose Companies LLC, a multidisciplinary real estate development, planning, and investment firm in New York City. Spurred by an acute sense of purpose and mission, Rose has become a highly successful real estate developer. Over the course of his career, Rose made an interesting discovery: "It came to me that the concept of temperament that helped Bach create harmony across scales could be a useful guide to composing cities that harmonize humans with each other and nature. . . . I call this aspiration the well-tempered city. It integrates five qualities of temperament to increase urban adaptability in a way that balances prosperity and well-being with efficiency and equity, ever moving toward wholeness."[48] Rose's five qualities of temperament demonstrate the application of ecohumanism to the community development process and stand out as combining the unique attributes of human and natural systems ecology, thus representing what can be accomplished. Welcome to the new ecological culture and its imperative in how to develop and redevelop our urban places for the twenty-first century.

Summarized, the qualities of temperament include (1) *coherence*, a framework that unifies, within a city, its disparate programs, departments, and aspirations that become a vision and a plan to integrate a number of elements, and (2) *circularity*, made possible by coherence, which replicates the embolic function of natural systems by allowing energy, information, and materials to flow through them; and since our current cities are linear and therefore must become circular, (3) *resilience*, the ability to recover when stressed (and an increase in urban resilience will occur when buildings consume less energy by becoming connected with parks, gardens, and natural landscapes that reincorporate nature into cities), (4) *community*, which acknowledges the benefits of improving the well-being of social networks to ameliorate such stresses as poverty, racism, trauma, toxins, housing instability, and inadequate schools, and (5) *compassion*, which provides a healthy balance between individual and collective well-being so that caring for others will become the gateway to wholeness not just for ourselves but for society as well.[49]

Rose is a systems thinker—and doer—in the tradition of R. Buckminster Fuller, Mumford, and McHarg, and he represents the new wave of incorporating ecohumanism in planning development projects that will be necessary for the ecological culture to succeed. As he says, "Thriving in the twenty-first century requires a cultural shift from an individual-

---

48. Ibid., 19–20.
49. Ibid., 20–22.

maximizing worldview to an ecological one, recognizing that our well-being derives from the health of the system, not the node."[50] He moves unabashedly from Bach to an ecohumanism philosophy to the world of real estate development: "Each project begins with objectives, from which the project organization and design flow. The green, walkable, transit-oriented, mixed-use, affordable and mixed-income projects we develop bring communities and nature into better balance, while rewarding our partners for their contributions and our investors with competitive returns."[51]

Ecohumanism in Design for the Ecological Culture

The pioneers of the Enlightenment have come and gone, and their place in history is secured. However, over the last several decades, we have witnessed the emergence of what may be identified as the first wave of pioneers to usher in the Second Enlightenment. Landscape architect James Corner summarizes an important premise behind such an advance: there is a "call for a new kind of social 'vision,' a 'new animism' in which human societies would see the world with new eyes—with wonderment, respect, and reverence. In social ecology, the ecological idea transcends its strictly scientific characteristics and assumes social, psychological, poetic, and imaginative dimensions."[52] Such a view captures the intent of Mumford's ecohumanism insofar as it incorporates into the design process not just form and function but spiritual awareness and aspiration. Relative to architecture, David Conrad summarizes Mumford's ecohumanism in this design art: "The most successful architecture combines form and function or, put another way, creative design and technical accuracy or, still another, symbolic meaning and functional integrity."[53]

The design approaches of landscape architecture and architecture are carving out new directions, yet a more comprehensive and holistic perspective requires acknowledgment. This approach strikes at the center of justifying how successful planning and design philosophies and methods will be in incorporating ecohumanism in the practice world. This challenge rests on the shoulders of the new leaders of the emerging ecological culture. Al-

---

50. Ibid., 373.

51. "Development as a Multi-purpose Process," Jonathan Rose Companies website, www.rosecompanies.com (June 1, 2017).

52. James Corner, "Ecology and Landscape as Agents of Creativity," in *Ecological Design and Planning*, ed. George F. Thompson and Frederick R. Steiner (New York: John Wiley and Sons, 1997), 94.

53. David R. Conrad, *Education for Transformation: Implications in Lewis Mumford's Ecohumanism* (Palm Springs, Calif.: ETC Publications, 1976), 57.

though many key people are spearheading the movement from the techno-logical culture to the ecological culture—from science to the arts—I single out one individual who has been an indispensable inspiration.

DESCRIBED AS A SYSTEMS THEORIST, inventor, architect, and futurist, R. Buckminster Fuller (1895–1983) had expansive interests that ranged from creating his own geometric space with the invention of the geodesic dome to championing the necessity of independent and visionary thinkers and doers. These would be people from all walks of life: from scientists to inventors, from artists to teachers, and from planners to designers. They would become the "Design Outlaws." They would not be anarchist or extremist but would engage the unknown; they would not be bound by conventional rules but rather strike out in creative, unlimited ways to make our world a more livable place. Design outlaws would be the successors to the inventive genius of Leonardo da Vinci and the Wright Brothers and the imagination of the Transcendentalists. "I think all humanity has crossed the threshold to enter upon its 'final examination,'" Fuller writes.[54] He is referring not to political or economic systems "but [to] the human individuals themselves who are in the final examination." He asks, "How much ingenuity do we have to solve the larger problems of society through anticipatory design rather than through outmoded institutions based on misinformation and the maintenance of the status quo for the vested in-terests?"[55]

Fuller's embracing of ecohumanism—although he does not call it that—is revealed in his concept of the design outlaw that will shape a human environment through anticipatory design. In fact, the basic understanding and functioning of ecology play a direct and essential role in Fuller's con-struct of systems that he describes as *synergistic*—"unique behaviors of whole systems unpredicted by any behaviors of their component functions taken separately."[56] Thus, according to Fuller, "we see that all life has been able to succeed owing to the anticipatory design of a regenerative ecological energy exchange. The mammals give off the gases that are necessary to the survival of the vegetation, while vegetation gives off the gases that are essential to the survival of the mammals. None of them knows that he is contributing gratuitously to vital support of the other."[57]

---

54. R. Buckminster Fuller, *Cosmography* (New York: Macmillan, 1992), 253.

55. Ibid.

56. R. Buckminster Fuller, *Utopia or Oblivion: The Prospects for Humanity* (New York: Overlook Press, 1969), 312.

57. Ibid., 144.

Are there really outlaw designers working and performing under the aegis of Fuller's description? Between 1990 and 1994, Christopher Zelov and Phil Cousineau conducted twenty-one interviews with such individuals. These were designers of alternative energy and transportation systems, inventive architectural and development practices, and total community system components. The interviews culminated in a film, *Ecological Design: Inventing the Future* (1994), and a subsequent book, *Design Outlaws on the Ecological Frontier* (1997). The purpose of Zelov and Cousineau's investigation was to highlight the achievements of "self-reliant thinkers in the Emersonian tradition, intent on forging the development of sustainable architecture and responsible technological change. Theirs is a tocsin call for design with rather than against nature."[58]

So what is the future of the design outlaw? And can we be convinced that a transition from conventional thinking to outlaw thinking—or visionary thinking—particularly in the fields of planning and design, can accelerate the move to the ecological culture?

OUR PRESENT TECHNOLOGICAL CULTURE has witnessed the infusion of new and innovative measures that have chipped away at the conventional way of doing things. The use of alternative building materials coupled with green architecture, the development of regenerative energy systems, the rise of urban agriculture, and the increasing use of recycling programs, as examples, have all affected the path to the ecological culture. If this trend is "the first generation of ecological design," then we are on "the threshold of a second generation[, which] is not an alternative to dominant technology and design; it is the best path for their necessary evolution."[59] Moreover, this second generation "must effectively weave the insights of literally dozens of disciplines. . . . It is time to bring forth new ecologies of design that are rich with cultural and epistemological diversity."[60] A convincing example rests in the multidisciplinary work of Pliny Fisk.

Inspired by the creative genius and whole systems philosophy of Fuller, the systems science thinking of Russell Ackoff, the architecture of Louis Kahn, and his education in the landscape architecture program under McHarg at Penn, Fisk established the Center for Maximum Potential Building Systems in Austin, Texas, in 1975. To some, he is a revolutionary—a

---

58. Christopher Zelov and Phil Cousineau, *Design Outlaws on the Ecological Frontier* (New York: Knossus Publishing, 1997), xvii.

59. Sim Van der Ryn and Stuart Cowan, *Ecological Design* (Washington, D.C.: Island Press, 1996), 31.

60. Ibid., 32.

design outlaw; to others, he is an indefatigable promoter of ecology and sustainability. Actually, he is both, combining the best of the worlds of humanism and ecology in his pursuit of systems thinking by taking a dedicated "holistic approach to solving problems and gaining insights into how things work . . . applied to everything from engineering to sociology."[61] He focuses on the areas of planning, architecture, and ecology from a single building to a city to a region.

Fisk received a bachelor's degree and a master's degree in architecture along with a master of landscape architecture (MLA) degree that was the culmination of his studies in the Department of Landscape Architecture and Regional Planning at Penn. He was especially influenced by the ecological planning and design of theory and method that McHarg pioneered. Yet in those days of graduate study, as Fisk was undertaking a thesis in landscape architecture, he pushed McHarg's method of ecological planning and design in a new direction. It would be a beginning for Fisk of his life's pursuit of challenging techniques, methods, and even the conventional wisdom in seeking out new approaches and projects that would work in concert with the notion of ecohumanism.

Fisk's assignment as a graduate student under McHarg was to address the Hackensack Meadows, an expansive polluted wetland across the Hudson River from New York City. As he explains to his biographer, Sam Martin: "The McHargian overlay process was only one of many ways of thinking about ecological restoration. In fact, the no-touch conservation procedure would not have worked in Hackensack Meadows or any other highly polluted environment where extreme change had already taken place." Fisk concludes, "We now had to think about time and the forces that created change. In other words, we had to think in systems dynamics terms."[62] As a result, he "mapped change, tracking where the system had been and where it was heading and how to intervene and steer that evolution."[63] Rather than fill the wetland for development or return it to nature, Fisk would "bring the area into some kind of balance by capturing that point in the evolutionary process and using it." This approach entailed using the invasive *Phragmites communis* species that had invaded the wetland and thrived on pollution. To Fisk, "From a systems standpoint, you ask the question: why was it there? It was there because it wanted the pollution. If it wanted

---

61. Sam Martin, *Pliny Fisk III: Creating a Maximum Potential Future* (Portland, Ore.: Ecotone Publishing, 2013), 41.

62. Ibid., 42.

63. Ibid., 43.

the pollution[,] why couldn't you use it to treat the water?"[64] He designed a model to convert the meadows into a wastewater treatment system, using the *Phragmites* to do the treatment. This approach and conceptualization of planning, design, and systems thinking would propel him on a creative and "outlaw" journey for his entire career.[65]

Ecohumanism in Education for the Ecological Culture

A Second Enlightenment to usher in an ecological culture is underway. The old rules are not just being questioned and challenged; they are being rewritten. At the soul of such a transformation is the high priority that must be placed on where we situate ourselves on the continuum of progress. We are on the threshold of reformulating how humans will fashion community, region, and nation. This movement is what Wahl calls a *regenerative culture* that "will have to facilitate the healthy personal development of a human being from ego-centric, to socio-centric, to species-centric, to bio-centric, and cosmos-centric perspectives of self. This means paying attention to how our culture and education system shape our worldview and value system."[66]

The essential framework for ecohumanism in education for the ecological culture must be predicated on systems thinking, not the reductive or segmented thinking that has been the dominant approach to learning. Most if not all of our higher education relies on analytical thinking, by which the parts are broken out and studied independently. For example, city and regional planning encompasses a number of components or fields, including land use, transportation, housing, community services, economic development, design, and theory, among others. From these components generally emerge a land use plan, a transportation plan, a housing plan, and a design plan that are brought together under the rubric of a comprehensive plan. A systems thinking approach would, by definition, provide a synthesis of these components to understand how the whole functions—in this case, the community or the region—and what interdependent role the components and the plans play.

---

64. Ibid.

65. Martin points out that Fisk's proposal was the largest wastewater wetland or "living machine" ever proposed at the time in the United States or anywhere else in the world, designed to treat the sewage resulting from 1.8 million people, using roads as control points and the dominant *phragmites* species to do the treatment. Ibid., 44.

66. Wahl, *Designing Regenerative Cultures*, 35.

In 1943, John Merriman Gaus, a professor of regional planning at Harvard University, presented an appraisal of the Graduate School of Design curriculum as it concerned the education of planners. After analyzing educational trends at a number of universities, Gaus's findings influenced not just the Harvard program but also other programs. He found that "in general, universities are recognizing their responsibilities and opportunities, and at the same time are keeping their new programs flexible and experimental."[67] He assessed that "we may say that we are in a period of regional study rather than regional planning and such planning as is attempted does not fall sufficiently within a single discipline or category to warrant our using the term *regional planner* as describing any one set of skills."[68]

In the same year, on the other side of the continent, Mumford, then a professor at Stanford University, was arguing that the humanities must be a priority on America's educational agenda. Mumford initiated a humanities program at Stanford, and his first course was called The Nature of Man. Ever the proponent of ecological balance, technological redirection, and regional planning, Mumford advocated for the humanities element as being essential in forwarding an educational balance. He maintained that "the humanities must educate for action as well as for contemplation: they must develop the citizen and the responsible leader no less than the connoisseur and the scholar: indeed, their highest aim is to create a balanced and unified personality capable of meeting the challenges of life on every front."[69]

Mumford would foster a systems thinking perspective to reforming education: "We have a new world to explore, to conquer, and to cultivate," he said, "the world of man's higher self, with all its myths and symbols, a new world which is also an old world: today a jungle which tomorrow we must transform into park, garden, and city."[70] Conrad has offered an overall perspective that "Mumford's reorientation of education to life-fulfillment [is] far-reaching."[71] As a true systems thinker, Mumford

---

67. John Merriman Gaus, *The Graduate School of Design and the Education of Planners* (Cambridge, Mass.: Harvard Graduate School of Design, 1943), 35.

68. Ibid., 20.

69. Lewis Mumford, *Values for Survival: Essays, Addresses, and Letters on Politics and Education* (New York: Harcourt, Brace, 1946), 229. Originally, this charge was included in Mumford's address, "The Making of Men," as part of the first annual conference held by the Stanford School of Humanities in 1943.

70. Ibid., 238.

71. Conrad, *Education for Transformation*, 88.

"would center on life itself, following Geddes, and approach all problems ecologically. Man and nature, the biological, social, and physical environments, would all be interrelated. The quality of life in cities, suburbs, and in rural areas would gain attention; urban planning, for instance, would become appropriate as a field of study, but not urban planning in any narrow professional sense."[72]

Insofar as curriculum development is concerned, McHarg tackled the specifics in suggesting that "three major subject areas should be included in a core curriculum. The first should focus on resources analysis and policies. The second should deal with the politics, process, and theory of planning decisions. The third should be in the area of social values and goals as they relate to resource development and planning."[73]

PLANNING EDUCATION has gone through quite a few iterations over many years. These versions have responded, in large measure, to changing views of the planner's role in society as it relates to the popular theoretical sentiment of the day. We have seen educational preferences move from the days of being physically or design oriented to a model that emphasizes comprehensiveness and rationality, from engaging in social advocacy to communicative theory, and from environmental to sustainability planning. All in all, planning education has not lacked a scarcity of areas to focus on.

Planning and design education stands at the forefront in equipping the next generation to be prepared to understand and solve community and regional issues. Steiner states simply, "The world needs more and better interior designers, architects, landscape architects, and planners." He continues, "Population, urbanization, and immigration trends demand the knowledge and skills of these professions."[74] If these are the challenges, then we are ripe for an infusion of ecohumanism into the educational process.

TODAY, there is a reinforced message that planning education specifically must be more community development based and pragmatic. This emphasis requires planning educators to have strong practice backgrounds and, very much in the Mumford tradition, to be generalist. As professor of the practice of urban design Alex Krieger holds, "Today's world is often suspicious of generalists, considering them ill equipped at specialized skills.

---

72. Ibid.

73. Ian L. McHarg, "Regional Landscape Planning," in *To Heal the Earth: Selected Writings of Ian L. McHarg*, ed. Ian L. McHarg and Frederick R. Steiner (Washington, D.C.: Island Press, 1998), 106.

74. Frederick Steiner, *Design for a Vulnerable Planet* (Austin: University of Texas Press, 2011), 252–253.

Yet those who can examine seemingly unrelated factors or phenomena and grasp their interrelationships—the hallmark of design education—are the most valuable professionals."[75]

The field of community development has carved out its own niche in applied planning and in educational preparation, offering programs and courses tailored to prepare professionals to work directly in or for communities. Effectively, community development has evolved over the last forty years to concentrate on certain key aspects. "First, efforts have been place based, with a special emphasis on minority and low-income neighborhoods and communities. Second, community development programs have emphasized public participation and community control."[76] It is an area of activism, training planners and allied professionals to have the skills to empower communities. A typical curriculum concentrates on participation in team projects, field research, service learning, and workshops. The intermingling of community with education is what research professor Lorlene Hoyt calls *the scholarship of engagement*, a type of inquiry in which research, teaching, and practice overlap and are mutually reinforcing. She proposes "a new epistemology known as reciprocal knowledge: development of knowledge and real learning on both sides, city and campus, achieved through a diverse, dynamic, and complex network of human relationships."[77]

"The training of planners requires a fresh approach," writes Barton. This change can be accomplished "with the various linked professions sharing a deeper and more ethically informed education. . . . Professional training should be focused on internationally transferable knowledge and skills, with an appropriate emphasis on practical planning and design exercises."[78]

More specifically, ecohumanism in education for the ecological culture will, by definition, have to be based on interdisciplinary connections functioning under the aegis of a systems approach to planning. This concept is not new, but what is new is how the interdisciplinary approaches will be integrated. This approach can and should take as its model the human ecological planning curriculum advanced by McHarg at Penn. McHarg's

---

75. Alex Krieger, "The Planner as Urban Designer: Reforming Planning Education in the New Millennium," in *The Profession of City Planning: Changes, Images, and Challenges 1950–2000*, ed. Lloyd Rodwin and Bishwapriya Sanyal (New Brunswick, N.J.: Center for Urban Policy Research, Rutgers University, 2000), 209.

76. Gary Paul Green and Anna Haines, *Asset Building and Community Development*, 3rd ed. (Thousand Oaks, Calif.: Sage Publications, 2012), 41.

77. Lorlene Hoyt, ed., "Reflections," in *Transforming Cities and Minds through the Scholarship of Engagement: Economy, Equity, and Environment* (Nashville, Tenn.: Vanderbilt University Press, 2013), 207.

78. Barton, *City of Well-Being*, 272.

genius was not that he created anything new but that he directed a synthesis of multidisciplines to perform in a way that they had not done previously.

We are at a point in history where the ecohumanism imperative in education offers a unique challenge to carve out an inclusive, dynamic, and creative direction. This unwavering thrust will usher in the ecological culture. No longer can educators rely on the old traditions of educational pedagogy if they truly desire their students to be intellectually and psychically prepared to confront the many worldly problems and issues of the twenty-first century. The educational challenge is this: enshrine an ecohumanism approach in education, at all levels, but most particularly at the university graduate level, with the mission of preparing the next generation of planners and designers. Arguably, this challenge will not be predicated on simply adjusting or modifying existing educational programs, curricula, or course offerings; it will require the invention of a new educational pedagogy.

The challenge is daunting, but it must be faced as a critical new direction in which to position ecohumanism as the guiding mantra of the ecological culture. Today, we are on the brink of doing something new—striking out in a profoundly important incorporation of ecology and humanism as the crux of an educational discipline. However, the path ahead will not necessarily be easy. As futurist and former associate professor of strategic foresight Peter Bishop writes, "Creating a new discipline is exciting, but exceedingly difficult. Not only must the founders create new methods and tools that are not guaranteed to work, but they also have to put up with suspicion and even disdain from the more established disciplines."[79]

An Ecohumanism Curriculum
for the Ecological Culture

In Chapter 12, I summarize future educational prospects for ecological planning that for the most part build on the human ecological planning and design curriculum that McHarg developed at Penn. However, another option could more vigorously integrate ecohumanism into a composite educational curriculum that would directly offer an interdisciplinary approach for the planning and design professions.

The pedagogical organization of this proposed curriculum would intentionally draw from and use already established college and university programs and courses. This approach does not suggest that new areas of curriculum development should not be considered or undertaken. New

---

79. Peter C. Bishop, "The Case for Foresight Education II," *World Futures Review* 10, no. 4 (2018): 151.

courses could be developed, or existing ones altered as needed, to supplement existing educational resources. Such a configuration might avoid the ups and downs that the ecological and human ecological planning and design curriculum faced at Penn. Moreover, if course offerings are effectively universal in breadth and scope, few aspects would need to be added and deleted. The wide range would offer an inclusivity that would provide the greatest latitude for student engagement. It would also build on the much-touted current view that higher education should be interdisciplinary. The ecohumanism curriculum would comprise four areas: foundational studies, planning and design studies, community development studies, and project-specific practicum or studio. Each area would include research, analysis, and field work. What follows is an outline of the proposed curriculum, with details to be worked out by each educational institution.

Foundational Studies

1. Natural sciences—biology, botany, geology, ecology
2. Social sciences—economics, sociology, geography, anthropology, political science
3. Humanities—history, art history, historic preservation
4. Ethnography—environmental psychology

Planning and Design Studies

1. Architecture
2. Landscape architecture
3. City and regional planning

Community Development Studies

1. Health and epidemiology
2. Transportation modes
3. Economic development
4. Affordable housing
5. Public participation and charrettes

Project-Specific Practicum or Studio

1. Work program
2. Research
3. Field work

4. Analysis
5. Presentation

An ecohumanism curriculum would consist of a multidisciplinary set of degree options combined with an interdisciplinary focus for each option. The fluidity of the curriculum is that it would encourage a total melding of studies, courses, studios, and practicum so that "mixing" and "matching" could be done and encouraged.

The following are the concentrations and degrees that the curriculum would offer, emphasizing preparation in the traditional fields of practice in city and regional planning, landscape architecture, and architecture:

- Master of ecohumanism in city and regional planning (MECRP)
- Master of ecohumanism in landscape architecture (MELA)
- Master of ecohumanism in architecture (MEA)

A new composite degree would be directed to preparing what Fuller called the "comprehensive generalist" and McHarg called the "Renaissance Man":

- Master of ecohumanism in community development (MECD)

MY CONCLUDING THOUGHT on this matter is that too often academics have a propensity to overintellectualize. In developing a curriculum, we might remember that much new learning is predicated on an individual's empirical experiences and intuition. Combining the two allows one to more fully understand and comprehend new ideas and forms of knowledge. It also permits the gut to speak. By bringing these components—experience, intuition, and gut—to any new learning endeavor, is it not possible to advance one's knowledge of what could be possible to achieve if we plan, design, and build ecologically? This question would justify moving ecohumanism into the forefront of the present and future education of planners and designers who could lead the way into the ecological culture. Our communities and regions need such leadership, and the path toward the Second Enlightenment will be ensured only if we embrace and advance creative approaches to planning, design, building, and education.

The educational component serves as the intellectual infrastructure to prepare the next generation. Those of us in the academy as well as in practice are responsible for advancing the educational legacy of Lewis Mumford and Ian McHarg. If we succeed, we will have finally achieved the ecological culture.

Selected Bibliography

The Selected Bibliography includes all published books and journal articles cited in the text and documented in the footnotes. Excluded are University of Pennsylvania catalogues and bulletins, various university reports and internal publications, archival and special collections documents, university and departmental memoranda, unpublished manuscripts, and personal correspondence.

Aberley, Doug, ed. "Weeds in the Cartesian Garden: The Context of Ecological Planning." In *Futures by Design: The Practice of Ecological Planning.* Gabriola Island, Canada: New Society Publishers, 1994.

Alexander, Ernest R. "After Rationality, What? A Review of Responses to Paradigm Breakdown." *Journal of the American Planning Association* 50 (1984): 62–69.

———. *Approaches to Planning: Introducing Current Planning Theories, Concepts and Issues.* Philadelphia: Gordon and Breach Science Publishers, 1992.

Alofsin, Anthony. *The Struggle for Modernism: Architecture, Landscape Architecture, and City Planning at Harvard.* New York: W. W. Norton, 2002.

Altschuler, Alan A. *The City Planning Process: A Political Analysis.* Ithaca, N.Y.: Cornell University Press, 1965.

"Art: Form of Forms," *Time*, April 18, 1938.

Auerbach, Karen. "His Work Continues, Naturally," *Philadelphia Inquirer*, April 20, 1997, B1, B6.

Barnett, Jonathan. *An Introduction to Urban Design.* New York: Harper and Row Publishers, 1982.

———. "What's New about the New Urbanism?" In *Charter of the New Urbanism*, edited by Michael Leccese and Kathleen McCormick. New York: McGraw-Hill, 1999.

Barton, Hugh. *City of Well-Being: A Radical Guide to Planning.* London: Routledge, 2017.

Bates, Marston. "Human Ecology." In *Anthropology Today: An Encyclopedic Inventory*, edited by A. L. Krober. Chicago: University of Chicago Press, 1953.

Beatley, Timothy, and Kristy Manning. *The Ecology of Place: Planning for Environment, Economy, and Community.* Washington, D.C.: Island Press, 1997.

Becker, Howard S. "The Epistemology of Qualitative Research." In *Ethnography and Human Development: Context and Meaning in Social Inquiry,* edited by Richard Jessor, Anne Colby, and Richard Shweder. Chicago: University of Chicago Press, 1996.

Bennett, John W. *The Ecological Transition: Cultural Anthropology and Human Adaptation.* New York: Pergamon Press, 1976.

Benyus, Janine M. *Biomimicry: Innovation Inspired by Nature.* New York: William Morrow, 1997.

Berger, Jonathan. "Environmental Ethnography for Landscape Planning." Ph.D. diss., University of Pennsylvania, 1984.

———. "Toward an Applied Human Ecology for Landscape Architecture and Regional Planning." *Human Ecology* 6 (1978): 179–199.

Berger, Jonathan, and John W. Sinton. *Water, Earth, and Fire: Land Use and Environmental Planning in the New Jersey Pine Barrens.* Baltimore: Johns Hopkins University Press, 1985.

Berry, Thomas. *The Dream of the Earth.* San Francisco: Sierra Club Books, 2006.

Bews, J. W. *Human Ecology.* Rev. ed. New York: Russell and Russell, 1973.

Bilsky, Lester J., ed. *Historical Ecology: Essays on Environment and Social Change.* Port Washington, N.Y.: Kennikat Press, 1980.

Bishop, Peter C. "The Case for Foresight Education II." *World Futures Review* 10, no. 4 (2018): 151–152.

Bloom, Allan. *The Closing of the American Mind.* New York: Simon and Schuster, 1987.

Boardman, Philip. *Patrick Geddes: Maker of the Future.* Chapel Hill: University of North Carolina Press, 1944.

———. *The Worlds of Patrick Geddes: Biologist, Town Planner, Re-educator, Peace-warrior.* London: Routledge and Kegan Paul, 1978.

Branch, Melville C. *Regional Planning: Introduction and Explanation.* New York: Praeger, 1988.

Brooks, Michael P. *Planning Theory for Practitioners.* Chicago: Planners Press American Planning Association, 2002.

Buder, Stanley. *Visionaries and Planners: The Garden City Movement and the Modern Community.* New York: Oxford University Press, 1990.

Bunkše, Edmunds Valdemārs. *Geography and the Art of Life.* Baltimore: Johns Hopkins University Press, 2004.

Bunster-Ossa, Ignacio. *Reconsidering Ian McHarg: The Future of Urban Ecology.* Chicago: American Planning Association, 2014.

Burchell, Robert W., and James W. Hughes. "Introduction." In *Planning Theory in the 1980's: A Search for Future Directions,* edited by Robert W. Burchell and George Sternlieb. New Brunswick, N.J.: Center for Urban Policy Research, Rutgers University, 1978.

Burmil, Shmuel, and Ruth Enis. "An Integrated Approach to Landscape Planning." *Journal of Architectural and Planning Research* 21, no. 2 (2004): 140–151.

Burns, James MacGregor. *Fire and Light: How the Enlightenment Transformed Our World.* New York: St. Martin's Press, 2013.

Cain, Stanley A. "The Conservation Program at the University of Michigan." In *Resource Training for Business, Industry, Government,* by Natural Resources Study Committee. Washington, D.C.: Conservation Foundation, 1958.

Chapin, F. Stuart, Jr. *Land Use Planning.* 2nd ed. Urbana: University of Illinois Press, 1966.

Clifford, James, and George E. Marcus, eds. *Writing Culture: The Poetics and Politics of Ethnography.* Berkeley: University of California Press, 1986.

Cohen, William J. "Envisioning a Second Enlightenment: Advancing Ecology in Planning, Designing, and Building City21." In *City21: The Search for the Second Enlightenment,* edited by Phil Cousineau and Christopher Zelov. Hellertown, Pa.: Knossus Project, 2010.

————. "Ian McHarg's Triumph." *Planning* 67, no. 5 (May 2001): 10–13.

Cohen, Yehudi, ed. *Man in Adaptation: The Biosocial Background.* Chicago: Aldine, 1968.

————. *Man in Adaptation: The Cultural Present.* Chicago: Aldine, 1968.

————. *Man in Adaptation: The Institutional Framework.* Chicago: Aldine, 1971.

Commoner, Barry. *The Closing Circle: Nature, Man, and Technology.* New York: Alfred A. Knopf, 1971.

Conrad, David R. *Education for Transformation: Implications in Lewis Mumford's Ecohumanism.* Palm Springs, Calif.: ETC Publications, 1976.

Corner, James. "Ecology and Landscape as Agents of Creativity." In *Ecological Design and Planning*, edited by George F. Thompson and Frederick R. Steiner. New York: John Wiley and Sons, 1997.

————. "The McHarg Event: An Unfinished Project." In *Ian McHarg Conversations with Students: Dwelling in Nature*, edited by Lynn Margulis, James Corner, and Brian Hawthorne. New York: Princeton Architectural Press, 2007.

Dansereau, Pierre. "An Ecological Framework for the Amenities of the City." *Diogenes* 98 (Summer 1977): 1–27.

————. "Megalopolis: Resources and Prospect." In *Challenge for Survival: Land, Air, and Water for Man in Megalopolis*, edited by Pierre Dansereau. New York: Columbia University Press, 1970.

Diamond, Jared. *Collapse: How Societies Choose to Fail or Succeed.* New York: Viking Penguin Group, 2005.

DiMattio, Vincent, and Kenneth R. Stunkel. *The Drawings and Watercolors of Lewis Mumford.* Lewiston, N.Y.: Edwin Mellon Press, 2004.

Dorman, Robert L. *Revolt of the Provinces: The Regionalist Movement in America, 1920–1945.* Chapel Hill: University of North Carolina Press, 1993.

Eiseley, Loren. *The Immense Journey.* New York: Random House, 1957.

Fábos, Julius Gy., Gordon T. Milde, and V. Michael Weinmayr. *Frederick Law Olmsted, Sr.: Founder of Landscape Architecture in America.* Amherst: University of Massachusetts Press, 1968.

Fairfield, Paul. *Education after Dewey.* London: Continuum International Publishing Group, 2009.

Firey, Walter. *Land Use in Central Boston.* Cambridge, Mass.: Harvard University Press, 1947.

Fishman, Robert. "The Fifth Migration." *Journal of the American Planning Association* 71, no. 4 (2005): 357–366.

Friedmann, John. *Planning in the Public Domain: Linking Knowledge to Action.* Princeton, N.J.: Princeton University Press, 1987.

Fuller, R. Buckminster. *Cosmography.* New York: Macmillan, 1992.

————. *Utopia or Oblivion: The Prospects for Humanity.* New York: Overlook Press, 1969.

Garrison, Jim, Stefan Neubert, and Kersten Reich. *John Dewey's Philosophy of Education: An Introduction and Recontextualization for Our Times.* New York: Palgrave Macmillan, 2012.

Gaus, John Merriman. *The Graduate School of Design and the Education of Planners.* Cambridge, Mass.: Harvard Graduate School of Design, 1943.

Geertz, Clifford. *Agricultural Involution: The Process of Ecological Change in Indonesia.* Berkeley: University of California Press, 1963.

————. *The Interpretation of Cultures.* New York: Basic Books, 1973.

Giliomee, J. H. "Ecological Planning: Method and Evaluation." *Landscape Planning* 4 (1977): 185–191.

Gillette, Howard, Jr. *Civitas by Design: Building Better Communities, from the Garden City to the New Urbanism.* Philadelphia: University of Pennsylvania Press, 2010.

Glikson, Artur. *The Ecological Basis of Planning.* Edited by Lewis Mumford. The Hague: Martinus Nijhoff, 1971.

Goffman, Erving. *The Presentation of Self in Everyday Life.* New York: Anchor Books, 1959.

Goist, Park Dixon. "Seeing Things Whole: A Consideration of Lewis Mumford." In *The American Planner: Biographies and Recollections,* edited by Donald A. Krueckeberg. New York: Methuen, 1983.

Gold, Andrew J. "Design with Nature: A Critique." *Journal of the American Institute of Planners* 40 (1974): 284–286.

Golly, Frank B. "Historical Origins of the Ecosystem Concept in Biology." In *The Ecosystem Concept in Anthropology,* AAAS Selected Symposium, 92 ed., edited by Emilio F. Moran. Boulder, Colo.: Westview Press, 1984.

Green, Gary Paul, and Anna Haines. *Asset Building and Community Development.* 3rd ed. Thousand Oaks, Calif.: Sage Publications, 2012.

Guha, Ramachandra. "Lewis Mumford, the Forgotten American Environmentalist: An Essay in Rehabilitation." In *Minding Nature: The Philosophers of Ecology,* edited by David Macauley. New York: Guilford Press, 1996.

Hagevik, George, and Lawrence Mann. "The 'New' Environmentalism: An Intellectual Frontier." *Journal of the American Institute of Planners* 37 (1971): 274–280.

Halprin, Lawrence. "Book Review of *A Quest for Life: An Autobiography.*" *Quarterly Review of Landscape Architecture and Garden Design Publications, Land Books* (Winter 1996): 8.

Harris, Britton. "New Tools for Research and Analysis." In *Urban Planning in Transition,* edited by Ernest Erber. New York: Grossman, 1970.

Hawley, Amos H. *Human Ecology: A Theory of Community Structure.* New York: Ronald Press, 1950.

Hayden, Dolores. *Building Suburbia: Green Fields and Urban Growth, 1820–2000.* New York: Pantheon Books, 2003.

Helm, June. "The Ecological Approach in Anthropology." *American Journal of Sociology* 67, no. 6 (1962): 630–639.

Herrington, Susan. "The Nature of McHarg's Science." *Landscape Journal* 29 (2010): 1–20.

Hersperger, Anna M. "Landscape Ecology and Its Potential Application to Planning." *Journal of Planning Literature* 9 (1994): 14–29.

Hills, G. Angus. "A Philosophical Approach to Landscape Planning." *Landscape Planning* 1 (1974): 339–371.

Holden, Constance. "Ian McHarg: Champion for Design with Nature." *Science* (New Series) 195, no. 4276 (1977): 379–382.

Holt-Jensen, Arild. *Geography: Its History and Concepts.* Totowa, N.J.: Barnes and Noble Books, 1982.

Hoyt, Lorlene, ed. "Reflections." In *Transforming Cities and Minds through the Scholarship of Engagement: Economy, Equity, and Environment.* Nashville, Tenn.: Vanderbilt University Press, 2013.

Hubbard, Henry Vincent, and Theodora Kimball. *An Introduction to the Study of Landscape Design.* New York: Macmillan, 1927.

Hudnut, Joseph. "Foreword." In *The Graduate School of Design and the Education of Planners,* by John Merriman Gaus. Cambridge, Mass.: Harvard Graduate School of Design, 1943.

Hunt, John Dixon. "Picturesque." In *The Dictionary of Art,* edited by Jane Turner. New York: Grove, 1996.

Jackson, John Brinckerhoff. *A Sense of Place, a Sense of Time.* New Haven, Conn.: Yale University Press, 1994.

Jacoby, Russell. *The Last Intellectuals: American Culture in the Age of Academe.* New York: Basic Books, 1987.

Jamison, Andrew, and Ron Eyerman. *Seeds of the Sixties*. Berkeley: University of California Press, 1994.

Janowitz, Morris. "Introduction." In *The City*, edited by Robert E. Park, Ernest W. Burgess, and Roderick D. McKenzie. Chicago: University of Chicago Press, 1967.

Johnson, Bart R., and Kristina Hill, eds. *Ecology and Design: Frameworks for Learning*. Washington, D.C.: Island Press, 2002.

Johnson, David A. "Lewis Mumford: Critic, Colleague, Philosopher." *Planning* 49, no. 4 (1983): 9–14.

Juneja, Narendra. *Medford: Performance Requirements for the Maintenance of Social Values Represented by the Natural Environment of Medford Township, N.J.* Philadelphia: Center for Ecological Research in Planning and Design, University of Pennsylvania, 1974.

Kaiser, Edward J., David R. Godschalk, and F. Stuart Chapin, Jr. *Urban Land Use Planning*. 4th ed. Urbana: University of Illinois Press, 1995.

Kellogg, Wendy A. "Review of *To Heal the Earth: Selected Writings of Ian L. McHarg*." *Journal of the American Planning Association* 65 (1999): 335–336.

König, René. *The Community*. New York: Schocken Books, 1968.

Krieger, Alex. "The Planner as Urban Designer: Reforming Planning Education in the New Millennium." In *The Profession of City Planning: Changes, Images, and Challenges 1950–2000*, edited by Lloyd Rodwin and Bishwapriya Sanyal. New Brunswick, N.J.: Center for Urban Policy Research, Rutgers University, 2000.

Kuhn, Thomas S. *The Structure of Scientific Revolutions*. 4th ed. Chicago: University of Chicago Press, 2012.

Kunstler, James Howard. *The Geography of Nowhere: The Rise and Decline of America's Man-Made Landscape*. New York: Simon and Schuster, 1993.

Laurie, Michael. "Scoring McHarg: Low on Method, High on Values." *Landscape Architecture* 61 (1971): 206, 248.

Le Corbusier. *Towards a New Architecture*. 13th ed. London: John Rodker Publisher, 1931.

Ledger, Marshall. "On Getting the Lay of the Land." *Pennsylvania Gazette* 85, no. 4 (February 1987): 30–36.

Lee, Brenda J. "An Ecological Comparison of the McHarg Method with Other Planning Initiatives in the Great Lakes Basin." *Landscape Planning* 9 (1982): 147–169.

LeGates, Richard T., and Frederic Stout, eds. *The City Reader*. London: Routledge, 1996.

Leicester, Graham. "The St. Andrews Conversation." In *City21: The Search for the Second Enlightenment*, edited by Phil Cousineau and Christopher Zelov. Hellertown, Pa.: Knossus Project, 2010.

Levy, John M. *Contemporary Urban Planning*. 5th ed. Upper Saddle River, N.J.: Prentice Hall, 2000.

Litton, Burton R., and Martin Krieger. "Review of *Design with Nature*." *Journal of the American Institute of Planners* 37 (1971): 50–52.

Lovelock, James. *The Ages of Gaia: A Biography of Our Living Earth*. New York: W. W. Norton, 1988.

Low, Setha. "A Cultural Landscapes Mandate for Action." *Cultural Resources Management Bulletin* 10, no. 1 (1987): 22–23, 30.

———. "Social Science Methods in Landscape Architecture Design." *Landscape Planning* 8 (1981): 137–148.

———. *Spatializing Culture: The Ethnography of Space and Place*. London: Routledge, 2017.

Low, Setha M., and Richard D. Walter. "Values in the Planning Process." *Ekistics* 49, no. 292 (January/February 1982): 137–148.

Luccarelli, Mark. *Lewis Mumford and the Ecological Region: The Politics of Planning*. New York: Guilford Press, 1995.

MacDougall, E. Bruce. "The Accuracy of Map Overlays," *Landscape Planning* 2 (1975): 23–30.

MacKaye, Benton. *The New Exploration: A Philosophy of Regional Planning.* New York: Harcourt, Brace, 1928. Reprint, Urbana-Champaign: University of Illinois Press, 1962.

———. "Regional Planning and Ecology." *Ecological Monographs* 10 (1940): 349–353.

Mandala Collaborative/Wallace, McHarg, Roberts and Todd. *Pardisan: Plan for an Environmental Park in Tehran.* Philadelphia: Winchell Press, 1975.

Mandelbaum, Seymour J. "A Complete General Theory of Planning Is Impossible." *Policy Sciences* 11 (1979): 59–71.

Margalef, Ramón. *Perspectives in Ecological Theory.* Chicago: University of Chicago Press, 1968.

Martin, Sam. *Pliny Fisk III: Creating a Maximum Potential Future.* Portland, Ore.: Ecotone Publishing, 2013.

Marx, Leo. "Lewis Mumford: Prophet of Organicism." In *Lewis Mumford: Public Intellectual,* edited by Thomas P. Hughes and Agatha C. Hughes. New York: Oxford University Press, 1990.

———. *The Machine in the Garden: Technology and the Pastoral Ideal in America.* London: Oxford University Press, 1964.

McClintock, Robert. "Review, *Design with Nature.*" *Main Currents in Modern Thought* 7, no. 4 (1971): 133–135.

McDonough, William, and Michael Braungart. *Cradle to Cradle: Re-making the Way We Make Things.* New York: Farrar, Straus and Giroux; North Star Press, 2002.

McHarg, Ian L. *Design with Nature.* Garden City, N.Y.: Natural History Press, 1969.

———. *Design with Nature.* 25th anniv. ed. New York: John Wiley and Sons, 1992.

———. "Ecological Determinism." In *Future Environments of North America,* edited by F. Fraser Darling and John P. Milton. Garden City, N.Y.: Natural History Press, 1966.

———. "Ecological Planning: The Planner as Catalyst." In *Planning Theory in the 1980s,* edited by Robert W. Burchell and George Sternlieb. 2nd ed. New Brunswick, N.J.: Rutgers University Press, 1978.

———. "Ecology and Design." In *Ecological Design and Planning,* edited by George F. Thompson and Frederick R. Steiner. New York: John Wiley and Sons, 1996.

———. "Human Ecological Planning at Pennsylvania." *Landscape Planning* 8 (1981): 109–120.

———. Letter to the Editors, *Landscape Architecture,* 80, no 4 (April 1990): 8–9.

———. *A Quest for Life: An Autobiography.* New York: John Wiley and Sons, 1996.

———. "Regional Landscape Planning." In *Resources, the Metropolis and the Land-Grant University,* edited by A. J. W. Scheffey. Proceedings on the Conference of Natural Resources, no. 10. Amherst: University of Massachusetts, 1963.

———. *Some Songs to the Stars: A Collection of Poems.* Cape May, N.J.: Knossus Project with Chelsea Green Publishers, 2001.

———. "Teaching the Ecological World View." In *Design Outlaws on the Ecological Frontier,* edited by Chris Zelov and Phil Cousineau. 5th ed. New York: Knossus Publishing, 1997.

McHarg, Ian L., and Frederick R. Steiner, eds. *To Heal the Earth: Selected Writings of Ian L. McHarg.* Washington, D.C.: Island Press, 1998.

McKelvey, Blake. *The Emergence of Metropolitan America, 1915–1966.* New Brunswick, N.J.: Rutgers University Press, 1968.

McKenzie, Roderick D. "The Ecological Approach to the Study of the Human Community." In *The City,* by Robert E. Park, Ernest W. Burgess, and Roderick D. McKenzie. Chicago: University of Chicago Press, 1967.

Meadows, Donella H., Dennis L. Meadows, Jørgen Randers, and William W. Behrens III. *The Limits to Growth: A Report for the Club of Rome's Project on the Predicament of Mankind.* New York: Universe Books, 1972.

Meller, Helen. *Patrick Geddes: Social Evolutionist and City Planner.* London: Routledge, 1990.

Meyerson, Martin, and Edward C. Banfield. *Politics, Planning and the Public Interest: The Case of Public Housing in Chicago.* New York: Free Press, 1955.

Miller, Donald L. *Lewis Mumford: A Life.* New York: Weidenfeld and Nicolson, 1989.

Miller, E. Lynn. "Environmental Conscience before Ian McHarg." *Landscape Architecture* 89 (1999): 58–62.

Miller, E. Lynn, and Sidónio Pardal. *The Classic McHarg: An Interview.* Lisbon, Portugal: CSER, Technical University of Lisbon, 1992.

Mitchell, William J. *e-topia: "Urban Life, Jim—But Not as We Know It."* Cambridge, Mass.: MIT Press, 1999.

Molella, Arthur P. "Mumford in Historiographical Context." In *Lewis Mumford: Public Intellectual,* edited by Thomas P. Hughes and Agatha C. Hughes. New York: Oxford University Press, 1990.

Moore, Charles. *Daniel Burnham Architect, Planner of Cities.* Vol. 2. Boston: Houghton Mifflin, 1921.

Morans, Robert W. "Neighborhood Planning: The Contributions of Artur Glikson." *Journal of Architectural and Planning Research* 21, no. 2 (2004): 112–124.

Morgan, George T., Jr., and John O. King. *The Woodlands: New Community Development, 1964–1983.* College Station: Texas A&M University Press, 1987.

Morris, Brian. *Pioneers of Ecological Humanism: Mumford, Dubos and Bookchin.* Montreal: Black Rose Books, 2017.

Muhlenberg, Nicholas. "Ecology, Economics, and Planning." In *Via 1 Ecology in Design,* 19–21. Graduate School of Fine Arts, University of Pennsylvania, 1968.

Mukerjee, Radhakamal. *The Philosophy of Social Science.* London: Macmillan, 1960.

Mumford, Lewis. "An Appraisal of Lewis Mumford's 'Technics and Civilization' (1934)." *Daedalus* 88, no. 3 (1959): 527–536.

———. *Architecture as a Home for Man: Essays for Architectural Record,* edited by Jeanne M. Davern. New York: Architectural Record Books, 1975.

———. *Art and Technics.* New York: Columbia University Press, 1952.

———. "The Automation of Knowledge: Are We Becoming Robots?" *Vital Speeches of the Day* 30, no. 14 (1964): 441–446.

———. *City Development: Studies in Disintegration and Renewal.* New York: Harcourt, Brace, 1945.

———. *The City in History: Its Origins, Its Transformations, and Its Prospects.* New York: Harcourt, Brace and World, 1961.

———. "Closing Statement." In *Future Environments of North America,* edited by F. Fraser Darling and John P. Milton. Garden City, N.Y.: Natural History Press, 1966.

———. *The Condition of Man.* New York: Harcourt, Brace, 1944.

———. *The Conduct of Life.* New York: Harcourt, Brace, 1951.

———. *The Culture of Cities.* New York: Harcourt, Brace, 1938.

———. *Faith for Living.* New York: Harcourt, Brace, 1940.

———. "The Garden City Idea and Modern Planning." In *Garden Cities of To-Morrow,* by Ebenezer Howard, edited by F. J. Osborn. Cambridge, Mass.: MIT Press, 1965.

———. *The Human Prospect.* Edited by Harry T. Moore and Karl W. Deutsch. London: Secker and Warburg, 1956.

———. "Introduction." In *Design with Nature,* by Ian L. McHarg. Garden City, N.Y.: Natural History Press, 1969.

———, ed. "Introduction." In *The Ecological Basis of Planning*, by Artur Glikson. The Hague: Martinus Nijhoff, 1971.

———. "Introduction." In *Lewis Mumford: A Bibliography, 1914–1970*, by Elmer S. Newman. New York: Harcourt Brace Jovanovich, 1971.

———. "Introduction." In *The New Exploration: A Philosophy of Regional Planning*, by Benton Mackaye. New York: Harcourt, Brace, 1928.

———. *The Myth of the Machine: Technics and Human Development*. New York: Harcourt Brace Jovanovich, 1966.

———. *The Myth of the Machine: The Pentagon of Power*. New York: Harcourt Brace Jovanovich, 1964.

———. *My Works and Days: A Personal Chronicle*. New York: Harcourt Brace Jovanovich, 1979.

———. *Sketches from Life: The Autobiography of Lewis Mumford*. New York: Dial Press, 1982.

———. "The Social Responsibilities of Teachers." In *Values for Survival: Essays, Addresses, and Letters on Politics and Education*. New York: Harcourt, Brace, 1946.

———. *Sticks and Stones: A Study of American Architecture and Civilization*. New York: Boni and Liveright, 1924.

———. *The Story of Utopias*. New York: Boni and Liveright, 1922.

———. "Survival of Plants and Man." In *Challenge for Survival: Land, Air, and Water for Man in Megalopolis*, edited by Pierre Dansereau. New York: Columbia University Press, 1970.

———. *Technics and Civilization*. New York: Harcourt, Brace, 1934.

———. "Technics and Human Culture." In *Human Futures: Needs, Societies, Technologies*. The Rome World Special Conference on Futures Research 1973. Guildford, UK: IPC Science and Technology Press, 1974.

———. "The Theory and Practice of Regionalism." *Sociological Review* 20, no. 1 (1928): 18–33, 131–141.

———. *The Transformations of Man*. Edited by Ruth Nanda Anshen. New York: Harper and Brothers, 1956.

———. *Values for Survival: Essays, Addresses, and Letters on Politics and Education*. New York: Harcourt, Brace, 1946.

Mumford, Sophia. Preface to *The Drawings and Watercolors of Lewis Mumford*, by Vincent DiMattio and Kenneth R. Stunkel. Lewiston, N.Y.: Edwin Mellon Press, 2004.

Nash, Roderick Frazier. *The Rights of Nature: A History of Environmental Ethics*. Madison: University of Wisconsin Press, 1989.

Ndubisi, Forster. *Ecological Planning: A Historical and Comparative Synthesis*. Baltimore: Johns Hopkins University Press, 2002.

Newman, Elmer S. *Lewis Mumford: A Bibliography, 1914–1970*. New York: Harcourt Brace Jovanovich, 1971.

Newton, Norman T. "A Report on the Department of Landscape Architecture, the School of Fine Arts: University of Pennsylvania." In *The Educational Survey of the University of Pennsylvania*. June 30, 1958.

Nolen, John. *New Town for Old: Achievements in Civic Improvement in Some American Small Towns and Neighborhoods*. Boston: Marshall Jones, 1927. Reprint, Amherst: University of Massachusetts Press, 2005.

Norton, William. *Human Geography*. 3rd ed. Toronto: Oxford University Press, 1998.

Novak, Frank G., Jr. *The Autobiographical Writings of Lewis Mumford: A Study in Literary Audacity*. Honolulu: University of Hawaii Press, 1988.

———. *Lewis Mumford and Patrick Geddes: The Correspondence*. London: Routledge, 1995.

Oberlander, Judith. "History IV 1933–1935." In *The Making of An Architect 1881–1981:*

Columbia University in the City of New York, edited by Richard Oliver. New York: Rizzoli, 1981.

Ogburn, William Fielding. *Social Change with Respect to Culture and Original Nature*. Gloucester, Mass.: Peter Smith, 1964.

Orr, David W. *The Nature of Design: Ecology, Culture, and Human Intention*. New York: Oxford University Press, 2002.

Osborn, Frederic J. *Green-Belt Cities*. New York: Schocken Books, 1969.

―――, ed. Preface to *Garden Cities of To-Morrow*, by Ebenezer Howard. Cambridge, Mass.: MIT Press, 1965.

Palmer, Arthur E. *Toward Eden*. Winterville, N.C.: Creative Resource Systems, 1981.

Passmore, John. *A Hundred Years of Philosophy*. London: Gerald Duckworth, 1957.

Pearlman, Jill. "Joseph Hudnut's Other Modernism at the 'Harvard Bauhaus.'" *Journal of the Society of Architectural Historians* 56 (December 1997): 452–477.

Petulla, Joseph M. *American Environmental History*. 2nd ed. Columbus, Ohio: Merrill, 1988.

Phillips, John. "The Biotic Community." *Journal of Ecology* 19 (1931): 1–24.

―――. "Ecology and the Ecological Approach." In *Via 1 Ecology in Design*, 17–18. Graduate School of Fine Arts, University of Pennsylvania, 1968.

Quinn, James A. *Human Ecology*. New York: Prentice Hall, 1950.

Ravaioli, Carla. *Economists and the Environment*, translated by Richard Bates. London: Zed Books, 1995.

Redfield, Robert. *The Little Community*. Chicago: University of Chicago Press, 1955.

Regal, Philip J. "Ecohumanism: Refining the Concept." In *Ecohumanism*, edited by Robert B. Tapp. Amherst, N.Y.: Prometheus Books, 2002.

Renne, Roland R. *Land Economics: Principles, Problems, and Policies in Utilizing Land Resources*. Rev. ed. New York: Harper and Brothers, 1958.

Ringger, Diane L., and Forest Stearns. "Nature's Landscape Architect." *Ecology* 51 (1970): 1109–1110.

Rose, Dan. *Energy Transition and the Local Community: A Theory of Society Applied to Hazleton, Pennsylvania*. Philadelphia: University of Pennsylvania Press, 1981.

―――. "Resource Competition in the Kennett Region of Pennsylvania." *Landscape Planning* 8 (1981): 175–192.

Rose, Dan, and Jon Berger. *Human Ecology in the Regional Plan*. Philadelphia: Department of Landscape Architecture and Regional Planning, 1974.

Rose, Dan, Frederick Steiner, and Joanne Jackson. "An Applied Human Ecological Approach to Regional Planning." *Landscape Planning* 5 (1978/1979): 241–261.

Rose, Jonathan F. P. *The Well-Tempered City: What Modern Science, Ancient Civilizations, and Human Nature Teach Us about the Future of Urban Life*. New York: HarperCollins, 2016.

Rosenbaum, Walter A. *Environmental Politics and Policy*. Washington, D.C.: Congressional Quarterly Press, 1985.

Sarles, Harvey B. "The Human in the Context of Nature." In *Ecohumanism*, edited by Robert B. Tapp. Amherst, N.Y.: Prometheus Books, 2002.

Schafer, David. "Time Is Not on Our Side." In *Ecohumanism*, edited by Robert B. Tapp. Amherst, N.Y.: Prometheus Books, 2002.

Scott, Mel. *American City Planning since 1890*. Berkeley: University of California Press, 1969.

Sears, Paul B. "Human Ecology: A Problem in Synthesis." *Science* 120, no. 3128 (1954): 959–963.

Seltzer, Ethan, and Armando Carbonell, eds. "Planning Regions." In *Regional Planning in America: Practice and Prospect*. Cambridge, Mass.: Lincoln Institute of Land Policy, 2011.

Shapiro, Harvey A. "What Happened to the Introduction of the McHargian Method to Japan." *Landscape Architecture* 69 (November 1979): 575–577.

Shoshkes, Ellen. "Jaqueline Tyrwhitt Translates Patrick Geddes for Post World War Two." *Landscape and Urban Planning* 166 (October 2017): 15–24.

Shulman, Ken. "The Gospel according to Ian McHarg." *Metropolis* 20, no. 1 (August/ September 2000): 86–89, 103, 105.

Spirn, Anne Whiston. "The Authority of Nature: Conflict and Confusion in Landscape Architecture." In *Nature and Ideology: Natural Garden Design in the Twentieth Century*, edited by Joachim Wolschke-Bulmahn. Washington, D.C.: Dumbarton Oaks Research Library and Collection, 1997.

———. *The Granite Garden: Urban Nature and Human Design*. New York: Basic Books, 1984.

———. "Ian McHarg, Landscape Architecture, and Environmentalism: Ideas and Methods in Context." In *Environmentalism in Landscape Architecture*, edited by Michel Conan. Washington, D.C.: Dumbarton Oaks Research Library and Collection, 2000.

Stalley, Marshall. *Patrick Geddes: Spokesman for Man and Environment*. New Brunswick, N.J.: Rutgers University Press, 1972.

Steiner, Frederick R. *Design for a Vulnerable Planet*. Austin: University of Texas Press, 2011.

———, ed. *The Essential Ian McHarg: Writings on Design and Nature*. Washington, D.C.: Island Press, 2006.

———. "Healing the Earth: The Relevance of Ian McHarg's Work for the Future." *Human Ecology Review* 23, no. 2 (2017): 75–85.

———. *Human Ecology: Following Nature's Lead*. Washington, D.C.: Island Press, 2002.

———. *Human Ecology: How Nature and Culture Shape Our World*. Washington, D.C.: Island Press, 2016.

———. *The Living Landscape: An Ecological Approach to Landscape Planning*. New York: McGraw-Hill, 1991.

———. *The Living Landscape: An Ecological Approach to Landscape Planning*. 2nd ed. New York: McGraw-Hill, 2000.

———. "Living Urban Landscapes." In *On Landscape Urbanism: Center 14, Center for American Architecture and Design*, edited by Dean J. Almy. Austin: University of Texas, 2007).

———. "Plan with Nature: The Legacy of Ian McHarg." In *Regional Planning in America: Practice and Prospect*, edited by Ethan Seltzer and Armando Carbonell. Cambridge, Mass.: Lincoln Institute of Land Policy, 2011.

Steiner, Frederick, and Kenneth Brooks. "Ecological Planning: A Review." *Environmental Management* 5 (1981): 495–505.

Steiner, Frederick, Gerald Young, and Ervin Zube. "Ecological Planning: Retrospect and Prospect." *Landscape Journal* 7, no. 1 (Spring 1988): 31–39.

Steinitz, Carl. "Landscape Planning: A History of Influential Ideas." *Landscape Architecture* 99 (2009): 74–83.

Steinitz, Carl, Paul Parker, and Lawrie Jordan. "Hand-Drawn Overlays: Their History and Prospective Uses." *Landscape Architecture* 66 (1976): 444–455.

Steward, Julian. *Theory of Culture Change: The Methodology of Multilinear Evolution*. Urbana: University of Illinois Press, 1955.

Stilgoe, John R. *Common Landscape of America, 1580–1845*. New Haven, Conn.: Yale University Press, 1982.

Strong, Ann L., and George E. Thomas. *The Book of the School: The Graduate School of Fine Arts of the University of Pennsylvania*. Philadelphia: University of Pennsylvania, 1990.

Stunkel, Kenneth R. "Vital Standard and Life Economy: The Economic Thought of Lewis Mumford." *Journal of Economic Issues* 40, no. 1 (2006): 113–133.

Sussman, Carl, ed. *Planning the Fourth Migration: The Neglected Vision of the Regional Planning Association of America*. Cambridge, Mass.: MIT Press, 1976.

Taylor, Nigel. *Urban Planning Theory since 1945*. London: Sage Publications, 1998.

Thompson, George F., and Frederick R. Steiner, eds. *Ecological Design and Planning*. New York: John Wiley and Sons, 1997.

Thompson, William. "A Natural Legacy: Ian McHarg and His Followers." *Planning* 57, no. 11 (November 1991): 14–19.

Toffler, Alvin. *Future Shock*. New York: Random House, 1970.

Toynbee, Arnold J. *A Study of History: Abridgement of Volumes I–VI by D. C. Somervell*. New York: Oxford University Press, 1946.

Tuan, Yi-Fu. "Space and Place: Humanistic Perspective." In *Philosophy in Geography*, edited by Stephen Gale and Gunnar Olsson. Dordrecht, Holland: D. Reidel, 1979.

———. *Space and Place: The Perspective of Experience*. Minneapolis: University of Minnesota, 1977.

Udall, Stewart L. "Foreword." In *A Quest for Life: An Autobiography*, by Ian L. McHarg. New York: John Wiley and Sons, 1996.

Van der Ryn, Sim, and Stuart Cowan. *Ecological Design*. Washington, D.C., Island Press, 1996.

Vaughn, Gerald F. "The Geography of Resource Economics." *Land Economics* 70, no. 4 (1994): 515–519.

———. "Sheffield's Richard P. Wakefield: Advocate for Human Values, World Futures, and the Environment." *Historical Journal of Massachusetts* 32, no. 2 (Summer 2004): 198–213.

von Weizsäcker, Ernst Ulrich, and Anders Wijkman. *Come On! Capitalism, Short-Termism, Population and the Destruction of the Planet—a Report to the Club of Rome*. New York: Springer, 2018.

Wahl, Daniel Christian. *Designing Regenerative Cultures*. Axminster, U.K.: Triarchy Press, 2016.

Wallace, David A. *Urban Planning/My Way: From Baltimore's Inner Harbor to Lower Manhattan and Beyond*. Chicago: Planners Press, 2004.

Wallace-McHarg Associates. *Plan for the Valleys*. Philadelphia: Wallace-McHarg Associates, 1964.

Watts, William. "Foreword." In *The Limits to Growth: A Report for the Club of Rome's Project on the Predicament of Mankind*, by Donella H. Meadows, Dennis L. Meadows, Jørgen Randers, and William W. Behrens III. New York: Universe Books, 1972.

Weller, Richard. "An Art of Instrumentality: Thinking Through Landscape Urbanism." In *The Landscape Urbanism Reader*, edited by Charles Waldheim. New York: Princeton Architectural Press, 2006.

Wilkansky, Rachel. "From Regional Planning to Spatial Planning: The Sources and Continuing Relevance of Artur Glikson's Planning Thought." *Journal of Architectural and Planning Research* 21, no. 2 (2004): 125–139.

Williams, Rosalind. "Lewis Mumford as a Historian of Technology in *Technics and Civilization*." In *Lewis Mumford: Public Intellectual*, edited by Thomas P. Hughes and Agatha C. Hughes. New York: Oxford University Press, 1990.

Windelband, Wilhelm. *A History of Philosophy: Renaissance, Enlightenment, and Modern*. Vol. 2. New York: Harper Torchbooks, 1958.

Wines, James. *Green Architecture*. Köln, Germany: Taschen, 2000.

Wojtowicz, Robert. "Lewis Mumford." In *The Book of the School: The Graduate School of Fine Arts of the University of Pennsylvania*, by Ann L. Strong and George E. Thomas Philadelphia: University of Pennsylvania, 1990.

————. *Lewis Mumford and American Modernism: Eutopian Theories for Architecture and Urban Planning.* New York: Cambridge University Press, 1996.

Worster, Donald, ed. *American Environmentalism: The Formative Period, 1860–1915.* New York: John Wiley and Sons, 1973.

————. *Nature's Economy: The Roots of Ecology.* San Francisco: Sierra Club Books, 1977.

Yaro, Robert D. "Foreword." In *To Heal the Earth: Selected Writings of Ian L. McHarg,* edited by Ian L. McHarg and Frederick R. Steiner. Washington, D.C.: Island Press, 1998.

Zelov, Chris, and Phil Cousineau, eds. *Design Outlaws on the Ecological Frontier.* 5th ed. New York: Knossus Publishing, 1997.

Index of Names

Page numbers in *italics* refer to figures.

General Subject Index

Page numbers in *italics* refer to figures.

ecological planning theory: evolution of, 34, 68, 71, 75–80, 84–92, 95, 97–101, 177, 187–188, 242; Ian McHarg on, 94–95, 126, 252. *See also* curriculum: ecological planning

ecological studies, 148–152. *See also* Medford study

Ecological Study for Twin Cities Metropolitan Region, Minnesota, 152

Ecological Transition, The, 25–27

ecology: concepts, 12, 15–16, 21–22, 25–27, 66, 75, 131, 135, 138, 144, 239, 242; Ian McHarg and, 75, 76, 78, 89–90, 100, 127–128, 132, 154–155, 158, 164, 188, 233–234, 261; Lewis Mumford and, 49, 57, 100; as scientific field, 21–26, 130, 143, 153, 160, 240–241, 259; social, 25, 29, 251, 258; theological, 19, 133. *See also* human ecology

economics: behavioral/human adaptation, 28; resource, 24, 27; theories, 45–46, 50, 61, 88, 175, *220,* 245–247

ecosystem, 22, 26, 97, 163, 190, 240–241, 246

education, 5–7, 10, 63–66, 120–121, 130, 235–237, 244–245, 262–267

Enlightenment, 3–8, 21, 65, 245–247, 258

environment: change to, 5, 9–11, 33–34, 40; natural, 21–22, 29–30, 36, 78, 100, 151, 160, 163, 187, 200; problems of, 76, 81, 110–111, 133–134, 137–138, 141–142, 173, 224, 244, 246; regulations, 175, 179, 185, 234, 243

environmental fitness, 167

environmental health, 252–253

environmental impact assessment, 152, 229

environmental impact statement, 152n55, 231

environmentalism, 16, 28–29, 85

environmental movement, 29, 45

environmental protection, 174–175

Environmental Protection Agency (EPA), 198

environmental statutes, 137n

environment-human relationship: adaptation of, 17–18, 40–41, 44–45, 75, 85, 100, 123–125, 127, 157; culture of, 23, 25–28; study of, 15–19, 32–33, 50–52, 66, 96–97

ethnography, 160–163, 187, 208, 218–219, 251, 253–255

evolution of species, 8, 15, 247

field-based learning, 180

501 studio, 145, 166, 179–186, 195–198, 201–203, 211, 213–215, 218–219

Ford Foundation, 129, 133

functionalism, 112–113

Gaia hypothesis, 13, 247

Garden City concept, 30–31, 52, 55–56, 58, 88

Garden City movement, 30–31

geographic information systems (GIS) 171, 180, 187, 196–198, 212, 214–216, 229–231

geography, 27–28, 54

GIS technology. *See* geographic information systems

Glasgow School of Art, 105, 112–113

Graduate School of Fine Arts: evolution of, 120, 189–190, 207–208, 215, 221–224; pedagogy of, 131, 134, 152–154, 200. *See also* Department of City and Regional Planning

greenbelt towns, 58

Harvard Graduate School of Design, 67, 106–113

health, 159–160, 168–169, 177, 200, 251–253

holism, xxi, 19, 62

holistic approach: to environments, 44, 62, 242; philosophy of, 29, 60, 133, 153, 168, 237, 252, 258, 261

House We Live In, The, 125–126, 205

Houston Area Research Center, 236

Hudson River school of painting, 20

human ecological planning: evolution of, 32, 80, 85, 222–224, 251; and Ian McHarg, 34, 50, 68, 100–101, 110, 160n, 211, 214, 218, 252; transition of, 71, 78, 80, 93. *See also* human ecological planning curriculum

human ecological planning curriculum: development of, 145, 156–163, 167–172, 174–177, 185–190, 197, 202–203, 219; Ian McHarg and, 208–214, 221–224, 234–237, 264; regional planning development and, 34, 113–123, 147–152, 164–166, 181–182, 198; theory of, 68, 71, 80, 140–141, 158, 172, 174, 189–191

human ecology: application of, 22–30, 162, 168; and Ian McHarg, 78–80, 100–101,

WILLIAM J. COHEN, a Fellow of the American Institute of Certified Planners, is an Associate Professor of Practice in the Department of Architecture and Environmental Design at Temple University's Tyler School of Art and Architecture. He is the editor of *People, Places, and Environment Reader* and author of *Swanendael in New Netherland: The Early History of Delaware's Oldest Settlement at Lewes*.